TRANSYLVANIAN VILLAGERS

TRANSYLVANIAN VILLAGERS

Three Centuries of Political, Economic, and Ethnic Change

KATHERINE VERDERY

UNIVERSITY OF CALIFORNIA PRESS

BERKELEY   LOS ANGELES   LONDON

University of California Press
Berkeley and Los Angeles, California

University of California Press, Ltd.
London, England

Library of Congress Cataloging in Publication Data

Verdery, Katherine.
  Transylvanian villagers.

  Includes bibliographical references and index.
  1. Transylvania (Romania)—Politics and government.
  2. Transylvania (Romania)—Economic conditions.
  3. Transylvania (Romania)—Ethnic relations.
  4. Peasantry—Romania—Transylvania—History. 5. Aurel
Vlaicu (Romania) I. Title.
  DR280.4.V47   1983   949.8′4   82-17411
  ISBN 0-520-04879-2

Printed in the United States of America

1   2   3   4   5   6   7   8   9

Aceasta carte este închinată
SĂTENIILOR DIN BINŢINŢI,
îndeosebi unuia care întruchipează
minunatele lor însuşiri:
Badea Petru Bota,
om excepţional, prieten iubit, sprijin nepreţuit.
Nepot de argat, el este acum bunic de "domni."
Fie ca aceasta cronică a schimbării celor din Binţinţi
să fie la înălţimea generozităţii lor.

TO THE VILLAGERS OF BINŢINŢI,
and especially to one who embodies
their wonderful character:
Badea Petru Bota,
exceptional man, loved friend, invaluable supporter.
Grandson of a landless servant, he is now
grandfather of "gentlemen."
May the present story of that transformation be worthy of
the generosity of these people.

A deputation consisting of a Magyar, a Saxon, and a Romanian was sent from Transylvania to Palestine to retrieve the body of the Savior. Upon reaching Jerusalem, they were dismayed to find the Sepulchre heavily guarded by numerous Roman soldiers, and they stopped to discuss what to do. The Maygar urged the others to let him cut into the soldiers at once with his sword, but the Saxon restrained him, observing that they were outnumbered and might be harmed: it would be wiser to try bartering for the body. The Romanian had still another solution: "Let's wait until nightfall and then just steal it."

— Story collected by Gerard (1888:124)
from travels in the 1880s

What do you get if you put three Magyars together?
    — *An insurrection.*
What if you put three Saxons together?
    — *A business enterprise.*
And if you put three Romanians together?
    — *A band of thieves.*

— Story told by villagers in 1980

Contents

PREFACE AND ACKNOWLEDGMENTS   xi

NOTE ON NAMES AND PRONUNCIATION   xvi

INTRODUCTION   1

State, Economy, Ethnicity: Overview of Themes   3
On Conducting and Reporting Fieldwork in Romania   18

PART I
TRANSYLVANIAN VILLAGERS IN THE
SOCIALIST PRESENT

CHAPTER 1   Sugar by the Kilogram and Cow's Tail by
the Piece: The People of Binţinţi under Socialism   29

The Economy of Romania under Socialism   39
The Rural Economy of Binţinţi in the 1970s   48
German-Romanian Relations in Present-Day Binţinţi   64
Epilogue: A Backward Glance   71

PART II
TRANSYLVANIAN VILLAGERS IN THE
HABSBURG POLITICAL ECONOMY

CHAPTER 2   On the Side of the Emperor: The Development
of the Habsburg State, to the Mid-Nineteenth Century   79

Hungary, Transylvania, the Empire, and Revenues   80
Centralization and Resistance I: Shifting Coalitions
*   Produce Horea's Revolt   93*
Centralization and Resistance II: The Pros and Cons of
*   Roman Catholicism   106*
Centralization and Resistance III: Nationalist Reaction   113

CHAPTER 3   Serfs of the Magyars: The Transylvanian
Economy Within the Empire, to the Mid-Nineteenth
Century   126

The Growth of the Imperial Economy   127
The Economy of the Hungarian Kingdom   133
The Transylvanian Economy to the Mid-1800s   141
Recapitulation   174

PART III
THE CLIMAX OF NATIONALISM AND
TRANSYLVANIA UNDER HUNGARIAN RULE

CHAPTER 4   "We've Been Here All Along": Nationalism
and Socioeconomic Change, 1848 to World War I   181

The Revolutions of 1848 in the Habsburg Lands   184
Developments in Hungary   195
The Economy of Transylvania, to World War I   201
Nationalism and Transylvania's Economic Development   222

CHAPTER 5   Paying Like a German: Turn-of-the-Century
Intergroup Relations in Binţinţi   230

Group Differences in the Organization of Agriculture   232
*Commercialization, Class Positions, and Interaction
    Between Groups   242*
Inheritance, Household Form, and Domestic Relations   245
Intergroup Perceptions and Village-Level Politics   256

PART IV
TRANSYLVANIAN PEASANTS IN
PRE-COMMUNIST ROMANIA

CHAPTER 6   Peasants into Gentlemen, and a Liking for
Cattle: The Transylvanian "Revolution" of 1918
and the Interwar Village Community   273

*The Interwar Romanian State and its Economic
    Policies   276*
The New Regime and Transylvania   287
*Binţinţi Between the Two World Wars: Changing Patterns
    of Migration, Fertility, and Marriage   291*
*Economic Relations and Agricultural Practices in
    Binţinţi between the Two World Wars   307*
Interethnic Relations and Social Differentiation   320
Interwar Village Politics   325
Conclusion   329
Epilogue: On the Threshold   333

CONCLUSION: That's How It's Always Been   338

   The State and the Peasants   339
   Economy   342
   Ethnicity and Nationalism   345
   *State and Ethnicity, State and Economy, and Empirical
      Synthesis   351*
   State, Economy, and Ethnicity: Theoretical Synthesis   360
   The Great and the Small: In Defense of Anthropology   368

NOTES   373

REFERENCES CITED   401

INDEX   421

Preface and Acknowledgments

This book is about political, economic, and social changes over three centuries in the lives of Transylvanian peasants — a specific community of them, but placed within a much broader set of transformations in Eastern Europe. There are many reasons why these people might be of interest, but one general reason is that for most of us, they are bathed in a silence we would not anticipate from their European location. The protagonists of this story lived in one of Europe's great empires, the Habsburg Empire, yet how many of us have ever heard of the Uniate church, or Horea's revolt? (In general, our western mentalities give less attention to peasants than to other groups, a slight that is magnified when peasants constitute nearly all of the population.) Most of us are amazed, not having known it before, when we discover that something one could arguably call "feudalism" persisted in this region until at last abolished by edict or law in 1785 and 1848. Although we understand a fair amount about the IRA and Basque nationalism, few Americans have the slightest idea how to comprehend the significance of full-page ads in the *New York Times,* protesting "ethnocide" of Hungarians in Transylvania. And while Western and Mediterranean Europe have become familiar through travel and frequent exposure, how many of us have an adequate sense of what daily life is really like in the "communist bloc" countries? Asked to draw a map, many Americans do not even know where Bulgaria or Romania or Hungary actually is.

Such silences, particularly when they concern areas that are fairly close, in geographical terms, are telling. They tell of systematic gaps in our experience, of skewed distributions of ethnic groups in western social structures, and of political biases in how the world is communicated to us publicly. Although in literature and art, silent spaces may be integral to the total aesthetic, in social science and history they are suspect, representing failures that embarrass our pretensions to knowledge, both of the world and of ourselves in it. This book invites us to hear from people and groups to whom we have not much listened. It tells something of how states were built around them and how their economies were affected by changes in patterns of economic activity far beyond their local horizons. It talks of how a principal component of their self-conception, their national or ethnic identification, was formed and transformed through time and acquired different meanings for different groups in society.

The book is organized as follows. An introductory chapter defines some terms and considers briefly the difficulties of doing fieldwork in Eastern Europe. Part I then describes the situation of some Transylvanian villagers in the present day, focusing primarily on economic and political organization and ethnic relations, and including information not only about the village but about the larger organization of Romania's socialist system. Parts II and III disaggregate in different ways the elements combined in Part I. Part II separates polity from economy, treating Habsburg state centralization (chapter 2) separately from the feudal economy of Hungary and Transylvania between the early 1700s and 1848 (chapter 3). Part III combines polity and economy, for the period 1848 to 1918, but separates the discussion of developments in the larger environment (chapter 4) from the reconstruction of village-level forms of social organization toward the end of the period (chapter 5). Part IV covers the years from 1918 to World War II; it recombines polity and economy, village and environment, and attempts to illustrate how prior historical processes have contributed to interwar social and economic organization. In an epilogue to Part IV, the changes that were to follow after 1945 are briefly recapitulated. A concluding chapter summarizes the major trends discussed in political and economic developments and in ethnic identifications for the whole period (early 1700s to the present), and seeks to integrate the themes into a broader interpretive synthesis, with special attention to the issue of ethnicity.

I have no reason to spare readers an extended listing of those whose contributions made the present work possible, or bearable, or better. This book exists through the help and forbearance of many persons and organizations. I am not ashamed of their numbers (which, customary disclaimers notwithstanding, may spread fringes of the mantle of responsibility a bit beyond my own shoulders), and I wish to thank them here.

My first and greatest debts are to the people and institutions in Romania that facilitated this research by extending to me the privilege of working in their country — above all, the villagers of Binținți

(Aurel Vlaicu), to whom the book is dedicated. Unfailingly cheerful and hospitable, these people gave themselves warmly to an enterprise they had not solicited and mostly found incomprehensible, and from which they had no reason to expect anything good. I gratefully thank all those who tolerated my interminable visits and welcomed me with affection as their friend. Sadly, some have died before seeing the fruits of their help in print. I must emphasize with vigor that I am responsible for the interpretations I have given these villagers' stories, interpretations with which they would not necessarily agree. To my village "family," Maria and Lazăr, I offer especial thanks for their services and love, essential to my well-being.

I am deeply indebted to Professor Mihai Pop, Romania's eminent folklorist and my principal research advisor, for tolerance, friendship, advice, and assistance far beyond my expectations and instrumental to my success. I benefited greatly also from discussions and generous help that I was honored to receive from Transylvania's outstanding historian, Academician David Prodan, in addition to the unparalleled inspiration I drew from his writings. Drs. Mihail Cernea and George Retegan are among the many other Romanian scholars who helped me with ideas and suggestions, for which I am grateful.

Among Romanian institutions, the one without which I could not have completed any part of this project is the National Council for Science and Technology, whose aid was invaluable in arranging all aspects of my two research visits to Romania and securing countless permissions for access to sources of data. Personnel in many other organizations too rendered vital assistance; I hope that recognition of their institutions will be adequate sign to them of my thanks. These include, in Bucharest, the Institute of Ethnography and Folklore, the Academy of Social and Political Sciences, the University of Bucharest, and the Library of the Romanian Academy; in Cluj-Napoca, the Academy Library, the Romanian State Archives, the Babeș-Bolyai University, and the Institute of History; in Deva, the People's Council of Hunedoara County, the Civil Registry Office, the State Notary, and the State Archive branch. I owe further debts of gratitude to the administrative personnel of the commune of Geoagiu for their exemplary courtesy and helpfulness, in a situation for which they had no precedent.

Before leaving my Eastern European hosts, I wish to thank Dr. Zsolt Trócsányi of the Hungarian State Archives in Budapest, who welcomed me very kindly on two brief occasions and made it possible to consult some documents that proved of great help to me.

Turning to people and institutions on this side of the Atlantic, I have enjoyed the intellectual assistance of many persons. First among these is Jane F. Collier, who has provided me with eleven years of stimulating critical conversation, from which many of the arguments in this book first took shape, and who read and commented extensively on each chapter as it was written. Carol A. Smith not only gave me frequent and thorough criticism but also, by sharing with me her own excellent writings on topics related to mine, stimulated me to refine my views. I was fortunate indeed in the conscientious and generous support of two excellent historians of Eastern Europe, Professors Istvan Deak of Columbia University and Keith Hitchins of the University of Illinois (Urbana); both sought tactfully to reduce my initial ignorance of Habsburg history and also read drafts of this work in full. G. William Skinner has given me helpful criticism and essential emotional support throughout my work on this project. Jane Schneider and Eugene A. Hammel offered numerous comments and encouragements; also helpful at various points were John Higham, Christopher Chase-Dunn, John Murra, Daniel Chirot, John W. Cole, Bernard J. Siegel, and Stephen M. Olsen. I owe much to colleagues and students in the Johns Hopkins Anthropology Department—particularly Sidney Mintz, whose frequent queries as to how my work was progressing finally embarrassed me into making it progress, and also Scott Guggenheim, Ewa Hauser, and Michel-Rolph Trouillot, for criticism. As for family and friends: my parents and siblings graciously accepted never seeing me relaxed—if they saw me at all—and my friends helped keep me alive with diversions. Special thanks to Rupe, B, and Andrew.

Were it not that I prefer to thank people before organizations, I would have mentioned much sooner the International Research and Exchanges Board (IREX), in gratitude for its exceptional support during my two trips to Romania (8/73-12/74 and 11/79-3/80), for which it was principal sponsor. Also of tremendous help during my field research were the services made available by the United States Embassy in Bucharest. The Eastern Europe joint committee of the American Council of Learned Societies and the Social Science Research Council contributed doubly to this project, first with a prize awarded to my doctoral thesis and integral to publication of this book, and second with a grant, financed in part by the National Endowment for the Humanities, that provided further research time at institutions in the United States during 1979-80.

Like the peasants of Binţinţi, whose indebtedness flowed into a circuit far beyond their immediate creditors, I owe much to a larger circuit of scholarly exchanges. Chief among those whose work has inspired my approach here are Immanuel Wallerstein, Charles Tilly, Fredrik Barth, and the anthropological tradition patiently cultivated over the years by Eric R. Wolf and Sidney W. Mintz. Whether or not they like the result of their influence, they, and those mentioned above, can perhaps draw comfort from the idea that at the very least, they have helped to nourish thought. Would that debt were always so nutritive.

Note on Names and Pronunciation

Some people referred to in this book bear their real names and some bear pseudonyms. Pseudonyms are given for all but two (noted in the text) of the peasant villagers who appear as examples or in anecdotes in chapters 4 through 6. (The pseudonyms consist of names once present in the community but not among the ancestors of those to whom they are given.) For Magyar names, I have not used the proper Magyar order (last name first) but have given the names in the order familiar to English readers.

Transylvanian place names are an author's nightmare, each place having Magyar, German, and Romanian versions. While it would be historically correct to use Magyar versions before 1918 and Romanian ones thereafter, I have simplified by using the Romanian version throughout, even for historical periods to which that choice is inappropriate. For the community of my research I use the older of two names the place has had — Binţinţi, rather than Aurel Vlaicu — because the latter refers to a real person who was born only in 1882. To aid the reader with the three place names that appear most often in the text, here is a phonetic approximation:

1) Hunedoara — Hoo-ned-wá-ra
2) Orăştie — Aw-rush-tée-yeh
3) Binţinţi — Bean-tséents (first syllable as in "lima bean") or, roughly, "been since," said as if imitating a Mexican. The residents of Binţinţi are sometimes called "Binţinţeni," pronounced "Bean-tseents-éñ."

Romanian is pronounced more or less like Italian, with the following additions:

ă = *u* as in *but* [ə]

î (also â) = a high central vowel with no English equivalent; the final *e* in *intelligent,* spoken rapidly, approximates it.

ş = *sh* as in *shot*

ţ = *ts* as in *fits*

final *i* is often not pronounced, becoming voiceless and/or palatalizing the preceding consonant.

As in Italian, front vowels soften *c* and *g* (to č and dj); hard *c* or *g* before front vowels is spelled *ch* or *gh*. (Thus, *chiuli*, to loaf, is pronounced "kyuli," but *ciuda,* spite, is "čuda.")

Most of the names that appear in this book can be pronounced using the following (*not* generally applicable) stress rule: stress is on the final syllable for words ending in a consonant and on the penultimate for words ending in a vowel.

Introduction

Even a half-mistaken historical perspective is worth a great
deal more than no perspective at all.
—Jakob Burckhardt, 1859

Past and present illuminate each other. If one observes
nothing but the limited present one's attention will be drawn
towards anything that moves quickly, shines brightly, shows a
new face, is noisy, or reveals its nature easily. A whole world
of events . . . is there to ensnare the hasty observer . . .

Any town, taken as a close-knit community that meets crises,
truncations and breakdowns . . . has to be considered within
the complex of its surrounding region . . . [and] within the
movement that gave life to the whole complex, perhaps far back
in time.   —Fernand Braudel, 1958

Evolutionary and ecological theory tells us that species survive
and expand partly by moving into new, sparsely inhabited niches,
often in response to cramped conditions within their older niche.
As anthropology's original niche in "primitive" or "tribal" societies
has grown more cramped, anthropologists have moved increasingly
into studying complex societies. There, we have tended to exploit
a niche underutilized by most sister disciplines: modern-day rural
or peasant populations, rather than urban or elite groups. Our
metabolic imperative remained the same as before—to render intelligible the ways of life and the organizational forms of these populations—but because the niche is new, fulfilling the imperative has
required some modifications. We have been moving into this niche
for several decades now, and we are still refining our adaptation
to it. To advance our adaptation is an objective of the present book.

Ecological analogies being only one of the tools by which I attempt this task, let me introduce a different analogy. Just as some
groups in the world have advanced their cause by establishing colonies among other groups, the rise of anthropology now requires us
to establish beachheads in, and draw upon the resources of, other
disciplines. We have enjoyed modest success by developing our own
talents, but as recessions set in we must become more aggressive if
we are not to go hungry, grow extinct, or become the colonials of
someone else. For readers who may find the phrasing uncongenial,
I have one that is more generous and sociable: this book seeks to

1

advance our understanding of peasant communities by an appeal to disciplinary ecumenism. It invites to the intellectual feast not only anthropologists but others, such as sociologists and historians, who have so much to give to this sort of inquiry. Their contributions have already—as will be seen—in half-baked form enriched the offering at hand.

The analysis of rural villages at first seemed deceptively simple. So much more compact, stable in composition, and territorially bounded than some of our tribalists, they appeared gratifyingly manageable. But we have come to see that the reality is much more complex, and that understanding it forces us to look not just at the communities themselves but beyond them (e.g., Cole and Wolf 1974; Collier 1975; Schneider and Schneider 1976). The present study looks farther beyond than most, in the belief that rural populations are intimately bound up with events of international scope extending far back in time. Therefore, I view my research community both from within and also from various external points of reference, stretching up to the imperial heights of Habsburg statesmanship in Europe; from the ethnographic present of the 1970s and also from various moments along a historical continuum, reaching back toward the refeudalization of Hungary in the sixteenth century. I extend my reach to this degree because I believe that with anything less, one cannot adequately render intelligible the actions of villagers or comprehend why their lives take the form they do. But it is obvious that so to extend our reach demands more than the usual techniques of anthropology: it requires help from macrosociology and history, at the least.

My approach to this study rests on a few assumptions. Territorial communities, as localizations of human action, have stories worth telling in their own right and their people deserve attention for their own sake. Yet they are constituted by, and derive their meaning from, social environments whose wider constraints they cannot escape. Human actors are individually complex and interesting; yet they achieve social significance as members of groups, of structures and systems of action that are more than the sum of individuals and that have collective, systemic "lives" of their own. The lives of these different kinds of social beings do not merely intersect on occasion in the form of familiar polarities such as "community" and "nation"; they unfold in continuous interactive relationships among the many layers of organization and activity in a social system. One task of the analyst is to specify the nature of the relationships obtaining among the layers, and then to ask how each serves as part of the context of meaning and action for the others in a continuing process through time.

Because relationships can be described in a variety of ways, it helps to be explicit about the view one is taking of them. This book treats three themes and weaves them together. It looks at villagers' relations with several layers in a political environment that culminates in the modern state; at relations within a global capitalist economy, whose subeconomies include Eastern European feudalism giving way to peripheral capitalism; and at relations among groups who differ in their ethnic or national identification. I take these three themes not only as central in Transylvanian society, past and present, but also as vital influences on the story's chief protagonists, Transylvanian villagers. Moreover, I see the themes as tightly interconnected: changing political and economic relations produced what became the paramount issue in Transylvania, namely, differences of nationality. To avoid awkward digressions in the flow of the analysis to follow, I will now take a moment to say what I mean by each of these themes.

STATE, ECONOMY, ETHNICITY: OVERVIEW OF THEMES

The population with which this book deals could be characterized, for most of its existence, as a village of "peasants." While this term has no generally accepted definition among anthropologists, most discussion of its characteristics has focused either on the position of these people in relation to external power-holders or extractors of surplus, including states, or on one or another aspect of their role in the economy (see, e.g., Dalton 1972; Firth 1950; Leeds 1977; Wolf 1966). Both foci contribute to how I treat peasants in my discussion. I begin, however, with power relations and the creation of states, a starting point that makes excellent sense for the part of the world in which this study is located (see Verdery 1979; also Rebel 1982).

THE STATE AND STATE-BUILDING

I do not intend to review polemics on the nature of the state — an area of increasingly vigorous argument, especially among Marxists (e.g., Miliband 1969; Poulantzas 1978) — but only to summarize the ideas upon which I draw in looking at state-building and its effects on peasants. States have been conceptualized in a number of ways.[1]

Some Marxists (more or less orthodox) see them as committees of the dominant class or as entities functioning to contain class conflict (Miliband 1969); world-system theorists see them as instruments used by economically dominant groups to pursue world-market oriented development at home and international economic advantage abroad (Wallerstein 1974); political conflict theorists see them as forms of organized coercion supporting the ascendant position of some groups over others (Tilly 1978*a*); and liberal political theorists in the tradition of Hobbes, Locke, and Rousseau see them as the expression of the will of the people, or as arenas of legitimate authority whose rules and policies rest not on coercion but on majority consensus (see also Skocpol 1979: chap. 1).

The problem of conceptualizing the state is complicated, in my opinion, because through time, there have been important alterations in what "the state" has been and therefore in how it should be defined.[2] Among the things that have changed are technologies of organization, the social strata providing recruits for state administration, the relations obtaining between the state and other groups in society, the areas of social life susceptible to state regulation, etc. These changes have been part of one of the most significant processes of modern times: the creation of what we call nation-states, a form "invented" in Europe and fully evident by the seventeenth and eighteenth centuries (see Tilly 1975). This process, which I refer to as state-building, was of indescribable moment for the populations—especially the peasant populations—within the purview of each state's attempted emergence.

But how can one characterize what it was that was being built, if the thing was changing character all the time? As a working notion, I view state-building as the growth of a type of organization in a society—better, of a cluster of linked organizations—whose agents sought to increase its capacity to manage and maintain order within a home territory, through a variety of subsidiary organs, and to compete with similar entities abroad in a number of ways, militarily and economically in particular (see also Skocpol 1979; Therborn 1978; Thomas and Meyer 1980). To increase these capacities required actions in both the internal and the international arenas. Success in either arena enhanced success in the other, contributing to the strength and consolidation of the state's component organizations. Success in both rested upon the ability of agents of the state to extract sufficient resources (revenues, technologies, talented personnel, etc.) and to utilize them effectively in building an efficient set of administrative organizations. These have enabled successful states to outmaneuver other entities of different kinds within their territorial borders and also to outcompete other states internationally.

A much debated point in discussions of the state is the degree of autonomy it enjoys from the interests of the "dominant class" in society. While there is some agreement that such a conceptual separation between state and dominant groups is necessary (Miliband 1973), precisely what affects the "relative autonomy" of the state from these groups, and how such autonomy is to be recognized and understood, remain unresolved questions. It seems wise to regard the relationship of state and dominant classes or class fractions as historically contingent. But especially for the earlier periods of my discussion—the era of Habsburg state-building—I find it useful to treat the state as not monopolized by any one class and as having "interests" of its own that are not identical with those of society's other groups, with whom it often competes for resources necessary to its existence. Such a view, emphasizing processes of competition, seems particularly apt for agrarian societies embarking on bureaucratic modernization, including the Habsburg Empire.[3] In these societies, the quest for resources (usually in the absence of a strong native bourgeoisie) has caused states increasingly to acquire their own independent character in interaction with—and sometimes at the expense of—other groups in the system, such as the peasants, the church, the nobility, the bourgeois groups that did exist, etc. (D. Smith 1978). In successful cases of state-building there was a trend for these revenue-garnering competitions to eliminate some of the aristocratic groups in society (ibid.), thereby changing the composition of the social field within which states acted.

For the early periods discussed, then, I treat the state as one of several conceptually separate actors in a broader social system, and I look for complex interactions in which the various social actors (including fractions of different classes) combined and recombined with one another in more or less overt, shifting coalitions to pursue their perceived interests more effectively. Such coalitions often directly involved or affected the peasantry and therefore constituted a crucial element in the peasants' social environment. The ways in which the conceptualization just outlined is less applicable to the socialist state than to earlier ones will be treated in the concluding chapter.

To speak of the state as "it" requires a suspension of one's critical faculties. As an "entity," the state consists of numerous organizations, groups, and other actors, which do not always act in perfect concert and whose participation in state processes changes both from issue to issue and more broadly over time. These constituents of the state include the bureaucracy (of empirically variable composition), branches of the military and police, the monarch or head of state and his advisors (representing a number of interests potentially quite diverse), the courts, the parliament, and so on. Any outcome, any decision, is not likely to be the will of any one of these interests, groups, or actors but the result of bargaining and shifts of coalition among them. (And the outcome may, of course, be further shaped by the expected reaction of other groups in society who do not take direct part in the decisions.) Despite the diversity of participants, differentially influencing the decisions to be made, however, states do eventually "act," giving off a single set of products in the form of a policy. This single set of products is the best foundation for viewing a state as "it."

These remarks on the "itness" of the state broach two problems encountered by anyone wishing to discuss the behavior of states in their internal or international environments. First, our vocabulary is such that nearly all ways of referring to the state involve reifications that one would rather avoid. To say "the state" excites the immediate retort, "but *who?*" "The monarch" is inexcusably personal; "the Court" evokes minuets, not government, and implicitly leaves out people we want to include; "some among the various organizations and participant groups in the state apparatus" may be fairly accurate but is impossibly pretentious and cumbersome. Having found no way around this problem, I nonetheless use each of the above expressions and several others (the ruling circles, imperial policy, etc.), and also overuse the passive voice. An objective of the present prologue is to clarify how I do and do not want these expressions to be understood.

The second problem, a related one, is that our vocabulary makes it very difficult to talk without imputing unified *intentions* to "the state," when what we want to do is describe the developmental tendencies of a social system and not the purposes its agents may have. I resolve this problem as follows. Social systems do have their own internal logics independent of the actions of any of their members, yet it is in part through the perceptions and actions of groups that the system's inherent possibilities are realized. Because it is beyond my present competence to rewrite the histories of the several social systems with which this book deals, revealing their internal logics, I concentrate on the reported and inferable behavior of their constituents. I assume, however, variable degrees of conscious volition behind these behaviors as well as constantly varying inputs into the policies that emerge, and I further assume that many consequences of such policies are fortuitous, not intentional. In sum, while I recognize that the growth of the state is, itself, a manifestation of systemic tendencies and not explicitly an intentional creation, I speak of it chiefly in its active role within its changing system.

In addition to its complex internal composition and development, the state has a further interesting feature: it not only collects and deploys resources but is also itself a resource, or an object of competition and struggle. This point is clarified using a distinction Thomas and Meyer make (1980) between the state as an organizational form and the particular regimes that occupy it. As a form, the state is a piece of social technology to which large numbers of groups in society would like access; the particular constellation of groups that enjoy privileged access to it at any one time makes up a regime. This variant of the old sociological distinction between positions and persons helps to separate the state as an element of the structure or as an actor with idiosyncratic interests proper to its structural position, from the processes internal to its action — processes that determine the specific course taken in pursuit of those interests, according to the will of no one man. My use of the term "state" does not follow Thomas and Meyer's distinction between state and regime but tends to lump the two together; the distinction nonetheless helps to show yet again how we might think of the state's autonomy from other social actors.

If we think of states as organizations or organizational forms, a logical next step suggested by organization theory is to ask about their environments, especially their external environments (see, e.g., Thompson 1967). States have interorganizational relations forming what we might call an interstate system. Even though processes internal to the state are, of necessity, intricately bound up with international processes, we have some suggestions that the behavior of states in their interstate system constitutes yet another level of action with its own properties, not entirely determined by merely aggregating individual states. One of the most intriguing such suggestions is this. When an interstate system containing especially powerful states comes into being, its very existence exerts pressure that inclines other entities wishing to interact with it to take on the organizational form characteristic of that system: to strive to become states (Thomas and Meyer 1980).[4] Thomas and Meyer have proposed this as a global organizational imperative in the present, in consequence of which a fairly uniform internal organization for states has become widespread even though many of the societies adopting it would, if left in isolation, quite possibly not have produced it endogenously and do not have internal resources adequate to sustain it. This view, however arguable it may be, encourages us to look beyond developments internal to states and to consider how the emergence of nation-states in Europe changed the rules of the game for all subsequent players, setting up imperatives that may have run counter to local developments in other societies.

The presence of an interstate system demands that questions of endogenous state formation be rephrased and poses problems that all other "actors" in the world must face. It adds a further dimension to considering peasants within the state, for we can no longer parochially regard all political developments affecting the peasantry as the resolution of merely internal problems. Thus, investigating any transformation of rural society necessarily entails contextualizing it in both its national and its international environments. Although "the state" was changing in form throughout the period to be covered in this book, I would argue that much of what proved decisive and revolutionary in the lives of Transylvanian villagers originated in actions by their state in its interstate system — actions themselves referable, in part, to changes in the development of the world economy.

Economic Change and Underdevelopment

The second theme of this work, as unmanageable as the first and as deserving of more extended treatment than it will receive, is how the economic environment and the type of economy changed in the eastern Habsburg empire, Hungary, and Romania. Two major questions make this theme unmanageable: how does one characterize and label the kinds of economic systems that prevailed in the Hungarian and Transylvanian parts of the Habsburg Empire through time and in the Romanian state to which Transylvania passed in 1918?; and, how does one conceptualize the relationship between the economies of these areas and other economies to which they are linked, in an encompassing economic system that became ever more global in extent, from 1700 to 1980? Both questions throw one into a thicket of terminological and theoretical argumentation that I do not aim to cut through. But I ought at least to clarify the position from which my analysis, especially that in chapters 3 and 4, will proceed.

All discussions must employ a vocabulary of some sort. The vocabulary I use derives largely from debates about the nature of Western capitalism and its historical and present relationship with other economic systems. This literature covers many issues important to understanding the behavior of localized populations within their larger environments, such as how "underdevelopment" comes about; whether the theater for its occurrence is a global capitalist one or something smaller; how to understand the transition from feudalism to capitalism and the indicators appropriate to each; and how different organizations of production within a single society are related to one another. For people familiar with these arguments and anxious to know my position on them, let me say that I am not a disciple of any one school but have been stimulated particularly (toward partial disagreement) by the literature on dependency theory and its variant, world-system theory.

Dependency theory has antecedents at least as far back as Luxemburg and Lenin, and arguments of its type have long been made not only by leftists but by the fascist right. Examples include the positions a number of Romanian political economists set forth in the early 1900s through the 1930s, concerning the nature of Romania's economic backwardness (Dobrogeanu-Gherea 1910; Voinea 1926; Zeletin 1925; see Chirot 1978a and 1978b).[5] Similar positions have been common since the late 1950s among historians from Eastern Europe trying to understand the nature of feudalism in that part of the world (e.g., Kula 1976 [1962]; Małowist 1958, 1966; Pach 1968, 1970). Western social science argumentation began absorbing this perspective with the work of Latin Americans, especially Raúl Prebisch (1950), as communicated more widely by Andre Gunder Frank (1967). With the publication of Immanuel Wallerstein's broad application of dependency theory to questions of global extent and considerable historical reach (Wallerstein 1974, 1979, 1980), critical debate of the thesis has reverberated among all social science disciplines. I refer to this as the world-system variant of dependency theory.

A basic premise of dependency theory is that those economic systems usually seen as "backward" or less developed — whether at, above, or below the analytical level of nation-states — are backward or imbalanced not because they have been isolated from the forces of modernization and development thought to inhere in a capitalist economic system, but because the workings of that very capitalist system have extended beyond the developed economies and distorted the developing economies to capitalism's benefit. Through one form

or another of neocolonialist domination, modernized economies
have progressed precisely at the expense of the others and are the
immediate cause of their backwardness. Dependency theory rejects
the Ricardian notion of comparative advantage and sees the international division of labor as the cause of advantage for only some,
not all. It rejects the idea of "stages of economic growth" (Rostow
1960), which in essence tells developing countries to be patient,
for their turn will come. It argues instead that any connection with
advanced capitalist economies is likely to be detrimental to the less
developed economies, for capitalism by its very nature expands
through dominating and using other economic systems, which are
more or less powerless against it.

The world-system variant incorporates all these premises. It
situates underdevelopment not just in bilateral (metropole-satellite)
relations but globally, viewing all development as occurring within
a single capitalist system of global extent. Within this system,
different kinds of damaging interactions occur between more- and
less-developed economies ("cores" and "peripheries"). The cores
and peripheries of these damaging interactions are not seen as
different modes of production but as entities holding different
structural positions within the global capitalist economy. Areas at
the core of the world system (the developed economies) monopolize
highly skilled, capital-intensive and technologically sophisticated,
highly remunerated industrial production. They exploit peripheral
areas (under- and undeveloped economies where most production
is unskilled, labor-intensive, and ill paid) through draining those
areas of labor and valuable raw materials, such as foodstuffs and
mineral resources, in a manner that transfers surplus value from
peripheries to cores. Stability in these complicated transactions is
provided partly by the occupants of a third structural position,
"semi-peripheral" areas. These areas contain a mix of developed
and underdeveloped economic activities (such as silk manufacture
plus grain exports); the mix shows the rising or declining status
of semi-peripheral areas in the world economy — usually achieved
at the peripheries' expense (Wallerstein 1974:349–350). Fundamental to the world-system view is the idea that once an area becomes
integrated into the capitalist world economy, capitalism's dynamic
takes over and suppresses internal developments specific to the
dependent areas. For this reason, one need not retain separate
labels for the dependent economies (like "feudalism") because they
are not driven by a logic other than that of capitalism.

This view has proved marvelously productive for understanding many problems, but it has been attacked and/or modified from various quarters as well. The objection most important to my arguments, and the one to which anthropologists have contributed more than to any other, is what I will call (after Mintz 1977) the "local response" objection. Its principal contention is that despite the obvious utility of a global perspective integrating areas hitherto (and unsatisfactorily) treated in relative isolation, the world-system view of Wallerstein and others gives too much weight to exogenous determination of local forms. Localized systems do, after all, have a life of their own. They may feed into the expansion of capitalism, but not just at capitalism's behest; they also do so according to their own internal dynamics. An early statement of this view formed part of the broader critique of Wallerstein offered by the historian Robert Brenner (1977). The most successful examples of the "local response" genre, however, do not deny the influence that global capitalism exerts on localized economies but look for the interaction between local developments and the larger capitalist economy (outstanding examples include C. Smith 1981, Trouillot 1982, and Kahn 1980).

The present work falls within the "world-system/local-response" dialogue. I take for granted the integration of areas of the world into a single world market dominated by capitalism, whose existence changes the "life circumstances" for all the world's constituent economies. Thus, I take a view of economic processes similar to my view of the interstate system: like the latter, capitalism's advance has changed the rules of the game for all those who interact with it. As for Wallerstein's three structural positions of core, semi-periphery, and periphery, although I regard the division as somewhat simplistic, I nonetheless consider it a move in the right direction. I hold, with world-system theorists, that to understand the internal workings of any economy, one must first "place" that economy in relation to the centers of capitalist expansion and to the rising, declining, or stagnant economies with which it is likely to be linked.

But I disagree that just because the world market operates according to a capitalist logic, this necessarily makes the entire world a "capitalist mode of production." Circulation of items in the world market can incorporate products from entirely different organizations of productive enterprise; profits can be reaped from them unintended by their initial producers — as when a villager gives, in payment for a lump of sugar, an egg that was not produced as a commodity but will circulate as one. Thus, although areas may become incorporated into the world economy, I do not regard it as inevitable that their own internal processes will be at once subverted by the logic of capitalism. Nor do I see capitalism's intrusion as the only cause of "backwardness," which sometimes also arises from causes historically internal to the local system in question. Interactions between global capitalist forces and smaller-scale, localized economies do not reflect only the "needs" of the former but also the historical particulars and internal tendencies of the latter. I see events in the world economy as the context of action, constraining only to a degree, for economic actors in social units that nonetheless have their own internal life. In seeking to understand specific local formations, I look both at their internal directions and at their relationship to other economic actors or to agents of capitalism in regional, subnational, national and international spheres.

This fence-sitting position raises for me the uncomfortable problem of deciding what to call the localized economies I choose not to treat as mere extensions of global capitalism. For example, in Eastern Europe from the early sixteenth to the mid-nineteenth centuries, there prevailed a form of economy often called the "second serfdom" (because it reemerged from the continent-wide feudalism of the Middle Ages, at the same time that Western Europe definitively ceased to be feudal). World-system theorists see this as just one of many forms capitalism took at this time. I demur and call it "feudalism" (following Banaji 1977) into the 1800s, when serfdom was formally abolished in the Habsburg areas; and after that I call it, for want of a better term, "peripheral capitalism." These choices are highly arguable.[6] I am not concerned about justifying them, inasmuch as I regard labeling something as less important than showing how it works. Despite retaining the label "feudal," however, I do see important connections between both feudalism and peripheral capitalism and the larger world-system processes within which their development occurred. It is part of the objective of chapters 3 and 4 to make these connections explicit.

My disinterest in labels helps me to skirt another murky area of discourse, that which treats the "articulation" of "modes of production." Scholars who write in this vein do not subscribe to the world-system theorists' insistence on a single global capitalist mode of production yet do consider (as do I) that capitalism's encounter with noncapitalist economic and social relations is among the most important of analytical problems. One way this problem has been posed has been to identify, label, and describe the workings of different modes of production that capitalism encounters, and then to show precisely how each intersects or "articulates" with the mode of production called capitalism (for an excellent summary, see Foster-Carter 1978). Work done under this rubric may or may not be compatible with some forms of the dependency thesis. (For example, the "articulation" can be shown to occur to capitalism's advantage through distortion—underdevelopment—of other local modes of production, draining the region in question of vital resources such that normal development becomes impossible.) While much of this literature is insightful and creative, it often bogs down in disputes over labels, over what is to be considered a mode of production, and so forth. Thus, in my analysis I eschew both the term "articulation" and the labeling of modes of production that engage in this sort of behavior. I find very useful, however, the notion that particular economies simultaneously contain capitalist relations in juxtaposition with other systems having different motive forces, which sometimes oil the motors of capitalism for their own reasons.

I also find very useful Arturo Warman's idea that a significant function of the state as an organization in at least some parts of the world system is to set the conditions for the meshing of such capitalist and noncapitalist, including peasant, economies (Warman 1980: chap. 6). The state may do more than simply this. It may actively promote some forms of activity that introduce new modes of production into the mesh and help them to flourish. This notion will appear, clearly substantiated, in chapters 1, 4, and 6; it forms the basis for a continuous relationship between state and capitalism from the nineteenth century directly into the socialist present.

Ethnicity and Nationalism

My third theme, ethnicity, would seem to refer to a different kind of relation between persons and groups, from the political and economic relations adumbrated above. In this book I argue that the form of ethnic relations is a precipitate of the other two sets. The treatment here accorded the subject of ethnic relations rests more fully on anthropological scholarship than is true of the themes already discussed. In particular, I follow trends begun in the 1970s, which see ethnicity as an interactional dynamic occurring among local populations within a wider system; the structure of that wider system directly affects the form of local ethnic interactions (e.g.,

Cole and Wolf 1974; Collier 1975; also Hechter 1975). Although anthropologists and some sociologists have reached a measure of conceptual agreement on how to approach this subject (not, however, on the results of analysis!), those in other disciplines less familiar with the concepts employed, especially historians, might benefit from a summary.

Following anthropological practice, I see ethnicity as a form of social organization among groups interacting within a society (Barth 1969). It entails, behaviorally, interactions across social boundaries and, cognitively, a set of categories that define those boundaries. The categories regulate interaction by establishing contrastive identities based on notions of "peoplehood"—what sorts of "people" are thought to exist, and how someone is to be identified as belonging to "people X" or "people Y" and treated accordingly. The precise content of these categorizations, what "peoplehood" is held to mean, and how it is recognized, are always historically specific. That is, we cannot assert that ethnicity always entails ideas of common origin and descent, common language, shared traditions, etc., because these particulars vary from case to case. Nor can we assume that ethnic identity means the same thing for one group in a social system as it does for other groups in that system, as chapter 4 will show (see also Domínguez 1977). And further, we cannot assume that the categorizations are in some sense "natural," based on observable characteristics of the populations in question. Research has amply confirmed that many of the traits used as ethnic markers emerge during the course of ethnic interactions, rather than existing prior to them (e.g., Golomb 1978), and has also often documented observable differences that are not made into contrasting ethnic identities (e.g., Rousseau 1975). So we cannot assume a priori that just because two groups speak different languages, they will view themselves as having different ethnic identities—even though in Western experience, at least, language has indeed proved one of the most frequently encountered ways of distinguishing peoples "ethnically." Ethnicity is therefore in no sense a natural or necessary aspect of human relations and identities but is a historically contingent social and cultural product.

Ethnic identities (and individuals can bear more than one) are not necessarily the most important of many social identities a person can potentially bear. Both the permanence with which an ethnic identity is "attached" and its contextual importance to the wearer are variables that are socially and historically conditioned. So also is the extent to which these identities pertain chiefly to individuals (albeit in reference to a putative group) and are manipulated and shed by individuals according to the situation they are in, or, rather, pertain to highly solidary collectivities, which may or may not manifest their solidarity in the form of overt collective action such as nationalist movements. Changes in this variable of ethnic "groupness" (relatively individualized identities vs. collective solidarity) are central to the discussion to follow. Among the factors shaping these and other variables are the kind of political economy in which ethnicity is being examined and, as part of this, the degree of centralization of the states that encompass it (see, e.g., Cole 1981; Coulon and Morin 1979). Alongside these structural variables, ethnicity also has a very important cultural dimension, the texture of meanings that constitute an inhabited ethnic identity. These meanings are difficult to recover from history, however, and are given less space in my discussion than they deserve.

Many of us are unaccustomed to thinking of ethnic identity as potentially temporary, fluid, multiple, or as having variable degrees of groupness; as not necessarily having to do with language or common origin; as social, and therefore in a sense arbitrary; as meaning different things in different times and places. To the degree that these propositions run counter to the reader's notion of what ethnicity is or means, I believe this reflects the extent to which the study of ethnicity as a phenomenon has been contaminated by ideological premises basic to Western (perhaps especially American) society. Most of us think we know what ethnicity is, know that it is "natural" and rests on real, common origin and preexisting, real differences like language; that membership in an ethnic group is unambiguous; that it is one of an individual's most perduring and salient characteristics even though it can be shed (by a long process of assimilation, in which the old ethnic identity gives way to a new one, equally perduring and salient), etc. These commonly accepted ideas bear a strong resemblance to Western notions of citizenship in a nation-state. That is, we tend to think of ethnicity as if it were like state citizenship. But this sort of idea is not especially applicable to many parts of the world, much less to most times in history. And only some aspects of it make much sense when applied to Eastern Europe, an area where ethnicity and nationalism are every bit as ideologically significant as in the West but in different ways (see Halpern and Hammel 1969 and Wilson 1976, for related discussions). Eastern European polities have shared Western concern with developing a loyal citizenry, but this has been coupled with two other phenomena somewhat foreign to the Western experience:

the recent emergence of "citizen" groups from different ranks in a rigid feudal estate system, and national struggles to justify territorial sovereignties in an area of highly unstable polities and long-standing ethnic heterogeneity. While Western European notions about ethnicity are apt in some respects for Eastern Europe, in other respects they are not; and Eastern European ethnicities have operated in social and historical milieux very different from the ones that nourished common Western conceptions.

I cannot hope to have cleansed all the ideological contaminants from my use of "ethnicity," but I do make an effort to explain its meaning in terms appropriate to Transylvania as well as in analytic terms. If I write as though the ethnic identifications of Transylvanians were perduring, "attached," and salient aspects of social life, inhering in group membership and entailing notions of descent, it is because in this particular context that is what ethnic identifications came to mean, at least some of the time. Chapters 2 and 4 will show in greater detail how the feudal history of these conceptions affected their development. Similarly, if I write in a manner that consistently implies ethnic *communities,* rather than individuals holding ethnic identifications, it is because in this particular context, ethnic identities emerged with a communitarian aspect wholly entangled with communitarian religious groupings and feudal status groups. The reader should not understand in these usages anything other than what is suitable to the case at hand.

I employ in the text one deliberate confusion that must be explained in advance: I insist on interchanging the terms "ethnicity/ ethnic identification" and "nationalism/nationality." Although some Western social scientists equate these terms (e.g., Wallerstein 1973), most would see them as phenomena of different kind, with "nationalism" implying far greater mobilizations of energy and collective political intent than does "ethnicity." Eastern Europeans also differentiate between the terms, seeing "nationality" as relating to culture at the national level and emerging from struggles for political unification, and "ethnicity" as referring to folk culture and nonessential local particularisms.[7] The Western and Eastern European notions overlap to a degree, but not fully.

From the Eastern European point of view, the groups I will be discussing are clearly "nationalities": their identifications emerged from the problems of nation-forming so common to this part of Europe. (Even today the Romanian government refers to them as "nationalities" [*naţionalităţi*] as I believe the American government would not.) For Western social scientists, however, the term "ethnicity" more suitably evokes the appropriate analytical concepts than does the term "nationality." In the present analysis, "nationalism" and "nationality" would probably be the better terms for the earlier historical periods and "ethnicity" for the later ones; and indeed, in chapter 4, where I discuss at length the rise of nationalism, I use that term more often, with its normal Western connotations suitably implied. To switch from one term to another halfway through would, however, be more confusing to the reader than to interchange them throughout. This device will serve as a reminder both that the meaning of what we discuss is shifting and that we are working at the interface of related but nonidentical conceptions, in contexts that give these conceptions an unusually heavy ideological charge from both the Western and the Eastern European sides.

State-building, world systems and economic transitions, and ethnic nationalism — these themes may appear inordinately grandiose to be examined in connection with a small Transylvanian village. But these peasants are very accustomed to such disproportionate tasks. For centuries they have been patiently bearing and giving life to awesome events: feudal transitions, imperial aspirations, capitalist expansions, socialist revolutions. A Transylvanian village is as good a place as any we could find to examine events such as these. For such events consist not only of abstract sequences occurring far above the ground but of concrete ones with real effects on the lives of small communities of people, which serve among other things as settings within which major social processes play themselves out — and are, sometimes, modified as well.

Which brings me to the role of anthropology. While I have stated above my enthusiasm for interdisciplinary endeavors, I nonetheless believe that anthropology has a distinctive and essential contribution to make to the larger enterprise of understanding social phenomena. Macrosociologists and historians, political scientists, and economists may give us the broad sweep, but anthropologists and local historians are the ones best equipped to demonstrate that sweep's particular, "on-the-ground" manifestations, and to show how events at the level of the particular often serve not just to reproduce but also to constrain the general processes of development and social change. It is our documentation of the specifics that verifies, amends, or invalidates larger theories about social process (see C. Smith 1981 for excellent illustration). In producing this documentation, historians have the advantage of a longer time span, but anthropologists have the advantage of covering a far more complete range of social life, as well as the possibility of questioning their populations for ever more detail (*ad nauseam,* as my own will be the first to confirm). Best of all is to marry the two.

The advantages of the anthropologist are predicated on the discipline's principal research instrument: immersion in the society being studied, through an extended period of fieldwork. This remains the distinguishing mark of anthropologists, even when they supplement interview data with archival and statistical research and with extensive reading of secondary works on the history and political economy of their areas. It is only recently that anthropological field research has become possible in Eastern European countries other than Jugoslavia. Even so, fieldwork is less possible in some of these countries than in others. Because such research poses special difficulties of a sort not often discussed by anthropologists working in other areas, it is important to speak of some of these difficulties, to make clearer the conditions out of which the following analysis arose.

ON CONDUCTING AND REPORTING FIELDWORK
IN ROMANIA[8]

The most common route to field research in Romania is through a grant[9] entailing bilateral agreements between Romania and the United States, rather than through funds that merely support the individual scholar. These grants are administered through Romanian government agencies and are, to my knowledge, the only way to do fieldwork there. With such a grant in hand, one generally has minimal problems with visas and with arranging fieldwork in the countryside. Difficulties are most likely to arise from hopes for access to some of the documentary and statistical sources anthropologists often consult. Even there, difficulties are not inevitable, and they often result (as in my case) from the researcher's lack of foresight or from bureaucratic bungling—hardly unique to Romania—rather than from any government wish to conceal data.

Because of the high degree of political centralization in Romania, researchers reach their destination by being handed down a ladder of command, legitimated at each rung by having come from someone on the rung above it. Some (though not all) fieldworkers find this principle effective right down to the level of the village, as I did. Once it was clear that "higher-ups" had approved my being there, few villagers were reticent to talk with me. A small number refused to be interviewed, some expressing doubts as to what I was really up to, and a few are still convinced that I was up to no good. On the whole, however, from very early in my stay I was received with remarkable cordiality and responsiveness by nearly everyone (reflecting in part the favorable attitude most Romanians have toward America). My efforts to interview and talk with villagers were in no way constrained, and it was clear from my second trip, in 1979, that there had been no intimidating inquiry after my 1974 departure. The only exception to this carte blanche was some indirect advice that too-close attention to the unsuccessful collective farm would create unnecessary embarrassments. Since my original research proposal called for little collection of economic data, neither I nor those who made the suggestion saw it as a hardship.

Given such hospitality from both government officials and villagers, the chief difficulties I met with in my fieldwork were typical ones for anthropologists everywhere, such as trying to justify incursions into people's lives for a project whose outcome one could not guarantee, or encouraging a conversation that might unexpectedly touch on subjects painful to one's hosts. I also found it uncomfortable to press for detail on any subject villagers seemed reluctant to discuss, particularly things like the process of collectivization. (A total of 16 months' residence in the community naturally produced information on even these topics.)

The problems became more serious, however, when I contemplated reporting and interpreting my data, as it is here rather than in the actual conduct of fieldwork that most of the dilemmas specific to this kind of work reside. Problems began with the very location of my research, the region known as Transylvania, whose history is one of the most politically explosive topics in any conversation with Romanians or Magyars (Hungarians) because both countries claim or have claimed rights of sovereignty over the region. The more I have read of Transylvanian history, the more convinced I have become that an objective rendering of this history is almost impossible.[10] There seems no position on any major issue in Transylvania's past that will not be found biased toward either the Romanian or the Magyar side and therefore unacceptable to the other. Among the subjects debated are: Which group occupied the soil of Transylvania first and thus has rights of earliest settlement in its arsenal of arguments? What is the "racial" origin of present-day Romanians (are they lineal descendants of romanized Dacians and Roman legionaries, as some Romanians claim, or are they returned stragglers from pure Dacian pastoralists whom the Roman conquest expelled

from Transylvania, as some Magyars claim)? And just how serious
was the discrimination against Romanians in Transylvania during
Magyar rule? Under the circumstances, an account of Transylvanian
history cannot avoid favoring one side, even as it strives toward
neutrality. The side whose view is overrepresented in my account
is the Romanian side, not necessarily because in any ultimate sense
I believe it is correct but because it is this population whose place
in and view of the world constitute the larger part of my inquiry.[11]
It also happens to be the side with which I am better acquainted,
since I can evaluate the counterclaims of Magyars only in French or
English translation (or in the correctives offererd me by judicious
scholars attempting to explicate what they see as reasonable in the
Magyar view).

This said, however, I wish to state my agreement with the Magyar
historian László Makkai, who offered perhaps the most ingenious
and intelligent assault on the problem: that Transylvania's indi-
viduality lies precisely in the intertwined evolution of its ethnic
groups, within parameters set by the geographical variability that
creates different ecotypes and correspondingly different conceptions
of the same overall geographic space (Makkai 1946:13, 16–18). I
am not concerned with whether Transylvania "really belongs" to
Romania or to Hungary—a point I have had to argue with countless people, from Romanian villagers to Budapest waiters to Hungarian car salesmen in Baltimore. I am concerned rather with the
intertwined evolution of its ethnic groups, which is the essence of
its history.

While such a lofty "value-free science" attitude is possible concerning Transylvanian history, it is less possible in the far more
delicate dilemma of how to report and analyze village life under
socialism. This dilemma has not horns, but antlers. One set of
problems concerns the tone to take in discussing the socialist period
in general; another, whether or not to report specific details, in an
effort to protect one's informants;[12] and a third, the difficulty of
determining *what* might jeopardize informants. All of these problems emanate from the fundamental fact that research in socialist
countries unavoidably involves both researcher and (inadvertently)
villagers and others in the struggle between so-called capitalist and
so-called socialist camps, fiercely engaged in propagandistic maneuvers to undercut one another.

The problem of tone creates ethical questions about one's general
responsibility to a place that has facilitated one's research. For
those who admire some of the ideals of socialism, the questions
extend to how one can provide an honest yet fair rendering of the

fate of those ideals, so far, in Romania. A discussion of any theme on modern Romania can adopt one of three emphases: how far Romania has come, compared with its situation in the past; how far it has fallen short of the goals espoused in its ideology; or, related to this, how messy everything is regardless of miserable past or betrayed goals. Even the most cursory exposure to the mass media and political rhetoric in the United States will provide excellent examples of the latter two emphases, coupled with a seemingly ungovernable urge to assess whether or not socialism "works." In the face of this imbalanced presentation, one is inclined to try something else. In my opinion, the question is not *whether* something works but *how* it works. Yet of course this cannot absolve us of the ethical responsibility to raise a protest if we encounter something whose human costs seem excessive.

I write as a sympathetic critic of Romanian society, an admirer of how many achievements have been realized when one compares the situation of the general populace in 1980 with that of 1930, or 1880, or earlier. I am critical of some of the means for realizing these achievements (a few points of criticism will be clear from chapter 1) and of what I regard as a repressive internal climate; and I recognize some unpleasant sides to life in Romania (as also in the U.S.), such as the shortages of commodities that our predictably commodity-minded Western press is so fond of underscoring. Yet my research in Romania gave me—a liberal Democrat with no interest whatever in socialism as a political solution, when I went to Romania in 1973—a hint of just how gargantuan is the task of social transformation envisioned by this regime and others similar to it. Although I am critical of government investment policy in agriculture (see chap. 1), I understand that the government cannot do everything at once, given its still-limited resources. I was convinced also that even if one insists on judging not *how* but *whether* socialism "works," the regime is still, in historical terms, in its infancy, and it is too early for a definitive judgment. If we could fix a year as the date of the Industrial Revolution, who writing thirty years thereafter could have called it the unqualified triumph and discerned the benefits that many now assess in it? Thus, my inclination is to tread somewhat lightly, against the widely prevalent tendencies to condemn in haste.

Though not the most serious ethical question I had to face, my desire to refrain from belittling Romania's socialism unfairly—that is, *not* to repay the hospitality of Romania's government and research organizations with the bourgeois propaganda they so justly fear—caused me much concern. The very existence of Western social science research must give Romanian officials constant nightmares. Yet they feel compelled to permit it because of their earnest wish to avoid total dependence on the Soviet Union and to obtain some of their needs, especially technology, from the West — access to Western technology being the Romanians' reward for these scientific exchanges. Research in Romania is as open to Westerners as it is largely because of Romania's difficult international position: attempting to maintain some independence of the Soviet Union while developing its own socialist economy, and hoping to fend off Soviet interference with proof that everything is moving along as planned. Given the propagandistic presentation that American media accord socialist states, Romanian officials have ample reason to be nervous that Western researchers will come in and, ignoring the achievements, expose the society's weaknesses, weaknesses they themselves often prefer to deny and surely do not want trumpeted abroad. One might think that social scientists would be a safer bet than other kinds of researchers, since we supposedly can recognize "ideology" and "propaganda" not only abroad but at home. Yet I have had enough arguments about socialism's "not working" with anthropologists, sociologists, political scientists, and historians to know this is a false supposition.

Romanian authorities may be surprised and dismayed to discover, after such a sympathetic prologue, that so much of my book deals with the past rather than the present and that in my conclusions, I give more weight to the continuities between past and present governments than to the revolutionary transformations, although the latter appear also. This is because although I see the shortcomings of the present socialist system as having two sets of causes, I am more competent to discuss one than the other. The causes are political and economic mismanagement in the present and the legacy of unresolved problems from the past, which have heavily constrained what the present leadership can attempt. Lacking an economist's tools for analyzing management in the present, I prefer to emphasize the contributions of the past.

While questions about the appropriate tone to adopt in discussing socialism are troubling, the more serious ethical issues lie in the possibility that subjects on which I touch, specific examples I give, or interpretations I offer will bring trouble to the villagers who received me with such generosity and support or to others who assisted my research. We assume a tremendous and inescapable responsibility in going to Eastern Europe and talking with persons who can later be made accountable for what they have said (or even for what they *might* have said) by a political system that holds values different from our own. This dilemma is not necessarily specific to research in Eastern Europe, but it is surely at least as grave there as anywhere else. And what makes it particularly distressing is that one can never be sure whether one's worries are reasonable, since so much of the social control exercised within this society arises not from known cases of retribution but from the fear of it as a possibility, a fear perhaps unwarranted by actual government intentions.[13] (This sort of anxiety, let it be noted, is far less often expressed by villagers such as those with whom I worked than by urban intellectuals, the persons most dissatisfied with Romanian socialism. I found in the countryside a consistently more favorable view of the government and a lower level of worry about the possibility of surveillance.)

Concern not to jeopardize innocent persons with illustrative examples is aggravated by the fact that it is not always easy to gauge what the government may find offensive, sensitive, or problematic. Two examples will make the point. When I first went to Romania, I intended to do a project on Romanian folklore (it was dropped, formally, because I found I had underestimated the research skills I would need), on the utterly mistaken assumption that folklore must be a fairly neutral and untroublesome topic and would get no one into hot water. I would not have made this ethnocentric assumption had I had much familiarity with Romania, but at the time I had no reason to judge otherwise. I soon began to reconsider the water's temperature, however, after an argument with political officials in charge of cultural activities, who had arranged for public presentation of some old folk customs from a community I had visited. When I suggested that those villagers saw their "old customs" as "for public display only" rather than as an integral part of the life cycle still being practiced, the officials became (to my view, inexplicably) irate. Only later did I begin to realize that I had stabbed close to the heart of nation-building. The second example comes from a subsequent research plan of mine, which involved what I thought would be unproblematic surveys of central-place functions in various settlements. I later learned that county officials were very distressed to hear I intended to ask where villagers went for various kinds of provisions. The reaction was, "Oh no! Then she'll discover that the countryside is poorly provisioned!" — which was the least of my concerns. (By the way, the countryside where I worked was adequately provisioned.) I would not have anticipated their sensitivity to this inquiry even after months of living in Romania.

The uncertainties created by such an environment complicate decisions about what to report, the more so as they involve persons not in a position to choose the degree of their association with me. Urbanites and academics who befriended me at least exercised some choice over the extent to which they pursued our connection, but not so the persons in my field site. The mayor and other officials of the commune where I resided were saddled with me without prior consultation or consent, yet for all I know they may be held accountable or their careers affected by what I say. (And then again, higher authorities may have no such impulse.) I hope it is clear from any critical views I express that my criticism comes from my own assessment of the system's tendencies overall and could not be shaped by information from petty functionaries and a handful of villagers.

It is very easy for us in the West to blame all this on the failings of communist[14] systems and the police terror on which they often rest. I think this conclusion false: we ourselves in the United States have helped to create this climate by our inordinate readiness to seize upon evidence of the inadequacies of communist systems, a readiness that feeds their defensive posture and inclines them even more to censor our interchanges with their citizens. My anxiety to protect my informants is not ultimately rooted in police repression, it is rooted in the Cold War, as is evident in the fact that I have not heard such extremes of concern about all facets of reporting data from anthropologists working in other repressive environments—say, in Guatemala or the Philippines (though these researchers doubtless face their own problems of protecting informants). The reason is that our media view those societies more benignly, even if sometimes disapproving of the repression itself. It is American readiness to see socialism fail, to grab at any clue of its bankruptcy with or without properly contextualizing these clues, that creates the environment in which I fear, perhaps needlessly, for those who have assisted me. I have my own theory about why the U.S. is so much more concerned with repression under socialism than with the unspeakable atrocities in Argentina in the 1970s or Guatemala into the present: because modern communist states explicitly restrict markets for our products as right-wing totalitarian ones do not.

I do not wish to imply any absence of serious problems in present-day Romania—problems of bad planning, of repression, of corruption and excessive bureaucratization. To insist that there are good historical antecedents for much of this is not to say these things deserve to be left unchanged. But I believe we obtain a better view of the sense and seriousness of these problems if we place them in both a historical and an international context than if we dwell at length on their present manifestations. I have not resolved the dilemmas of reporting on fieldwork in Romania by suppressing information about how things "really are" but rather by selecting particular subjects, as they "really are," and then discussing the processes and events that shaped them.

This strategy poses several difficulties of exposition and analysis. First, because I am convinced that international conflicts between socialism and capitalism create the ethical dilemmas discussed above, I am even more firmly committed to placing the banalities of fieldwork into their international setting rather than viewing them from a more modest perspective. This, however, is no simple task, for we are not accustomed to connecting a tiny village with its international environment. Although the result sometimes seems strained—such as when Binţinţi pops unheralded into a paragraph on Habsburg salt policy and then disappears again—I believe the objective justifies the regrettable infelicities. Second, my analytical predilection for understanding the present in terms of its history produces a work whose form is more than a little peculiar for an anthropological monograph. And the choice entails using fewer data of reliable quality and more data whose validity is sometimes questionable: no amount of careful inquiry into what crops were sown in 1935, or how relations were then between Germans and Romanians, can substitute adequately for exact figures from the present or actual events and interactions witnessed and discussed with those on hand. Extensive reliance on informants' memories, rather than on observing and questioning what occurs today, raises many questions about the validity and accuracy of information recalled through the screen of intervening years and events. Nonetheless, the problems are not so great that we should abandon the effort to reconstruct earlier patterns as best we can.

I turn, with relief, to a final and much less taxing choice concerning the form of my presentation. An Eastern European reader of earlier drafts of this work objected to my speaking with the voice of an outsider, as in chapter 4, where I call "mind-boggling" a combination of alliances that, from the point of view of an Eastern European, makes perfectly good sense, or describe other events as if there were something peculiar about them (there is, to *our* sensibilities) rather than simply as the way they were.[15] Implicit in this objection is the opinion that a good report should make the view-point of the "natives" so integral to the mode of writing that the reader is seduced into comprehending it as is the anthropologist in the field; a report that treats its "natives" as objects somehow demeans them.

While I agree with this opinion in many respects, I have elected not to abide by it. I cannot presume to tell the story of these people from their point of view, to speak for them (as, for example, Arturo Warman can and so eloquently does, in his book). I can hope only to convey to readers my own understanding, emergent from an environment unlike the one being described, of the things that we might find peculiar or mind-boggling in this place. Although it is these villagers' story I wish to relate, I cannot do it in any voice other than my own. The schematizations and interpretations that might offend belong to me and not to them.

So also do the assumptions that make it impossible for me to ask some of the questions they or other Eastern Europeans might ask. For example, I encountered not long ago a summary of principal themes in recent Czech literature, whose writers emphasize the irrationality of history as opposed to its rationality, an idea so impor-tant to many of us. While I can ask why we have such stake in the notion that the movement of history is rational, and can speculate that it has something to do with the sense of efficacy that attaches to our position in recent world history and to the desiderata of orderly control and mastery so central to our thinking, I could not set aside this assumption of history's rationality and write from the Czech point of view. Anthropologists cannot permit themselves the degree of confidence in their imagination that such an effort would require: it would threaten our confidence in the scientific validity of the enterprise. I present this historical ethnography of Binţinţi, then, as the most inside of outsiders, but an outsider nevertheless.

PART I

TRANSYLVANIAN VILLAGERS IN THE SOCIALIST PRESENT

CHAPTER 1

Sugar by the Kilogram
and Cow's Tail by the Piece:
The People of Binţinţi
under Socialism[1]

Vom realiza cincinalul în patru ani jumate cu orice preţ,
chiar dacă ne trebuie zece ani.
 (We will complete the 5-Year Plan in 4½ years
 at any cost, even if it takes us a decade.)

Ei se fac că ne plătesc, noi ne facem că muncim.
 (They pretend they are paying us, and we pretend
 we are working).
 —Romanian sayings from the 1970s

The small community of Aurel Vlaicu, formerly known as Binţinţi,
lies in the Transylvanian region of the Socialist Republic of Romania. Now one of Romania's three major regions, Transylvania
has appeared in many guises over the past several centuries. It
constituted the core of the province of Dacia in the Roman Empire;
it was an integral part of the medieval Kingdom of Hungary, then
an autonomous principality under Turkish protection; incorporated
later into the Habsburg Empire, it passed into the nineteenth-
century Hungarian state and thence into Romania in 1918. A
colorful, complicated, and significant history shaped this region,
rather demeaned by its inevitable and sole association, in Western
minds, with tales of Dracula.

The landscape of southern Transylvania, which contains Binţinţi, is pleasantly varied. Through the center of an accidented
terrain flows the river Mureş; it springs from the northern branch
of the Carpathian Mountains and runs west and south into the
Danube via the river Tisa. From its southern banks the floodplain
rises into the southern arc of the Carpathians, the whole Carpathian
chain forming a wall that dramatizes Transylvania's separateness
from the rest of Romania and yet allows movement, by easy crossing,

29

among the country's different parts. North of the river, the massif of the Apuseni or Western Mountains helps to mark off the Transylvanian plateau from the plains of Hungary. The whole region is one whose natural possibilities range from pastoralism and settled agriculture to forestry to the mining and processing of diverse metals.

These possibilities are all particularly prevalent in the county of Hunedoara (Hunyad, under the Magyars). One of the most heavily industrialized counties of Romania, center of coal mining and steel processing, Hunedoara's mountainous terrain is hospitable to animal husbandry while the valleys of its two water courses, the Mureş and the Strei, invite grain cultivation. Hunedoara contains several cities and large towns, among them Orăştie (population 14,994 in 1973). It also contains, near Orăştie, one of Romania's most significant places: Sarmizegetusa (now Grădiştea de Munte), capital of the Dacian Empire until the Roman Emperor Trajan took it in A.D. 106 and a vital symbol to Romanians of a history they claim links them directly to both these noble ancestral peoples.

A few kilometers beyond the outskirts of Orăştie begin the lands of the commune of Geoagiu.[2] As an administrative unit, this commune has a population of 7,338 (in 1973) in eleven villages, four of them collectivized, and occupies a territory of 157 square kilometers. It borders against two State Farms that were formed partly with lands taken from several of the commune's villages. One of those villages, which lost a third or more of its original lands to the State Farms, is Aurel Vlaicu, or Binţinţi.

This village of about 900 people is known among villages in the area for several things. First, it is the birthplace of Romania's famed equivalent and contemporary of the Wright brothers, aviator Aurel Vlaicu, whose natal home has been turned into a museum visited by tourists from other parts of Romania. Second, by reputation it has the worst collective farm in the whole eastern part of the county. Nonvillagers attribute this variously to the lack of unity among its inhabitants (partly a function of high immigration, owing to the village's proximity to good public transport), to its having been a very rich community before it was collectivized, and to its past centrality in the feudal economy of Transylvania's lowlands. Even today it is sometimes referred to as a "village of serfs" by other villages that were more or less free. Third, it is one of only two communities in the area to contain Germans as well as Romanians. And fourth, it is said to be unusually modernized and, therefore, lacking in the picturesqueness and folk traditions that lure researchers and tourists to other parts of Romania.

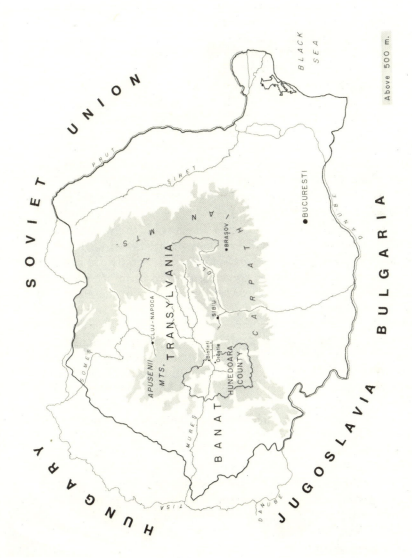

MAP 1. Binţinţi and Transylvania within present-day Romania.

The road into Binţinţi (paved since 1971) joins the national highway nine kilometers east of Orăştie. Along the main street are numerous television antennas, which confirm both the presence of electricity and the opinions about the village's modernization. Fields stretch out from the center, their expanse unbroken by any markers separating them — no stone walls, no breaks of trees, no hedges — a clear suggestion that the 600 hectares of arable land in this place know no private owners. Only small portions, within and close by the area built up with houses, have individualized personalities, and the quick repetition of the same crops in them — patches of maize and squash, patches of fodder beets and potatoes, then more patches of maize and squash — betrays these portions as the private plots of collective farm members. Houses are not widely scattered but sit close to one another along the main road and along the dirt ones that go off from it at periodic intervals.

Both the layout of streets and the form of houses present an aspect of heterogeneity. Varied in design, date of construction, and degree of completion, the houses are sometimes unfinished brick, sometimes brick covered with stucco and painted one of a variety of colors: green, yellow, blue, grey, red or white. Some are squares internally quartered and some go straight back from the street in a single line of rooms; courtyards are sometimes visible from the street, closed in only by wrought-iron gates and fences, and sometimes wholly private from the viewer's eye behind high walls and solid wooden gates. Grapevines climb along trellises or trail from wires stretched across courtyards. Two immense dwellings announce themselves as special by their size and their distance from the street, partway up a hill. These were once inhabited by Magyar nobles, owners of village serfs, and the peculiar tumulus behind them is said to be the place from which feudal nobles could survey all their holdings and laborers at one glance.

Upon reasonable acquaintance, the people of this village prove to be hospitable and (at least as important) garrulously sociable. If they feel confident of their listener they rarely hesitate to offer forthright opinions on a tremendous range of subjects. Let us select from this range a few opinions — as well as some topics on which talk flows less freely — and then examine more fully the national and local contexts from which they emerge.

We used to be serfs, you know. We were under the Hungarians. But Romanians were in Transylvania first; don't let anyone tell you otherwise.

We have a collective farm here, but it isn't very well run — they just don't pay enough. They bring in outsiders at higher wages but when we complain that we should get more they say, "It isn't allowed (*nu e voie*)." Who'd want to work in the farm when you can get a regular and decent salary in the factory, instead of an occasional load of maize and a miserable pension? And steal! Why there isn't a soul there who doesn't have his hand in the till.[3]

We have Germans here, it's not all Romanians, and they've been here so many years they're almost like natives. Things weren't always good between us but everything's fine now; we're all the same, there's good and bad of them just like us, they're very hardworking, and their kids are all professors and engineers. But the people who bring this place down [in the view of a native-born villager] are all these newcomers (*veniți*); they've moved in here from the hills and brought their backward ways and hordes of kids to mess up our beautiful village. And now, with the government not allowing abortions any more, they're bound to multiply even faster.

This business about no abortions is terrible, really, since we have no other good ways of preventing children. It makes life very tough for couples if they don't want a mob of kids to raise, or for foolish girls who get themselves in trouble. If the government didn't give people an allowance for extra kids, things would be even worse.

But you know, all governments are both bad and good, and this one is a lot better than most we've had. The state does a lot for us, and our leader Ceaușescu is for the people. No government here ever helped people before, you just did what you could on your own. Sometimes the collective farm doesn't pay us our pensions, but we don't really worry, because our government won't just let us die.

Collectivization, now that's another story. It was dreadful when they took away our land, and it's a scandal how this farm works. But even so, things were never so good before as now.* And a lot of people will say the same, even though some are still dissatisfied — those who want it all to drop into their laps. Before, we peasants were dirty and poor, we worked like dogs all summer and then a hailstorm would come and destroy the whole crop in a second; we took all day to go to market to sell eggs and a chicken for a little cash. Now the bus comes and you go to the factory and get your salary. Was that a good life? No sir, it wasn't. Now we can get good jobs if we want, we can send our kids all the way through university if

---

*The opinion cited here is from the 1970s, before the food shortages and rationing of the early 1980s, which resulted from mismanagement and the global economic crisis and which provoked deep discontent among rural as well as urban Romanians.

Pl. 1. Binţinţi house in style of serf dwellings (built nineteenth century).

they're smart and it hardly costs us anything. Even the collective farm wouldn't be so bad if only people would work in it properly, instead of just leaning on their hoes until lunchtime and then leaning on them again until dinner.

And believe me, back in the old days we didn't buy sugar by the kilogram as we do now, we bought it by the lump. Today everyone's a gentleman, everyone's dressed in fur, you don't see a poor person anywhere. I was a miserable sharecropper and my son is an engineer. That's really something.

A similar mix of views comes from all groups in the community, Romanians and Germans, locals and newcomers, men and women: enthusiastic about improved standards of living and opportunities for employment and education, calmer about interethnic relations than about attitudes between locals and newcomers, disgruntled with the performance of the collective farm. The sentiments are genuine and are freely volunteered, the most uniformly enthusiastic often coming from those who used to be among the village poor. It is only after more intimate acquaintance that some silences begin to become eloquent amid the friendly chatter. These people do not

Pl. 2. Newly built Romanian house (ca. 1970).

like remembering or speaking of the unpleasant sides of socialism before life under it began to improve; and their reluctance is not simply from mistrust of their visitor, it is from old pains and uncertainties best left in memory's closed rooms.

Despite their reticence, one eventually learns something of what happened in those earlier years. Binținți villagers confronting a new Communist-controlled government after World War II could scarcely know what to expect. On the assumption that at the very least, no government could take away their land, they settled into life as before: working hard, marketing livestock and grains and dairy products, and trying to scrape together income to buy more land. Early indications concerning the future were mixed. On the one hand, the Germans who had lived in the village for over fifty years were declared enemies of the people, along with all of Romania's Germans, for their association with the Nazis; their lands were completely expropriated, and nearly all between ages eighteen and thirty-five were deported for war-reparations labor in the Soviet Union (75,000 Germans in all were deported from Romania).[4] Even though Germans and Romanians had not been on the friendliest terms in previous years, Romanian villagers were still sobered to

see Germans being loaded onto trains at night with no word as to
where they were going, or if and when they would return. On the
other hand, the misfortune of the Germans meant a windfall for
poor Romanians, who received their lands. Because Germans had
held the largest farms in Binţinţi, village Romanians fared unusually well in this reform: 250 hectares were distributed in a village
of 225 households, many of whom were not entitled in the reform
(the national average was 1.2 hectares per recipient). This 1945
reform, like an earlier one in the 1920s, rescued many peasants
from pauperization and increased their production for market.
It seemed a promising start.

While the poor peasants became beneficiaries of the new government, the richer ones became its victims. About fifteen among the
village's wealthier households were named *chiaburi,* or "rural exploiters" (the *kulaks* of similar policies in the Soviet Union), and a
variety of measures were applied to eradicate them as a class. The
state's rationale for this was to eliminate the elite rural stratum,
which, while not constituting a class of landlords, tended to capture
economic benefits at the expense of poorer peasants. Although
this role of the wealthy peasants is amply attested in Romanian
literature from before the war, its applicability is unclear in Binţinţi, where the richest peasants had less than fifteen hectares at
the time.[5] The label of chiaburi did not necessarily reflect actual
exploitation within this village: a few wealthy households escaped
the designation by influencing party officials in their favor, while
other households were the perhaps inappropriate victims of old
grudges and envy borne them by one or another of the now-
championed poor peasants. Although the Party hoped to foment
antipathy toward the "rural bourgeoisie," the result here was largely
the opposite. Many of these "class enemies" were the persons of
highest prestige in the community, godparents of numerous poorer
families. Already highly respected, they won sympathy rather than
enmity for their struggles under levels of taxation and harassment
that strained them to the limit (see also Kideckel 1982: 327–328).
It was, in fact, precisely this ability to win villagers to their side
that encouraged the regime to eliminate wealthy peasants, so as to
reduce the political threat they represented. Even today, however,
villagers protect these families with a reluctance to single them
out by naming them.

One of the most important measures taken against chiaburi was
the imposition of progressive mandatory quotas of agricultural
produce each household had to deliver to the state at below-market

prices. These quotas were required of everyone, but they increased in ever-steeper increments for peasants owning more land. A hardship for all, they were ruinous to the wealthy. Quotas were imposed both on all products customary for this village (wheat, maize, milk, vegetables, meat) and on crops not customarily planted here, such as tobacco and sugar beets. Following an initial period in which villagers gave graduated proportions of their actual yields, the quotas were fixed according to the *expected* yield for a given surface area. While this system might have encouraged innovations to increase productivity, villagers say this did not occur, insisting that they had nothing left over to invest in modernizing agriculture and could do no more than intensify their labor inputs, already very high. There was thus little change in agricultural practices well into the 1950s.

Villagers who do not determinedly avoid the subject speak of the era of quotas as among the worst of times. They do not even hasten to report with amusement and pleasure, as they do in many other circumstances, the stratagems they devised for getting by. Some families were quick enough to have their extended households split on paper and recorded as separate nuclear families, each farming a portion of the total; this would save them the extra increment assessed on larger properties. Because the persons responsible for setting and collecting quotas changed from year to year and were outsiders whom one otherwise never saw, and because rural incomes were very low, few villagers could manage to improve their fates by influencing or bribing the officials. Instead, some people resorted during the initial period to declaring less than the actual amount harvested—until villagers saw just how perilous this could be when the village mayor himself, a member of the Communist Party, underdeclared his harvest, was denounced, and ended up in jail. A variant of this strategy remained attractive, however, because the collectors had full control over no crop but wheat, which had to be threshed in public where agents could take the quota on the spot. For all other products, the minimum necessary for subsistence could be hidden away, and if the remainder was below the expected yield, then some peasants pleaded a poor harvest and listed themselves as debtors for the following year. But many did not dare take such a gamble and risk the huge fines that loomed as deterrent; instead they would give their last kilogram of wheat, or borrow or buy the produce to fulfill their quota. To earn the cash for this, some worked temporarily in industry. For all peasants in this period, the main objective recalled today was to keep as much of their production as possible, and never mind about trying to get ahead, modernizing farms, or buying land.

Only the Germans, dispossessed altogether, were free of the burden of quotas. Those who returned to the village spent their first couple of years sharecropping from Romanians, in a perfect reversal of prewar roles, or working for Romanians as day-laborers, paid in kind. "We were the Romanians' serfs," they say. Some Romanian villagers who had received German lands in the reform offered small pieces back to the former owners, otherwise destitute. Other Romanians turned over to Germans enough land to fill the tobacco quotas assigned by the state, and in exchange for the very intensive labor investments necessary to this crop they would also give the Germans an extra quarter-hectare or so, to use as they saw fit. Germans could supplement these marginal opportunities once construction began on a national highway at the village border, and they hired on as wage laborers in roadbuilding. With the highway completed (ca. 1947), most of the German heads of household entered the unskilled industrial labor force at the large steel mills in Hunedoara City, continuing to sharecrop in their spare moments though more from habit than from necessity. Romanians say, "They cut the cow's tail off for the Germans in one single whack, but ours they took off piece by piece."

In 1956 the compulsory deliveries of produce were ended for all items but meat (partly because the revolution in Hungary had made clear that discontented peasants could raise hazardous resistance, which must be preempted [Turnock 1974:133]), and peasants enjoyed a brief respite. But they had no hope of a return to the normality of prewar days: all around them for the preceding four years, settlements had been being made into collective farms during a national campaign to collectivize agriculture (to be discussed more fully below). Instead of building up their stock after 1956, many villagers quietly sold off horses and oxen and kept only cows for plowing. In 1958 some Binţinţi families were encouraged to form a peasant association (*întovărăşire*), a preliminary to collectivization, in which villagers were to pool their implements and work the fields jointly while still retaining title to their lands. The following year, this association was relabeled a collective farm, or more properly, an agricultural production cooperative (*Cooperativa Agricolă de Producţie*, or CAP), in which individual title to land was relinquished. A drive was begun to enroll all households, with the initial exception of the chiaburi and Germans.

Nearly everyone resisted the effort. Commune officials aver that Binţinţi was the most recalcitrant community in the whole area;

but several pressures encouraged them to consider collectivizing nonetheless. Informers were used to gather names of all villagers who owned pistols; these people were then disarmed and urged to join the collective. Party agents would come daily into the village and go from house to house, explaining and persuading as best they could. After three or four wealthy peasants were inexplicably arrested and jailed for several months, villagers began signing up at a faster rate. Some were reminded that their children's enrollment at *gimnasium* was at stake. Others were worn down by being called to headquarters for persuasion, sent home when they declined, and sent for again as soon as they had reached their fields, so that day after day they could make no headway with their farming. At length, everyone approached, except for three widows, saw the wisdom of donating to the cooperative their main implements, their draft animals, and the lands many had painfully amassed over a lifetime of backbreaking labor. By the end of 1959, when Binţinţi was declared a full cooperative (three years before the national campaign ended, in 1962), only 26 percent of Romania's arable land remained in the hands of private farmers (Montias 1967:92). Collectivization had been achieved here as elsewhere in the country with a minimum of overt violence, a major lesson learned from the Soviet experience.

The state had won its war against the peasants, but many of them chose not to participate for long in the instrument of their defeat. Although the first villager to serve as president of the farm was a widely-respected man, who carefully refrained from collecting more of the donated implements and animals than he could house on farm property, it was not long before villagers began abandoning the cooperative farm for jobs in industry. The meaning of this transfer of villagers from agriculture into industry will be clearer, however, if we stop listening to the stories of villagers themselves, for a moment, and obtain a broader view of the state's economic plan during these years and of agriculture's position in it.

THE ECONOMY OF ROMANIA UNDER SOCIALISM

The Communist government that assumed power after World War II faced an economy not only devastated by war and subordinated to Soviet designs but also chronically underdeveloped. A determined but unsuccessful push for industrialization during the 1930s had left Romania still a peripheral economy dependent on agricultural exports and imports of manufactures. Although the new government intended to change this situation, its room for maneuver was potentially constrained by the decisive role of the Soviet Union. It is of great significance for Romania's subsequent development that the Soviets did not initially obstruct but in fact supported the Romanian leadership's goal of industrializing (Jowitt 1971:83–84).

The initial congruence of objectives that gave Romanian industry its start was not to last, nor did it imply an egalitarian relationship between the two countries. Joint Soviet-Romanian companies (*sovroms*) were set up, which enabled the Soviet Union to channel toward itself a number of crucial raw and processed goods from Romania, particularly petroleum products. Techniques of processing were advanced with especial rapidity in the economic branches important to the Soviets, and although the gains would be useful to Romania later on, this was not their initial motivation (Turnock 1974:129). In some cases the drain on Romanian products was felt right down to the village, as the state utilized resulting shortages to try to extract necessary items from the peasants. (Villagers in Binținți remember a period when lamp oil was almost impossible to obtain and could be gotten, if at all, only by paying for it with eggs. From this circumstance there arose a jingle they still recall, loosely translated as "Long life to you, my little hen, for my light comes from your ass-end."[6])

Stalin's death inaugurated a less imperial relationship between Romania and the Soviet Union, as *sovroms* were dissolved and new policies adopted to encourage more equal relations among bloc members. Meanwhile, Romania's industrialization had progressed significantly if unevenly, with a strong emphasis on heavy industry (steel manufacture, in particular) necessary to modernizing other sectors of the economy, including agriculture. Increasing attention also went to exportable manufactures that might earn foreign exchange (Turnock 1974:130, 133). By the late 1950s the Romanian Communist government was obviously pursuing a policy very similar to that of some political parties from the interwar period: autarkically protectionist, opposed to any specialization within a larger division of labor, and aiming at forced-draft industrialization as the means for achieving economic independence and greater equality (Turnock 1974:112, 284–285).

This policy ramified into other East-bloc economies, especially that of Czechoslovakia, whose high industrial output Romania had helped to support by sending foodstuffs in exchange for large imports of machinery. By 1957, their trade had markedly declined

(Montias 1967:46–47). Perhaps for this reason, Romania's economic program now began to draw complaints from Czechoslovakia and East Germany, in particular (Turnock 1974:285; Jowitt 1971:200), who pressed for a new bloc policy that would emphasize further integration and specialization of economies within the bloc rather than equal development for all. Their view became increasingly persuasive to the Soviet Union and an anathema to the Romanians, who were able to nourish their rebellious cause by skillful manipulation of the growing Sino-Soviet rift (Turnock 1974:135). By the early 1960s, autarky held pride of place in Romanian economic planning, and when East-bloc suppliers tried to obstruct by withholding necessary materials, the Romanians turned to suppliers in the West (ibid.: 133, 284–285). Around the central issue of economic self-determination there emerged a strong nationalist stand on the part of Romania. By 1964, the leadership was making explicit its implicit view that planned management of one's own economy is a fundamental right of the sovereignty of socialist states (Jowitt 1971:209). A nationalist insistence on rounded and self-determined development, rather than complementary economic specialization, has characterized Romania's economic policy into the 1980s, despite changes in the definition of priorities.

The consequence of this insistence was an economic growth rate that in the late sixties and early seventies was second only to Japan's (Spigler 1973:4; Wagner 1977:115). By 1970, industry and construction were providing 70 percent of the national income, as opposed to 57 percent only five years before (and less than 40 percent before World War II, when most of the GNP came from agriculture); two-thirds of the nation's requirements for machinery were being furnished by domestic production (Turnock 1974:136). Whereas in 1950, only 19 percent of the total labor force was employed in the industrial sector, in 1975 that had risen to 49 percent (Tsantis and Pepper 1979:139). And whereas interwar industrialization had consisted mainly of import substitution, the new regime has aimed to develop an export trade in manufactures. Exports of Romanian machinery and products of the chemical industry exceeded agricultural exports throughout the 1970s (ibid.: 378–389).[7] Romania's economic growth now depends largely on trade with Third World countries—exporting finished goods and importing raw materials—rather than on exchanges with other Comecon countries. The pattern of imports and exports proves that Romania has definitely shed its former role of peripheral agrarian neocolony (see Chirot 1976) and has become an important importer and exporter of both raw and finished goods, with a broad range of clients.[8]

These results have not been without cost. Romania ransoms its independent spirit with strict ideological adherence to official Soviet views and to orthodox Marxist-Leninism (Turnock 1974:7). And the model adopted — a Stalinist one in which broad productive capacities are mobilized through forced savings that rely on holding down private consumption and wages — has some adverse effects on popular morale (Spigler 1973:xi, 9). The proportion of the national income reserved for accumulation rather than consumption stood at an unprecedented 34 percent for the 1971–1975 Five-Year Plan (Tsantis and Pepper 1979:82), although this occurred within a budget 75 percent larger than that of the quinquennium preceding (Turnock 1974:137). The tremendous rate of growth and the insistence on "multilateral development" — meaning that rather than specialize in some products and import others, Romania intends to cover as many of its own needs as possible — require guarantees of an adequately large labor force, which is assured by treating the population as a collective resource and removing control over it from individual citizens. Emigration is stringently curtailed, contraceptives are unavailable, and abortions are illegal. These intrusions into people's freedom of choice, especially in the most intimate matters, are among the most widely resented of government policies.[9]

Aside from such human costs, the program of forced industrialization has been conducted at the further expense of agricultural development. Even Romania's president has frequently admitted, since 1970 (Larionescu 1980:16), that agriculture has been forced to bear a disproportionate share of the burden of industrialization, receiving inadequate investments as shown in a growth rate slower than that in any other sector of the economy (see Tsantis and Pepper 1979:78). Through the early 1960s especially, this made for perfect continuity with interwar priorities, which had starved agriculture of investment so as to support industry. Thus, to depict agriculture as the runt of the economic litter is not contradicted by a 5 percent average increase in agricultural output between 1955 and 1977, one of the highest rates of increase in the world (ibid.:40), because pre-Communist agricultural productivity was one of Europe's lowest. Although investment in agriculture has steadily grown since the mid-1960s, problems with output and productivity still abound and help to depress the standard of living. The victimization of agriculture is apparent in the insufficient incentives for agricultural labor and in the inequitable prices for agricultural goods (Spigler 1973:10), which diminish agricultural incomes and undermine performance. One of many vicious circles set up by inadequate investments in agriculture concerns livestock production, where output is very poor, below other East-bloc countries; part of the reason is fodder shortages (ibid.), themselves caused by poor increments in the productivity of grains, whose surface areas thus cannot be appropriately reduced to accommodate more fodder (Turnock 1974:226).

The agricultural population has been asked to bear heavy costs for industry since the regime's early days, the one initial benefit being the 1945 land reform, intended to win support from the poorer peasants. The first stage of these demands was the compulsory agricultural deliveries (quotas) that Binţinţi peasants recall with such distaste. For a state whose top priority was to build a solid urban industrial population, guaranteed food supplies were an absolute necessity, and the government was apparently unwilling to bank on taxation and market mechanisms, as had its predecessors, to provide the necessary urban food supply at sufficiently low cost. Quotas would assure food for workers until the eventual creation of fully collectivized agriculture, the epitome of state control over the food supply. Throughout the first phase of collectivization, begun in the late 1940s but suspended in 1951 because of violent reaction from all sectors of the peasantry, peasants consistently held down their consumption so as to deliver the quotas that fed industrial growth.

This solution could not last indefinitely, however, for the growth of industry required increased productivity in agriculture, through improvements and investments; and the testimony of Binţinţi villagers has already shown that under the regime of quotas this did not occur (see also Montias 1967:89). Something had to be done to resolve the longstanding agrarian problems, defined by Romanian analysts as excessive fragmentation, outmoded tools, undermechanization, and a generally "backward" peasant mentality marked by a subsistence orientation and a lack of concern for efficiency, specialization, or technological innovation (Larionescu 1980:13–14).[10] Collectivization was deemed the only policy that could assure "rational" farming, with specialization and machine inputs to raise productivity (ibid.).

The effort to collectivize entailed a variety of organizational patterns aimed at reducing the number of family farms. When popular resistance showed that an advanced form of collective was unacceptable, there was a retreat to a simpler and much less radical form, the peasant association (*întovărășire*). This aroused less opposition and constituted a sort of training ground, accustoming peasants to the idea of relinquishing individualized cultivation. After 1955 collectives were gradually reintroduced, now named cooperatives; the population was more resigned, and in the all-out campaign to collectivize (1958–1962) there was not just coercive pressure but a serious effort at persuasion through economic arguments about the superior promise of mechanized collective farming. Cadres sought to adhere at least formally to the notion of free consent. (This is not to deny, however, that "administrative violence" had also been exercised. See Cernea 1974:98.) The campaign was declared closed in 1962, leaving about 4.7 percent of arable land still in private hands, in mountainous regions unsuited for mechanization.

The Romanian push to collectivize agriculture should be understood from several different standpoints. Clearly, given the total commitment to industrialization, adequate control over food was necessary, especially in the face of peasant stratagems to reduce their contributions. At the same time, however, the all-out campaign coincided with two important events: the withdrawal of Soviet troops from Romania, and the beginnings of Romania's dispute with other Comecon members concerning the industrial plan. Collectivization can thus be seen, on the one hand, as signaling Romania's intention to follow Soviet precedents both for agricultural management and for the ideological treatment of class differences in the countryside (Turnock 1974:31) and, on the other hand, as signaling the regime's determination to mobilize all its resources and energies toward industrial development regardless of the opinions of others (Jowitt 1971:213).

As a mobilization of resources, collective agriculture meant several things. First, it permitted consolidation of fragmented agricultural holdings and made them amenable to mechanized work. Second, it provided a labor pool that industry would otherwise have had trouble recruiting, since the low level of capital accumulation caused the state to begin its industrial program with very low wages (Turnock 1974:31). To collectivize agriculture and keep agricultural prices low was therefore tantamount to the full and rapid proletarization of the agricultural labor force, and it assured that a growing industry would have a steady supply of workers as agriculture became ever more fully mechanized. It also helped to accustom those future workers to a more industrialized labor regime (ibid.:43) by training a population with centuries-deep roots in agriculture to take on new rhythms and work disciplines. Third, putting together these two effects, collectivization guaranteed that agriculture would support some sectors of industrial production with internal markets as peasants had failed to do in the period before 1945. The newly enlarged farms with their diminished labor motivation became certain customers for machine manufactures and the products of chemical industries (fertilizers), which had not been in much demand before, when the tiny plots and plentiful animal manure of small-holding peasants made tractors and chemical fertilization unnecessary and irrational. Fourth, by eradicating the "irrationality" and subsistence orientation of a small-holding peasant sector, collectivization contributed to integrating the entire economy more tightly around uniform principles of calculation and of value, despite the persistence of a few private farms in the mountains.

Beyond all these effects on the economy, however, collective agriculture had implications for political relationships as well. It placed peasants inside an organization that, although not (yet) outright state property, was directly managed by the state. Thus it brought peasants into an unprecedentedly close relationship with the bureaucracy, in an increasingly bureaucratized economy. It broke down their independence and exposed village communities directly to government agents (Turnock 1974:212). If to collectivize agriculture was the ultimate in proletarizing peasants, it was also close to the ultimate in bureaucratizing them. The two effects worked together: in making the state and Party the direct instruments for extracting surplus (and enabling the state to extend its surplus-extracting capacities to all sectors of the economy), it created an entirely unprecedented relationship among peasants, means of production, and polity.

A single reality can always be described from different slants, permitting either favorable or critical assessment. So also with Romanian agriculture in recent years: depending on the slant one wishes to take, agriculture has either made great strides forward or remained the economy's most backward sector. If one compares agricultural production with its prewar state, the increase in yields and improved, "rational" cultivation techniques—mechanization, field consolidation, etc.—cannot be denied (although one wonders, "rational" according to what set of norms?). But compared with gains made in industrial production in the postwar period, agriculture is indeed behind. Viewing the entire economy as a system, agriculture has clearly suffered from the priority given to industrial development. The discussion below will outline only a few of the trends in agricultural development during recent years; for more extensive treatment, the reader is referred elsewhere (Cernea 1974; Francisco et al. 1979; Kideckel 1979; Montias 1967; Turnock 1974).

Overall agricultural output has increased about fourfold during the past thirty years (Larionescu 1980:16), reflecting state investments that may lag behind those in industry but have nonetheless risen tremendously in absolute values (from 6.4 billion in 1951–1955 to 77 billion in 1971–1975, a 1,100% increase). The state has undertaken massive projects in agriculture, including drainage and irrigation works. It has increased supplies of equipment, invested in industries producing tractors and fertilizers for agricultural use, invested in education for specialized agricultural personnel, and enacted social legislation aimed at improved pensions and pay scales and a standard of living more similar to that of industrial workers (Larionescu 1980:20). While detractors will assess these measures as insufficient, their improvement over the past cannot be doubted.

The state has also attempted to motivate more productive labor in the cooperative farms (hereafter, CAPs) by developing incentives. The most important such innovation was the change, beginning in 1970, from a system of remuneration based on workers' labor inputs (calculated in terms of days worked, or *zi-muncă*)[11] to one based on crop yields, called the contract-payment system (Cernea 1975) or *acord global*. In the newer system, working units (usually household heads) make a contract with the CAP obliging themselves to produce specific quantities of various crops on lands assigned them and prepared by the CAP. Their payment is a set proportion of each crop for the amounts specified and increasing proportions for harvests in excess of those amounts. Instead of the collective brigades and teams of the earlier system, the basic labor unit in the contract-payment system is the individual household, which can organize the work of all family members including those who commute to factories and are rarely available for daily labor in the CAP, so as to focus on tasks and time periods that maximally require labor. Because farm members would ostensibly benefit more from their efforts than under the earlier system, the new arrangement was expected to raise labor inputs, production, and thus rural incomes too. Ironically, the new system was so successful that within two or three years the government reduced the incentives, inasmuch as peasants were earning more than the labor force salaried in industry

(Cernea, personal communication), which threatened to diminish the labor force eager for industrial employment and embarrassed the "workers' party" plan of keeping industrial labor attractive.

The state has sought further to boost agricultural efficiency by periodically rearranging the organizational links within agriculture's system of production, which is not all of a piece. Until recently, there were three major and separate components: State Farms (IASs), which are fully state property with salaried employees; agricultural collectives (CAPs), each of which is in theory the collective property of its constituent members only; and machine-tractor stations (SMAs), the centers that provide machinery, for which CAPs pay them by the work done. In addition there are the private farms in the hills, integrated into the socialist sector through contracts of produce. Organizational relations both within and among these various components, especially between the CAPs and SMAs, have created numerous complications (Cernea 1974 provides an outstanding analysis of these and other problems in the organization of Romanian agriculture). In an effort to resolve these difficulties, the state has redefined interorganizational relations several times. Beginning in 1973, "intercooperative associations" consisting of four or five CAPs were created with the aim of specializing each one along different lines within a single remunerative system, toward increasing rationality of land use and investments. In 1979, all three major components were merged with other kinds of enterprise into single entities called "Agro-Industrial Councils" to be managed uniformly and, it is hoped, more efficiently. The trend is now toward setting minimum guaranteed salaries in cash and kind, giving members of CAPs something of the stability of income enjoyed by industrial workers.

A further and crucial feature of socialist agriculture in Romania is the personal usufruct plot granted to members of CAPs. As of a 1972 statute, each CAP member who worked a set minimum in the farm would receive a plot of 0.15 hectare (Cernea 1976:99), which amounts to a bit less than one-third of a hectare per couple if both spouses work in the farm. These plots are of major significance in two respects. First, they serve to hold down the permanent migration of agricultural labor into industrial centers and help to equalize rural and urban food consumption. Villagers use their plots to grow either a large part of their yearly food needs or items that can be marketed for extra income. Many are reluctant to forgo this opportunity by moving to cities, where they will have to stand in food lines and sometimes find the produce exhausted before their turn comes. Thus, a population proletarized by collectivization is held on the land, to provide needed labor as long as agriculture is insufficiently mechanized to do without so many workers. Second, these plots, worked almost entirely according to the desires and for the benefit of those who farm them, account for a disproportionate share of all agricultural production (true of other socialist countries as well). Just as some analysts see capitalist economies retaining and being nourished by noncapitalist economic systems (see, e.g., Rey 1973), one might see these plots (along with the uncollectivized mountain farms) as integral to the survival and growth of the socialist economy (Preobrazhensky 1971 [1924]). Personal plots occupied about 8 percent of the arable surface in the 1970s, as against 19 percent for State Farms and 68 percent for CAPs excluding the plots (Tsantis and Pepper 1979:636–637); in 1975 their output of cereals was roughly proportional—10 percent—but they produced a full third of the country's entire meat output, 36 percent of all potatoes and vegetables, 38 percent of the milk, 40 percent of the fruit, and almost half of all eggs (ibid.:250–251). The usufruct plots are thus a locus for producing labor-intensive items with high output values per hectare, and they are vital in easing shortages caused by state policies for production and distribution.

We can flesh out this skeletal description of socialist agriculture by bringing it down to the level of a particular farm and briefly discussing economic activities and the CAP in Binținți. The discussion does not pretend to completeness, for two reasons: first, the poor reputation of the Binținți CAP makes it both an inapt example of general processes and an unfair choice for analysis that might be broadened into criticism; and second, because my research concentrated on other subjects, adequate data on the rural economy and the CAP were not gathered. An excellent and detailed discussion of the workings of a collective farm in the 1970s is provided by Kideckel (1979).

THE RURAL ECONOMY IN BINȚINȚI IN THE 1970s

THE COOPERATIVE FARM

The Binținți CAP has a fairly diverse profile, specializing first in cereals and second in dairy cattle, with additional concentrations in vegetables and, of necessity, fodder crops. The CAP has three subfarms, one for field cultivation of grains and some fodder crops, one for cattle, and one for the vegetable garden; each of them is worked collectively by brigades and teams. The vegetable and cattle brigades are largely self-recruiting, while the field teams are formed from the remaining households. Farm officials explicitly recognize that groups of neighbors and kin (who are usually neighbors as well) work better together than groups without these ties; in consequence, territorial subdivisions produce the two village brigades, each further divided into teams. The officials who oversee the farm's operation (e.g., president, accountant, cashier, party secretary, brigade leaders, and various advisory boards) are all from Binținți, except for the specialists: agronomists and veterinary personnel. In some farms one of these specialists does double duty as president but such is not the case here, where the president is elected (usually against no opposition) by the farm's general assembly.

In 1980 the CAP had about 530 head of cattle, about 60 percent of them lactating and the rest heifers. (Male calves are sent to a different farm to be fattened for export, chiefly to Italy.) The cultivation plan for the approximately 600 hectares of arable land varies each year. Maize and wheat between them usually take up 55 to 60 percent, in roughly equal proportions; fodder crops (clover, lucerne, fodder beets, etc.) increased their percentage from about 15 percent in 1973 to 30 percent or more in 1980, reflecting an increase in the dairy component; vegetables and sugar beets occupy varying amounts, at least 10 to 15 percent.[12] Extensive natural hayfields provide an additional crop of importance.

These products move within diverse circuits. Wheat and maize are used both to pay CAP members—thus, redistributed on the spot—and to fulfill the farm's obligations to the state for use of machinery, for fertilizer, etc. The portion paid to the state goes to warehouses in Orăştie, whence some of the maize is sent to the pig-raising facilities of nearby State Farms and the remainder is processed for sale in state stores in the county. Milk produced in Binținți is transported to a processing center (Simeria) about twenty-five kilometers away, where some of it is turned into butter and cheese. Most of the products from this center are distributed within Hunedoara for direct consumption, with only a small amount of butter and cheese going into export (destinations named include Austria and Italy). Vegetables and potatoes are also destined primarily for consumption within the county, except for some potatoes and onions that head for West Germany and the Soviet Union. Fodder crops and hay are consumed by the CAP's dairy cows and are, even so, inadequate for the needs of the farm, which must purchase fodder from elsewhere (an additional expense often reimbursed in cereals).

The fact that so little of this farm's output goes to export, in a country with still-considerable agricultural exports, is explained by the economic profile of Hunedoara County. According to Romania's economic plan, every county is expected to provide for its own food needs insofar as possible, and only the excess over internal requirements enters a larger circuit aimed either at other Romanian counties with deficits or at international trade. Hunedoara, being one of the most populous, industrialized, and urbanized counties of all, has high domestic food needs and thus contributes little to the larger food circuits. For Binţinţi peasants, this marks a change over prewar marketing patterns, which linked them directly to an international export trade.

To illustrate some of the workings of this farm and its relations both with higher-level power centers and with its members, let us inquire into a few topics: the vegetable farm, the method of remuneration used, the link between usufruct plots and the socialist economy, and the problem of fodder. The objective of these examples is not to indict the operation of the farm but to show how conflicting demands from different quarters work out in practice.

In both 1974 and 1979–80, several villagers expressed their opinion about the folly of planting the huge quantities of vegetables cultivated by this CAP—carrots, peppers, onions, cabbage, etc. Villagers cannot comprehend why so much land that is excellent for cereals should be given over to vegetable farming; they justify this complaint with the several years of poor vegetable harvests (actually due, in considerable part, to inadequate supplies of well-motivated labor for this arduous cultivation). The failures reinforce villagers' disrespect for a centralized economic plan that does not take into account the suitability of higher-level directives for local conditions. This vegetable plan does, however, have its own rationale. One reason for the desired county self-sufficiency in foods is to reduce the need to transport food long-distance. This cuts costs for fuel and appropriate facilities (Cernea, personal communication; see also Skinner 1978, for a very different example), which frees state funds for application elsewhere and, perhaps most important, economizes on precious fuel supplies.

Unfortunately Hunedoara, with its large urban population, has one of Romania's lowest percentages of arable surface for growing cereals and vegetables. As vegetables are the more perishable item, with greater transport problems, the plan very reasonably shifts some of the arable surface from cereals to vegetables, while additional cereals are freighted from the extensively mechanized grain-farming areas south of the Carpathians. Because Binţinţi has very high quality arable areas, it is a good candidate for this substitution. Yet villagers are scornful because in their view this is not the best use of land. (This does not prevent them from signing up for the vegetable brigade, however, even though their performance in it is lax. Their eager recruitment may come from the better pay for vegetable cultivation in this CAP and from the fine opportunities presented to those who wish to engage in petty theft of vegetables for themselves, friends, relatives, and neighbors.)

Not all of the farm's surface area is worked by the animal, vegetable, and field brigades, however. A large proportion of it is given out by rotating lot, providing villagers with what they refer to as their "portion" (*porţie*) to be worked according to the contract-payment system (*acord global*). The two systems of remuneration outlined on page 47 above are therefore applied simultaneously in this farm, producing an exceedingly complex result. Work in one of the three brigades is paid by the number of days worked, work on "portions" is paid by output, and each farm member except for dairy workers has labor obligations of both kinds (as well as their usufruct plots). In terms of crops, this means that most vegetables and wheat, as well as dairying, are remunerated by days worked, while the higher-incentive contract-payment system is used for the more labor-intensive crops: maize, potatoes, and sugar and fodder beets grown on members' portions (*not* the same as their usufruct plots). These latter crops are paid in a percentage of the yield, variable by crop and by year, while the brigade labor in wheat, milk, and vegetables is paid in cash and a small amount of grain. As if this mix were not complicated enough, the actual calculation of earnings, as explained by a CAP clerk, is almost impossibly tricky. What counts as a day's work varies by the task; basic payment, set in cash, differs for each kind of product cultivated, and a percentage is automatically withheld from the basic pay, to be paid only if the farm meets its production targets. An additional part of the basic pay is converted into produce at a rate most villagers are unaware of (see Kideckel 1979: chaps. 5-7 for extended discussion of payment systems).

These and other complexities make the determination of payment for members a herculean task even for the clerk whose job it is, much less for villagers hoping to keep track themselves. This leaves much room for abuse by farm officials eager to fulfill their obligations to state organs like the machinery stations. Befuddled workers are easy prey to the shrugs and "it-isn't-allowed" of farm officials. Although villagers themselves seldom complain that the CAP leaders are cheating them of rightful earnings (only that the farm pays very badly), subterfuge by the leaders is not an unreasonable suspicion.

Yet one must also recognize that the CAP officials face a bind of their own. Yields are often lower than expected, not just through mismanagement but because of natural disaster, poor worker performance, or (at least as important) problems in the farm's relationship to machinery. For example, tractor drivers from the machine stations, over whom farm leaders exercise no authority, often devote insufficient time to preparing CAP fields, which will yield less because they are poorly plowed; this leaves drivers time to plow the usufruct plots of villagers, who pay nice bribes for the service.[13] Or again, CAPs having financial difficulties may opt to contract for only two of the three accustomed plowings, to reduce what they must pay for machinery; and this too diminishes yields. (The Agro-Industrial Councils of 1979 are intended to resolve some of these dilemmas.) Whenever the leadership of this village's CAP finds its harvest inadequate to cover both their contracts to the state and their members' pay, they have always chosen to fulfill contracts upward — necessary to keeping their jobs — at the expense of paying members, to whom they are not directly accountable. Then, to avoid the full consequences of this alienating choice upon village labor, they hire seasonal laborers from mountain areas, who are paid a good wage and are fairly reliable, as CAP members are not. The poor pay of which members so often complain is thus a result of the peculiar integration of machinery stations and CAPs, and of the economic centralism that sacrifices members' interests to higher-level obligations.

This discussion suggests why members say that of the two kinds of work they owe the CAP (that is, excluding work on their usufruct plots), they much prefer working their portion in the contract-payment system to labor in the brigades. One might think this preference comes from the greater motivation provided by incentives for personal gain in the contract-payment system, but this is not so. Both the CAP members and an actual example of the work contract make it clear that production minima on the portions are set so high that members barely achieve the amounts stipulated and never enter the range for more favorable remuneration.[14] Work on the portion is preferred partly for its convenience — members say they can work whenever they want, instead of when the team leader calls them. In addition, however, they prefer working their portion for contract payment because this allows them greater, though far from complete, control over the pay they receive, reducing the chance for farm officials to tinker with output figures and, thus, with remuneration.

This possibility gains force from one villager's report of what happened in the early years of the contract-payment system. A successful trial year (1972) was followed by a second in which the CAP officials collected members' yields from their portions and then later announced that there would be no pay in that system for the year because overall production targets (increased over the previous year) had not been reached.[15] A few villagers raised a pro-test, for their contracts explicitly stipulated remuneration for amounts many were sure they had produced. In a rare show of defiance from an otherwise apathetic group, CAP members voted in the next general assembly meeting that henceforth the officials would weigh each member's production at the harvest site and turn over the stipulated remuneration then and there, rather than col-lecting all produce without measuring it and then figuring payments later. With this innovation, members know whether or not they have fulfilled their individual contracts, and they are no longer wholly at the mercy of some centralized accounting system that unreliably pays a pitiful remittance whose figuring they cannot comprehend. The degree of control over earnings is much greater than is possible in the day-labor payment system.

One side effect of villagers' preference for working their portions is that they apply themselves more conscientiously to the more labor-intensive crops, which, given the problematic and costly linkages with machinery, works to the overall benefit of farm yields. But there is even more potential for increasing yields, and it is not likely to be realized. Since each person's portion is reassigned randomly every year (and they themselves favor this, for it eliminates perma-nent yield discrepancies caused by soils of different quality), people have no interest in long-range improvements on their portion to raise its productivity. Any manifest concern with long-range pro-ductivity goes chiefly to members' small, permanently assigned usufruct plots, and even there it most often takes the form of crop rotations and intensified labor. Households that still keep cows reserve their soil-enriching organic fertilizer for these plots, using the CAP's chemical fertilizers (which, they say, are inferior to manure) on their portion.

In Binţinţi, the usufruct plots are for the most part not used to plant marketable crops,[16] as they are in some areas, but to supplement household food requirements. Villagers grow maize, fodder beets (if they keep cattle), squash (for pigs), potatoes, and vegetables for their own use rather than for sale. The main exception is that those households that keep cows will sell milk, butter, and cheese to other villagers or in the market for extra cash. Many couples are able to provide a surprisingly large portion of their food from their plot. They raise one or two pigs, large numbers of barnyard fowl, and sometimes also rabbits; and they fully cover their use of potatoes and vegetables, leaving only bread, some wheat flour and corn meal, and perhaps dairy products as their chief necessary purchases.

Although technically speaking, members use the products of their plot as they wish, the socialist economy has ways of integrating some of those products into its plan. As with the difference between the products and labor motivation characteristic of the fields versus the portion, the state takes advantage of members' motivation on their usufruct plots to extract items with high labor investments, this time animal products. Meat and dairy products are among the items most essential to Hunedoara's economic plan. Needs are partially but far from completely covered by pig-raising facilities in some CAPs and State Farms and by dairy installations such as the one in Binţinţi. The state (via county agents) covers the considerable shortfall by stimulating private livestock rearing through guaranteed purchase of pigs, cattle, and milk or cheese, from CAP members and from farmers in uncollectivized upland areas. Through advance contracts with the state, individuals agree to deliver milk, cheese, or animals for a set price by weight, sometimes augmented with bonuses in the form of grain or of fodder items otherwise difficult to obtain. In general, the contract prices for live cattle (many destined for export) are competitive with market prices, but contracts for milk and pigs (consumed internally) are much less favorable. Party officials in each commune are therefore responsible for obtaining assigned quantities of pigs and dairy products from the inhabitants of their commune's several villages. This amounts to shoring up socialist provisioning of the industrial work force by incursions into the subsistence fund the villagers maintain with high labor inputs. It is yet another example of how agriculture carries industry on its back through the state's formidable capacity for extracting surpluses, necessary to developing a once-backward economy with minimal recourse to autonomy-reducing foreign aid.

Because Binţinţi villagers do not overwhelm their commune officials with voluntary contracts of pigs and milk, officials turn to a number of persuasive devices. One of the simplest is an appeal to patriotism, in which villagers are urged to help assure their country's independence from "outside powers" by seeing that it does not need to rely on external sources for basic provisions. This appeal is effective but cannot be used routinely. Beginning around 1973, it was combined with a proposal that villagers should join together in groups of four or five households to contract a pig, cooperating however they wished in order to provide it. Various tactics encourage them to accept the proposal. When someone tries to arrange plowing through the CAP or goes there for the ticket without which he cannot market anything (see below), he may be refused if he has not helped to contract a pig. Similarly, political leaders may deny the permit that entitles villagers to cheap vacations in one of Romania's many health spas, or may fine households repeatedly for minor infractions like a clogged ditch.

The proposal to join together for a contracted pig cleverly enables villagers to fulfill their patriotic obligation without the tremendous effort that would have been required if a pig were expected of every family, for then everyone would have to keep at least two pigs, the one each household already raises for itself and the one for the state. Since pigs are fed on maize, potatoes, and squash from usufruct plots, fattening an additional pig would be a highly visible and alienating drain of private resources into the socialist domain. Instead, households either chip in to feed a common pig, jointly reimburse one of their group for raising it, or—most often—combine to buy a pig at open-market prices, resell it on contract, and split the loss among them. Ironically, this stimulates the open market for pigs sufficiently that some households now raise two pigs, sell one in the market at a good price, and use part of the proceeds to absorb the loss incurred by buying another pig to sell at low prices to the state. Although they have invested extra food and labor, they have made money overall, more than if they contracted the second pig to the state directly.[17] The catch, however, is that commune officials are gradually reducing the number of families permitted to cooperate in providing a pig. Ultimately, then, the original alienating proposal may insinuate itself into reality. Pieces are still being cut off the cow's tail.

Any household with a plot to support a pig (and that means most of them) is fair game for persuasion into pig contracts. Contracts of milk and cheese are trickier to obtain, however, since fewer households keep cattle, and they do so under conditions that give officials little leverage. Furthermore, undue pressure runs the risk that these families will decide to stop keeping cows altogether and save themselves a lot of trouble. The crux of the matter is the difficulty of procuring adequate feed for cows. Exploration of this problem gives a close view of one of the many vicious circles that stymie this CAP.

If one asks villagers how they manage to feed their cows on a third of a hectare of land, the reply may be a red face. In the summer, cows graze with CAP cattle on common pasture (for a fee); their winter diet includes fodder beets and maize from the household's personal plot, plus wheat bran obtained in exchange for milk that is contracted; but this is far from enough. A very few households are fortunate to abut onto natural grass fields from which they can reap almost enough hay for the year. An additional source is the extensive hayfields of the CAP, which fills some of its own hay needs by allowing members to reap as much as they wish, keeping one-quarter of it or less and turning over the remainder to the farm. Most villagers find this a derisory percentage for the labor involved, yet the farm leadership refuses to increase the reaper's take and has in fact decreased it, over the past decade. In consequence, the farm often finds itself with unreaped hayfields ruined by autumn rains, and its cows lie hungry on bare cement floors, while villagers steal hay from various sources, sometimes outright and sometimes with the bribed connivance of officials at the source in question.

It is a neat bind indeed. CAP officials want to retain as much of their own hay as possible, to cut the expenses they must incur for purchasing hay in a CAP that is (like most others) chronically in debt. They therefore refuse villagers' requests that reapers be given more than 25 percent. At that rate, however, most villagers will not do the work, so the CAP must pay seasonal workers a hefty wage to reap what villagers disdain. Meanwhile, the locals steal hay, usually from one or another *socialist* sector — CAPs or State Farms — with the result that private cows live secretly off public goods, and the CAP must further augment its supplies with purchases or see its cows starve. When commune leaders come around asking for milk to contract, some (though not all) villagers resist by saying that as long as the CAP is so tightfisted with its supplies of fodder, they see no reason to comply, since they need the income from higher market prices for milk in order to buy feed! One sees with this example how the interests and resources of CAP officials, state agents, and individual members work at complete odds with one another to produce wholly unsatisfactory results (see also Cernea 1974:245–246). The state's desperation for adequate dairy (and meat) supplies for its cherished industrial workers, and the CAP's desperation to avoid overspending (further motivated by its necessary payments to the state), lead them to obstruct supplies of fodder that villagers must have in order to fulfill patriotic obligations and feed their cows legally.

Romanians at all levels explicitly acknowledge the problems in agriculture and offer many reasons to explain them. Commune officials blame incompetence and factionalism within the management of the Binţinţi CAP. The CAP's leaders blame the apathy and poor performance of villagers. Villagers agree with both, blaming the president and agronomists and veterinarians as well as the work of the inadequately paid CAP members. In the words of one woman, "The leaders are no good, but the people aren't any good either." Sociologists and economists blame the state-determined system of agricultural prices, patterns of sectoral investment, and the organizational linkages among components of the agricultural sector. Each of these explanations has credence and is supported by systematic processes at one or another level of analysis; appropriate remedies lie at all of them. Agricultural production would be improved by any of the following changes: less infighting and greater competence among the CAP leadership, new organizational links between CAPs and machinery, decentralization of the economic plan, higher agricultural prices, or better pay and stronger commitment from members—especially, higher returns to labor for women, who constitute two-thirds of the agricultural work force.

None of these solutions, however, address the truly fundamental problem: the overwhelming priority given to multilateral industrial development at any price, so as to avoid the perils of dependency on either capitalist or socialist great powers. This priority has expectable consequences. It is impossible to develop all sectors of the economy equally at the same time, given Romania's initially low level of capital accumulation and economic development. It is pointless even to expect collectivized agriculture to work well in a system that commits the bulk of its resources to industry when, historically, agricultural development had never been adequately supported. Even the priority given to industrialization is understandable: this economy has long been dominated from outside and has often suffered from that fact—for example, during the

1930s, as markets for its agricultural products dried up, precluding imports of manufactures upon which the country depended. The leadership can readily justify its desire to reduce dependence on manufactured imports and raw agricultural exports. And Romania is well enough endowed with varied natural resources to make an autarkic policy at least remotely feasible.

While the priority given to industrialization may be understandable, however, it cannot yet be said whether that priority is defensible or whether its fundamental premise is in error (and perhaps in this respect more than any other, Romania's economic development constitutes one of the era's most significant experiments). Analysts are far from agreed on the extent to which the world division of labor inherently creates underdevelopment, best remedied by autarky. Even if there were agreement on an answer, Romania's leaders might not care: their position is one more of belief than of cool analysis, and it has a respectable lineage in Romanian economic history (see Montias 1967:231; Roberts 1951). One can trace the history of this belief, show its implications for agriculture and its human costs, and ask whether the end justifies the means; but whether or not its premise is erroneous cannot yet be demonstrated decisively. One can merely point to the greater success of agricultural policy in such other socialist states as Bulgaria and Hungary, and suspect that Romania's people would be better served by more balance and moderation in the industrial plan.

"Peasant-Workers" and Rural Incomes

Binţinţi villagers do not bother themselves with such questions. From their perspective, the issues are simple: their pay is lousy, they have no personal attachment to collective fields, and the state offers more attractive prospects in its beloved industry. Residents of Binţinţi are in an unusually favorable position to take advantage of these alternatives,[18] for living very near a main highway and railroad line, they have frequent bus and train service to five towns and large cities (maximum commuting time: two hours) that offer a variety of jobs, largely as skilled industrial workers. Table 1-1 provides a rough breakdown of the village labor force in 1973 (defined as all men and women between the ages of 18 and 64 inclusive, except for young people still in high school).[19] This table shows that 52 percent of the entire labor force (a full 85 percent of the men in it) work in occupations other than that of cultivator, mostly outside the village. Not all of the 37 percent whose principal occupation is in agriculture (93 percent of them are women) work

TABLE 1-1. The Labor Force in Binţinţi, 1973 (N = 510)

Principal Source of Income or Occupational Classification	MEN		WOMEN		BOTH	
	Within total labor force					
	N	%	N	%	N	%
Solely from agriculture (women: includes "housewives")	13	2.5	174	34.1	187	36.7
Work outside agriculture[a] (industry, white-collar)	204	40.0	62	12.2	266	52.2
Pensioned from industry, or CAP before age 65 (plus women recorded as "ill housewives")	23	4.5	34	6.7	57	11.1
	240	47.0%	270[b]	53.0%	510	100.0%

[a]Includes functionaries and CAP employees who practice a skill (e.g., tractor drivers) but do not depend on field labor in the CAP for their living.

[b]There are more women than men in the labor force as I have defined it because (1) more 18-year-old males are still in school, while 18-year-old females are either working while waiting to marry or doing nothing; and (2) many couples consist of a wife under age 65 and a husband over 65.

actively in the collective farm: many till no more than their private plots and call themselves "housewives."[20]

The basic pattern of livelihood in Binţinţi, then, is a "peasant-worker" pattern. Large numbers of villagers—primarily men—commute daily to work as skilled industrial laborers while other members of their families—primarily wives and elderly parents—stay at home, working in agriculture at least to some extent. A number of households consist of extended families in which both husband and wife of the junior couple hold outside jobs while the senior couple works in the fields and minds the grandchildren. These extended households—13 percent of all households in Binţinţi in 1973—constitute the best all-around adaptation to the "peasant-worker" employment strategy, for they permit family members to benefit maximally from the opportunities for both wage earning and food provisioning, without excessively taxing anyone's labor.[21] Far more heavily burdened are women in nuclear families with young children and commuting husbands, for an inordinate amount of labor falls upon them as wives and mothers who must also work in the CAP and private plot to make ends meet (see Cernea 1978; Hann 1980:144-146).

In schematic terms, the "peasant-worker" pattern creates a new norm in which nearly all households support production in two spheres, agriculture and industry (in earlier times, only some households supported production outside agriculture). But although family members' spheres of production differ, the products from their activities move in larger circuits that are similar. Like agricultural production, much of Romania's industrial production is geared to internal needs, while a portion of it goes to export. The factories that employ people from Binținți make items with variable destinations. Steel from Hunedoara's mills is important domestically but also goes abroad; sewing machines made in Cugir are sold both internally and to socialist-bloc partners like the Serbs and Chinese; about 10 percent of the production from Orăştie's mechanical works goes to Africa and Asia, clothing from its leather-working outlet is sold on domestic and foreign markets, and its furniture factory serves chiefly local consumption.[22] What distinguishes the peasants from the workers of Binținți more than the circuits of their products is their slightly different relationships to the means of production: workers work in enterprises owned by the state in the name of the whole society, while CAP property is still the common possession of its members only. This distinction has little practical importance, but in theoretical terms it suggests greater "exploitation" of peasants than of workers, for the state extracts surplus at least as stringently from CAPs it does not "own" as from workers in industry.

The movement of Binținți villagers between agriculture and industry is not without precedent. During the interwar period, especially in the 1930s, some villagers found in temporary industrial employment the means necessary to keeping themselves in agriculture; and during World War II additional numbers were able to stay in their fields by taking on factory work in Cugir, which was then manufacturing weapons and entitled its workers to army exemption. But whereas in those times the factory provided income supplements that shored up a primarily agricultural livelihood, the relationship is now reversed: work in agriculture provides food supplements to peasant-worker incomes, freeing city food stocks for city-dwelling labor and freeing peasant-worker industrial wages to purchase industrial products.

The shift from primarily agricultural to primarily industrial employment of Bințințeni is not just a measure of the state's favoritism of industry, which prevailed in the period before 1945 as well as now. One important contributor to the shift is increased infrastructural support for moving rural labor, chiefly through investments in the transport network. Another is that industrial earnings are relatively better than they were before or than agricultural earnings are now. Wages are especially good in some of the factories near this village. Of the 229 commuters in 1973, about half worked in highly strategic and well-paid industries in Cugir and Hunedoara City (40 percent and 10 percent respectively). And a third contributing factor, linked to the second and to the failures of the CAP, is a complete shift in how villagers assess the relative desirability of agricultural and industrial employment. Before the 1940s, peasants looked down on industrial work as evidence of a person's marginality to or failures in the more valued agricultural sphere, but now the occupation of "CAP peasant" falls very near the bottom of their evaluational scale.[23]

Given the flight from agriculture (in which individual investments of funds are now pointless), the socialist ownership of most other enterprises,[24] and the home agricultural supplements that save workers' earnings from having to purchase food, to what do cash incomes go? Their primary use is one form or another of conspicuous consumption, much of it serving to absorb the output of Romanian industries. Villagers build new houses or remodel old ones to create ever more imposing residences. Glossy and costly furniture adorns at least the sitting room used for guests, if not other rooms as well. People buy radios, TV sets, refrigerators, gas stoves, and washing machines domestically produced, as well as leather jackets, fur caps, and new watches.

Second, informants note a trend toward ever greater public displays at major rites of passage, especially weddings and, increasingly, baptisms. It is not just that the wedding feast itself has expanded, outgrowing the houses of its participants and moving into the village hall or even into a local restaurant, with larger and larger numbers of guests. Almost more telling evidence of display is the gifts collected from wedding guests, who once gave a chicken, a fancy loaf of bread, or some sausage but now give cash; and reports are that the size of the gifts is escalating. The very manner of the giving is occasion for display, and even for competition. The gift (*cinste*) is given to an official of the wedding party, who goes from guest to guest and calls out in a loud voice to the assembled company each donor's name and the amount given. Since participants are not uniformly attentive to this time-consuming operation, especially generous gifts from donors toward the end of the rounds must be trumpeted with especial vigor. From the often mammoth sums thus acquired, expenses of the feast are paid off and the remainder is given to the bride and groom to launch them into a lifetime of spending. Villagers observe that during the 1970s, not only weddings but the births of children began to be marked by larger feasts, and the public *cinste* had started to make its way into the baptismal celebration also.

The element of display in the two forms of expenditure noted so far is undeniable. A third form of expenditure is more complexly motivated: the sums spent on higher education for one's children. Under the socialist government, higher education costs a fraction of what it once did. No truly bright child is deprived of schooling because of financial inability, and most high school and university students have at least partial scholarships. Students nonetheless have expenses for transportation, clothing, and supplies, such as calculators for aspiring engineers, and their families must bear these costs from budgets to which the students (unlike their employed age-mates) do not contribute. Expenses of providing adequately for children at university may even cause mothers to leave the CAP for factory work. Parents who spend earnings in this way act largely from a wish to help their offspring into desirable careers that utilize their talents properly. But there are benefits that make these expenditures partake of display also: the very high prestige of their children's occupations — engineer, teacher, researcher, doctor — is contagious and gives the families a big boost up the local status ladder.

The three forms of expenditure mentioned above are the most common for Binţinţi, but a fourth merits mention: various forms of bribery. Less conspicuous than the other forms, it is not usually treated as "consumption" but is nevertheless an important way of spending cash. A social custom with a distinguished tradition in Romania, bribery once flourished mainly in cities, but now rising rural incomes are enticing it into the countryside as well. One finds petty bribery in the form of gifts to tractor drivers for plowing gardens, to collective farm officials for recording excess workdays or for being inattentive when hay is stolen, to employees of the furniture factory for slipping into the village with a load of sawdust (used as fuel in kitchen stoves), to doctors, who it is thought would not give concerned treatment without a "little attention." There is even talk, although little apparent practice, of bribes to improve the grades of children in school or to influence their entry into university.[25] Usually regarded as evidence of the corruption and bureaucratic decadence inherited from the days of Turkish rule or as a sign of the failures of socialism, bribery can also be seen as yet another kind of investment, like houses and furniture, in an economy that has few profitable uses for surplus earnings, the magnitude and circulation of which are constantly increasing.

The social orbits and aspirations of most Binţinţi villagers direct their cash largely to the three more conspicuous forms of "investment." These investments require fairly intensive inputs of labor in both industry, whence the wages come, and agriculture, which reduces expenses for food and releases income for other ends. High labor inputs notwithstanding, however, the possibilities for adequate earnings mark the present era as perhaps the turning point in a centuries-old process of constant labor intensification, whose lineaments succeeding chapters will present. Production in the current system still, of necessity, rides on intensive applications of labor because Romania lacks both the foreign currency and the indigenous capacity for generating capital-intensive high technology. But the volume of fixed assets and of funds for reinvestment has risen sufficiently that the system's main source of accumulation is no longer increases in absolute surplus labor. Elderly Binţinţeni have their own way of expressing part of this change: "Today everyone has money. In the old days you never saw much money because prices were so bad. Now you can buy anything. But the problem is, now no one wants to *work* any more: they come home from the factory and sit in front of the TV instead of going out to the fields. *We* used to work *all the time*."

This discussion of village livelihood has left aside one important group of villagers: the Germans. Their patterns of livelihood are similar to those of Romanians, with a few minor departures. Because of the expropriation of German lands in 1945, Germans had nothing to turn over to the CAP.[26] Efforts were eventually made to include them in the CAP labor force, using the private plot as incentive: those having sizable gardens around their houses could keep them only as CAP members, and those who had no such gardens would be given some if they enrolled. By this time, all able-bodied German men had been working in the steel furnaces at Hunedoara for a decade; they had no intention of returning to agriculture, and only two or three of them signed on (but rarely work) as collectivists. A slightly larger number of women did, and are now among the farm's most conscientious members. Aside from proportionately less involvement than Romanians in the CAP, German employment patterns differ in that all German commuters are skilled workers while some Romanians are unskilled (e.g., janitors, guards), and some German men draw fat industrial pensions from long employment in factories, while many Romanians of comparable age barely subsist on the miserly and irregular pensions of the CAP.

Such disparities in patterns of livelihood are, nonetheless, of minimal importance, and this is — as will be seen — a major change from
the past. Another major change, partly linked to this one, is a
reported shift in the character of relationships and attitudes between these two groups in the village. Because relations among
ethnic groups have been a central issue throughout Transylvanian
history, and because the present change in these relations is analytically significant, we should examine the present situation in
some detail.

GERMAN-ROMANIAN RELATIONS IN
PRESENT-DAY BINŢINŢI

We have already learned, in sampling the opinions of Romanian
villagers, that the community contains Germans also (about 10
percent in the 1970s, as high as 20 percent earlier in the century),
and that although relations used to be more troublesome the groups
get along fine now. Germans concur in this assessment. Some Germans even describe wartime discoveries that identification with
Romanians could be a positive advantage. The first postwar intermarriage (1945) occurred on the eve of their deportation for the
Soviet Union, and through it the German wife, with her new Romanian surname, escaped being shipped off. Several Germans
relate how, as prisoners of war in Russia before 1945 or as travelers
on public transportation while Romania was still occupied by the
Soviet army, they avoided harsh treatment from the anti-Nazi
Soviets by assuming Romanian identity, speaking nothing but Romanian among themselves. One woman was so impressed with this
discovery that she officially changed the religion on her marriage
certificate from Lutheran to Romanian Orthodox, in 1946. And
several had cause to be grateful for prior cordialities with Romanians
who now did them good turns. While these events are not sufficient
to have revised interethnic relations, they perhaps inaugurated the
warming trend that both sets of villagers have noticed.

Observation and a sharp ear nonetheless produce evidence that
"getting along fine" does not mean a complete absence of ethnicity
as a social issue. Ethnic identifications and notions of ethnic difference are very obviously alive, in spontaneous comments from
both groups, in stereotypes expressed, and in occasional mixed
events.[27] If you tell a Romanian that you have been visiting a
German family, the inevitable rejoinder will be, "I bet they didn't

give you anything to eat or drink" (untrue). Germans will talk disapprovingly of Romanians' propensity for clever theft and duplicity. Both groups will offer stories about some German parents who threatened to disown a son or daughter planning to marry a Romanian. Passersby may overhear German being spoken by a small knot of women working in the CAP, while Romanian women call out in irritation, "There you go again with that German jibber-jabber. Why don't you speak Romanian so we can understand too?" And at a German social gathering, when two men intermarried with Romanian women add a Romanian song to the festivities, a German has been heard to remark at the end in Romanian, "That was real nice," in a tone dripping with sarcasm. Germans will clearly imply that if Romanians were a less disorganized and more disciplined people, the CAP would work better. When a German dies and is buried the next day, Romanians will offer frosty observations about how hastily the dead person was disposed of, rather than being given a sociable send-off such as Romanians give, holding their two-day wakes with food, card playing, and amiable chatter around the corpse and finally burying it with loud displays of grief instead of with tight-lipped tears and Lutheran hymns. And although Germans rarely display drunkenness, a few have been observed brawling tipsily — in Romanian, a telling commentary.

Yet these images are countered by others. Tipsy Germans may sometimes brawl in Romanian, but they also tell jokes interminably in Romanian as well, averring that German just doesn't have many good jokes. At the funeral of a "hastily" buried German, the priest delivers double sermons, one in German and then a Romanian version for Romanian guests and affines (this innovation appeared in 1979). At one such funeral in 1980, a German visitor sang traditional Romanian mourning songs, which moved Romanians to tears (but seemed to disconcert some of the Germans present). Some Romanians say, "If it weren't for these Germans, we'd be as backward as hillbillies." And some Germans disliked a recent TV serial from East Germany because the fathers treated their children so brutally — a significant opinion, given that both groups say German fathers in the old days would never even buy their sons a drink in the pub, and given German comments about Romanians' generous spirit, especially with their children. The (Romanian) tax collector says admiringly of a particular Romanian, "He pays his taxes just like these Germans, one visit and you're done. Not like most of these other Romanians, whom you have to visit ten or twelve times before the whole tax is finally paid."

Concerning the Germans who turn their backs on intermarrying offspring, it emerges that reconciliations were effected partly through pressure from other Germans, who chided them for making a laughingstock of themselves with such intransigence on this issue. Real changes in German attitudes and behavior concerning intermarriage are revealed when we learn that only 3 percent of Germans married Romanians between 1893 (when the Germans arrived) and World War II, but since then the figure has risen to 32 percent; and since 1970, over 75 percent of village Germans have chosen Romanian spouses. The change has further ramifications. The child of one mixed marriage was baptized in 1974 in both Orthodox and Lutheran churches (its grandmother exclaimed cheerily, "God knows what religion she is!"), with godparents from both ethnic groups.

These indications of ethnic ambivalence are accompanied by other evidence of the changing significance of ethnic identity. Among Romanians this appears in their responses to questions about what distinguished the two groups in past and present. While Romanians most often characterize past differences between Germans and themselves in terms of wealth rather than by ethnic markers, most of them speak of present differences in terms of language, religion, and various aspects of "national character" (orderliness, diligence, etc.). Beyond this, however, if one examines the contexts in which Romanians spontaneously bring up the subject of ethnic differences, these prove to be very similar to the contexts in which social status in its broadest sense is assessed. Romanians eagerly point out how much finer their houses and furniture are than those of the Germans (it was once the other way around). But this is not to invoke a truly ethnic difference, since among Romanians modernization of houses and purchases of fancy furniture are major competitive arenas for negotiating status. Romanian observations that all German offspring are now professors and engineers (whereas before, these Germans rarely pursued higher education) are part of a more general interest in upward mobility. Finally, when Romanian women complain about the clannishness of German women in the CAP, the issue is not ethnic isolation so much as the inaccessibility of German gossip. Romanian village women exert great efforts to establish well-informed ratings of the moral qualities and overall character of everyone else, a job for which liberal applications of gossip are essential, and they are very frustrated by Gemans' reluctance to contribute their fair share in comradely fashion.

If Romanians now appear less explicitly concerned about inter-ethnic relations per se[28] than all their comments suggest them to have been in the past, to what extent is this true also of Germans? The question is better phrased in terms of German conceptions of ethnic identity in the abstract and of how actively they seek to maintain it. The answer is, in brief, that although elderly Germans are more concerned with a wider range of ethnic markers than are younger ones, even the latter retain an explicit commitment to some aspects of their ethnic identity.

When asked how someone is to be recognized as "German," most Germans mention language and religion, although Lutheranism is not a perfect indicator because some Germans are Roman Catholic. To determine how to categorize persons whose identity is ambiguous, a German asks whether they were baptized in or (in some cases) married in the Lutheran church or in the Romanian Orthodox church; whether they speak German, and whether they greet other Germans in German if Romanian witnesses are present; and how they classify themselves. Germans chart declining consciousness within their own ranks by the following indices: Do the children speak German among themselves while playing? Do adolescents consistently seek German rather than Romanian sweethearts? What language do the children of a mixed marriage customarily use, and what identity do they claim? Do people go out of their way to find and associate with German friends, or do they mix with more or less anyone? Do they know the traditional German songs and dances? Do people spell their names in the German manner or opt for Romanian spellings (e.g., Schmidt or Şmit, Pfeiffer or Faifăr)? All these are useful signs for gauging the persistence of identity among Germans who have moved to cities, as well as among those still in the village.

No German in Binţinţi lacks spoken facility in some variant of the German language (although younger ones often are ill-equipped to write Hochdeutsch). Most of them use German speech except in mixed company—and sometimes even then. All are nominally Lutheran, but church attendance among those under fifty is waning. The older generation, but not all of the younger, knows traditional songs and dances. Older Germans tend to associate among themselves, the middle generation does so to a lesser extent, and adolescents more often have friends among the Romanians than strictly with their German age-mates. Nearly all spell their names in the German manner,[29] with a few exceptions. On some wedding invitations sent even by the older German generation to Romanian guests, a Romanian spelling is used, and one German with political ambitions and a Romanian wife often fails to double the consonants in his surname (Romanian doubles no consonants). Some members of the oldest generation remain strongly opposed to intermarriage, while those in their thirties and forties (many intermarried themselves) appear to regard the prospect with equanimity, and most adolescents are loud in their opinion that the ethnicity of a sweetheart is inconsequential. The 32-percent figure for postwar intermarriages substantiates these different views amply.[30]

The fact that Germans under middle age are less attentive than their elders to some of the markers of German identity should not mislead us into thinking them careless of their identity on the whole. All these Germans, whether intermarried or not, are concerned that their children learn German. They are sent to German-language schools wherever possible (the state supports schools in minority languages in any settlement that produces a minimum of twelve pupils per class) or are tutored in German. In some mixed households, the non-German parent learns some German, and much German is spoken both within the family and among children at play. Even the German who has dropped his double consonants sends his children to spend time with their uncle and grandparents, where they will have to speak German. There is no German of Binţinţi origin, including those who have intermarried and moved to cities, whose children are not fully conversant in the language.

Most important in reducing the salience of German ethnic identifications is the overall transformation of the economy and its supporting educational and occupational structures. Upward mobility now depends on a largely homogeneous set of institutions centering on education, to which all groups have equal access, and societal development has diversified both the contexts for different social identities and the kinds of identities possible within them. For many citizens of Romania, a person's occupation is more significant than ethnicity in the context of work and often of marital choices also, even if ethnic identifications remain important in selecting schools for one's children, or friends with whom one associates. Overall, the former social system linked German identity with favorable class and status characteristics (more so than did Romanian identity), but today one's most broadly salient social attribute is position in an occupational hierarchy within which Germans and Romanians are similarly distributed. Many village Germans see the heightened social importance of occupation as a source of ethnicity's decline.[31]

There are also three major processes that work in the opposite direction. First, the official ideology of the Romanian government is that Romania is a multiethnic state in which all ethnic groups share the same political (socialist) values but have the right to free expression of their cultural differences (not, however, to organized political articulation of ethnic claims). In their linguistic loyalty Binţinţi Germans are, therefore, well within their rights. Despite some pressures toward assimilation, felt more acutely by Romania's 8 percent Hungarian minority than by its 2 percent of Germans, the state guarantees and supports some degree of schooling in minority languages, proportional representation in political bodies and in the Communist Party, minority-language publications, and various artistic and recreational activities. Some of these guarantees are overseen by the state-facilitated Councils for Working People of German and Magyar Nationalities, created in 1968.[32] As an example, Germans in Hunedoara hold an annual festival, impressively organized and very well attended, at the time of their traditional pre-Lenten festival. Organizational snafus that threatened to jeopardize one year's celebration were resolved through successful appeals to high Party officials in Bucharest, testimony to the active concern for supporting such events.

A part of what motivates this concern, however, is the second process keeping German ethnic identity alive: emigration to West Germany, assured for a given number of families each year by the Helsinki Conference of 1977 and also built into trade agreements between Romania and West Germany since the *Ostpolitik* of the 1960s.[33] When the steady stream of emigration petitions grew into a flood in the late 1970s, Romania sought to encourage its Germans to remain at home by creating a supportive cultural environment for them; West Germany also exerted some pressure, especially through priests, to staunch the flow somewhat. Nonetheless, as of 1980, Germans were still submitting tens of thousands of petitions to emigrate, or even fleeing on their own. The prospect of emigration is, I would argue, basic to Germans' interest in maintaining their language, without at the same time posing impediments to intermarriage, since spouses are permitted to leave regardless of their nationality. One German urbanite confirmed this view: when questioned about his careful arrangements for his son's German schooling, he replied, "I want to give him the means to choose."

The third force encouraging German identity, and the one most difficult to assess in its effects, is Romanian nationalism. Although nationalism has been a central theme in the politics of Romanians since the days of their unfavorable subjection within the Habsburg and Ottoman Empires, in recent years the nationalist defense of Romania's right to sovereignty has become so shrill and all-pervasive as to discomfit some members of the non-Romanian minorities. The effects of this nationalism are mitigated somewhat by the state's emphasis on the dignity, integrity, and historical necessity of the Romanian *state*, defined by its coresident groups, rather than of the Romanian *people*. But tension still inheres in the minorities' positive identification with the peoples of national states other than Romania, and it is deepened by the implicit romanianness of some of the current preoccupations. Much is made, in the media and in the classroom, of the Dacians—a historical population in whom the non-Romanians have little interest and from whom they cannot claim direct descent, as Romanians do. In the late 1970s Dacocentrism was everywhere, including on the official calendar of the Romanian Orthodox church, which was headed by portraits of the two Dacian kings Burebista and Decebal as well as by quotations from classical sources extolling the virtues of Dacian "relatives" (the Getae and Scyths) as peoples "most brave and intelligent" and "full of faith and wonderful in their Christian goodheartedness."

The minority groups have no public forum for self-aggrandizing counterstatements, and it is difficult for them to forget their separate identities in an environment saturated with such talk. Moreover, they must deal with a Romanian population puffed up by infusions of constant chauvinist rhetoric. A result is that at least one Binţinţi-born urbanite, raised with admirable evenhandedness in a German-Romanian home, is now a self-ascribed German in explicit reaction, and other Germans wonder anxiously where this nationalism will lead. The subject points up one of the most sobering dilemmas faced by the Romanian state: perceiving itself as potentially threatened both by Hungarian irredentism concerning Transylvania and by the ever-watchful Soviets with whom Romania shares a long border, it overplays its right to independent existence at the price of alienating some of its own citizens and placing its internal legitimacy on a shakier footing.

The preceding view of Binţinţi under socialism has touched on only some of the subjects one might expect from an ethnographic account. Nothing has been said, for example, of religion, kinship, socialization, or inheritance. And it has taken up its subjects under the heading of a paradox. "Sugar by the kilogram" suggests villagers' awareness of the great improvements in their standard of living under socialism, while "cow's tail by the piece" suggests the price they have paid for it, in an ever more complete and often bewildering divorce from their traditional means of production and habits of livelihood.

The paradox captures the essence of the development strategy of Romanian socialism: to reduce the agricultural population through various means, to build up industry, and to increase incomes sufficiently to create an internal market for the products of industry and for other items of consumption, leading to a better life for the Romanian people. The state sees these elements as integral parts of a single program: a better life is impossible without industrial development; national economic advance is measured not just in radios per capita but in the creation of a self-sustaining productive infrastructure; and agriculture must bear the burden for this. It is a terribly costly undertaking and exacts a heavy toll from its population, many of whom do not comprehend why the price is so great. If they occasionally complain, the cause is sometimes their incomprehension (or shortsightedness, or greed) and sometimes their having been asked to sacrifice far more than is humanly expectable.

The outside observer, rather like a therapist, can understand why things are as they are and have come to be so, while feeling they do not have to remain so forever. Sympathetic to alternative strategies for development and to the difficulties faced by Romania's leadership, one can nonetheless be concerned for the consequences this leadership's strategy will have upon villagers whose opinion has for centuries been solicited too seldom.

EPILOGUE: A BACKWARD GLANCE

This excursion into Binţinţi has exposed only some of the facets of this place, and even so it has begun to satisfy curiosity only by creating further mysteries. The following chapters will attempt to unravel a few of these mysteries; it would be well to pose the questions explicitly, for greater ease in seeking clues toward their solution.

Relations between the Germans and Romanians in the village are puzzling. There is something peculiar about the mixture of admiration and hostility, visible especially in the disjunction between a German who can tell a child, "If you marry a Romanian, never set foot in my house again," and the Romanian who observes, "Without these Germans we'd be as backward as hillbillies." The clearly implied change from harsher relations in the past to relative calm in the present ought somehow to be explained. It is not an issue of merely parochial interest, for one of the subjects most widely discussed in literature on modernization is the conditions that contribute to the rise of nationalism and ethnic self-consciousness in some circumstances and to their seeming decline in others. In following the relations among groups in Binţinţi, we will encounter both rising and declining nationalism, and our efforts to understand it will draw us far beyond the limits of this village.

Further puzzles concern the relationship between villagers and the political environment or state, another central issue in studies of social change. The reluctant participation of Binţinţi villagers in their collective farm betrays their resistance to a role created for and imposed upon them, without consultation, by the Romanian state. Their recalcitrance is not inconsequential: it is one — although far from the only — cause of the farm's miserable performance. One might reasonably wonder whether their behavior is just a phenomenon of the present (popular opposition to socialism, as uninformed social analysis would have us believe) or something of longer standing, merely the most recent phase in a protracted antagonism between autocratic polity and stubborn peasants. There are without doubt some unprecedented elements in the current situation: today's state is right in villagers' midst as it never was before, and it has effectively decreed their disappearance altogether qua peasants, through collectivization and the development of industry. Yet there are hints of continuities with the past nonetheless, for the Romanian state was building up industry at the expense of agriculture well before 1945. And going back even further, one finds that the thrust of state policy under Transylvania's eighteenth-century Habsburg rulers was also to erect an imperial great power on tax revenue from already overburdened serfs.

There is the further peculiarity that villagers have often not perceived as such the antagonistic relationship between themselves and the state that might be structurally identifiable. Just as peasants resisting the CAP nevertheless speak of this government as "a lot better than most we've had," in the chaotic revolutions of 1848 peasants loyally took up arms on behalf of the tax-hungry Habsburg dynasty under the slogan, "We side with the emperor." What, then, characterizes the relationship between these villagers, today and in the past, and the various states to which they have been subject since the days of the emperor? Is there a discernible trend, and does it say anything more general about processes of modernization? Does the state's eradication of peasanthood bear at all on the changing relations between Germans and Romanians?

A final set of puzzles concerns the constant present-day references to serfdom. What sense can it possibly make for Binţinţi to be called, in the 1970s, a "village of serfs"? How plausible is German villagers' view that the Romanians' feudal past explains the high rate of theft from the CAP, as well as the Romanians' prewar technological inferiority to themselves? What do we make of German comments about being "serfs of the Romanians" after their return from deportation to the Soviet Union? A villager listening in on a discussion of feudal times volunteers the opinion, "It was a lot like the CAP then, you know. Just like now, peasants had no interest in improving land or in getting as much production as possible. And the lord gave everyone a little piece of land just like our usufruct plot, in exchange for working his large fields." People point to the headquarters of the CAP, located in the house of a former feudal noble, and joke, "It was a mess before, and it still is today." And some of the proverbs they quote in reference to daily affairs come straight from the days of the feudal economy.

This association becomes richer the more one explores it. In 1980, as in 1820 (the year of a major feudal census), villagers own some cattle but no land, they work as little as possible on large fields with which they have no identification (even though these fields are now technically their collective property), they return home in clothes bulging with goods stolen from the "estate," and they work intensively and with far greater productivity on the small parcel given them in usufruct. The village enterprise is, as before, not a single self-sufficient unit but part of a larger division of labor; this "estate" is combined with others near it in a set of partially specialized and complementary activities. The labor on the estate is supplemented seasonally by workers coming from more mountainous districts, just as occurred both in feudal times and also under the pre-collectivization peasant economy of the twentieth century. In 1820 villagers were obligated, as they are now, to present the overlord with produce—eggs, a chicken, some milk—and (if they had plots below the minimum size) they were to associate in groups of two or three households to provide the pig that was required of everyone (Enea and Botezan 1969:116–117). As this list lengthens one begins to wonder if Transylvanian feudalism ever ended at all.

Phrased so baldly, of course, this question must be answered in the affirmative. Similarities of form do not imply continuities of system. To take an example, the present emphasis on display and on spending income for conspicuous consumption—for fancy houses, furniture, clothing, and entertainment—reminds one of a past in which feudal nobles entertained lavishly in palatial dwellings and spent income on display; both of these have occurred in economies having little room for profitable (i.e., entrepreneurial) investments of income. There are, however, crucial differences underlying the superficial similarities of form, differences not just in the social class of those doing the spending but also in the place of origin of the goods being displayed: largely foreign (except for victuals) in the case of feudal nobles, and largely domestic in that of socialist villagers. The contrast is enormous. Villagers of today are encouraged to be consumers in a home market that the state hopes to develop even more fully, while nobles of yesterday hoped to prevent the emergence of any local manufacturing at all (see chap. 3). The processes of accumulation implicit in the two scenes are therefore worlds apart. The third set of questions, then, concerns the Transylvanian economy, agriculture in particular, during these three centuries from feudalism to socialism, and the meaning of these superficial similarities of form within their different contexts in history.

One afternoon in December 1979, as I was talking with an old lady about prewar agriculture, her ten-year-old niece came in with a problem. "Auntie, sing me a Christmas carol, I need one for school." The old lady began:

> "We shepherds three are on our way
> To Bethlehem this holy day
> With gifts for Jesus Christ our King.
> O joy! Our Lady, joy we sing."

Before she could begin another verse she was impatiently interrupted, "No, no, auntie, Comrade Teacher said we shouldn't have any of those with religion in them. Sing one without religion." Scarcely missing a beat, the old lady resumed the same tune:

> "We shepherds three are on our way
> To Bucharest this holiday
> Gifts to Comrade Ceauşescu we bring.
> O joy! Our happy joy we sing."

It made a perfectly good song, with the rhythmic twitch absent in the original Romanian. But the meanings of the two variants, although linked, are scarcely comparable at all.

This vignette and the image of the feudal economy in modern Romania aptly represent the central questions asked in this book. They are questions not primarily about present social forms but about how present forms are framed by processes in the past. Their guiding assumptions are that the social phenomena we encounter have meaning and can be understood only in specific contexts, and that to examine both changes and continuities in those phenomena requires an account of the contexts as well. This book aims to understand the local forms of some phenomena often discussed in connection with processes of modernization and economic development: changes in the political environment of peasant populations, the rise and decline of nationalism and ethnic consciousness, and the transformation of local economies. It aims to clarify the historical context for the information set out in this chapter, about the social life of villagers in socialist Romania. Like all things social, these forms and processes do not exist in the abstract but in concrete locations. In this case the vantage point for examining them is a very parochial one indeed, a community of 600 to 900 souls in a little-known corner of Eastern Europe.

While the vantage point may be parochial, its present significance and the contexts that frame it are not. Inquiries enabling us to comprehend the historical processes from which socialist revolutions struggle to realize their objectives are far from trivial, at whatever level we can achieve them; for attempted transformations of this kind have become a fundamental part of modern reality. As for how these historical processes themselves are framed: understanding the character of ethnicity, economy, and the state as lived by these villagers requires us to begin with two related but separable contexts. The first is provided by the processes of state-building in Europe and in the Habsburg empire as it reacted to European state formation. The second is provided by the transformation of Eastern European economies from feudalism to peripheral capitalism to socialism. No explicit attempt will be made to justify such an ambitious choice of contexts. If our understanding of the problems posed here is deepened by inserting them into so large a frame, that understanding will be justification enough.

PART II

TRANSYLVANIAN VILLAGERS IN THE HABSBURG POLITICAL ECONOMY

CHAPTER 2

On the Side of the Emperor: The Development of the Habsburg State to the Mid-Nineteenth Century

Copilul cu multe moașe rămîne nebotezat.
(The child delivered by many midwives remains unchristened.)

Politica e o mare curvă.
(Politics is a big whore.)
— Proverbs quoted by informants.

Every man wills something different,
and what happens is what no man wills.
— Lenin

Villagers subject to a powerful and omnipresent Communist state in the 1980s are heirs to a long tradition of state-building, in which one after another aspiring central organization has striven to incorporate them into its plans. While not denying the importance of earlier attempts, I focus here on the efforts of the Habsburg rulers beginning in the eighteenth century,[1] with only a brief glance at the past upon which these rulers built, and which impeded their success. I begin with the eighteenth century somewhat arbitrarily—rather in the manner its rulers would have liked!—as a time when Habsburg monarchs made decisively new advances in centralizing their rump-of-a-Holy-Roman Empire within a Europe crowded by newly centralizing nation-states (see Tilly 1975).

This was the era of the enlightened absolutists Maria Theresa and Joseph II, who jointly endeavored to raise their state in the estimation of other European powers that, in the early 1700s, viewed it with derision and anticipated its imminent and impoverished demise (Ardant 1975: 201-202). As of about 1700, the empire's territories and population roughly equaled those of France but its tax revenues were five times less; Maria Theresa and Joseph II between them increased those revenues from less than 30,000,000 florins in the 1730s to 80,000,000 by 1780 (ibid.: 200, 202n). The increase would not prove sufficient to win the Habsburgs their desired estate within Europe; but producing it involved them intimately in new kinds of relations with the estates within their territories, which is the process examined in the present chapter.

The internal composition of the eighteenth-century empire was, depending on one's point of view, refreshingly or distressingly varied, divided into numerous historically independent entities with divergent pasts. In social terms, the empire consisted of a heterogeneous group of aristocrats emergent from or still depending upon agricultural livelihood, small and scattered bourgeoisies, and a huge peasantry; all these were subdivided within the historically separate territories, producing regional class segments that often had little in common with class equals in other areas. The dynasty's plan for state centralization depended upon a set of complex, frequently shifting alliances with one or another group in each territory. Its most entrenched and regular opponents increasingly proved to be the agrarian aristocracy of Hungary and Transylvania, in the empire's eastern half.

Although the struggle between monarch and nobility in these eastern lands had numerous dimensions, they can be simplified by looking specifically at the problem of revenues, which brought the two groups into direct conflict over the surplus that both sought to extract from the third main participant, the peasantry. But the tale of the eighteenth-century courtships and estrangements among and within these groups cannot be told without first locating them, at least provisionally, in space and time. To do so, let us regard the succession of three sovereigns from the village point of view and then inquire about the entities over which these sovereigns ruled.

HUNGARY, TRANSYLVANIA, THE EMPIRE, AND REVENUES

8 December 1506, Buda

We, Uláslzó, by the grace of God King of Hungary, Bohemia, Dalmatia, Croatia, etc., keeping in memory the services done us by our faithful subject János Corvin of Lipova and all his line, do freely give, donate, and confer upon his widow Beatrice and her daughter Elisabeth all properties held in his name: the holdings in Binţinţi, Vingard, Cut, Draşo . . . (Pataki 1973:132–138)

The Hungary over which King Ulászló II reigned in 1506 had been a feudal kingdom for five hundred years and had seen periods of strong kingly authority alternate with resurgences by the feudal aristocracy.[2] These fluctuations grew partly from internal struggles for power but were aggravated by frequent nomadic invasions from the Eurasian steppes (see McNeill 1964). Until the thirteenth century, the Hungarian kingship had been one of Europe's strongest, but it then suffered a decline relative to the power of the nobility. The shift was marked by a document called the Golden Bull, a sort of compact signed in 1222 by King András II, upon which an unwritten constitution evolved much as happened after the Magna Carta in England. With this document, the monarch sealed his submission to the lesser nobility, in particular; and by its terms the Hungarian nobles became a privileged and separate estate, entitled to such rights as trial by a special judge, immunity from taxes, the right to rise up against a king considered unjust, and guarantee of a parliamentary role. The monarch's power was thus constrained by noble privilege but was also preserved and consequently did not decline further, as happened elsewhere in feudal Europe (Marczali 1910:xxxiii).

This peculiar contract between king and nobility persisted even after the expansion of the Ottoman Empire brought about the dismemberment of the Hungarian Kingdom in 1526, when the victorious Turks killed King Ulászló's successor Lajos II. When the Habsburgs later acquired Hungary from Turkey in the 1690s, they were to wrestle interminably and in vain with the powerful Hungarian aristocracy and its constitutional rights, guaranteed and enforced since 1222.

28 February 1670, Alba Iulia

We, Michael Apafi, by the grace of God Prince of Transylvania, lord of parts of the Hungarian realm, and Count of the Szeklers, in consideration of the lamentable misfortunes of the noble lady Sara Gámány of Binţinţi, widow of Miklós Macskásy—himself driven into our realm by Turkish conquest of his city[3]—do freely give, donate, and confer upon her two serfs, to serve her and her heirs in perpetuity. (Macskásy Collection #238; hereafter designated "MC")[4]

The Transylvania over which Apafi ruled (1660–1691) had been the region at medieval Hungary's eastern frontier. Constituting, as it did, the outpost against raiding nomads, Transylvania had great strategic importance. As part of its defense, Hungary's kings settled colonists along the southern and eastern foothills of the Carpathian

Mountains, whose watershed demarcated Hungary from the steppes. The colonists included Teutonic Knights, groups of cultivators from the Low Countries—to this day called "Saxons"—and Szeklers, a group related to the Hungarians in a yet-undetermined manner. In further fortification of Hungary's heartland, the kings also made Transylvania into a special military zone, ruled by a *voievod*, or governor and commander general. An appointee of the king, this noble enjoyed perquisites of office that included huge estates making him the richest lord in Transylvania. The voievod's exceptional powers and wealth—products of Transylvania's strategic location—would prove sufficient for him to sustain serious claims to the Hungarian crown.

These claims acquired greater substance after Ottoman forces defeated Hungary in 1526. The next one-and-a-half centuries were to see the two aspirant empires, the Habsburg and the Ottoman, stalemated across the body of Hungary, while the voievods (now princes) of Transylvania nimbly juggled allegiances to both the emperor and the sultan. Turkish influence prevailed in Transylvania but complete control was never established; Transylvania remained a nominal vassal and payer of tribute, whose princes gained their throne through a combination of internal struggle and Turkish favoritism.

From at least 1530, these princes realized that the Habsburg and Ottoman forces would neutralize each other, leaving the principality much room to maneuver (Makkai 1946:177). During the late 1500s and early 1600s, a nearly autonomous Transylvanian state emerged and was strengthened.[5] Precocious absolutism blossomed in the reign of Prince Gábor Bethlen (1613–1629), a monarch whose conception of enlightened despotism resembled that of his Habsburg successor, Joseph II, 150 years later. Bethlen centralized his rule with the support of the gentry and undermined the power of the great aristocracy by confiscating their estates; the revenues from these estates maintained a standing mercenary army, freeing the prince from dependence on the traditional armed levy of the nobility. Internal trade and commerce were increased by mercantilist policies; foreign artisans and miners and Moravian Anabaptists were imported, state trade was organized with monopolies, and urban growth was encouraged (Pamlényi 1975:151; Makkai 1946: 230–231). Under Bethlen's reign huge herds of animals moved toward Viennese markets. Prices were internally controlled and related to prices abroad. For the first time, serfs could send their sons to school, and in the 1600s Transylvania was one of Europe's very few zones of religious toleration. Transylvania's status during this period is symbolized by the signature of Bethlen's successor among those of other sovereign signatories to the Treaty of Westphalia (1648).

During the 165 years of Transylvania's relative independence, the region's already complicated social structure developed the final complexities that have brought despair ever since to politicians and scholars—and, as will soon be discovered, to readers as well. There is no single way to characterize this complex social system, for at different times in history different categorizations have been employed by the residents and by their observers. I will discuss five of these, partly overlapping, and outline how they intersected: territory, jural privilege, religion, language, and class.

By the middle of the thirteenth century, Transylvania had become divided into three allogenic territories with separate administrative regimes. I will call these the Counties, the Szekler lands, and the Saxon lands, although a number of other names exist for them.[6] The Szekler and Saxon areas covered most of the border territory along the mountains between Transylvania and areas to the east and south; they had been colonized, as mentioned above, to fortify the frontiers of the Hungarian kingdom. To make this strategy efficacious, King András had found it necessary in the 1200s to create completely separate spaces for the two main groups of colonists and to grant them separate administrative regimes; otherwise, the wholly divergent economies of these two peoples—the Szeklers being quasi nomads and the Saxons sedentary cultivators—produced frictions impossible to resolve within a uniform administration and perilous to a strong defense (Makkai 1946:57–58). These two territories each occupied about one-sixth of the surface of Transylvania; the Counties occupied the remaining two-thirds and had still another administrative regime.[7]

To delimit these territories and give them names is fairly simple; it is more difficult to describe who lived in them. Most generally, each territory was associated with a group holding a particular jural status, all members of which enjoyed the privilege of liberty; each of these groups, called *natio,* conferred the status of citizen (as opposed to subject) upon its members, and all were regarded as noble. The Saxon and Szekler areas were each associated with internal rule by those two natios, and the Counties were associated with rule by what came to be called the Magyar natio. These three groups constituted what are known as the three "nations" of Transylvanian history, associated *grosso modo* with three regions. But members of these three "nations" were not the exclusive residents of their lands, for a very large group of subjects (as opposed to citizens) lacked the status of natio, had no territory, and was interspersed among the other three. The Szekler, Saxon, and County lands therefore had people who were not Szeklers, Saxons, or Magyar nobles, although privileges and rights in those lands were enjoyed only by those who were.

Complications proliferated with the Reformation in the sixteenth century. Until that time, citizens with privileges were Roman Catholic, and subjects were partly Catholic and mostly Eastern Orthodox. The Reformation brought in Calvinism, Unitarianism, and Lutheranism, which together with Catholicism were legally declared the "four received religions" of Transylvania, leaving Eastern Orthodoxy a merely tolerated creed. Conversions did not settle within the existing boundaries of territory and natio fully, although they did in part. The most perfect coincidence was that of the Lutherans, the Saxon natio, and the Saxon lands. Unitarianism was largely confined to the Szekler natio, some of whose citizens were Calvinist instead, and a few Catholic; noble Magyars in the Counties were Catholic and Calvinist. The subject population, scattered throughout, remained partly Catholic and overwhelmingly Orthodox until the late seventeenth century (see section 3 below).

These religious diversifications blurred some of the boundaries between natios; differences of language, which later served as the main marker for what became the *ethnic* meaning of "nation," blurred the boundaries differently. Again the most neatly bounded were residents of the Saxon lands, who were the only Lutherans and German-speakers. People of noble status in the Counties were Catholic and Calvinist and generally spoke Magyar (although many of them were ennobled from the ranks of the other tongues). Residents of the Szekler lands too spoke Magyar, or turned to it from a related language very early in their history, and therefore could be treated together with nobles in the Counties for linguistic purposes. Among the subject peoples some spoke Magyar and the large majority spoke Romanian. Map 2 shows roughly the distribution of the three administrative territories and the groups inhabiting them. (The map combines religion and language, clarifying but also oversimplifying, and it gives only a rough idea of the proportional admixtures of groups in the different zones.)

Although for this period privileged status within a feudal estate system was more salient than class, it is possible to describe loose groupings that had varying relations to the means of production.

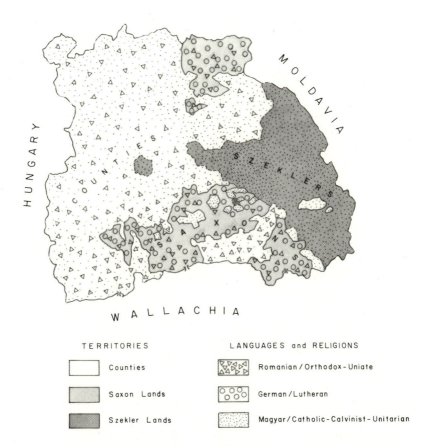

TERRITORIES

Counties

Saxon Lands

Szekler Lands

LANGUAGES and RELIGIONS

Romanian / Orthodox - Uniate

German / Lutheran

Magyar / Catholic - Calvinist - Unitarian

MAP 2. Administrative divisions of Transylvania, mid-eighteenth century, showing rough distributions of groups (religion and language combined).

In the Counties one can speak of privileged (citizen) landowners and subject serfs. Technically, in the Szekler areas there were no subject serfs; in fact, however, by 1600 the Szekler areas also had landowners and landless serfs, as well as some free smallholders. In the Saxon lands there were a few wealthy landowners and merchants, a larger number of artisans and small-scale merchants, and a large group of peasants, most of them free to own land despite marked differences in the amounts held. Transylvania as a whole, then, comprised a feudal aristocratic landowning class with rights to labor (this class being largely Catholic or Calvinist, Magyar-speaking, and resident in the Counties); a collection of bourgeois groups

—artisans and merchants—(largely German-speaking, Lutheran Saxons, though a number of locally resident merchants were Greeks, Armenians, and Wallachians); free smallholding peasants (some were Magyar-speaking Szeklers of various religions, more were Romanian-speaking Orthodox and German-speaking Lutherans); and various kinds of dependent cultivators—serfs and cottars (a very few German-speaking Lutherans, some Magyar-speakers, of various religions, and large numbers of Orthodox Romanian-speakers). Readers who find themselves overwhelmed by these multiple confusions will be dismayed and relieved to learn that there are still others, which have been mercifully left aside.[8]

Transylvania's period of relative autonomy gave it nearly two centuries of historical development very different from that of the Hungarian Kingdom whose eastern fortress it had earlier been. Yet its prevailing political and economic order of privileged noble estates and subject serfs remained similar enough to that of Hungary to hold open the possibility of recreating a single kingdom. Transylvania's ruling groups often perceived their interests and their situation differently from Hungary's aristocrats (Makkai 1946:9) and were somewhat different in socioeconomic composition from the Hungarian nobility—including far fewer great landowners and a large number of nobles with scarcely any land at all. But not only did aristocrats in Transylvania have lands also in Hungary, they all considered themselves Hungarians (Magyars)[9] once the issue of nationality came onto center stage. These similarities would help unify the nobles of Transylvania and Hungary against the Habsburgs, who were soon to become their overlords.

27 July 1735, Vienna

We, Charles VI, by the grace of God august and elect Emperor of the Romans, King of Germany, Spain, Hungary, Bohemia, etc., Archduke of Austria, and Prince of Transylvania, do hereby decree that the contesting parties from Binţinţi, Captain Farkas Macskásy and his relatives, in particular Mr. Ferencz Olasz, must, either through their own good will or through proper legal channels, resolve their quarrel, so that Captain Macskásy's relatives will cease and desist from interfering in the peaceable maintenance of his estates in Binţinţi by stealing his harvest, especially his wheat, to dramatize their claims against him. (MC #2838-2839)[10]

The Habsburg Empire ruled by Emperor Charles (1711-1740) was a sorry remnant of the great Habsburg Empire of the Spanish explorations and conquests. That earlier empire, having spent itself in inadequately financed wars, split apart in 1556 and then crashed in 1557 when its emperor declared bankruptcy, bringing financial ruin to all the territories included in the once-great Holy Roman Empire or dependent upon its prosperity. The more modest and streamlined Habsburg Empire of the 1600s (see map 3) contained, in the terms of a later era, "Austrian" provinces (Styria, Upper and Lower Austria, the Tyrol), "Czech" provinces (Bohemia, Silesia, Moravia), and an "Italian" province (Lombardy). By 1815 it would have acquired Venice as well as "Polish" and other eastern provinces (Galicia, Bukovina). But no acquisition augmented its territory, resources, and difficulties as much as the gain of the ancient kingdom of Hungary (including Croatia-Slavonia), together with Transylvania, from the Turks. The process of incorporation was begun under Emperor Leopold in the 1690s and concluded under Charles in 1711.

The Habsburgs were forced, however, to swallow their prize whole, and it would prove an indigestible morsel. Frequent reversals in Habsburg victories against the Turks in the 1680s and 1690s benefited Turkey's Transylvanian protégés: a war-weary Emperor Leopold took Transylvania in 1691 but under circumstances that left it nearly intact. His Diploma Leopoldinum guaranteed the autonomy, internal constitution, and jural order of Transylvania and did not attempt to regulate its formidable internal complexities. This entailed accepting an oversized and anti-Habsburg Magyar nobility augmented by refugees from the areas of southeastern Hungary upon which the Turks had preyed; a bewildering array of three privileged nations (Magyar nobles, Saxons, and Szeklers) and unprivileged subjects, the four "received" religions (Unitarianism, Roman Catholicism, Lutheranism, Calvinism) and one tolerated religion (Eastern Orthodoxy), and representatives of cities and walled towns; a decentralized system of county administrations (paralleled separately in Hungary); and an aristocratic Diet independent of the monarch and holding rights to appoint functionaries. The powers of the nobility and of this Diet, undiminished because international politics had weakened the Habsburg Empire and fostered the survival of a strong Turkish protectorate up to 1691, would come to thwart every Habsburg design for centralizing imperial power and would retard for decades the dissolution of Transylvania's feudal order. One might say that the Transylvanian nobility was the Turks' vengeance on Austria—a refractory and temperamental stepchild reared in the interstices of parental discipline.

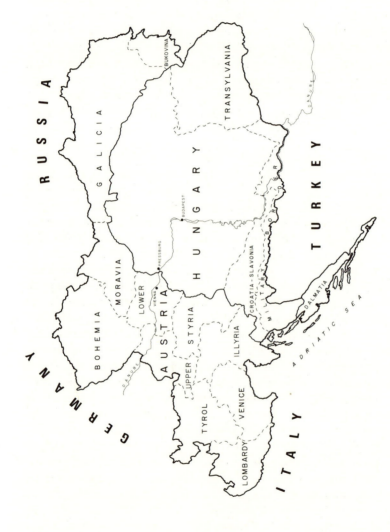

MAP 3. The Habsburg Empire in the early 1800s, showing Hungary and Transylvania along with other regions of the empire.

The affinity of these nobles with those in Hungary doubtless fed the Habsburgs' determination to incorporate Hungary separately when the Turks ceded it in 1699. Again, however, imperial exhaustion brought Hungary in on terms favorable to itself and unpropitious for the dynasty's hopes of building a unified European state. From the anarchy of the Turkish period emerged a Hungarian nobility undomesticated to normal centralized rule; and the Turkish occupation itself had followed upon a reassertion of the power of the great aristocrats against the gentry and the king. The Habsburg emperors, while they had ruled Hungary's northeastern corner during Turkish suzerainty over the rest, had sharpened the nobles' resistance to central rule by periodically trying to bring them more firmly under control. This involved infringements of the aristocracy's "constitutional rights"—that medieval set of conceptions deriving from the compact between King András and the nobles in 1222—and provoked a wariness not relaxed even after the final agreements of 1711, in which Charles recognized and guaranteed Hungary's administrative autonomy and the independence of its aristocrats.

Concerning the effects of Habsburg state-building on Hungary and Transylvania, I should point to a source of possible analytic confusion, arising from the fact that the two areas were incorporated separately and given differential treatment but were nevertheless similar in structure. It is probable that constant hostilities between the empire and Turkey entailed a special imperial policy toward Transylvania as a border region.[11] Thus, although the Habsburgs frequently engaged in intricate maneuvers against the nobles in Hungary, they were not always as aggressive in their explicit handling of Transylvania (see section 2 below). But because the two nobilities were similarly situated, had the same historical concern with constitutional privilege, communicated extensively with each other, and overlapped in their membership, policies aimed at Hungary could easily flow over into Transylvania. While the Habsburgs may have been less overtly oppositional to Transylvania's nobles, however, they were more concerned with the strategic importance of Transylvania's (as opposed to Hungary's) peasants, as a possible counterweight to noble resistance in this crucial zone. These speculations, which I deem well founded, clarify puzzling differences in Habsburg treatment of the two regions; the subtleties should be kept in mind, for they are sometimes obscured in the discussion to follow.

Habsburg monarchs hoping to consort as equals among Europe's other powers faced a daunting task. In playing by the rules of the time, they would waste much strength in military contests; and they would confront the necessity of rationalizing their administration and centralizing, disciplining, and technologically modernizing their army and finances. The trajectory was to be very uneven, as military defeats hindered internal centralization and as internal conditions unsuitable to centralization contributed to international failures.

The most serious internal obstacle was the inadequacy of existing revenues to build a bureaucracy and support a standing army without resort to plunder. Increased tax revenues required a more widely commercialized economy, better transportation networks, and more reliable collection procedures than existed in the empire. Of signal weight was the constitutional tax exemption for the Magyar nobility, which required state-builders to look to a cash-poor peasantry for revenues beyond those gained from mining, customs, and tolls. Emperor Charles's success in securing Magyar aristocratic assent to the creation of a standing army (1711), to be quartered and supported by the populace through permanent taxes, scarcely relieved imperial coffers—the less so as the emperor was obliged several years later to reaffirm his commitment to noble tax-exemption. The simultaneous pressures of war with France and problems of succession compelled retreat by the forces of centralization in favor of the territorial nobility. This scenario would be often repeated, until in 1867 the nobility and middle classes would decisively rout the Habsburg forces of centralization and create their own.

Denied a share of the wealth in noble pockets, for the time being, Habsburg state-makers turned to alternative sources. One tactic was to increase and regulate the trade in salt coming from the east. The long-standing importance of this trade within Europe had made control over it a cornerstone of the Hungarian Kingdom as early as the tenth century (Makkai 1946:39). In the principality of Transylvania and the adjacent county of Maramureş in eastern Hungary lay Eastern Europe's richest salt deposits (Dordea and Wollmann 1978:136-140)—indeed, an Austrian official noted in 1708 that salt was the crown jewel of Court revenues from Transylvania (ibid.:141). To benefit maximally from this resource, the Crown first consolidated ownership over all salt mines and then propped up the price of salt (so that smuggling along the Carpathians became a very lucrative by-employment among mountain dwellers). Salt production in Maramureş doubled from 1700 to 1750 and quintupled between 1700 and 1800 (ibid.:136). With overpriced salt, the clergy and nobility were drawn gradually into contributing revenues. At first they had been entitled to free supplies (only peasants and burghers had to pay the inflated price), paying one buffalo hide per eight centners of salt (about 450-500 kg) and something for the army horses used in transporting salt to their estates. This price gradually increased throughout the 1700s, and after 1765 all citizens were required to pay the official price (ibid.: 140n).

Transylvania's nobles were not enthusiastic about state interference in the salt trade. Many of them had grown rich from renting salt rights or using their free access to profit from selling salt — one such noble had sold 100,000 salt blocks in 1699 alone (ibid.:138). Transylvania's Diet opposed all Court plans for reorganizing the salt trade; individuals sabotaged Court efforts and charged tolls for salt transport along their rivers (ibid.: 141, 163). State interest in salt threatened more than the nobles' earnings from it, however. The Habsburgs faced the difficult problem not just of controlling salt in the east but of getting it out, for transport was miserable. To increase salt revenues meant regulating rivers and improving roads, largely with the labor of serfs, and then increasing the transport of salt along these routes, also with serf labor, labor thus withdrawn from the estates of the nobility. As the official Salt Commission was enlarged, as ever more villages along the main rivers were drawn into the trade (Binţinţi first appears in a list from 1804), as censuses were made of expert boatmen among the serf population (1774, 1777, 1784, 1810), and as regulations were passed (1784) that exempted any serf involved in transporting salt from his labor dues to his lord (Bassa 1970:141), nobles became fearful. Their labor supply in jeopardy, they began to protest that the state was exploiting the serfs.

For the aristocracy as a group, the salt trade was a threat in another sense: salt revenues were among the incomes considered the Crown's private property, thus not subject to Parliamentary control in their disbursement. These unmonitored monies were not negligible: of all the revenues managed by the Hungarian royal chamber in 1780, salt alone yielded 61 percent of the total (3,500,000 florins), or almost the whole amount of taxes voted on the populace by the Diet (Marczali 1910:319). Imperial success in building up so large a discretionary fund on resources from the east constituted a major triumph — one of the few — in state-building activities against a recalcitrant citizenry. It was only much later that the nobility came to see the personal benefits they might draw from the improved transportation opened in the name of salt.

In their perpetual quest for revenue, the state authorities lavished expectable attention on the tax system in the empire, especially as this affected their main tax-producing population, the peasants.

First, to increase the odds of extraction, taxes were assessed not just in cash but also in kind, particularly in the hinterlands of towns where troops were billeted (Binṭinṭi was in such an area). Thus, we find tax registers like the following one set up for Binṭinṭi in 1720:[12]

TAX ASSESSMENT IN:[a]

Tax on:	Cash (Rhenish florins)	Wheat	Oats	Hay
		(approximation, in liters[b])		(carts & lbs.[c])
Households	25	460 l.	1240 l.	5 cts. 200 lbs.
Animals	25	460 l.	1240 l.	5 cts. 200 lbs.
Agricultural income	25	460 l.	1240 l.	5 cts. 200 lbs.

Source: Magyar Országos Levéltár, Vegyes Összeírások (miscellaneous conscriptions), file F49, nr 7/22.

Notes:

[a]The form of this table is mine, not that of the assessors. I am indebted to Dr. Zsolt Trócsányi for translating the headings in the original document. The totals are presumably the tax burden for the village as a whole.

[b]The document gives these amounts in a complex manner that I have converted to the above approximations in liters. The figures are approximations because measures were inconsistent both across space and through time.

[c]A cart of hay is a cubic fathom, or about seven meters by volume. Additional assessments by weight were of variable volume, depending on how dry the hay was required to be.

In addition, tax assessments became increasingly individualized, a move that reflects the bureaucracy's increased capacity and determination and that would raise revenues further. Prior to 1730, taxes were assessed by "portals." This had been intended to mean households, but in practice it usually meant aggregates of about nine households, sometimes totaling fifty or more persons. Changes introduced in 1730 and then consolidated in 1750 by further changes replaced taxation by "portals" with a head tax. This greater bureaucratic penetration brought the state into unmediated contact with the individual producers, rather than with collectivities (villages or domains) wherein taxes were more easily dodged and tax liabilities irregularly apportioned (Prodan 1979 I:46–47).

Tax revisions and other means of extracting revenues were often opposed, indeed sabotaged, by the nobility, who competed with the state and with one another as well. One trick was to encourage the peasants to misreport their incomes and animal inventories so their assessed tax would be less—and thus their surplus for the lord correspondingly larger. For villages very susceptible to administrative supervision and control, the conflict was particularly acute. This likelihood was greatest in lowland settlements like Binţinţi rather than in remote upland villages, and the lowland areas were at the same time the most agriculturally productive ones, where the lords would most zealously protect their serfs against imperial predation. Two examples from Binţinţi provide a glimpse into how this conflict proceeded.

> 14 May 1736. Legal preliminary directed to the Imperial Tribunal.
>
> The villagers of Binţinţi testify that twelve serfs of Ferencz Olasz have been excused of their tax obligations, to the detriment of the other landlords [whose serfs would have to make up the shortfall—ed.n.] and that ten others have tax immunities, which some of them make up in labor services to their masters. (MC #2848)[13]
>
> 1820. Imperial Enquiry into the Conditions of Serfs.[14]
>
> We, the serfs of Binţinţi, declare that we have never paid our tithes (*dijma*) to our masters or to the Emperor, in our own memory or from what we heard from our ancestors. Our masters told us that even though many villages around here pay the tithe, and we are supposed to follow the law of the land too, our masters wanted to spare us serfs by taking no tithe so we could do more work for them at harvest time.[15]

These peasants' plain speech testifies eloquently to a fierce struggle between lords and state-builders for control over the products of serf labor.

CENTRALIZATION AND RESISTANCE I:
SHIFTING COALITIONS PRODUCE HOREA'S REVOLT

> 9 November 1749. To the Empress from the County Magistracy.
>
> The serfs of Binţinţi have given testimony concerning the flight of some serfs belonging to Peter Macskásy—one Bortes Avram and his three sons—who fled about 60 years ago from the Macskásy estate in Binţinţi. We know that they went into Wallachia and then returned with changed names to Transylvania. Some of them settled on ecclesiastical estates and others on lands belonging to

the Royal Treasury. Agents of the government came looking for them but could not track them down. (MC #2865)

28 October 1771

Seven serfs of Binţinţi pledge themselves as guarantors for eight serfs belonging to Farkas Macskásy, in Binţinţi. The eight serfs fled his estate and attempted to take refuge across the borders in Wallachia, but they were caught by the army. Their guarantors undertake to post bail and to prevent them from fleeing again. (MC #2901)

Tax revisions availed nothing if serfs continually fled across the mountains; it became a major concern of imperial authorities that flight would seriously enfeeble the rural tax base (Prodan 1979 I:15). This concern, together with the cameralist variant of mercantile theory to which the Habsburgs adhered — that welfare is best increased by increasing the tax-generating capacity of the agricultural population (Blum 1978:309) — brought the state into direct, repeated, and prolonged confrontation with the territorial nobility over the conditions of servitude. While it may be true that the Habsburg monarchs did more to reform lord-peasant relations than did the rulers of any other major servile economy (Blum 1978: 73, 221), an important motive for this was the general paucity of alternative sources of revenue at the monarchy's disposal. Any reductions that did occur in the burdens of the serfs stand as testimony to the progress of the centralizing state against its aristocratic rivals.

The Habsburgs and their advisers took several steps that solidified their tax base in rural areas. Among the most significant of these for Transylvanians was the establishment of Border Regiments among the peasant population, in 1761, using pieces carved from Transylvania's three "lands" (as well as parts of Hungary) and placed under a separate administration. Serfs enlisted in these regiments were freed of feudal obligations to their lords, becoming surer contributors to their empress. The Border Regiments were intended to hinder flight by increasing surveillance at the frontiers, and, doubtless, to lower the costs of maintaining an imperial armed force in such difficult conditions when external wars threatened constantly. The Border peasants fed themselves, paid their taxes, and served their empress's growing state, all for the price of a little manumission. And even that was cheap, for many of the areas mobilized were marginal for agriculture and were either minimally integrated into a manorial economy or in fact not technically (although often actually) of servile status at all. The formation of the Border Regiments had a number of unforeseen effects, among them that peasants suddenly realized serfdom was not an ineluctable fate (Prodan 1979 I:49); but emigration from the empire was scarcely staunched. It seemed necessary, then, to continue and intensify efforts to regulate serf-master relations in the serfs' favor, to interpose the state between peasant and lord in such a way as to curb the lord's power, to the state's advantage.

The Habsburg Empire of the 1700s was not the sort of place in which this would be easy. It had not been sufficiently centralized to incorporate the Magyar nobility of Hungary and Transylvania with the ruthlessness required to eliminate their obstructions to state-building. Consequently, the balance of power between the imperial government and the nobles was constantly in flux, resulting in well over a century of shifting internal coalitions, both intentional and fortuitous. The main participants, in the eastern half of the empire, were the peasantry, the nobility, and various organs of the state, but internal divisions within each of these multiplied the possibilities for alliance.

The nobility was so major a power within the empire that the imperial authorities could not do without some measure of its support. In what appears to have been a conscious imperial policy, Habsburg monarchs — especially Maria Theresa — set out to woo a segment of the Hungarian aristocracy. Through ennoblements (not only of Hungarians but also of others such as Italians, including the forebears of Binţinţi's Ferencz Olasz), donations of huge estates in the Hungarian Plain, offers of sizable loans that were cheap and secure, strategic appointments to the chief positions in expanding state agencies, county administrations, and church offices, and with other such enticements (see Marczali 1910:112-125), the imperial circles created among the most powerful Hungarian magnates a group that participated in the state and worked to further its development. Historically speaking, an alliance between monarch and magnates was unusual; it had normally been from the lesser, not the great, nobility that Hungary's kings and Transylvania's princes had drawn sustenance in solidifying their position. But throughout the eighteenth and nineteenth centuries, it was magnates, not gentry, who were the state's loyal agents and frequent contributors to policy formation. In the Hungarian and Transylvanian Diets this group tended to take stances less oppositional to the central government than did the gentry, who led every major reaction to Habsburg policy from at least the mid-1700s on. The division between magnates and gentry was not a phenomenon of Habsburg rule—it had been apparent since medieval times—but Habsburg policies enhanced the split, to good effect.

The effect was less marked in Transylvania than in Hungary, one of several important differences between these two branches of the Magyar aristocracy. Transylvania's noble families were, on the whole, older than Hungary's. Ennoblements and donations producing a grateful clientele in Transylvania were a sixteenth- and seventeenth- rather than an eighteenth-century occurrence and supported Transylvania's princes rather than some grander monarch (Makkai 1946:275; Oțetea 1970:233). Older donations made for a poorer aristocracy, as subdivision through inheritance worked itself out across additional generations: few Transylvanian magnates rivaled even a middle-sized Hungarian noble in wealth. Imperial authorities had little land to give out in Transylvania after 1700, and it seems that they did not manage to seduce many Transylvanians with other blandishments. For Transylvania's nobles remained more uniformly opposed to the Habsburgs than did the nobles of Hungary, a reality neatly captured in the fact that 30 percent of the convicted revolutionaries of Louis Kossuth's Hungarian revolution in 1848 were Transylvanians, who made up only 15 percent of Hungary's and Transylvania's combined populations.[16] However, authorities did not cease trying to woo the greatest Transylvanians whenever possible.

If the courtship of nobles had dire consequences only when pursued with inadequate ardor, the same cannot be said of the state's occasional romance with the peasantry. I have already attributed this romance in part to official concern with revenues, revenues unrealizable from an oppressed people with no cash income. Clearly, to shift the destination of peasant surplus required reducing their oppression. Peasants must be made to pay taxes, not *robot* (labor dues), which meant having their feudal burdens gradually relieved to make paying taxes feasible; and they must be made the subjects not of their lord but of their emperor, while perceiving the nobles as more oppressive than the state, the state as more benevolent and deserving of loyalty than the nobles. Meanwhile, these two forms of predation coexisted and made the lives of the peasants particularly dismal, from one point of view; yet from another, because the relationship had now become three-way (a situation always less stable than a dyad), it gave them unprecedented opportunities.

Experiments toward regulating feudal relations dated from at least the 1600s, but it was Empress Maria Theresa who breasted the formidable difficulties involved in this task with the greatest vigor and effect. Her most explicit reasoning appears in a late memorandum (1770), where she wrote, "The peasantry, who are the most numerous class of the citizenry and who are the foundation and greatest strength of the state, should be maintained in such a condition that they can support themselves and their families and in addition be able to pay their taxes in times of both peace and war. The rights of the seignior must give way before these considerations" (cited in Blum 1978:221).[17] In 1747, decrees had set maxima for the labor dues that landlords could exact from their serfs, but the reluctance of the nobility to publicize these regulations nullified their potential effects (Prodan 1979 I:47). Following several fruitless attempts to secure these so-called urbarial regulations with the help of the Hungarian and Transylvanian Diets, the empress ceased to summon the Diets after 1764 because they did nothing but obstruct. In 1767 the imperial Council of State (formed in 1761) issued a set of urbarial regulations for Hungary over the heads of the Diet (i.e., unconstitutionally), and its implementation was entrusted not to the usual aristocratic county administrators but to a special state commission (Blum 1948:50). This Urbarium fixed the number of days' *robot* for different categories of serfs, set minima for the size of a serf's usufructuary holding, established conditions within which work should take place, and so forth.

But the Urbarium was not applied to Transylvania, for reasons that remain obscure. Perhaps because Transylvania produced other revenues (salt and precious metals), it was less crucial to tap peasant agriculture—the more so as conditions for agriculture in Transylvania were much worse than in Hungary. Perhaps it reflects more generally a special state policy toward this strategic and sensitive border province, which, while it would not be spared any of the state's centralizing initiatives, might on occasion be treated a bit leniently. Whatever the cause, the imperial Council of State accepted the Transylvanian Diet's long-standing definition of labor dues: four days' manual labor or three days' labor with animals, per week, for serfs; two days per week for cottars with some land, and one day for those without. The Council left it to the lord's good judgment to determine what size holding would guarantee the serf an acceptable living (Prodan 1979 I:54).

The lords, for their part, responded in several ways. First, they proclaimed themselves distressed (as indeed they were) at the amount of work their serfs had to do for the state: quartering troops, carting salt, serving in the army, transporting taxes in kind, doing construction work, paying exorbitant taxes, and ruining their cattle with wartime transports of material and produce. Nobles set themselves up as the protectors of the peasants against exploitation by the state and decried the disruption of harmony and mutual affection between serf and master. They emphasized that the basis of governing should be law and precedent (their specialty) rather than the arbitrary whim of a single autocrat (Prodan 1971:31). One noble later expressed these views succinctly in a petition of 1790-91: "As for the condition of the peasants, no one has more at heart the defense and safeguarding of the peasants than their landlords, whose duty it is to protect them if only that their fortune should remain untouched and as large as possible" (cited in Prodan 1971:27). The nobles were especially anxious that minima not be set for the size of serfs' holdings — minima that would surely exceed the amounts already held — for the trend had been for landlords to enlarge their domains at the expense of peasant tenures. They served this end and also subverted government plans by advising their serfs not to declare the full amounts of usufructuary holdings to agents of the government censuses (1785, 1820) that were designed toward urbarial regulation, suggesting to them that their taxes would be increased (Grimm 1863:23).

Thus, despite the numerous urbarial edicts that emanated from the imperial council, in Transylvania these were ineffectual. This being the case, how can we say that the state's endeavors influenced coalitions among groups in the empire? Regardless of the outcome of state interference, it was now clear that feudal relations had become an affair of state rather than a private matter. The government had declared its interest in making the serfs its wards; this declaration put the nobility urgently on guard and alienated especially those who perceived in such regulations (correctly, as it turned out) their own probable ruin.

At the same time, a historically revolutionary idea had been planted among the peasantry: the idea that they might have an ally. The emperor won the ideological battle for the serfs' loyalty simply by opening to them the possibility that their burdens — and their lords — were subject to regulation. True, Transylvania's peasants complained about high taxes and the hardship of billeting troops, but they complained more about the difficulties of their lives as serfs, and they unquestionably saw in the emperor a benevolent patron siding with them against their masters' demands. The belief in the "good emperor" is clearly evident from at least the late 1700s until at least 1848. Time and again during this period, peasants supported their protests by invoking the emperor's presumed protection. They circulated the news that he had proclaimed them free or granted other benefits, but that the nobles were hiding the truth and refusing to implement it (Cherestȩşiu 1966:142). In the chaotic year of 1848, when the rumor spread that the Hungarians had overthrown the old emperor and raised up a new king of their own, the response of the peasants and their leaders was to counterorganize under the slogan, "We side with the emperor" (Noi ţinem cu Împăratul — Cherestȩşiu 1966:296).

While the delicate balancing act, the coalitions and ideological battles, among these three principals continued well into the nineteenth century, perhaps the best place to see it happening is in the reforms of Emperor Joseph II, who ruled jointly with his mother Maria Theresa from 1765 to 1780 and then alone until his death in 1790. It was from these reforms that there erupted a major peasant uprising in 1784. This uprising was produced, in my view, precisely by the shift in the overall field of power within which peasants acted (see Wolf 1969: Conclusion), a shift caused by the state's incursions upon noble prerogative, to the peasants' benefit. It was Habsburg centralization and the changing coalitions among peasants, nobles, and state that generated this most significant of Transylvania's peasant rebellions. The serfs rose up to attack the feudal system, indeed, but they did so in the emperor's name, with his supposed blessing, and on his supposed orders to extirpate the nobility from Transylvania's soil.[18]

Emperor Joseph II represented the epitomal enlightened despot of the late eighteenth century. His reign, like that of his mother, gave succor to the agricultural population, though in a very paternalistic way (his motto was "Everything for the people but nothing by the people" [Prodan 1971:234]). At the same time, however, he and his advisers hoped to disarm potential middle-class revolutions by anticipating them with policies to facilitate the growth of a bourgeoisie (Prodan 1971:229) and the development of a market economy. The authoritarian absolutism of Joseph II exemplifies the reforms and paths to centralization that an intelligent analyst of the times deemed necessary for more effective participation in the continental economy and state system. That his government could even contemplate these ambitions testifies to the relative success of state centralization earlier in the century; that he was forced to revoke most of his major reforms underscores how discrepant were the internal possibilities for political evolution and his perceptions of the demands posed by the international order.

For present purposes, among the most important of the Josephine reforms were those aimed at centralizing the administration (thereby angering local representatives of the county administrations he hoped to set aside) and those directed at regulating the conditions of the serfs. The general philosophy of his administration was to reform, not overthrow, feudal relations and to retain the old compact with the nobility (Prodan 1971:243). But imperial policy on further centralizing the state so irrevocably estranged a major segment of the aristocracy that the compact with the nobility was imperiled. This regime wished to streamline the bureaucracy far in excess of anything hitherto seen. In the interests of efficiency, the government declared in 1784 that the language of administration throughout the empire would be German rather than "dead" Latin (or, as it had been in Transylvania since the sixteenth century, Magyar). Following this assault on local administrative custom came an order dissolving the system of administration by autonomous counties and introducing a centralized bureaucracy with completely new territorial divisions and many German bureaucrats. This was an abomination to the lesser nobility, whose preserve and chief livelihood the county system had become. Imperial policies concerning the serfs further outraged this group of nobles as well as many magnates whom the administrative changes might not have distressed. Although during the course of the nineteenth century many magnates would come to favor the emancipation of the serfs, this was not their frame of mind in the 1780s; Joseph's determination to abolish serfdom met with united opposition among all groups of the nobility.

While the nobles were accurately perceiving their conflict-ridden compact with the Crown as being in jeopardy, what were the views of the apparent Court favorites, the peasantry? Let me speak only of the peasants in Transylvania, for it was they who offered their views most vocally. To say "peasantry" is, of course, to oversimplify, for there were several different kinds of peasants in Transylvania; but given how little internal evidence there is for the attitudes of each of them, I must let the simplification stand. The rural population of Binţinţi and villages like it saw, in 1773, with their own eyes and for the first time in history, the emperor whose subjects they were. He had traveled on horseback along the Mureş River valley (the road passed through Binţinţi), stopping to inquire into the living conditions of the people and collecting thousands of petitions thrust into his hand along the way—a total of 19,000. They had heard of his visits into peasant dwellings in other villages, where consternation had been visible in his face as his Saxon interpreter translated for him the peasants' answers to his questions: we serfs of Count Farkas Kuun of Geoagiu must work five and sometimes six days a week for our master, who never gives us so much as a crust of bread all day; we serfs of Count Gergely Bethlen give four days a week of manual labor and then two to three weeks' uninterrupted work with animals (Prodan 1979 II:236); we serfs of Baron Antal Orbán of Binţinţi were tied for twenty-four hours by our necks and hands to a post when we couldn't manage to raise it for him (Prodan 1979 II:263).[19] They saw in the emperor's reactions the first sign that they themselves might have some rights and that their landlords were not, after all, sacrosanct and omnipotent but subject to laws, like themselves (Prodan 1979 I:70-71, 78).

After this first visit, peasants occasionally heard of some edict the emperor had issued in their favor. A second visit from him in 1783, along the same route, reassured them of his continued sympathy and concern. More complaints were encouraged, more petitions received. After this visit, word went around that he had proclaimed further regulations which, since no effect was visible, must be being obstructed by the nobles. Clearly the emperor was on their side and wished to improve their lot; clearly he did not know that his good intentions were being thwarted by the lords and the local authorities.

Since the emperor had proved so receptive to the grievances of his people and since the authorities were untrustworthy, a few peasants took it upon themselves to journey to Vienna to seek audiences with him. Two in particular—a cottar known as Horea and his companion known as Cloşca, from a mountain village about seventy kilometers from Binţinţi—went, indeed, several times, and word traveled that they had seen the emperor and had been encouraged to take matters into their own hands.

In the summer of 1784 peasants learned that volunteers were being sought for the army and were to present themselves in Alba Iulia, thirty kilometers east of Binţinţi. The news spread like fire; the imperial recruiters found themselves deluged with peasant volunteers. Everyone who presented himself was told to give his name and then return home, continue his labor dues, and await further word. The populace rapidly understood this as part of the emperor's plan to free them, for all knew well that serfs taken into the Border Regiments two decades before had been freed. Then suddenly peasants heard that the recruitment had ceased. They suspected treachery and subversion of the emperor's wishes. The suspicions were fueled by the evident opposition of the nobility to recruitment: serfs from Sîntuhalm belonging to Ferencz Macskásy, who also had properties in Binţinţi, complained to authorities that since they signed up he had treated them harshly, had put two serfs in irons, taken the crops and animals of two cottars and tossed their wives and children into the street, and threatened to punish everyone with fifty lashes and send them to prison (Prodan 1979 I:249).

When residents of Binţinţi heard that on November 2, 1784, the serfs in the nearby mountains had risen up under their leaders Horea and Cloşca and a third, Crişan, they had no reason to doubt the rebels' claims that these were orders from the emperor. They were told, the emperor ordered our enlistment, and now he has ordered us to kill all the Hungarians and nobles and burn all noble properties (Prodan 1979 I:289); and as for anyone who does not join us, the emperor is coming along behind us with his troops and will put to the sword all those who hang back, and their wives and children with them (Prodan 1979 I:318). Peasants in Binţinţi saw some of their nobles flee in panic to cities some distance away.

None too soon, for at six o'clock in the morning four days later, the rebels arrived in Binţinţi, entreating and commanding locals to take up the torch. The core of the rebel army swept onward, leaving the villagers to murder, loot, and burn. The serfs of Binţinţi, in all likelihood convinced that they were doing the emperor's bidding, wrought terrible devastation on the properties of at least eleven nobles and the Calvinist minister. They cut off the head of the Savior in the village church. They attacked the castle of Baron Orbán with especial fury, setting it on fire, destroying the flowers and fish ponds, raiding cellars and granaries, opening wine casks until wine flowed ankle-deep (Prodan 1979 I:339). Orbán and two others reported to authorities, upon their return from Sibiu where they had fled, "We saw such ruin as neither Turk nor Tartar ever wrought in Transylvania" (ibid.:340).

In the midst of this debauch, an armed force surprised about one hundred Binţinţeni and their comrades; thirty-six people died, forty-two were wounded and taken prisoner to Deva, where many were summarily beheaded, eight of them Binţinţeni (Densuşianu

1884:188). This effectively ended the destruction in Binţinţi, though rampaging serfs continued to pillage and burn in surrounding settlements.

For ten days the violence continued, with few further reports of armed intervention like the one in Binţinţi. Then word was spread that the army had proposed, and the rebel leaders accepted, an eight-day truce until the emperor's response should arrive. The peasants became quiet, but not docile: serfs of Count Gergely Bethlen, with properties in Binţinţi and many other villages, refused to work, Bethlen's agents reported to him (ibid.:422). Peasants in other villages nearby complained to the authorities that their landlords had pushed them out of their own dwellings and had installed themselves and their retinues on the excuse that they now had no other shelter. Peasants feared this boded ill (Prodan 1979 II:114). Some peasants, finally, heard rumors that members of the nobility, alarmed at the casual attitude of the army, had called for an armed insurrection of the nobles according to medieval custom, but this insurrection did not materialize.

By the expiration of the truce, the rebels realized they had been tricked into marking time while imperial forces could be gathered. Discovery of this deception triggered a second rising, but now the rebels more often encountered troops. With each such encounter a question began to gnaw at them, more and more insistently: since the emperor's army was definitely moving against the peasants, whose side was the emperor on? The question was more or less answered when the rebel leaders were captured, tried, and sentenced to death. Before their execution, at the emperor's orders they were paraded in chains through all the villages in the Mureş River valley—through Şibot, Binţinţi, Geoagiu, and all the rest between Deva and Alba Iulia—to prove to those who had taken part that the instigators were indeed captive and about to die at the emperor's command. The emperor had further ordered each village in the rebel region to send six serfs to witness the executions. We can assume that six Binţinţeni watched while Horea and Cloşca were broken agonizingly on the wheel and then carved into pieces. How they explained this event to themselves there is no way of knowing; but that it was not a lesson in humility is clear from the fact that five months later the authorities undertook an inquiry into why serfs refused to resume their labor dues, and the inquiry was begun in Binţinţi (Prodan 1979 II:557).

From the nobles' point of view, there had been no doubt about whose side the emperor was *not* on: their own. The treatment they had suffered at his hands made them quite ready to believe that the peasants truly were acting with his support—were even secretly inflamed by him. They were angered but probably not surprised when Joseph refused his chancellor's proposal that the despoiled nobility be given aid—he retorted that their sudden penury was their own fault (ibid.:19–21). Even more infuriating was that the imperial commission investigating the revolt treated the rebels so leniently as to encourage future disobedience: hundreds of prisoners taken in the rebellion were closely questioned about its causes and then released under amnesty. And many nobles thought they saw the emperor's fine hand at work in the manner of Horea's execution: though sentenced to be broken on the wheel until dead, he was given the coup de grâce after only a few moments' torture. Some of the spectators complained that his execution had been suspiciously brisk.

More than anything else, the nobility abhorred the government's delay in bringing the rebels to heel. And it is in trying to understand this delay that we see simultaneously at work the problems attendant upon centralizing the state and the chaotic effects of the Court's tacit alliance with the peasantry. From the evidence and the analysis given in David Prodan's monumental work on the subject (Prodan 1979), it is clear that internal rivalries and the institutional differentiation of administrative organs were what allowed the revolt to achieve the amplitude it did. These complex processes can be schematized as follows.[20]

Joseph's determined pursuit of state centralization had made important inroads into Transylvanian autonomy. The commanding general of the army in Transylvania, formerly the unquestioned subordinate of the Transylvanian governor, was now rivaling him for primacy in running Transylvania's affairs. Both offices were filled by Court appointees; yet the governorship, despite its supposed integration into the newly created unified bureaucracy, was still marked by Transylvania's historical autonomy. It was not yet the office of a Habsburg career bureaucrat but instead joined imperial service to the earlier tradition of independent action. Furthermore, the separate administrations of the Counties were not yet streamlined into working in concert with the other administrative organs and were still dominated by the intransigent lesser nobility. The governor, the Counties, and the commanding general were thus imperfectly coordinated and internally at odds, the product of old hostilities among various bodies and among the social groups that monopolized each of them. In a word, the new administrative machinery was too recently installed to be functioning without hitches.

The Imperial Command, for its part, worked in harmony with the emperor yet hesitated to act without his explicit orders, which were impeded by the backward state of communication in Transylvania. When the revolt erupted, the nobility and civil organs demanded armed retaliation. The Imperial Command did not, however, see itself as the tool of civil authorities, and the general, like many of his predecessors, actively sympathized with the peasantry, whom he saw as having every reason to rebel. In fact, the army had often warned the government of the possibility of revolt, hoping thereby to advance the rectification of serfdom's abuses (Prodan 1979 II:13). The Imperial Command had no taste for sacrificing to serve the nobles nor for summarily smashing an aggrieved populace in whom the emperor had shown great interest and who, it was clear, were not at all raising an anti-imperial rebellion. Given these latent coalitions among monarch, army, and peasants, the commanders chose to wait for the emperor's express orders before moving against the peasants (Prodan 1979 I:264, 460-61).

The commanding general therefore sent news of the outbreak to Vienna, maneuvered his troops but tried to avoid engaging the rebels, was deaf to the irate demands of the nobles and County assemblies, set in motion the possibility of a truce, and waited. His report took ten days to reach Vienna; the order to suppress the rebellion took another ten to return—probably record speed, for those times. The institutional malintegration of the various spheres and the rivalries among them are perfectly captured in a single image: separate requests, that of the army for orders and that of the administration for military protection, move toward the emperor along the same roads, at the same pace, from the offices of the Transylvanian governor and the Imperial Command, which stand one block apart in the city of Sibiu. While Prodan sees this as purposeful separation of powers in the interests of effective domination by the center, I see it rather as the fortuitous result of the imperfect bureaucratic rationalization and insecure position of supremacy that plagued the Habsburg state of that day.

The rebellion left many problems in its wake. First, its very occurrence persuaded imperial circles of the need for some sort of urbarial regulations, and these were passed and maintained in force despite the vigorous objections of the nobility. That the regulations were far from comprehensive nonetheless betokens the state's inability to carry to conclusion what it thought necessary. And the regulations caused further trouble among the serfs, who did not understand that to be legally unbound from the soil did not mean the end of feudal dues. Second was the problem of indemnifying landlords for their ruined property. Claims from 489 looted estates in just one county, that containing Binținți, exceeded 775,000 florins (Jankovich Commission, microfilm, fasc. VI #684), in a day when a pair of draft oxen cost at most 30 florins. Two nobles with properties in Binținți sustained some of the heaviest damage of all; these two submitted 0.4 percent of the county's claims (2/489) but their damages amounted to 5.7 percent of the registered total. The Court decided that any damages not recouped by peasants returning stolen goods would be submitted to the state for consideration.

So much for the nobles and the state. The peasants returned to an existence almost as miserable as before, but with an occasional insubordinate and cunning exception:

30 April 1788. Legal preliminary.
Thirteen Bințințeni testify concerning the behavior, over the past few years, of one Josef Sfirlus, steward and serf of Ferencz Macskásy. We know he was arrested in the uprising and taken prisoner to Deva for having been caught while looting the castle. We heard his master, Ferencz Macskásy, say that if he himself had not posted bail, Sfirlus would have lost his head in Deva like most of the other captives. But he returned to Binținți, and very high and mighty he's become. We've heard him bossing and swearing at Master Ferencz Benkö and seen him try to bash in Benkö's head with a club once when he was drunk. And he seems to have stashed away a fair amount from those manors he robbed. And we remember that before the revolt all his friends were poor men and he often had nothing to eat for supper. But now he seems to be eating and living quite well. (MC #446)

CENTRALIZATION AND RESISTANCE II: THE PROS AND CONS OF ROMAN CATHOLICISM

If, until the suppression of Horea's revolt, the serfs of southern Transylvania had imagined themselves the sometime friends of the Habsburg monarch where feudal relations were concerned, the two were, in the religious sphere, decided (though partly unwitting) opponents; in this, peasants shared sentiments with some other Transylvanians.

Before rising up in the emperor's name against the nobles in 1784, these peasants[21] had caused several disturbances over the subject of religion. The reason was the Habsburgs' drive to catholicize their subjects, using the Church as an instrument to achieve the unity so conspicuously absent in the empire.

Transylvania was the Habsburg land least likely to muster a receptive attitude toward such intentions. Not only was much of its peasant population Eastern (largely Romanian) Orthodox, but its Lutheran German burghers and its Calvinist and Unitarian Magyar and Szekler nobles were accustomed to religious freedom. During the Turkish occupation, Hungary and Transylvania had become strongholds of Protestantism. The Turks did nothing to hinder Protestantism's spread (Macartney 1934:77), for such conversions helped to ensure that the nobles would not form a subversive compact with Catholic Austria. In Transylvania the legitimacy of Protestantism was codified by the beginning of the 1600s. It was, therefore, a fact of life that the Habsburgs had to accept when they covenanted Transylvania's autonomy (a fact that rankled, too, for Protestantism had become for Magyar nobles in Hungary and Transylvania a symbol of opposition to Habsburg centralism). Their acceptance did not, however, exclude their making vigorous efforts to foster Transylvania's toleration of ever larger numbers of Roman Catholics.[22]

The population most solicited in this drive was the Romanian Orthodox peasantry. One can imagine several reasons for the government's serious desire to catholicize the Romanians. Certainly a conscious aim was to win souls to the true faith, but the policy had several further effects, inadvertent or not. First, Transylvania's unsubdued status in the empire—its autonomy, its laws, its social structure all being protected—clashed strikingly with the objectives of imperial rule and centralization, and this dissonance was even more alarming given Transylvania's strategic location in the empire's defense. Prodan suggests (1971:113-114) that the Court purposely elected to leave Transylvania privileged so the nobility would not weaken the empire by rebelling, but at the same time chose to advance imperial unity by catholicizing Transylvania's population. Other analysts see in the campaign yet another facet of a consistent policy to wear down all local particularisms, in the interests of bureaucratic modernization, and to check the power of the Protestant Estates (Hitchins 1979: 216; Oțetea 1970:275). The Transylvanian Chancellery gave its view of the imperial position thus, in 1782: to catholicize Romanians had two objectives, the theological one of bringing schismatics back to the fold and the political one of breaking connections with foreign powers (i.e., the Romanian principalities across the mountains) so Catholic Romanians would incline toward their emperor and not toward a foreign prince (Ciobanu 1926:6–7).

The means selected for the task was the Uniate church, a hybridization of the Roman Catholic and Orthodox faiths. Tested earlier among the empire's other Orthodox peoples (e.g., Ruthenians), it was inaugurated in Transylvania in 1692, accepted with revisions by the Orthodox archbishops in 1697, and codified by an imperial diploma in 1699. To become a Uniate (and therefore a "catholic") required accepting four points of doctrine on relatively arcane matters, but the conversion formula wisely left untouched the rituals— icons and saints' days—so central to the peasants' faith. The state dared hope that Romanians would become Uniate to improve their status: for several centuries the Orthodox population in Transylvania had been merely tolerated and had never been privileged like members of other faiths; their priests were not *ex officio* members of the nobility but were of serf status; their flock had no access to educational institutions or other benefits. Authorities focused attention on the Orthodox clergy, whose conversion would, it was hoped, ramify downwards. And they anticipated ready conversion by the clergy, enticed by liberty from bondage and upward movement into noble status.

Early signs pointed to a successful project, as clerical conversions proceeded fairly well. But if at first the rural congregations were confused or even ignorant of the change—since the rites and liturgy remained nearly identical, parishioners whose priests did not tell them of the new arrangements often did not even know they were technically converts—this confusion soon resolved itself into outright rejection among many Romanians, especially those in the southern region. Peasants began to leave the Union en masse as of 1744, when a visionary Serbian monk appeared among them and preached against the Uniates. Centers of counteractivity sprang up in towns along the Mureș valley from Sibiu to west of Deva (Hitchins 1979:230); protests flew to Vienna; communities moved against their Uniate priests, throwing some out and restricting others' rights of village membership; villagers swore that they had never been Uniate in fact. And again, many of the actions against the Union were made in the sovereign's name. Let us see something of the Union's progress in one rural settlement.

1 January 1745, Binținți

Three nobles of Binținți draw up a contract, at the request of the villagers, and in response to the petition of the Uniate priest, Toader

Popa, to use the land, grain, and animals pertaining to the properties of the church. The villagers grant him use of the church lands
until April 24 but refuse permission to use the wine or cereals produced thereon after that date. The priest in turn renounces the
normal parishioners' obligation to keep his shed and hayrick in good
repair. (MC #2862)

20 June 1745, Binţinţi

Six serfs of Binţinţi stand as guarantors, against heavy property
forfeit, for the pledge extracted from George Popa, serf of Lt. Col.
Farkas Macskásy of Binţinţi, that he will not flee from his lord's
domain, will not study, and will not prepare himself to enter the
priesthood. (MC #2863)

1747, Vienna

The Empress Maria Theresa presses ahead with the campaign against
orthodoxy and requests a list of all the schismatics. She further orders
the arrest of two leaders of Orthodox opposition to the Union, one
from Alba Iulia and one from Binţinţi, who will stand trial for
having incited the populace against the Union, even defying military
orders as they did so. (Dragomir 1920:175–176)

1751, [Blaj]

The Uniate bishop [Aron] writes the empress that nearly all villages
in the refractory county of Hunedoara have returned to the Church.
This includes Binţinţi, a powerful nest of Orthodoxy where much
agitation occurred and which was regarded by the Court as particularly troublesome. But it has now repented its errors and become a
good and obedient example to neighboring villages. (Dragomir 1920:
Annex, 104)

1755, Orăştie

Villages in the district petition the Court for damages suffered in
the course of reestablishing the Union, especially for restitution of
money paid to Orthodox priests. We the headman and village council
of Binţinţi, in the name of the whole village, request 25 florins'
compensation for the loss of two oxen during the disturbances.
(Dragomir 1920: Annex, 140–142)

10 April 1756. To the Roman Catholic [Uniate] Bishop in Alba Iulia.

Esteemed Sir, my benevolent patron, and my lord:

In recent days as I was walking around my estate in Binţinţi, I
happened upon a Romanian who was publicizing to the villagers a
circular from a priest in the Saxon districts. The circular had the
following content: that each village of the Orthodox faith should
send a delegate to Sibiu by Easter, at the latest, where two Orthodox
bishops from Serbia and Your Excellency's predecessor in office,
Bishop Klein, will reinstate the Orthodox creed. This circular was
brought into Binţinţi secretly with instructions to pass it on in secret

to other villages and to understand it specifically as a Patent from Her Imperial Majesty. It is thus quite possible that a new movement of resistance is in the making; even the village headmen have absented themselves—only they know where. In order that we not suffer a calamity as disruptive as the previous one [1744—ed.n.] I, your Excellency's humble servant, have taken the liberty of informing you concerning these events, in hopes that you will be able to take appropriate countermeasures.

Your faithful servant,
Ferencz Olasz, Binţinţi
(Dragomir 1930: 314-315)

1760, Vienna

The empress publishes a new decree reminding the Romanians that they are not at liberty to renounce the Uniate faith in favor of Orthodoxy, and she orders that in the following 158 villages the churches must be given back to the Uniate priests: Binţinţi, Gelmar, Pişchinţi, Rapolt. (Dragomir 1930: 143-144)[23]

, The peasants of Binţinţi, and many other villagers like them, were not moved. In the Buccow census of 1760-1762, whose objective was to learn the precise state of religious affairs in Transylvania, Binţinţi is listed as having eighty-seven Orthodox families and one Orthodox church, while the priest to which it pertains is a Uniate (Ciobanu 1926). Continued agitations in this decade further provoked the miscarriage of the Union. Despite an imperial edict of toleration (1781), Joseph II continued issuing patents to staunch the flow of returnees to Orthodoxy; but these were inefficacious. In 1805 Binţinţi had not only eighty-five Orthodox families and one Orthodox church but also its own permanent Orthodox priest (de Etéd 1911: Dosa conscription).

Although resistant peasants had ample cause for dissatisfaction, some of their resistance was in all likelihood emboldened by the nobility. It is unclear how seriously the nobles wished to sabotage catholicization, but it is very clear from the documents relating to the religious struggles of the 1760s that Calvinist nobles, in particular, encouraged villagers against the Uniates (Hitchins, personal communication). Since several of the nobles of Binţinţi were Calvinist, we can imagine a tacit support on their part—or even an active one—that might have had something to do with the village's troublesomeness to the Court. One motive for encouraging the resistance was labor: the Binţinţi nobles who wanted George Popa not to become a priest had every desire to prevent him from achieving the status that would lose them his services. Another was a wish to reduce claimants to privilege, for Uniates could claim rights not open to the Orthodox populace. A third possible motive was enmity to Habsburg centralization in any of its guises, which may account for why Calvinists (who were anti-Habsburg almost by definition) were especially active. Roman Catholics among the nobility were likely to be of two minds: on the one hand catholicization was ideologically congenial to them, but Habsburg centralization was not, and neither was the disorder caused by it. When Ferencz Olasz wrote to his bishop, he was probably driven by anxiety at the specter of rural unrest, so disruptive to the manorial economy.

The nobility's opposition to the Uniate church encourages the view that the Union's relative failure[24] was in part a setback to Habsburg state centralization, or at least a sign of state weakness. This was not a state that could satisfactorily manage angry peasants in the east while requiring its troops for wars on western fronts. Indeed, it was precisely at a time of local religious ferment and the Seven Years' War that Maria Theresa created the cheap surveillance instrument of the Border Regiments, mollifying some peasants as she did so. The same impression of faltering state development emerges from considering one of the very few of Joseph's reforms that did not provoke a great aristocratic outcry: the religious tolera-tion edict of 1781. By this edict, the Habsburgs retreated from the aggressive catholicization that had marked this century, even though they would continue to shore up the Union and to regard the Church as a crucial unifying force.

The motives that gave rise to the edict of 1781 are open to several interpretations. Hitchins (1969:49-50) sees it as another imperial maneuver to sap the power of the Transylvanian Estates, under-mining them by giving the Romanian Orthodox population privi-leges hitherto denied. An alternative interpretation emerges from looking beyond Transylvania to the edict's potential effects in Hungary. Much of the Magyar gentry was Protestant rather than Catholic. Until 1781 those who were Protestant were barred from holding public office — in Hungary, but not in Transylvania, where the constitution had long guaranteed religious toleration and allowed its large Protestant gentry into public service. Toward the end of the eighteenth century there grew up in Hungary an influential group of intellectuals of gentry origin who were Protestants. Many were educated in Western Europe and in the Enlightenment tradition, and they understood and favored the emperor's conception of the state (Király 1975:34-35). It is at least plausible that the edict attempted to cultivate this receptive segment of the Hungarian gentry even as other reforms alienated other segments (those gentry employed in the formerly autonomous counties). At the same time, it would have dramatized the Court's conciliatory intent by retreating from the catholicization that both Hungary's and Transylvania's Protestants had always liked to see as purposely designed to persecute not Protestants but *Hungary,* as a Protestant redoubt (Makkai 1946:214).

This interpretation would contradict the idea that state development was faltering, for it shows the monarch doing what had not been adequately accomplished to date: luring members of the landowning class into the state apparatus as public functionaries loyal above all to the dynasty (see Anderson 1974:321). If in this one respect Joseph advanced the centralization of his state, however, it could scarcely make up for the countless other respects in which his ambitions failed. For despite this monarch's determined efforts to create a modern state, his many reforms were not to stand. In the late 1780s, imperial ambitions in the international sphere embroiled the empire in an alliance with Russia and thence in a war with Turkey, in which Austria at first fared ill. At the same time, news of the French Revolution awakened monarchical anxiety that the revolution might spread. To prevail against these menaces required restoring the compact between monarch and nobility, the hand of the latter having been inadvertently strengthened by international events. The coalition was indeed repaired, but its price was the repeal of nearly all the reforms so hazardous to aristocratic contentment. The emperor rescinded all of them except three. The rejoicing that ensued defies description; it symbolized the restoration of an older balance, a weaker state, reflecting internal compromises compelled in spite of, and contradictory to, tendencies toward centralization prevailing in the interstate system.

The nobles were particularly delighted with the rescissions that reinstated the autonomy of the Diet and of the County administrations (reestablished within their old boundaries), abrogated the German bureaucracy and language, and restored seignorial monopolies and tithes. Of the measures not rescinded, one was the toleration edict, with its anticentrist symbolism; the second affected only the clergy; and the third was the urbarial provisions arising from Horea's revolt. Despite loud protest by all segments of the nobility, this last measure, timid though it was, remained in force. Apparently the other concessions were enough, however: the Court managed to mollify the nobles without completely betraying the peasants — the basis of the state — and thereby created a fragile but balanced triad among contenders.

In their experiments with religion the Habsburgs had aimed to unify their empire or, failing this, to build a coalition with Orthodox populations like that in Transylvania, who might serve as a loyal ally should other state actions trigger revolt among the nobility. The state had hopes of winning over not just a Catholic peasantry but an elite emergent from the disenfranchised Romanian people, the Uniate clergy. This elite nourished itself on resources the Habsburgs gave along with Catholicism — noble status and access to institutions of learning (otherwise denied to Romanians) in centers as distant as Rome and Paris; they were expected to prove grateful clients and to promote the stability of the state as they ministered to their flock.

But aside from the refusal of many peasants — encouraged by nobles friendly to their views — to accept the proffered alliance, the Uniate clergy were soon to clash with Magyar nobles and show the Court what remarkably unintended consequences could emerge from the religious and administrative policies adopted in the name of state unity. The chief of those consequences was the eruption of nationalism, a phenomenon not restricted to the Habsburg Empire but bearing, in its manifestations there, all the marks of the peculiar history of state-building in its Habsburg variant. The nationalism that surfaced in the late 1700s would prove, when bonded with the continued dominance of the agrarian aristocracy in the east, the tip of an iceberg against which the Habsburg ship of state would collide in 1848 and 1867, to be severely disabled and then sink into the sea of new nation-states in 1918.

CENTRALIZATION AND RESISTANCE III: NATIONALIST REACTION

The subject of nationalism in the Habsburg lands is not one to be introduced blithely. Many tomes have been devoted in full or in part to one or another aspect of this problem (e.g., Cheresteşiu 1966; Deak 1979; Hitchins 1969, 1977; Jászi 1929; Macartney 1937, 1968; Makkai 1946; Pascu et al. 1964; Prodan 1971). No discussion of the Romanian peasantry, in its relation to other groups or to its own historical development, can avoid this difficult subject. Its all-pervasiveness and inescapable importance will become ever more obvious as it recurs in the chapters to follow. In the present section I will outline some of the parameters of nationalism in the empire through time, most particularly for the nationalisms in the empire's eastern half.

It may help to preface my outline with a schematization of how I view the historical "facts" analytically, with specific reference to Hungary and Transylvania. As of about 1700, the empire's various regions differed from one another in terms of such objective traits as language, cultural traditions, and history, but their differences had not yet been brought into sufficiently sustained contact to have become overly politicized. Regions also differed in their degree of commercial and manufacturing development, but each region's internal composition was grossly similar to others in containing a feudal aristocracy, a dependent peasantry, and a very small bourgeoisie engaged in crafts and petty trading. Within Hungary and Transylvania these social groups tended to differ from one another in terms of both their principal economic activities and their objective cultural attributes. These objective cultural attributes had not yet acquired political significance, however, although the process whereby they would become frozen into exclusive ethnic or national identities was already unfolding. The compartments containing different economic and cultural configurations were still fairly isolated from one another, forming noncompetitive niches (Cole 1981) between which persons sometimes moved, adopting the cultural characteristics of the new compartment without regarding this as contrary to nature. Culturally different groups rarely jockeyed for access to the same compartments, though they often argued over just where the boundaries of one niche ended and another began (ibid.).

Two simultaneous processes changed this situation. First, imperial competition with other states pressed toward centralization and toward unifying and homogenizing the population in cultural terms —what is often called "nation-building." The empire's internal heterogeneity rendered this highly problematic, yet its place in the state system made the task essential. Second, the empire's economy, linked to a larger economy beyond its borders, was gradually transformed. Small disparities in economic development widened into complementary regional specializations, under state initiative, and regional social structures consequently diverged. As the various regional elites now found themselves pursuing interests that were in conflict, their conflicts led them to compete with one another for influence or control over the formation of imperial economic policy. Each monarchical attempt at further centralization invigorated these conflicting regional interests; the state—or something state-like—and control over it became what groups in each region wanted most to capture (Verdery 1979:392). These struggles over the imperial and regional economies affected intergroup relations inside Hungary and Transylvania also. The balance between agrarian and commercial interests in Transylvania came into dispute, bringing groups formerly in adjacent and noncompetitive niches into direct confrontation over the shape of the local economy.

State centralization and economic transformation had mutually reinforcing effects on the development of nationalism. While these processes interacted in Western European states to transform class systems within unified nation-states, they gave rise in the empire to the emergence of "nations," or, better, aspirant nation-states, out of old classes inadequately transformed. The process of turning the empire into a modern state then unleashed problems that began at the top and ramified downward. What Austria perpetrated on Hungary would color Hungary's response both to Austria and, as a by-product, to its own internal minorities, caught in Hungary's own struggle to build and control a state. At each step along this chain, the aspirations of any one entity necessarily affected its internal relations with its peasants, in ways similar to those exemplified in the preceding two sections of this chapter. Each presumptive "state" sought to appropriate the model of successful state creation that had emerged from different conditions elsewhere in the world; the search involved building internal alliances and balancing conflicting claims. The continuation of nationalist problems into the present day is a legacy of this set of developments, rooted ultimately in Habsburg state-building.

For the moment, I can only allude to some of these processes, whose lines will become clearer in subsequent chapters. My ultimate quarry in this pursuit is to understand how Magyars and Romanians could have, and could continue to have, such wholly divergent views on the question of Transylvania as to be irreconcilable. Since inspecting the two views themselves will not lead to much progress on this issue, I can at best ask two questions: What is the nature of the sociopolitical system within which two such opposite conceptions could emerge?; and how are the nationalisms of Magyars and Romanians related to their respective places in a transforming system of production? I will engage the first question now and approach the second in chapters 3 and 4.

The fact that the first great nationalist crisis — one having cultural overtones rather than being just an aristocratic backlash — emerged in the wake of the Josephine reforms reinforces the idea that somehow state-building and nationalism are linked. This crisis had two main ramifications: the Magyar gentry led a reactive movement articulated in nationalist terms, and the Uniate clergy produced a set of petitions in the name of the Romanian people. The roots of the former lay buried deep in medieval Hungarian history, in the constitutional privileges won by the nobles in 1222. The roots of the latter had taken hold more recently, as the Habsburgs gave Romanian Uniates access to the educational opportunities and the religious organization that were to serve as their first political resource in Romanian struggles with Transylvania's natios.

Habsburg efforts to centralize their state had constantly run aground on the constitutional privileges of Hungary's nobles, from as early as the partition of Hungary by the Turks in 1526, which left a piece of Hungary in Habsburg hands. A possible solution to this conflict would have been for the emperor to cease convoking the Hungarian Diet and gradually let the constitution lapse. The empire needed funds, however, and to obtain some of them required the vote of the Hungarian Diet. Since the constitution could not therefore languish and expire from neglect, it would have to be trampled. Yet the Habsburgs were not strong enough to trample the constitution and survive the consequences. Each time the emperor revoked or jeopardized constitutional rights, the nobility rebelled in the name of the constitution and of their privileged status; each time, the emperor backed down.

To link nationalism with these constitutionally based and jealously guarded privileges, one must examine the concept of natio by which the noble estate had come to be defined. By the early 1700s, the concept of natio (which I will carry further in chapter 4) had two senses in Hungary: it meant both an ethnic/territorial grouping and a jural one, in the sense of *populus:* citizens as opposed to subjects, the privileged rather than the plebs, the free versus the unfree, those with the right to exercise power over those who suffered its exercise (Prodan 1971: chap. 4). This latter, jural meaning became attached to the idea of natio and acquired increasing prominence, overshadowing the ethnic sense, during the sixteenth and seventeenth centuries — a change especially evident in Transylvania. The conjunction of the jural with the ethnic meaning had dire consequences, worse when later combined with developments in Western Europe — the Enlightenment and the rise of nation-states — that naturally had echoes farther East. Once natio became not just ethnic but jural as well, ethnic groups came to be differentiated in their jural and then in their political status; thus, some ethnic groups — Romanians — came to be excluded from the polity.

When the spread of Enlightenment ideas restored the ethnic meaning of natio as the primary one, it was fatally combined with the idea of privilege. Only some, not all, natios counted: the noble ones. "The people" consisted of the populus; the "nation" of Magyars was the jural natio of nobles. Inasmuch as in both Hungary and Transylvania the different natios were originally associated with different territories (within which, of course, one also found coresiding non-natios, or unfree persons), the scene was set whereby the eighteenth-century reassertion of an ethnic meaning would play into the idea of nation-states.

This reassertion of an ethnic sense to natio in the eastern Habsburg lands, however, clearly drew inspiration from the emerging bourgeois sense of "nation" as it grew up in Western Europe, whose social environment and conceptual medium were wholly different from those of the areas infected by it. "Nation" became "nation-state" in Western Europe as part of the process of state-building within territories more ethnically homogeneous, and upon bourgeoisies more substantial, than those of the empire. The discrepancies were unfortunately lost on those Magyar nobles for whom the idea of nation was attractive and easy to comprehend, resembling as it did their own political sense of natio. Reading French philosophers, they understood them more in the manner of people such as Herder (product of a Prussian social system much like Hungary's): nature creates nations, not states; the right life for man is in communities united by common culture, where the prime bond is attachment to family land, to the traditions and historical memories of one's people; "whom nature separated by language, customs, character, let no man artificially join together by chemistry" (Berlin 1976:xxii, 157–159, 163). Magyar aristocrats understood the Enlightenment concern with "the people"—but qua populus, not qua populace. They read Rousseau and were entranced with the idea of a social contract to which the nation must consent—but only the nation qua nobles (Makkai 1946:281).

Habsburg state-builders, hoping to create a state along Western European lines, walked innocently and blindly right into this intellectual snare. Their desires to centralize entailed, of necessity, infringing on noble privilege. To this the nobles had an absolutely natural though historically inaccurate response: if the nation is natural, and the nation is noble, and the state is an abominable machine, its extension an artifice crippling to the human spirit, what more predictable outcome than that the "nation" of the nobles in Hungary should oppose Habsburg centralism by reacting against the state on behalf of the Magyars as a nation? To resist Habsburg state-building was to promote, in the name of constitutional liberties, the withdrawal of the natural Magyar nation from the artificial empire. The nobles (the gentry, in particular) whose obduracy finally forced revocation of all the Josephine reforms — the uniform administration, the death of autonomous counties and county governments, the abrogation of constitutional liberties and parliamentary rule, the introduction of German — were reacting both as nobles whose positions of power and influence had been attacked on every side and also as those members of the nation who could preserve Magyar national character from obliteration within the state. The most "nationalistic" — in the ethnic sense, now — of their demands were linguistic ones, and by these one can diagnose the shift from noble resistance to nationalist reaction. For the next century, noble resistance and nationalist reaction would be inextricably intertwined in Hungary, but the idiom would be liberal nationalism and the chief vehicle would be language. This was the easier as there was no substantial non-Magyar bourgeoisie to carry on a social struggle for which the nationalist idiom might have proved inapt (Prodan 1971:382–383).

If the matter had stopped with reaction in Hungary, that would have been enough,[25] but of course it did not. The Magyar nobility in Transylvania were as exercised as their Hungarian counterparts by the Josephine reforms, and since they had been using not Latin but Magyar administratively for two centuries, the germanization of the bureaucracy was especially offensive to their ethnic sensibilities. Like the Hungarians they began to press for greater magyarization. From their actions emerged what became the stickiest issue in Transylvania's national politics: demands for directly incorporating Transylvania into Hungary, which would facilitate magyarization and strengthen the position of the Transylvanian aristocracy. Expectably, this aroused great alarm among Transylvania's other ethnic groups, who saw any expansion of Magyar or noble rights as necessarily reducing their own. Transylvania's Saxons — constitutionally as "noble" as the Magyars — began airing nationalist counterclaims resuscitated[26] by the nationalistic idiom of the Magyar nobility.

Magyar nationalism had its gravest implications for the non-natios, in particular the Romanians. The concept of natio had evolved through a fateful semantic trick, producing the formula that the state can be national only as it is nobiliary, that the only true state is the state of the "nation," that is, of the nobles. Because "national" retained in its semantic field the meaning of "noble," the state created by withdrawing Hungary from the empire would be built upon a social contract to which nonnobles — the populace — would not be invited to consent. This formula meant that in the Transylvanian part of the new state, over half of the population would be nonparticipants. Their only hope was to *become noble* by becoming "of the nation": to become Magyar. For otherwise there was no place for them in a Hungarian state at all.

This deadly logic set the terms of the argument within which Romanian nationalism was a reply, although the reply was aimed at several audiences. The Romanian national movement was in part directly provoked by Habsburg centralization and by the rescission of Joseph's reforms. It was indubitably aggravated by the extremity of Magyar demands. But it had also been growing on its own, and its chief irony was that the Habsburgs had themselves provided Romanians with the necessary organizational conditions for reaction in forming the Uniate church and giving Uniate clergy a privileged status, access to education, and a legal institutional framework. More than this, the education to which Uniates now were entitled was to provide them with the ingredients for the Romanian national ideology. While studying Latin, philology, and history, Romanian clergy-intellectuals became convinced of the Latin foundations of the Romanian language and, thus, of the Roman ancestry of their people. Descent from the Romans was to become the basic premise of Romanian nationalism, a claim to give Romanians dignified, equal footing with the natios of Transylvania who excluded them. It is therefore highly probable that without the Uniate church, that is, without Habsburg assistance, organized Romanian nationalism in the late eighteenth century might not have arisen.

If Horea's revolt in 1784 revealed the attitudes of Romanians as a class, the action that advanced the cause of Romanians as a nation was a series of petitions drawn up by intellectuals and members of the clergy, chiefly Uniates but with Orthodox support. The series culminated in a document known as the *Supplex Libellus Valachorum* (Humble Petition of the Wallachians), which was sent to Emperor Leopold II in 1791. This petition asked, on behalf of the Romanians of Transylvania, for confirmation of the civic rights that belonged to them as members of an empire concerned with the rights of man in society, rights of which they had been increasingly and systematically deprived during the "unjust times" of recent centuries. It requested that Romanians be recognized as the fourth "nation" in Transylvania and that Romanian Orthodoxy become a fully recognized rather than a merely tolerated religion. Very carefully constructed, the petition based its claims on appeals to law; it sought to justify them by asserting and trying to prove on linguistic grounds that Romanians were the first occupants of Transylvania, with the Romans among their ancestors (this to a monarch whose titles included "Holy Roman Emperor"). It appealed to principles of enlightened equity and reposed absolute confidence in the emperor's adherence to those principles. The emperor read the petition and sent it, acknowledging its importance, to be taken up by the Transylvanian Diet. There it caused a frightful uproar, its claims were rejected, and it was buried.

Space is inadequate to detail the antecedents of the petition or describe the century-long, painstaking struggle by members of the clergy to bring the plight of Romanians to the attention of the Court. It is important to emphasize, however, how Romanian nationalism emerged from Habsburg state centralization. First, as already mentioned above, the vehicle for the Romanians' action was one set in motion by Habsburg state-building: the Uniate church. Second, the centralizing reforms of Joseph II's administration, while they alienated the nobility and other groups, generally worked in favor of Romanians; thus, the petition was intended to expand the promise newly held out to these people by the Habsburgs, rather than to protect a niche under assault, as was the case with Magyar nationalism. Third, this petition was the direct product of state-building policies but in a different way from the reactions of the other nationalities: Magyar nationalism aimed to restore the constitutional order that had existed *prior* to Joseph II; Romanians aimed to restore progress *obtained under* Joseph II and then revoked at Magyar insistence, as well as to restore "ancient rights" eroded during times of aristocratic hegemony. Both nationalisms therefore appear like efforts at restitution, both speak in a similar idiom, and in this sense one can see the Romanian action as provoked by the spirit of other nationalisms. But the order to be restored was precisely opposite. The difference shows how clearly the centralization of the state had worked in favor of the nonnobles and helped to turn them into allies (see Prodan 1971: chap. 3, for extended discussion of these issues).

The petition bore no fruit, for at least two reasons. The Transylvanian Diet rejected its arguments by invoking the older rather than the more recent meaning of "nation": they said that the Romanian petition was pointless because Transylvania's constitution was concerned not with *nationalities* but with *estates,* that is, nobles (Seton-Watson 1963:190)—a status to which some Romanians had been raised, which proved they had rights. The ambiguity inherent in the polysemous concept of "nation" thus enabled the Diet to reject the petition as groundless. But the petition met this fate only because the emperor refused to act on it himself, throwing it instead to the Diet. And his reason for doing so stemmed from the need for a rapprochement between nobles and Court. By deferring to the authority of the autonomous Transylvanian Diet, the emperor demonstrated the sincerity of his intentions (Prodan 1971:39). Thus, the petition fell victim to the inadequacies of state-building that prevented zealous absolutism from crushing a determined and powerful aristocracy.

The late 1700s were, then, the period when the politics of nationalism first emerged as such. They were to create problems of the highest order for over a century, as the Magyar nobles, defending their privileged position, worked to create a unitary Hungarian national state separate from the Habsburg Crown. The Hungarian language laws of 1790-91 were the first in a long series of linguistic measures by which the aristocracy hoped not only to revivify their language but also to impose Magyar speech upon the rest of Hungary's population. The Magyars constantly agitated to make Magyar the language not only of internal administration but also of Parliament and of communications with the imperial bureaucracy. These were but a few of the forms Magyar resistance took.

Once the Hydra of nationalism had raised its heads in the empire, the path to state centralization became even more perilous than before. The Magyar nobility was now fully politicized and had a consistent response to each centralizing effort. When Emperor Francis (1792-1835) yielded to some of their linguistic demands—in Deak's analysis, as a sop to the gentry to buy their support for taxes and for the army (Deak 1979:20)—he created further means for the Magyars to oppress and assimilate the ethnic populations within their own jurisdiction; this of course added to his own difficulties. One or another national minority was being obstreperous for the entire nineteenth century, either directly against the Habsburgs or in appeal to them against the Magyars.

Under so relentless an attack, state centralization not only ground to a halt, it retreated. Credit for this "achievement" usually goes to Metternich, chancellor and chief architect of imperial policy from 1814 to 1848. But the policies of Metternich and his supporters (probably, judging by their views, members of the old provincial nobility) merely articulated one set of tendencies inherent in the imperial system's evolution. Habsburg policy in Metternich's day illustrates well the internal confusion and dissension from which single decisions at length struggled forth. Metternich advocated decentralization, Emperor Francis, centralization. Metternich recognized the government's incapacity to centralize and wanted to salvage what he could by reversing the trend (Taylor 1942:36–40). His proposals included giving official sanction to the independent life of the "historic provinces," turning over to them the welter of daily detail and freeing the imperial government to craft overall state strategy. The emperor and his supporters, however, favored no diminution of central authority. Part of Metternich's conception was that giving in to nationalisms would undermine their resistance to the center: he aimed at a new federalism, breeding strength (ibid.:41–43). But because the emperor and his faction were never wholly persuaded by these arguments, the resultant policy was a hybrid. Increased autonomy was accorded some of the provincial Diets, especially those that might counterbalance Hungary, but the full Metternichian plan was not implemented.

If the Metternichian and imperial factions disagreed on the wisdom of centralization and the means for unifying the empire, they agreed in a fundamental respect: they fully believed in the historical reality of the separate provincial traditions under their scepter, rather than seeing these traditions as, in part, the recent creation of their own policies and of action by provincial elites. They gave credence, for example, to Slavic intellectuals' dreams of "reviving" a South Slav literary language that had never existed (Taylor 1942:52).

It would be inaccurate to find in this a conscious effort to differentiate peoples so as to divide and conquer, empty statements of the sort by Emperor Francis notwithstanding.[27] To see divide and conquer as a purposeful strategy of government is to posit a uniformity and clarity of vision that did not exist in ruling circles. Nevertheless, the very existence of sentiments like these—the subventions of Slavic poets and the summoning of provincial Diets, encouraged to press demands similar to those of Hungary and to claim "traditional privileges" (Taylor 1942:141)—created a climate in which provincials could utilize tradition and cultural difference toward political ends. The climate, the mentality, was set within which *all* conflict could be fought out in nationalist terms. This outcome was reinforced by the degree to which other social conflicts were so tightly entangled with "national" differences as to be inextricable, displacing onto the national plane all manner of other issues (Prodan 1971:362). The ultimate effect was to divide the emergent bourgeoisie and reduce the strength of its challenge to both absolutism and feudalism (Chereşteşiu 1966:128–129).

In the following chapter I discuss the economic conditions that evolved together with developments in the sphere of state-building. I do not plan to rest with the simplistic conclusion that capitalism's development in the empire was impeded because the bourgeoisie was weak and divided by nationalist conflict. My intention thus far has been to show that a large part of what emerged as nationalism, the empire's Waterloo, came from the exigencies of state-building; and some evidence for this is that nationalist conflicts were the proximate cause of the empire's two breakups—in 1867 and 1918. An understanding of the growth of nationalism is not much advanced by asking whether the state schemed to divide and conquer, for we cannot attribute sufficient unity of will to substantiate such an argument and make it believable. What can be seen clearly, however, is that out of state-building there evolved a language for the articulation of conflict. It was a language that all peoples of the empire found easy to learn, and it proved one whose categories have constrained much of their thinking even to the present day.

All social actors face a social environment that is more or less indeterminate, within which they must behave as if rational choices were possible and uncertainty minimal. The more complex the social actor, the more readily the potential sources of indeterminacy multiply and the more imperative it becomes to seek to reduce them.[28] For those most complex of social actors, states, a prime way of reducing indeterminacy in the international system has been to consolidate internal power within their societies. This has meant improvements in organizational design—bureaucratic rationalization, centralization, increasing the reach of the state over the power of other internal groups. The eighteenth and nineteenth centuries were times when the Habsburg state's constituent policymakers wrestled among themselves for a workable formula toward these ends. With the brief exception of 1848–1859, when the Hungarian revolution and other centrifugal forces were (temporarily) extinguished, the general trajectory moved shakily upward through the late 1700s and then decisively fell.

This chapter has presented three examples to illustrate how Habsburg state-builders struggled to consolidate their organization within the imperial social system. My way of describing these struggles has emphasized the state's changing alliances with and oppositions to various groups within a constantly fluid internal field. I have suggested that protecting the tax base — the rural population — by regulating feudal relations established the right of state-makers to intervene in these affairs, a right that extended the sphere of action defined as legitimate for the state. The scheme ended, however, in only qualified victory for the Habsburgs and their restless protégés, the peasants, as a powerful nobility prevented further-reaching urbarial reforms. I have argued that in Transylvania, Habsburg efforts to enlist the Catholic church in the enterprise of centralization and cultural unification fell victim to both the power of the aristocracy and resistance by some of the peasants. And I have proposed that the most crippling by-product of state-building, from the state's point of view, was the rise of nationalism, a victory for the lesser nobility in particular and a defeat for the state and to some extent also for the Transylvanian peasant, at least in the short run. The development of nationalism altered the possibilities for maneuver by the state as it tried to build its strength in the larger arena: coalitions that involved tax-paying peasants or budget-controlling nobles were now precluded in some areas (though not in Transylvania) by the nationalist appeal of budget-controlling nobles to tax-paying peasants. The agents of the state were left, at best, with shifting their alliance from one nationality to another.

Power, in this case the power of the state vis-à-vis its internal competitors, can be seen as the reciprocal of dependence: a state acquires power to the extent that it obtains alternative and abundant sources of supply for its needs, rather than relying on a single source (Emerson 1962; Thompson 1967). For the growth of state power, at least two sets of resources are crucial: techniques of organization and control, and revenues. The Habsburgs had several sources of organizational technique, none of them unique to Austria but no less significant for that: continental philosophies (the Enlightenment) as understood by the rulers and adapted to local circumstances; bureaucrats imported or welcomed in refuge from other places (Metternich, Belcredi); internal processes of trial and error built on a long history of imperial rule; and the direct borrowing of forms from other European polities, as when Joseph II pointed directly to the constitutions of Western Europe in his attempts to regulate servitude in his domain (Blum 1978:310). Revenues had several potential sources also, but these proved easier to name than to pry open. The rulers tended to concentrate on one: a rural populace that practiced inefficient agriculture (by Western standards) and was insulated from direct siphoning by a reactionary lesser nobility, ensconced in administration and controlling the allocation of funds. Insofar as the state depended on few and niggardly sources of revenue, its power was curtailed.

Was this bad organizational management? Perhaps, but more than that it showed the impossible situation in the empire, in which powerful groups stymied one another's growth and hindered the emergence of alternative suppliers of abundant resources. The empire proved an infelicitous laboratory for experiments in centralization because its bourgeoisie was weak, relative to its miserly aristocracy. In other words, state centralization was not adequately supported by developments in the economy. We turn, then, to that economy, to ask about the nature of the nobility against which Habsburg rulers could not adequately prevail and about the kind of livelihood they pursued; and to wonder how they managed to retain so entrenched a position for so long, and how they finally lost it.

CHAPTER 3

Serfs of the Magyars: The Transylvanian Economy within the Empire, to the Mid-Nineteenth Century

Stăpînul zgîrcit învață sluga hoață.
(The stingy master makes his servant a thief.)

Pune negru pe verde că stăpînul nu vede.
(Cover the weeds with dirt, for the master isn't looking.)[1]

— Proverbs

It can be asserted without hesitation that Transylvanian serfdom was among the most oppressive ever known.

— Prodan (1979 I:46)

The agents of the Habsburg state in the eighteenth and early nineteenth centuries were concerned not only with extending central power over other groups in society but also with regulating and encouraging diversification of the economy. And just as the state's centralization had radical consequences for the peasantry and other groups, so also did its economic policies. The Habsburgs strove to nourish manufacturing and to enliven economic exchange both within and across imperial borders, enhancing revenues from taxes and trade. Because these activities were associated with specific groups, and because these groups proved to be unevenly distributed across the landscape, economic policy-making created new fields for alliance and opposition, as well as new intragroup oppositions, as modes of livelihood diverged. When combined with the effects of nationalism, the result was a transformation — a turning sideways — of the prevailing system of privilege. A more or less horizontal layering of society, characterized by mechanical solidarity within each layer and organic solidarity between them, gave way to differentiated regions joined to one another organically but dominated by groups asserting (with highly variable accuracy) mechanical solidarities based on real or hoped-for ethnic homogenization. Some of these regions would enjoy higher economic priority than others.

This general transformation, covered in the present and the following chapters, is not itself the focus of analysis; but it is so crucial a frame for developments in the Transylvanian economy that its lines will be drawn as a preliminary. The overall objective of the present chapter is to show how changes in the organization of the imperial economy shaped the economic environment of peasants in southern Transylvania. The line of argument that connects these two terms is, however, a crooked one indeed, as crooked as the empire's internal history is complex. I hold that developments at each identifiable level — the global economy, the imperial economy, the economic system of the eastern lands, and the economy of Transylvania — conditioned the possibilities at levels internal to it. At the same time, each of these economic systems had its own inner logic, its own life course, and was determined as much by its own past as by its larger surroundings.

I will describe in sequence (and in progressively greater detail) the general economic profile of the empire from 1700 to 1848, the economy of the eastern (Hungarian) lands, and the Transylvanian economy, the last seen in part through the eyes of Binţinţi villagers. The reader is forewarned that the time periods covered in each description are not identical, and that each new section asks one to jump backwards in time (uncomplainingly) from the mid-nineteenth century to an earlier era. The chapter's final section summarizes the effects of these sequences of events and levels of economic activity upon the environment of Transylvanian peasants like those in Binţinţi.

THE GROWTH OF THE IMPERIAL ECONOMY

Many of the economic changes that affected groups in the empire did not emanate wholly from state control but from the empire's participation in a pan-European economy, whose capitalist development was constantly quickening throughout this period. This encompassing economic system influenced the growth of the imperial economy rather as the pan-European state system influenced the growth of the Habsburg state. The consolidation of strong nation-states in Western Europe and their interaction with others in an interstate system changed the rules of the game for all potential players; so also did the advancement of capitalism in the core areas of an integrated world economy change the rules for others interacting with it. Thus, the place of the Habsburg economy in its broader economic environment must be reckoned with in trying to understand events inside the empire itself, for this broader environment exercised constraints on the possibilities for internal economic change.

Within the global system the empire's economy was intermediate. It contained both industrializing zones and unmodernized agrarian zones linked to other more and less advanced economies in Europe and beyond. In Immanuel Wallerstein's terms, it was a "semi-periphery," neither as advanced as the economies of England or France nor as undeveloped as those of Poland or the Romanian principalities. But the empire had a definite edge over these latter areas and even over what would become Germany and Italy: it was a large and variegated entity, centralized and state-like enough to craft policies aiming at overall economic development.

During the eighteenth and nineteenth centuries, the empire's economic actors, encouraged by its state-makers, tried but failed to achieve elite status among the core powers of the global economic system. The sixteenth-century bankruptcy of the Spanish Habsburg Empire, and of all its associated territories in the east, had dealt a blow that proved fatal to full modernization of the Austrian Habsburg economy. While financial crises and Turkish invasions prostrated the realm, the northwest European states had gained a developmental edge amounting to a gap the imperial economy could not close. Even important developments in mining, in textile production, and in the capitalist modernization of agriculture after 1800 were not enough to make the empire more than a second-rate economic power. More-developed West European economies (England, France) would begin to support it with loans as early as the 1700s,[2] and these and other advanced economies would increasingly invest capital in the empire throughout the following century (see Rubinson 1978:43; Berend and Ránki 1974a:93).

Imperial policymakers seemed to recognize the empire's inability to compete on equal footing with the more advanced Western European economies, and they used the state apparatus to create and maintain an internal environment as protected as possible from the hazards of international trade. One of the objectives most consistently pursued was to develop internal self-sufficiency in manufactures and foodstuffs — in other words, to promote autarky. (This, of course, presupposed the preservation of territorial unity (increasingly problematic as nationalist sentiments swelled), another objective often evident in policies of the time.

Diversifying the economy in hopes of making it more self-sufficient was a difficult task, for as of about 1700 the chief economic activity throughout the Habsburg lands was agriculture, much of it of very low productivity. Not until 1820–1830 did the empire undergo the agricultural revolution that had already been increasing productivity in England as of 1700. Such nonagricultural activities as existed were concentrated in the north and west. The provinces of Bohemia and Silesia were the sites of textile and glass manufacture, crafts, and trades that had been developing since the sixteenth century, despite the periodic devastations of war. One found some manufacture of wool and other textiles on a smaller scale in Moravia and the Vorarlberg. Mining, especially of silver, was important in Lower Austria, northeast Hungary, and parts of Bohemia; and the iron mines of Styria fed the production of light hardwares, such as nails and scythes, in Styria and Carinthia. But skilled crafts developed very slowly, much artisan production was hampered by guilds, and the nobility consumed luxury items deriving not from local industry but from Italy, Germany, and France (Kann 1974:122).

Given this imbalance, throughout the eighteenth century the state pursued mercantile policies designed to increase industry, promote self-sufficiency, and create an exportable surplus. Among the measures were protective tariffs, prohibitions on imports of luxury items, and embargoes on a number of raw-materials exports. For example, as of 1702, state orders allowed no one but nobles, functionaries, and doctors to wear fine textiles of foreign origin and permitted no exports of wool, thread, or rawhide, all to stimulate local production (Moga 1973:141–142). Luxury imports continued, however, constantly upsetting the balance of trade. These policies were probably premature, being applied before adequate local demand had been awakened, and their results were therefore somewhat disappointing (Kann 1974:123), but they undoubtedly helped to consolidate and diversify the economy from mid-century onward.

The state furthered diversity in other ways, such as through Maria Theresa's success in wooing industry to relocate within the empire after the empire lost Silesia, the most industrialized of its regions, to Prussia in 1740–1742. As a consequence, textile production surged forward in Bohemia, Moravia, and Austria. In the absence of sufficient capital accumulation in private hands, the state itself founded factories directly, many of them producing for the army (Macartney 1968:40). Alongside all these policies the state opened an active search for markets in Turkey and Russia (ibid.: 39).

In 1764 the empire's unity as an economic system was sealed by erecting a tariff wall that included all provinces but the Tyrol (whose place in the transit trade was too important to risk). During the next two decades this economic unity was cemented with a customs union in which duties were not levied across any internal frontier except the one between the Hungarian lands (including Transylvania) and the other provinces. The tariff wall entailed further prohibitions, import quotas, and exceedingly high duties on luxuries and primary exports. Its principal aim was again to encourage economic self-sufficiency (Gross 1973:240), in hopes of insulating the empire from deindustrialization by maximally protecting its internal industry from external competition.

The tariff wall and the internal customs line may have helped assure autarky, but they also rigidified internal complementarities among regions so that manufacturing (and some mining) became associated ever more firmly with the west while agriculture and the mining of precious metals became the duties of the east—each region being expected to share its products with those specializing in something else. Table 3-1 gives an idea of the extent of these regional disparities in production and demand as of 1831. The table shows that in comparison with population, both trade and industry were overrepresented in the western half and underrepresented in the east.

From 1800 on, regional differences sharpened as factory industry took off—largely in Bohemia and lower Austria, leaving other regions behind (Blum 1948:42). The continental blockade of the Napoleonic wars boosted textiles in the western lands and grain production in Hungary. This was followed by a lag, in the 1820s, and then by another textile boom between 1830 and 1847.[3] During this period the state began a vast program of railway construction, using investment and loan money and, doubtless, industrial goods from England, France, and the other advanced economies, just as it had imported from them the machinery used in local textile mills. At the same time, the empire began building up its own iron-producing capacity alongside the increase in textiles. These two branches, iron and textiles, remained the most important, most protected, and best organized branches of industry in the empire.

It is necessary to add that until mid-century most of the industrial products were consumed within the empire, "exported" largely across the internal customs line into Hungary (Gross 1973:261-263), where industrial growth had been almost nil. Looking closely at this internal discrepancy, one is forced to consider the extent to which the "underdevelopment" of the eastern regions had been engineered by Habsburg colonialism. How much did the Court, determined to maintain Austrian supremacy in the realm, force Hungary into dependence on agriculture and, ultimately, into economic backwardness? Until very recently, Hungarian historians—to say nothing

TABLE 3-1. Regional Differences in the Distribution of Trade and Industry in the Lands of the Habsburg Empire, 1831, Compared with the Distribution of Population within the Empire

| | Region | TRADE INDEX | | | | INDUSTRIAL INDEX [a] | | |
| | | % of value of all goods | | | | | | |
		imported	exported	% population [b]	balance [c]	% of manufacturing and trades enterprises	% population [b,d]	balance [c]
W/N	Austrian lands*	35	31	15	+	30	23	+
S	Italian lands†	36	36	14	+	29	22	+
N	Czech lands§	13	21	18	-/+	28	27	+
Ctr	Hungary	9	5	34	-	-	-	( )
NE	Polish Galicia	5	5	13	-	5	20	-
SE	Transylvania	3	2	6	-	6	9	-
		101	100	100		98	101	

(W comprises W/N, S, N; E comprises Ctr, NE, SE)

Source: Calculated from Austria, Statistische Zentralkommision, *Tafeln* 1831.

*Upper and Lower Austria, Tyrol, Styria, Karstland, Carynthia.

†Lombardy and Venice, plus Dalmatia.

§Bohemia and Moravia-Silesia.

[a] Total figures for the categories "Gewerbe" and "Fabriken und Manufakturen" in the 1831 *Tafeln*, for each region, divided by the totals for the empire. Hungary was not included in the official count.

[b] Excludes the Military Border, which had no trade and little industry.

[c] "Balance" refers to whether the figures for trade and industry are in excess of or less than the figure for population; that is, trade is overrepresented in the Austrian lands when their proportion of the imperial population is taken into account. The "balance" definitely favors the western lands over the eastern ones.

[d] A different figure is given here for "% population" inasmuch as Hungary was not included in the official statistics; the figure in this column is each land's percentage of the total for the empire minus the population of Hungary.

of the Hungarian gentry of previous eras—tended to see the empire's regional specialization as intentionally designed to disable Hungary and its troublesome aristocrats. Hungarian historiography and its gentry forerunners have been very fond of the colonial metaphor, regarding Vienna as an imperialist power and Hungary as the "crown-jewel of Austrian quasi-imperialism" (Gross 1966:95; see discussions in Jászi 1929: 185–212; Marczali 1910:37–99; Deak 1979: 27; Pamlényi 1975:192–193). This view justifies Hungary's rebellion in 1848 and blames the deficient economy on Austrian oppression rather than on choices made by members of Hungary's own dominant class. The colonial imagery therefore has the virtue of rallying all sectors of the noble Hungarian natio in Hungary's defense, instead of inquiring (divisively) into how local groups might have contributed to retarding the economy.

This picture is very one-sided. Aside from the possibility that it might have been sensible to develop the economy around initial complementarities among regions, one must remember that the nobles of Hungary were, and adamantly insisted on remaining, exempt from taxation, long after aristocrats in the western zones had lost this privilege. Because of this exemption, the empire derived disproportionately low revenues from the economic activities carried out on Magyar estates. Hungary and Transylvania together comprised about 38 to 39 percent of the empire's population and an equivalent share of the value of all agricultural production, yet they contributed only 13 percent of the total tax on agricultural products until as late as 1831 (calculated from data in Austria, Statistische Zentralkommission, 1831). For the nobles, tax exemption was a symbol of their status as a special estate within the imperial aristocracy; they would resist taxation as long as they had the power to do so. For the authorities, it meant that Hungary was not pulling its weight; the internal customs line rectified this, by taxing all agricultural produce that passed out of Hungary (and no industrial products that passed into it). This is not to deny that the outcome discriminated against Hungarian industrialization, but the responsibility for that result does shift rather more onto Magyar shoulders.

The problem of tax exemption ramified beyond the immediate revenue concerns of the state, however, and agitated other groups with vested interests that the state wished to protect. Developments in the early eighteenth century had begun to turn some segments of the Austrian and Bohemian aristocracy from agricultural livelihood toward industry and commerce, where they found that their interests no longer corresponded with those of their fellow aristocrats in Hungary. These industrializing aristocrats did not share the tax exemption of the Magyar nobles. In their worried opinions, tax-exempt Magyars might develop lower-cost products that could eventually beat out manufactures in the western lands, where not only taxes but higher wage levels inflated the price of goods. The Austrian and Bohemian magnates exercised significant influence on the imperial economic council (precisely because the empire was seeking to reduce its reliance on peasant-based taxes?). By 1763 they had established with the empress the principle that the state would not found manufactures in Hungary. Moreover, applications for licensing new enterprises had to be approved by this council, which often found reason to reject applications from Hungarian entrepreneurs (Macartney 1968:43-44).

Thus, the de facto discrimination against Hungary's economy arose from a split within the empire's dominant class, the aristocracy. Several factors occasioned the split: the state's interest in industrialization, its alliance with aristocrats engaging in that activity, the empire's poor competitive position internationally, which dictated internal self-sufficiency and complementary organizations of production, and a complex history of state centralization that left the Magyar aristocracy with special privileges it refused to relinquish. If the Hungarian economy was ultimately underdeveloped, compared with those of Austria and Bohemia, it was not because of a conspiracy by the Habsburg Court. With this background, we may now examine what became of Hungary's regional specialty, estate agriculture.

THE ECONOMY OF THE HUNGARIAN KINGDOM[4]

The lands of the Hungarian Crown—Hungary, Croatia, and Transylvania—corresponded roughly to the drainage basin of the middle Danube, forming an integral geographical unit. Complementing this unity was the fact that the Hungarian Kingdom had enjoyed centuries of existence, even if sometimes in abbreviated form, and its nobles were accustomed to having a hand in shaping its economy and its politics. These lands (together with the province of Galicia farther north) were the areas within the empire in which a feudal economy persisted longest before agriculture began to be transformed along capitalist lines.

Before describing the characteristics and development of this agrarian economy, however, I must defend my use of the term "feudal." Many scholars would deny that Eastern Europe in the eighteenth century was feudal: I use the term because it implies several features I wish to emphasize and is more apt than might be thought, especially in referring to the economy of eighteenth-century Transylvania.[5] For some scholars, "feudalism" applies only to the Western European Middle Ages and refers to an uncentralized political system in which the feudal warrior receives his fief through the central institution of military vassalage. "Feudalism" ceases to obtain, this view holds, when relations of serfdom come to be backed by the state—often considered characteristic of Eastern European feudal systems.

Even by these stringent criteria, eighteenth-century Hungary and Transylvania were not far from being feudal. The basic feudal institution of the armed noble levy was abolished there only when a standing army came into being in 1715, and even then it was rein-stituted and called up four times between 1790 and 1807, during the Napoleonic wars. The chief difference was that now each armed noble was no longer expected to bring a retinue of foot soldiers. Monarchical donations of large "fiefs" in exchange for service or loyalty occurred frequently in Hungary (but not Transylvania) well into the eighteenth century. Only after land for such donations ceased to be available did the main mechanism for acquiring lands become inheritance—the other main mechanism for acquiring land in medieval Europe also. The lineal connection between military service and constrained inheritance appears in the 1742 will of a Binţinţi noble, which concluded, "In making out this testament, I consulted officials to confirm that the lands I leave to my sons are, as I believe, donations won by the sword and therefore by law can be inherited only in the male line, not willed to my daughters" (MC #359). As for the enforcement of serfdom by the state, bondage to the soil was not of this type in Hungary and Transylvania. Never legislated through the central authority, serfdom remained a matter of agreement among nobles and was enforced within the domain of private law. Eighteenth-century records of the Transylvanian gentry family Macskásy illustrate this: unlike documents concerning rights to land, which are addressed to local, provincial, or imperial tribunals, all the documents referring to the family's relations with its serfs are merely private notes addressed to no external authority. Only with the Habsburgs' attempts to regulate feudal relations did laws about serfdom appear on state ledgers. These laws signify the central power's intrusion into the lord-serf nexus and mark the belated decline of a feudal system in Hungary, even later in Transylvania.

This is not, of course, to deny differences between the medieval and the eighteenth-century Hungarian and Transylvanian feudal systems. There were indeed differences, just as there were between Bloch's first and second feudal ages in Western Europe. As the state gradually acquired institutional independence and usurped the military functions of the nobility, these nobles changed from a warrior caste into a status group concerned with display and conspicuous consumption.[6] Marc Bloch notes this for late Western European feudalism also: the feudal nobility was always distinguished by its mode of life, but this shifted from the profession of arms to other signs of high status (Bloch 1961:311). Even under classic Western feudalism, display had been a way for nobles to increase their followers, whom they would equip and lead on military adventures to seize land and augment their productive resources (Brenner 1977:46). Kula writes, for Polish feudalism, that crucial to a nobleman's rank was the number of clients he had to feed and the level of pomp exhibited in consuming his surplus product, directly or transformed into luxury goods (Kula 1976:51). Kula does not say that pomp helped to collect clients, but the connection is a plausible one. Banaji goes further still: he sees the nobles' drive to defend and improve levels of consumption as the primary mechanism of expansion within late feudal economies (1977:19, 27) — in short, as their motive force, much as the drive for entrepreneurs to accumulate profits serves as the motive force within a capitalist economy.

I follow Kula and others in seeing feudalism as a system (possibly one of several) based on large landed property and relationships of personal dependence (Kula 1976:15), "dependence" being construed to mean serfdom and also clientage, importantly cemented through consumption and display. All feudal systems rest ultimately on collecting land, which implicitly collects those nonowners of land who come attached to it. The nonowners produce what the lord consumes, transforms into luxuries, offers his followers, or, in earlier times, used for arming himself and his retinue. Whereas in medieval days one collected land largely by the king's donations, outright seizures, and inheritance, in eighteenth-century Hungary and Transylvania donations declined, laws of entail shored up inheritance, and other mechanisms appeared, most especially the pawning of lands by serfs and nobles to other nobles. Whatever the mechanism, however, mere accumulation of land was not the noble's ultimate objective, any more than the accumulation of fixed capital is the objective of the capitalist entrepreneur. The capitalist aims to accumulate profits; the noble aimed — no more irrationally — to accumulate visibility, status, and prestige.

To see how display helped to preserve noble status would require an excursus into history that is beyond my scope, but a few possibilities suggest themselves. First, where landed property passes to some extent through women as well as men (as was true for Magyars), ritual display may build up landholdings by attracting desirable marriages (Therborn 1978:43). Second, where pawning of lands is a significant mechanism of expansion for a noble, display may win clients among the indebted nobility and encourage their turning to their lavish patron should they wish to pawn an estate. Hugely visible stocks of grain were also a way of luring serfs who needed grain loans, for which serf lands (even if they technically belonged to another noble) might be pawned and perhaps lost altogether, as discussed below. The collection of followers through conspicuous display is so amply attested in anthropological literature that the point needs no further illustration.

Display might also have taken on a third function in eighteenth-century Hungary and Transylvania, a function that converted prestige into another valued good: access to political power. Election to office in the County administrations required wealth and standing (Király 1969:111-112) and, one can assume, a following: likewise, appointment by the emperor to the governing circles of the Habsburg realm, in which many wealthy Magyars came to serve. As the discussion of regional complementarity has shown, access to power was an increasingly valued possession in the imperial political economy, a circumstance that meshed with the age-old involvement of Magyar nobles in the political life of their kingdom and their County administrations. Perhaps these pretentions to influence and power make it easier to understand why so many nobles raised such appalling debts so as to maintain their standards of consumption during the eighteenth-century crisis in their revenues.

I must emphasize, however, that in calling this economy "feudal" and focusing on conspicuous display as the nobles' principal cultural concern, I am not arguing either that nobles were unconcerned with businesslike management of their estates or that no other forms of activity took place in the Hungarian Crown lands. A preoccupation with income (if not precisely with profits) automatically accompanies any concern with conspicuous display. Indeed, a prolonged crisis in income will press nobles to seek new sources of revenue, by increasing agricultural production within existing social confines or by experimenting with nonagricultural pursuits; the options available have something to do with what nonfeudal forms of activity coexist with the feudal forms, and how. Thus, the manner in which the feudal economy interdigitates with other economic activities will shape the preservation or replacement of feudal forms (this, more importantly than any simple change in attitudes).

Here lies the significance of the empire's regional division of labor, which developed in consequence of status-conscious nobles' insistence on their tax exemption. In Hungary, the imperial division of labor restricted income-hungry nobles to agricultural commercialization and prevented the rise of indigenous manufacturing. Let us see briefly how this result was conditioned, and then turn to a more detailed inquiry into the very different development of the economy of Transylvania.

The sixteenth century was a time of gradual but extensive reorganization in Hungary's economy. The period began in prosperity: the growth of Venice, Vienna, and south German cities provided new markets for Hungarian cattle. From the cattle export there resulted labor imbalances that, in my view, contributed to the reimposition of serfdom on Hungary's peasants in the wake of a peasant uprising (1514).[7] By the early 1600s, however, the economy was stagnating, undermined by the bankruptcy of Phillip II (1557) and by changes in international trade routes, which slowly reduced both the luxury trade passing through Hungary and the export of Hungarian cattle and copper. The consequent arrest of urban development enhanced the power of the nobility at the expense of urban groups but also choked off urban food markets for produce from the countryside. More than a century passed until Hungary's economy — then part of a greater imperial economy — began to pick up again. Internal grain markets opened with the creation of a standing army and with improvements in water transport to Vienna and other areas of enlivened demand. Throughout the 1700s, the growth of wool manufacture elsewhere in the empire spurred Hungarian sheep raising. The state imported Merino sheep during this period, and sheep eventually surpassed cattle in the sphere of animal husbandry — which headed the list of Hungary's exports in the 1700s, well ahead of grains. Hungarian grains were consumed within the empire, but they did not travel much beyond.

The balance between Hungary's two main market commodities, livestock (especially sheep) and grains, fluctuated over the next hundred years in both internal and international trade, mirroring transport improvements that moved grains long-distance as well as price trends in the various agricultural products and in the textile market. During the first decades of the 1800s, the period of the Napoleonic wars and the continental blockade, grain prices skyrocketed everywhere, and the embargo on English wool made room for new suppliers. The consequent expansion of the Austrian textile industry created local markets for both Hungarian grains and Hungarian sheep. From 1814 to 1824 grain prices plunged, England reasserted itself over Austrian wool manufacture, and Hungarians exported their raw wool to England via German merchants (Blum 1948: 98–99). Sheep raising remained Hungary's number one export industry until the 1840s. At that point, Russian, South American, Australian, and South African wool began to undersell Hungarian wool, and rising grain prices from the Crimean War in the early 1850s drove up Hungarian grain production (Blum 1948:102; Gaál and Gunst 1977:12–13). But grains were to fall again later in the century in favor of cattle, though Hungarian grain had by now become indispensable to the empire's internal economy. Production of these goods, whether for internal exchange or for export, rested increasingly on demesne farming instead of peasant production, which had earlier been the chief source of commodities sold.

It seems appropriate to see in this period of Hungary's economic history, from about 1800 onward, the definitive emergence of a peripheral-capitalist economy in Hungarian agriculture. The cause of this development was a crisis in seignorial incomes, which had been deepening throughout the eighteenth century for a variety of reasons. Habsburg mercantilism had driven up the price of many luxury imports, precisely as the entry of Magyar nobles into the Court at Vienna escalated their standards of consumption. Various forms of state interference in feudal relations further squeezed noble incomes, as did the prospect of war in the late 1700s, with consequent tax increases, requisitions, and recruitments. Changes in terms of trade may have worsened the difficulties. For nobles who had not already confronted a yawning chasm between incomes and consumption costs that was unbridgeable within the technology and accounting habits of a feudal economy, the crucial event in forcing a reorientation may have been the devaluation of currency in 1811–1813. This reduced the value of banknotes (as well as of loans and debts) by 80 percent and, insofar as it wrought havoc on incomes from the previous years' brisk sales of grain and wool, could have helped sway landowners to new economic practices. All these factors show how the incorporation of Magyar nobles into the empire, with its weakly developed economy, created a new environment in which their old economic practices would have to be modified.

One can find, in a few anecdotes, some signs of how this modification proceeded. Marczali (1910:84-85) writes of the consternation bred among local nobles when the emperor, anticipating war with Turkey, ordered in 1782-82 that the Drava, Sava and Danube rivers be regulated. Towpaths cut for military purposes aroused aristocratic anxieties at the additional implications of these new routes. The emperor soon learned that local nobles had destroyed the towpaths, an act Marczali attributes to their fear of increased export trades that would drain wealth from Hungary. Marczali also quotes a poem written by a more progressive aristocrat of the day to satirize the view of these backward nobles; its last stanza was:

> In the counties of Zemplén, Bereg, Ungvár, Szabolcs,
> There is money, food, and wine in the cellars:
> What more is needed? Why should the Hungarians
> Live a life of uncertainty to fill their purses further?[8]

Blum observes that the nobility of this same period were unmoved when Empress Maria Theresa imported pureblood Merino sheep into the empire in 1773: "In the latter part of the eighteenth century Hungarian lords cared so little about sheep raising—or any other profitable agricultural activity—that they rented the pastureland of their estates at extremely low rates to German herders . . ." (Blum 1948:98).

This indifference evaporated, however, once the Napoleonic wars stimulated Austrian wool production for export—an export trade that was "further encouraged by the continuing depreciation of Austrian currency" (ibid.)—and nobles realized they could amplify their incomes more by raising sheep themselves than by renting out their pastures. Not only did landlords begin laying out capital to purchase the new breeds; they "outdid themselves in their efforts to improve the blood strains of their flocks" (ibid.), paying exorbitant sums for fine rams at auction. Paget records, also in connection with sheep raising in the 1830s, the calculations that led his Hungarian host to turn to it as the most profitable form of agriculture, for its labor requirements were low, its market was certain, and its export was not taxed (Paget 1850 I:282). Subsequent years saw the beginnings of aristocratic investments in industry (some in sugar beet factories, for example) and heard the first heretical suggestions that the forced labor of serfs was less efficient than hired labor (Blum 1948:198-199).

If these snippets bespeak changes ramifying through the entire economy, let it be noted that the economy at issue is almost wholly agrarian. Industrialization would not begin to take hold in Hungary until the mid-nineteenth century, and even then, the industries would be based chiefly on processing of foods, thus continuing to give the economy an agrarian cast. As the revolutionary mid-century approached, Hungarian proponents of industry decried in ever shriller tones the "backwardness" that their land's agrarian economy signified, a situation they imputed to Habsburg imperialism.

We have already seen that Habsburg imperialism was only part of the story. The Magyar nobles' unwillingness to relinquish their tax-exempt status—whether from defense of political traditions, economic interest, or status consciousness—had contributed greatly to taxing estate agriculture through tariffs and to excluding industry from Hungarian soil. If Hungary's nobles solved their revenue crisis by gradually turning to capitalist agriculture, the primary causes were neither colonialism nor the modernization of their outlooks and habits of reckoning. Rather, imperial and foreign markets developed for products suited to Hungary's natural endowments. These markets provided new options in an environment otherwise optionless because of noble intransigence.

The intransigence was similar in Transylvania, but the economic outcome was not the same. To begin with, Transylvanian nobles seem to have felt their revenue crisis later, or less severely, than did those in Hungary, and its resolution was therefore postponed. Perhaps sumptuary standards escalated somewhat less sharply for remote Transylvanians than for Hungarian nobles close to the Court. Perhaps the state's less rigorous interference in Transylvania's feudal relations—especially the failure to extend there the Urbarium imposed on Hungary in 1767—gave landlords more freedom to continue extracting absolute surplus labor from their serfs. The result was an unusually oppressive and long-lasting feudal order and minimal modernization of agriculture by the mid-1800s.

Transylvania's economy was also more diversified than Hungary's, however, and when nobles did finally confront their crisis, many turned to other than agricultural pursuits. The extent of diversification is surprising, given what we have seen of Hungary and given that Transylvania's agrarian regime was as unremittingly feudal as any in Europe. This juxtaposition made Transylvania unique in the empire and shaped the environment of its peasants differently from the environment of any other peasantry in the realm.

THE TRANSYLVANIAN ECONOMY TO THE MID-1800s

Transylvania had defining administrative boundaries within the early Hungarian Kingdom, but these boundaries took on new significance in 1526 when the Turks conquered central Hungary, leaving Transylvania as a tributory vassal. The boundaries that then acquired substantial historical reality remained "real" until 1918. This historical reality is what warrants my treating Transylvania as an economic entity. The ruling Diet, functioning at least nominally until 1867, was controlled by a feudal aristocracy similar but not identical to that of Hungary, and this Diet influenced economic development within the principality both by its own decisions and by its successful opposition to many initiatives of the Habsburg state. Acting first as its own agent (sixteenth and seventeenth centuries) and then as an obstacle to Habsburg interference (eighteenth and nineteenth centuries), the Diet gave Transylvania's economy its own peculiar character. The region was actively developing while Hungary stagnated yet was comparatively more feudal by 1800. Hence the necessity of treating the two economies as linked but separate.

As a new member of the empire in the early 1700s, Transylvania occupied a structural position not dissimilar to the position of the empire in the global economy: it was an internal semi-periphery of an international semi-periphery. As described in chapter 2, it was a recently powerful though declining quasi state, the only entity of its kind in the empire that absorbed it. Like the imperial economy, the Transylvanian economy contained both a zone of predominantly estate agriculture and another in which farms supported manufacturing and commercial enterprises. This latter sector, located in the region's southern part,[9] was the remnant of that brisk mercantilistic era (see chap. 2, p. 82) when small processing industries had accompanied the growth of exports in cattle and metals (iron, gold, silver, copper, mercury, and tin, as well as salt). Also like the imperial economy, Transylvania had important trade relations with both more- and less-developed economies: luxury goods and raw materials were imported, and finished goods were exported into the wholly agrarian economies south of the Carpathians.

It would be plausible but mistaken to call this a typical feudal economy with a dynamic interaction between seignorial and free urban sectors. The inordinate size of the latter and its capacity to sustain itself largely with free-peasant farming, together with the seignors' preference for imports over local products (see Hintz

1846:429), reduced the interaction of the two. Because such sectoral malintegration of the agrarian and manufacturing spheres would characterize this economy until the twentieth century, one should look at their earlier relations. In doing so, it is helpful to recall Transylvania's division into three distinctive administrative zones — the Counties, Szekler lands, and Saxon lands — and to look briefly at the kinds of activities concentrated within the first and third of these, in particular.

Table 3-2 shows the distribution of some of Transylvania's main social categories within the three zones as of 1767. Because of the way data are grouped in the table's source, the major urban centers (3 percent of the population) are missing from the table, with only minor centers included (see line 7). I must therefore add that the most economically active Transylvanian towns were in the Saxon lands, which, even without the largest centers, already contain nearly half of Transylvania's bourgeois groups within less than a quarter of the overall population. The table illustrates graphically the concentration of aristocrats, serfs, and cottars in the Counties, and of burghers and free peasants in the Saxon lands, as well as the near absence of feudal categories from Saxon areas and of free peasants from the Counties. One can also see from the right-hand column that, overall, feudal categories make up two-thirds of the population, and free peasants and burghers just over a quarter.

One other indicator gives evidence of the differential distribution of activities, this time within the processing sector alone, as of the end of the period discussed here. Looking at the number of enterprises of different types per 1,000 inhabitants as of 1844 in the Counties and the Saxon lands, one finds that for consumer industries in the Austrian statistics (butchers, brewers, bakers, flour millers, food vendors), the number per 1,000 persons is equal for the two zones (8.7/1,000). For non-consumer industries (painters, glaziers, tailors, printers, soap- and candle-makers), there are 7.5/1,000 in the Counties and 11.2/1,000 in the Saxon lands, a disproportion that increases for commercial industries (linen finishers, silver- and gold-workers, spinners, hosiers, watchmakers), where the Counties show only 7.4/1,000 while the Saxon lands have 18.1/1,000 (calculated from information in Hintz 1846).

The bourgeois characteristics and free peasantry of the Saxon lands (which, we must remember, contained other nationalities besides Saxons) were a consequence of the strategic location in which the Saxons had been colonized in the twelfth and thirteenth centuries. The passes between the Hungarian Kingdom and lands

TABLE 3-2. Territorial Distribution of Major Social Categories within Transylvania, 1767

| Social Category | LOCATION | | | % in Total Transylvanian Population |
| | % of each category's total that is in:[a] | | | |
	Counties[b]	Szekler Lands	Saxon Lands	
1. Great aristocracy	74.0	12.6	0	.1
2. Small-medium aristocracy	75.9	24.0	0	1.7
3. Dwarf (tax-paying) nobles	73.5	26.0	0	5.0
4. Serfs	80.8	9.9	9.1	41.8
5. Cottars	86.7	8.0	3.3	17.6
6. Free peasants	6.6	30.0	61.4	21.4
7. Tax-paying burghers	20.9	.2	47.5	4.6
8. Other (Greeks, priests, gypsies, saltcutters, miners, etc.)	64.5	8.3	19.0	7.9
% in Total Population	61.4	14.3	21.2	

Source: Calculated from Csetri and Imreh 1972:204–205.

[a] I have not included all categories or all locations from the tables in Csetri and Imreh; thus my figures do not total 100%.

[b] Includes Partium, Chioar, and Făgăraş districts.

to the east and south were militarily vital enough to warrant granting the settlers administrative freedoms. This enabled them to exclude from their territory the feudal relations for which most of them had fled their German homelands. Later, their settlements became the chief customs points in the long-distance trade that linked the West and the Orient from the fourteenth century on, and upon this trade Saxon town life flourished. Long-distance trade — passing through Transylvania because Ottoman conquests altered prior routes — gave rise to a local trade between Transylvania and Wallachia, the Romanian land immediately south of the Carpathians. Saxons in and near the towns began producing manufactures to supply this local trade: clothing, cutlery, weapons, and paper in exchange for rawhides, animals, and cotton from Wallachia. In this way the Saxons created their own commerce and crafts on the back of fortuitous changes in global trade. The towns drew chiefly upon free-peasant farms for their food, rather than upon noble estates.

The Saxons' hold on commerce soon came under attack, however, as the nobility began to favor merchants from the Turkish territories. In 1576, with the nobles' help, Greek traders received trading rights in Transylvanian towns (Meteş 1920:206). Other merchant groups followed in their wake, and by the mid-1600s Saxons had lost control of the long-distance trade to Greeks and Wallachians. The reasons for their ouster are uncertain, but one can make a few guesses. First, nobles may have grown alarmed at Saxon prosperity and wished to undermine it. Second, new trading patterns in the early 1500s favored the Orient over Western Europe as the new major source of luxuries; Oriental traders may have offered nobles better contacts, prices, and goods than did Saxons, linked to cities north and west.

These circumstances were in all likelihood what produced the first signs of ethnicity among Saxons, who had voluntarily called themselves "Hungari" but now began to behave as "Germanissimi Germanorum" (see Makkai 1946: 174, 266-267). Although this might be seen as a defensive reaction against those whose politics were threatening the Saxon specialty, more probably Saxon ethnic closure was a vehicle for competing against trading groups from outside. Ethnic monopolies have proved especially effective instruments for managing long-distance trade, in many times and places (see A. Cohen 1969). Given that trade along Transylvanian routes was in gradual decline during this period, competition for it would have become unusually sharp, requiring that Saxons strengthen their ethnic organization to beat out Greeks, Wallachians, and other foreign traders.

As things turned out, the Saxons were no match for the outsiders, especially when local nobles became opponents also. The Saxon community did not sink into economic nothingness, however, and leave nobles to rule the economy unopposed. Their local manufacturing and some short-distance trade survived, though in a weakened state. To account for this is to underscore Transylvania's semi-peripheral (rather than peripheral) status inside the empire: Saxon industry survived because of its proximity to the unindustrialized grain-producing economy of Wallachia, beyond the Carpathians and outside the empire. Wallachian markets kept Transylvania's indigenous manufacturing and commercial groups in business to oppose the agrarian nobility.

If Transylvania's economy remained less overwhelmingly feudal and agrarian than Hungary's, then, it was because a territory containing one-fifth of the population remained immune to feudalism's fullest effects. Income there passed through hands not wholly given to lavish spending. The cause of this, in turn, was the privileges granted the Saxons as members of a medieval feudal estate. Never feudal in practice, they were nonetheless fortunate in having their economy rest on a feudal foundation, which gave them the means to isolate themselves administratively and economically as no group in the rest of Hungary was able to do.

COMMERCE, INDUSTRY, AND MINING

Contrary to our expectations from looking at Hungary, then, agriculture was not the only meaningful economic activity in Transylvania between 1700 and 1848, even though a feudal aristocracy prevailed in general. Within and to some extent outside the Saxon lands there was persistent commerce and industry, especially mining. These deserve closer attention, for as the economy shifted toward capitalism during the nineteenth century, one finds several variants of capitalism juxtaposed. Each of these—capitalism in mining, mercantile capitalism, and industrial capitalism—affected the peasants around it in slightly different ways. And the mix of these variants changed across the landscape, creating multiple microenvironments for a peasant population whose feudal existence might be mistakenly viewed as grimly uniform. The immediate environment of the peasants of Binţinţi contained all these variants, with important consequences for the feudal system that was this population's most intimate daily reality.

At the beginning of the 1700s Transylvanian commerce was largely in the hands of foreign merchants located in Saxon cities. Throughout the century Saxon merchants waged a battle with the Transylvanian Diet and the Habsburg Court for more favorable trading conditions and for import restrictions that would expand markets for Saxon wares. But either the Diet or the imperial circles consistently opposed them, the Court doing so at least partly because arrangements with Oriental trading companies assured the necessary raw materials and outlets for imperial manufactures (Cernovodeanu 1972:411). The Saxons struggled without interruption to recapture control of the trade until the early 1800s, when they finally won preferential licensing for commerce in at least a few categories of Viennese wares (Moga 1973:194). This time, the Court may have taken their side in order to counter Transylvania's obstinate nobility.

Although the state and Diet largely sided with the foreign merchants against the Saxons, the Court did heed the Saxon complaint that foreigners were emptying the land of capital that could be put to good local use. By 1740, the state was encouraging and pressuring the foreigners to settle in Transylvania, threatening otherwise to cut back their trading privileges. Some of these settled Greek, Armenian and Wallachian merchants later provided the capital that opened several manufacturing enterprises, from which both the state and some local nobles would draw income.

The Saxons were the only indigenes to express much concern about controlling commerce; the same was not true for small-scale manufactures. Early in the 1700s the Habsburgs, in their eagerness to promote industry, had encouraged several projects that resulted in the appearance of glass, paper, and potash manufacture. Much of it arose on aristocratic estates and used serf labor, with merchants supplying any needed capital (Daicoviciu et al. 1961:316; Oțetea 1970:272). After several decades, however, the state withdrew from many of these ventures, having decided to oppose the growth of most local manufacturing in Transylvania (Surdu 1960:138–139). The Austro-Bohemian manufacturing interests on the imperial Economic Council probably had a hand in this reversal, for a number of Transylvanian industries (glass, textile, and iron) duplicated enterprises in the western regions and the competition was not welcome. Thus, the same group that kept Hungary agrarian also moved to undercut feudal and other manufactures in Transylvania.

The orphaned enterprises were turned over to lessees, some being Armenian and Jewish merchants (Surdu 1964:194), who gradually acquired controlling shares in their management. By century's end many of the industries that had remained in aristocratic hands were defunct, the main exception being alcohol manufacture (Surdu 1960:126). Manufacturing enterprises that persisted had mostly been revived by substantial mercantile capital, in large part from outside, which transformed them from a moribund state to healthy capitalist ventures (Surdu 1964:149).

The Saxons' textile manufacture probably would have disappeared down the same path, had they not protected it with determination. They increased restrictions on entry into guilds, excluded non-Saxons, tightened their monopolies on raw wool and hemp, and allowed guild members to sell directly (Moga 1973:217). These moves may have retarded modernization of the textile industry but they also kept it alive and in Saxon hands (well into the nineteenth century). Using the inexpensive labor of free peasants who engaged in cottage weaving of wool and linen, Saxon textile production was still functioning to take advantage of enlarged markets in Wallachia (from 1821 on) and of heightened demand for fabrics during the Crimean War. By the mid-1800s, well-financed Saxon textile manufacture was the principal branch of Saxon industry. Factory production was not yet widespread, but Saxons had ways of changing that: one of "their" factories had been established with merchant capital by a local merchant from Wallachia, but its operation was imperiled by Saxon boycotts until the owner finally leased the factory to them (Surdu 1964:187).

Other small-scale manufacturing in the early 1800s included a few paper and sugar mills, candleworks, alcohol manufacture, tanneries, and production of glass, furniture, and gunpowder. A few shops were opened between 1830 and 1850 to produce agricultural machinery. Many of these establishments were run as joint-stock companies, their shareholders including members of the local and imperial aristocracy, the Austrian bourgeoisie, and bourgeois groups in Transylvania (Cherestești 1966:27). Overall, early nineteenth-century processing sustained itself on combinations of local capital, state support, and investments by foreign merchants. All industry, however, suffered from the general lack of local capital (to say nothing of the terrible state of the transport network), a problem apparently less severe for the Saxons than for others. Helped perhaps by increased overland trade during the Continental Blockade (Imreh 1955:11), the Saxons managed to erect sound financial institutions by the 1830s and 1840s. It may be for this reason that many of the small manufactures were located in Saxon territories.

At least as serious for Transylvanian industry was the absence of an adequate internal market. The only support for production in this period was the existence of markets in the Romanian principalities, the destination of Transylvania's paper, textiles, leather goods, and many other products. According to Iorga (1925 II:95), this market was enlarged after 1821, and Transylvania increasingly took on the role of processing raw materials for the principalities. Cotton, wool, and hides were brought in from the south and sent back as fabrics, clothing, and finished leather goods. Iorga does not explain the timing of this market expansion: one might see it as significant that at precisely this time, Wallachia became firmly tied to Western Europe as a grain-producing "colony" (Chirot 1976), which must have raised the purchasing power of at least some segments of its population.

The economic activity that yielded the greatest value in Transylvania and was most solidly grounded by the mid-nineteenth century was industry based on mining. Full development of the iron industry would not begin until rail transport reached Transylvania in the 1860s, but the foundations in mining had been laid long before. Indeed, given that only one-fifth of Transylvania was reckoned arable as late as 1848 — with pastures and forests making up over half and the remaining quarter considered unproductive except for its mines — mining rather than agriculture was often thought to be the region's future (Cherestesiu 1966:20). Mines had already been significant in its past, at least since the gold mining of Roman times, which gave way to booms in silver, lead, and other precious metals later on. Iron production was also very old, one of its major centers being the domains of Hunedoara castle, where serfs mined iron ore and turned it into implements for their feudal masters, on whose estates the mines lay. The use of serf labor in mines located on feudal properties was a common practice until the seventeenth century, when merchant capital from the Levantine trade began to buy up and transform some of these mining operations away from their feudal roots (Otetea 1970:232).

Nobles relinquished their proprietorship of mines at a much faster rate once the Habsburgs took Transylvania. The state rapidly gained control of salt and gold mines, in particular, acquiring most other mines from their noble proprietors in the process. The state also brought in miners from the Tyrol and Bohemia and made major investments in upgrading production. Although the acquisitions began in the early 1700s, they intensified greatly after the empire lost Silesia, its most developed region, in 1740. Capital for these purposes came first from state funds and then from shareholders' investments in the joint-stock companies formed in several of Transylvania's mining regions as early as the mid-1700s. Among the shareholders were the empress, other outsiders (including doctors, tradesmen, and merchants, especially Armenians), many aristocrats from other parts of the empire, and a few Transylvanian magnates (Neamțu 1970:227–229).

The investments were lucrative ones. In the first half of the nineteenth century, Transylvania produced more gold than all the rest of Europe combined (Cheresteșiu 1966:32), and the merchant capital that went into iron mining nourished what was becoming Transylvania's number one industry: iron production. Capital inputs into mining accelerated during the nineteenth century and the number of joint-stock companies rose, again composed mostly of non-Transylvanians and a few local magnates (Tóth 1955:225). With increased processing of the extracted ores, mining and metallurgy became the principal sectors in the Transylvanian economy and the heart of Transylvania's capitalist development. As of 1844, Transylvania had fifty-six iron works and would add fourteen more in the next decade (Wagner 1977:112). Highly concentrated production in coal and iron (especially after 1848), together with relatively advanced technology and very inexpensive labor, brought the state and other shareholders large revenues from these industries (Vajda 1967:173).[10] In Transylvania's mining, then, there were signs of capitalist development — even in the late 1700s — evident in no other branch to an equal degree. This impression is reinforced by the high proportion of miners who were wage-earners rather than serfs.

What effect did this mining, commerce, and industry have on the peasant population?[11] Above all, any area adjacent to these activities was more likely to include production of agricultural commodities than were areas more remote. Urban artisans, merchants, and tradesmen had to be fed, largely by the peasants in their hinterlands. Production of agricultural commodities was especially likely in the Saxon lands, which not only contained most of the urban industry but also had a free peasantry capable of devoting its full labors to its own agricultural tasks rather than to those of feudal

lords. Beyond this, peasants in those lands who had holdings inadequate to their subsistence needs could participate in cottage industry, which may have reduced their agricultural production but gave
them incomes to purchase commodities from their wealthier neighbors when necessary. Several authors observe these possibilities for
commodity production. Marczali, for example, notes that in a cash-
poor era when many settlements were in arrears, taxes were paid in
full wherever local industry was near to provide a local market for
produce (Marczali 1910:23–25; see also McNeill 1964:100, and
Hintz 1846:437).

Mining areas provided a slightly different impulse to agricultural
commodity production. Here the internal market came from miners,
a large percentage of whom were landless; for example, Neamțu
(1971:257) says that landless miners amounted to 80 percent and 97
percent in two Hunedoara settlements in 1780. Salaried landless
miners had to feed themselves from their wages. Since most mining
areas had no rich peasantry, the food that fed the miners must have
been produced either by the wealthier serfs nearby—even though
mountain land was not very bountiful—or by more distant noble
or serf farming. There is some evidence of agricultural commodity
production among mountain peasants, such as the early replacement of labor dues by money rents in mining areas (Botezan 1970*b*:
38). I nonetheless incline to the belief that production by the nobility
supplied at least a goodly share of the food commodities purchased
by miners.

Thus, both mining and industry simultaneously encouraged
commercialization in the countryside and did not compete for the
land on which crops were grown. Wherever mines or processing
works were located, one could expect to find an increase in peasants'
market orientation and in opportunities for marketing produce
from noble estates. Given the size and distribution of mines and
industry, the principal commercial agriculture would be within the
free peasantry of the Saxon lands and among noble estates at their
margins. In the Counties, the few urban centers, industries, and
mines would provide occasional spots of market agriculture on the
landscape, but these were far rarer than in or near Saxon areas.

One might expect that serfs would be among those producing for
such occasional markets, but the likelihood of this depends on the
size of serfs' usufruct plots. As will soon be seen, these were not very
large. The suppliers of markets in the Counties, therefore, howso-
ever modest these markets were, would be the nobility. This did not
necessarily mean that nobles would become capitalist farmers; it

meant only that they had new opportunities to expand incomes toward maintaining lavish display. And insofar as they did seek to increase their incomes, it was upon the backs of their serfs. For the true feudal noble, if Banaji (1977:21) is right, reckons as "costs" only cash outlays and as "profits" all cash receipts. This noble would thus not diminish his "income" by paying out wages. Rather, he would increase his exactions of absolute surplus labor directly, and to the maximum.

THE AGRICULTURAL ECONOMY

In turning to the feudal economy, we move the focus downward from Transylvania in its totality and examine more closely the organization of life in the Counties, containing not quite two-thirds of the region's area and population. The essence of Transylvanian feudalism was land ownership, together with peasant bondage to the soil by customary law and with very tight controls restricting property ownership itself to members of the natios or feudal estates. This feudalism rested less on extra-economic coercion of peasant labor than on peasant nonownership of land, which the lord gave "in exchange for" labor so serfs could reproduce themselves and thereby recreate their labor. Transylvanian feudalism itself was not reproduced over time primarily through legal enforcement of the relationship between lord and serf. Rather, it was reproduced through legal controls on property transmission, in particular through rules of entail that precluded a lord's alienating from the patriline any land from his ancestral holdings; he could alienate only what he acquired himself, such as by clearing land or by dispossessing serfs. This is very close to classic medieval feudalism, unaltered by state assistance to the lord. For this reason, serfdom's true end in Hungary and Transylvania did not come with the edict by which Joseph II untied serfs from the land in 1785 but with the abolition of entail and other property restrictions during the upheavals of 1848.

Incomes and Markets

The remainder of this chapter depicts Transylvania's eighteenth-century feudal regime, with illustrations from documents for some estates in Binţinţi. The picture is a fairly static one, for research into this period is not yet advanced enough to answer with certainty many of the obvious questions about social and economic processes. Much current scholarship insists that the latter part of the 1700s witnessed the inexorable penetration of capitalism into Transylvanian agriculture. There is good reason, however, to be skeptical of this view, one difficulty being that it is by no means clear what market expansion could have fueled such a shift.[12] Because this issue bears on my interpretation, I will begin by summarizing the likely trends in eighteenth-century commercialization that seem to emerge from inconsistent and varied scholarly sources. The effects of many factors mentioned would have fluctuated across space; I direct myself chiefly to Transylvania's southern parts.

Indications of a squeeze on noble incomes, which might have led to increased market production, suggest countervailing tendencies. First, throughout the eighteenth century nobles were being gradually forced away from alternatives to estate agriculture, as the Habsburg state bought up mines on noble properties and made decisions that undercut small-scale feudal manufactures. (The few nobles who acquired interests in mining and processing concerns, however, thereby augmented incomes without recourse to agriculture.) Second, Emperor Joseph's assault on County administrations as he revamped the bureaucracy in the 1780s temporarily threatened the salaries of some nobles, but this was resolved in 1791 in the nobles' favor. Third, between 1700 and the early 1800s the tax burden on the peasantry quintupled (from 0.3 to 1.5 million florins), rising much faster than population and cutting deeply into surpluses for lords. Yet falling prices for at least some imported luxuries in the late 1700s, such as English textiles, would have somewhat eased expenditures for consumption. Fourth, an increased rate of population growth in the late 1700s would have raised the take from feudal dues in kind; but army recruitments and requisitions in the 1780s and 1790s may have more than canceled out the difference. Imperial intrusion into feudal relations being more insistent in Hungary than in Transylvania, incomes probably suffered less overall in the latter area. A general trend is, however, difficult to identify with certainty.

Given that we do not know the rate at which consumption standards were escalating, we cannot conclude definitively that noble incomes were or were not in jeopardy. My own view is that nobles probably had reason to be very concerned with augmenting their incomes, increasingly so over the long run, but were not in such protracted danger as to necessitate radical changes in their social economy until after 1800. The one clear trend is that it became less and less possible to diversify activities beyond agriculture but still remain within the feudal framework. In the second decade of the 1800s real disaster struck, as devaluations (1811) and tax increases crippled incomes, and a terrible famine (1815-1817) reduced the labor supply in the Counties by 22 percent (see Csetri and Imreh 1972:150). At this point nobles indubitably faced a crisis and were forced to choose among alternative ways of increasing incomes within agriculture or switching into other sectors of Transylvania's developing economy.

For nobles concerned with augmenting incomes before this crisis, what were the possibilities for their main option — that is, marketing agricultural products (their own or their peasants')? Let us look at export markets first. The state of transport and the superior grain potentials of areas to the west and south meant that Transylvania would not export grains, with the possible exception of a few brief years during the Austro-Turkish war (1788-1791). This war may have created a short-lived market for exporting maize from southern Transylvania into Wallachia, devastated by the occupying Russian troops (Hitchins, personal communication). As for the more plausible export, cattle, I found no mention of this possibility in secondary sources, little evidence of it in documents (see below), and small expectation on logical grounds. The eighteenth century was not a period of expanding urbanization in Eastern Europe generally, and the few urban centers (Vienna, Istanbul) were better provisioned by cattle from agricultural areas near to them than from Transylvania. It is possible that wool was exported, but more from mountain areas than from the feudal lowlands.

It is more likely that Transylvanian estates served only internal markets. These did expand somewhat — although not remarkably — during the 1700s, especially from population growth without increased productivity (Surdu 1960:110). The chief loci of industry were in or near the Saxon lands, provisioned by free peasants and, perhaps, a few noble estates at the margins. There was only modest urbanization even as late as the 1840s, much of it from influxes of persons having landed incomes and not wholly market-dependent (Csetri and Imreh 1966a). The most obvious internal food market was salaried miners, but although this population did grow, it amounted to no more than 2.7 percent of the population up through the early 1800s. And these people did not always take their business to urban markets. The peasants of Binţinţi reported to conscriptors in 1820 that they could sell produce in several places, but that foresters and miners often picked up wheat directly from them in the village (Cziráky, Question 4). It is known from other sources that these purchasers may have bartered ceramics, fruits, or wooden barrels rather than paying cash.

An additional possibility is the army; the evidence here is that its demand was probably steady but small, and not growing. Much of Transylvania's defense was in the hands of the self-supplying peasant Border Regiments. The number of regular troops stationed in the region was never more than 5,000 to 10,000 during the eighteenth century, and more than half of this was cavalry, billeted among the peasants and at their expense, rather than infantry, garrisoned in towns and fed by markets (Deak, personal communication). Even then, troops were often fed by peasant taxes in kind rather than by commodities from the estates. Only during the military campaigns of Joseph II against the Turks, near the century's end, would the army's demand have risen and boosted markets temporarily. The army more readily expanded markets for manufacturing than for agricultural commodities, through increased demand for weapons, gunpowder, and uniforms.

Finally, lords may have turned to consumers within their very midst: poor peasants marginalized by land-hungry nobles, peasants pushed to the brink by famines or bad harvests, peasants living on increasingly fragmented holdings as population climbed throughout the century, mountain peasants whose land was poor and who needed to find grain.[13] However, we cannot assume a cash flow among these peasants sufficient to sustain market purchases. Forced labor, not salaried labor, prevailed in agriculture; payments in kind and loans of cereal against labor were frequent in the late 1700s, as one learns readily from documents listing quantities of cereals, hay, and straw paid out for labor on György Macskásy's estate (residents of upland villages receive their wage in wheat, lowlanders in hay or straw [MC #471]). A fair portion of the grain stockpiled in estate granaries went to these purposes; only some of it went in carts to market.[14]

There must have been at least some cash in the countryside, for in 1782 Ferencz Macskásy of Binţinţi was reaffirming to his innkeepers his insistence that the wine sales he monopolized must be paid in cash rather than in wheat (MC #432). Just how much room did Macskásy have to expand the internal consumer's market? Scholars concerned with how commercialized the peasantry was do not much illuminate this problem, indicating that there both was and was not a fair degree of commercialization in the countryside (see Botezan n.d., 1976; Botezan and Enea 1970). Moreover, it is not certain whether the objects being produced were exchanged for cash (which could nourish aristocratic incomes by purchasing wheat or wine) or bartered. A few conclusions nonetheless seem safe.

First, circulation of money and chances to exchange produce were most extensive for peasants in the Saxon lands, where seasonal labor was also often engaged for cash (Chereşteşiu 1966:60; Botezan 1976: 164–165, 168). Wage labor was better paid there than elsewhere, including the mining regions (Botezan n.d.: 385). These opportunities affected both the residents of the Saxon lands and the residents of serf villages close enough to profit from occasional work. Second, there is a chance that serfs living near the margins of the Saxon areas could have been involved in cottage industry for Saxon textile production, as were poor peasants within the Saxon lands. Third, peasants not subject to *robot* obligations — largely uplanders — were more likely to be producing goods for exchange than were *robot*-owing serfs. Among the latter, the most commercialized were wealthy serfs in fertile areas who managed to keep extended households with large labor reserves for their own use. Although it is certain that *all* peasants sold such items as fowl, eggs, and dairy products in market towns or mining centers (Botezan and Enea 1970:153), the richer serfs might also have earned cash by selling some cereals or livestock.

These conclusions make it clear that although cash did not flow in abundance among the serf population, there were nonetheless peasant consumers for noble intoxicants. And the list suggests who were the most reliable such consumers: wealthy serfs with ready access to town markets, and landless peasants (who thus had low *robot* obligations and more labor time of their own) near mining centers, near the Saxon lands, and near vineyards, where wages were more common than for other kinds of day labor (Botezan n.d.: 381). Peasants in other categories would have had to be more abstemious — that is, all those with subsistence-minimal lands and small nuclear-family units for fulfilling onerous labor obligations. With few adult workers and few draft animals, they could work their own land but poorly and produce little extra to sell for cash. Village populations in which these peasants predominated were doubtless the ones who replied to Cziráky's questions about cash income by saying, "We could sell things if we had anything left over to sell, and we could earn cash if it weren't for all the labor we give our lords" (see Botezan and Schilling 1970, 1971, 1973). They must have constituted a challenge to lordly distillers eager for increased sales.

It seems safe to conclude from this survey that market opportunities existed and remained fairly constant throughout the eighteenth century and into the nineteenth but did not much expand. When combined with conclusions about noble requirements for income, this implies that fluctuating and intensifying income needs faced a fairly inelastic environment for increased commercial farming on noble estates. In my view, this suggests a gradual involution of the feudal economy, a slow intensification of the ways of exploiting labor and of turning peasants into consumers, all within the confines of the feudal system. Putting this dynamic together with exogenous influences (prices of luxuries, tariffs, war-induced inflations and devaluations), with the Court's reluctance to intervene too forcibly in Transylvania's manorial affairs, and with the modest sizes of many noble estates, one gains some insight into why Transylvanian serfdom was among the most oppressive ever known.

Characteristics of the System: Display, Land, Labor, and Products

The basic characteristics of feudalism in the Transylvanian Counties in the 1700s, to be expanded upon below, were as follows. A large population of nobles, 8.2 to 9 percent of the total County population (Prodan 1979 I:36), struggled on small estates to maintain a suitably aristocratic life-style on incomes provided not by rents from a comfortable tenantry but by the labors of serfs, under conditions breeding extremely low productivity. The size of the subsistence plot — the wage-in-kind — granted these serfs was so small as to constitute for many of them barely enough to reproduce themselves. This made landlords virtual dictators over the production process. Because many factors, including the fragmentation of their own estates, reduced labor productivity and the possibilities for improvement, the chief tendency of these nobles over the eighteenth and early nineteenth centuries was to expand their incomes by increasing the areas at their disposal and the labor of the peasants they controlled. I do not hold that these nobles were incapable of raising agricultural productivity but that the possibilities for doing so were, given the history of Transylvania's property structure, extremely limited. This kind of landlord had a different attitude toward labor, and consequently a different behavior toward it, from his peripheral-capitalist counterpart: he was not interested in "saving" labor or in revolutionizing the labor process but in maximizing labor input.

Since my analysis of Transylvanian feudalism presupposes a nobility preoccupied with incomes and conspicuous consumption, I should offer some evidence for this image. Prodan observes that the entry of Transylvania into the Viennese orbit inflated the consumption standards of local nobles. New houses were admired, new forms of luxury proliferated; urban residence became preferable to the village manor (Prodan 1979 I:35). Some of the new standards were propagated by Transylvanian nobles who also owned property in Hungary and regularly traveled to the Hungarian capital or to Vienna. Peter Macskásy, who bought himself a house in Orăştie before he died in 1712, was no backward gentryman: among his effects in Binţinţi he left — along with a carriage and pillows and a silver bridle manufactured locally in Sibiu — fourteen measures of English cloth with collars of marten, some belts of snakeskin, a fine saddle blanket made of English cloth and embroidered with swallowtails, a pair of London summer gloves, and a lined black English mantle (MC #2819). Klara Gyulai was pretentious enough to address a letter (in Hungarian) to her relative Ferencz Macskásy in the city of Deva, in 1775, "Monsieur le Francoise Macskasi de Tinkova mon tres chere frere" (sic), proposing a meeting upon her return from Vienna (MC #433). Yet the Macskásys were at best a good gentry family, not aristocrats at all.

Travelers' journals from the nineteenth century present an incontrovertible picture of aristocratic display (Gerard 1888; Paget 1850; Tucker 1886) and report on the tremendous indebtedness of the nobility that tried to sustain it. The Englishman Paget, visiting Transylvania in 1835, found Baron Miklós Wesselényi keeping a courtyard full of pheasants (not native to those parts) and raising English thoroughbreds to sell expensively to his fellow liberals, while his serfs performed their accustomed *robot* around him and hindered his sales of grain by throwing themselves on his mercy during years of poor harvest (Paget 1850 II:213-225). Paget also notes in his travels the number of nobles wearing clothes cut after the latest London fashion. These observations confirm what we might guess from the earlier negative trade balance of eighteenth-century Transylvania, thrown off by importing "all sorts of luxury items for the nobility" (Surdu 1960:132). As further confirmation, we learn that in the currency devaluation of 1811, Transylvania exchanged less than a fifth of the number of banknotes that would have been proportional to its population and area — a datum reflecting the low circulation of cash in the economy but also the expenditure rather than accumulation of income, "wasted" on gambling, parties, and fancy houses (Botezan n.d.:399).

These were not easy times to uphold inflated life-styles, for inflation and currency devaluations cut into incomes even as standards spiraled upwards — and conceptions did not change accordingly.

"The rich Hungarians . . . prefer to use their money to acquire immovable goods than to consign it to commerce or risk it in industrial enterprises," Demian tells us (1809 II:451). A Magyar gentlewoman in Cluj complains (as late as 1880) to her guest William Tucker, "My eldest son, István, has disgraced our family by becoming a merchant . . . and ruined himself beyond retrieve, by marrying . . . the low-born child of a wealthy manufacturer" (Tucker 1886:59–60). Paget finds in the 1830s that his aristocratic hosts keep their accounts in total disarray, reckoning nothing as income or expenditure if it is not *money,* and remarks on their hoarding gold and jewels (Paget 1850 II:398–400). It is rare that he meets a noble like the baron who had recently (in 1830) had his Scottish bailiff introduce crop rotations and begun calculating the profitability of raising sheep, given the difficulty of selling grain (Paget 1850 II: 230–231). More characteristic than Paget's baron was the mentality that seems to emerge from the instructions Pál Macskásy's widow sent to her new estate administrator in 1798. These manifest, at most, a businesslike orientation but surely not one concerned with sales, profits, markets, or investments:

30 v 1798, Cluj
1. Survey and inventory all goods and possessions.
2. Anything taken in should be inventoried with a signature.
3. Run the properties so as to have neither losses nor postponements.
4. Prepare reports concerning workers (their number, contracts if any exist) and take steps to see that they work when they are supposed to.
5. Behave well with the workers, neither beating them nor shouting at them.
6. Keep accounts fully up to date, and be prepared to render a report on the state of affairs at a moment's notice. (MC #460)

Let us accept as a guiding assumption, then, that the nobility of Transylvania in this period was concerned with lavishness and with bigger incomes toward that end, and let us look at how their economy developed through the early 1800s. We will begin with one of their most reliable, if not quite universal, sources of income — office-holding — and then turn to land ownership and serf labor.

The status of noble entitled men to two important privileges: ownership of land, and public office. For those with important official functions, urban residence — and appropriate display — were mandatory and usually entailed leaving one's estate in the care of a manager, whose talents and rectitude then affected one's fortunes.

Public office was an especially important means of livelihood for those nobles with modest holdings; many of the nobles of Binţinţi enjoyed it, both in the 1700s and later.[15] The Macskásy family produced at least two county high sheriffs (the most important official in the local administration of Hungary and Transylvania), one lieutenant sheriff, and one or more county prefects; in addition, several of their members were army officers, one achieving the rank of general. Other Binţinţi nobles of the 1700s were assistant prefects, lieutenant sheriffs, and officials in the Salt Commission, and one was chief notary. Proprietors of the 1800s held as many titles of Count and Baron as those of the 1700s and occupied offices equally illustrious — indeed, more so: one Binţinţi proprietor (Elek Nopcsa) was the Transylvanian Chancellor in Vienna.

The possession of a salary did not make one neglect one's agricultural affairs, however, as is shown by the fact that most of the documents in the Macskásy collection were kept by three who were high sheriff, county prefect, and army general. There is a hint that the salaries of these positions were not always sufficient to their occupants' appetites but that without them their holders would have starved on their meager estates. In 1734, when future General Farkas Macskásy attained the rank of captain, he pawned his Binţinţi estate to his relatives to raise money for the expenses incurred by his promotion (MC #2836). And the financial state of chief notary Mihály Olasz, before he achieved his position, was embarrassingly revealed in 1737 after his death, when his fellows testified in a court case that at his marriage he had been so poor he could not pay for his wedding but borrowed the money for it (a debt later paid off by his wife [MC #2854]).

While office was frequently an important supplement, for most the foundation of status and income was landed property. The preoccupation with land ownership reveals itself in many places, among the best of them being estate records like those of the gentry family Macskásy in the village of Binţinţi. Their preoccupation with land is visible in simple percentages: of the 250 documents I consulted[16] (about two-thirds of the family's archive for Binţinţi), 60 percent concerned landowners' dispositions of their land or violations of their rights to it. The remaining 40 percent encompassed all other kinds of landlordly concerns: relations among serfs and between serfs and landlords; notes about enserfment or serf sales, exchanges, or flight; loans of money or grain to serfs or other proprietors; records of crops sown; instructions to estate managers; inventories of household effects; and a few items indicating how landlords encroached not only on each other's lands but on those reserved for the use of serfs.

There is much to be said about land under Transylvanian feudalism, including the stratagems of landlords for increasing the surface areas at their disposal and the problems caused by the fragmentation of estates, but these require preliminary discussion of the land's most important attribute: the serfs who came attached to it. Because none but nobles could own land, its possession automatically entailed the labor of nonnobles. Landowners divided their estates into two portions, known as "urbarial" (or rustical) and "allodial" (or dominical) lands, the ratios between them varying considerably from estate to estate. The urbarial lands were subdivided into serf holdings (*sessiònes*) on which serfs had rights of usufruct and in exchange for which they gave both dues in kind and labor dues (*robot*) on the allodia, or lord's demesne. A "full holding" was divisible into halves, quarters, and eighths, thus introducing differentiation within serf ranks. Landlords also had special labor contracts with peasants who were not expected to give dues in kind but received a patch of land for subsistence. These contract serfs, whose condition was not hereditary, sometimes arrived in flight from elsewhere (a frequent enough occurrence) or were even lured from other nobles, or they might come from the ranks of the estate's regular serf population. There were other categories of labor besides these two.

A serf holding had to feed the serf, his animals (which were his only real property), and his family, generate money for taxes, and produce extra for dues and tithes in kind. Serfs had no right to dispose of this holding with the single exception that they could sometimes pawn (Rom. *zălogi*) their lands within the confines of the estate, usually as collateral against loans of cash or grain from a landlord.[17] And a serf had no right to move or marry without the lord's consent and could be moved from his plot to another or thrown off it altogether, at will, especially if he failed to maintain the animal inventory necessary for fulfilling both his *robot* obligations and the requirements of tilling his own plot. Lords themselves kept a minimal inventory: they relied on the animals and implements of the serf for cultivating their estates.

The serfs' labor obligations were far more stringent in Transylvania than in Hungary, where urbarial regulations had been passed and where at least the Diet recognized the right of serfs to redeem their obligations, as Transylvanian serfs could not (Cheresteşiu 1966:31). The Transylvanian Diet in 1714 set such high limits on feudal exactions that lords could easily commandeer serf labor for over half of each week throughout the year: four days' *robot* was the norm set for serfs, three days for cottars. A major lordly abuse of *robot* was the effort of some lords to requisition this amount per working adult rather than per household head, as was the intent (Surdu 1960:116–117). Another was simply to coerce more labor than the Diet's maximum, an abuse for which serfs had no recourse.

Although one finds reports of lords who demanded and got five and six days' labor per week (see chap. 2, p. 101), the obligations that peasants in Binţinţi declared as of 1820 are closer to the set limits. These declarations, part of an (unsuccessful) Habsburg attempt to remedy excesses in Transylvanian serfdom, show that even within this one village the obligations varied widely:

> We seven serfs of Baroness Antál Orbán work two days each week with oxen and two more days' manual labor; during harvest we work more often, if we are called to, and we each do a full week's carting per year. These obligations have been in force for 35 years. Before that we worked whenever our master ordered us to.
>
> We five serfs of Count Benedek Lázár work two days each week with oxen and do a week of carting per year.
>
> We seven serfs of Lajos Macskásy work two days each week with oxen or two days' manual labor if we have no oxen, and they use us for harvesting and carting until the work is done.
>
> We three serfs of János Macskásy work one day each week with four oxen, two days with two oxen, and two days manually. Our wives do fifteen days' sifting each year.
>
> I the serf of Moses Györffy do one day's manual labor each week.
>
> . . . Adding up all our obligations, we [41 serfs] give 884 days with four oxen, 1,040 days with two oxen, 2,288 days' manual labor; 82 hens, 82 chickens, 420 eggs; our wives spin all together 164 pounds of hemp . . . (Cziráky, Question 3)

The total declared holdings[18] (arable, hayfields, and houseplot) of the serfs responsible for these labors in 1820 ranged from 1.75 hectares to 9 hectares, and it seems from the reports that although technically speaking the obligations were supposed to be roughly proportional to the size of a serf's plot, they varied more from lord to lord than from rich to poor serf. Thus the poorest serf in the list worked four and sometimes more days a week for Baroness Orbán in exchange for his less than 2 hectares, while the two richest worked two days and a bit extra at harvest for their 9-hectare plot.[19]

The holdings reported above are, if anything, on the large side of the norm, and this is yet another respect in which the lot of serfs in Transylvania was harder than in Hungary. While urbarial regulations had set the minimal size of a full serf holding in Hungary at 14 to 18 hectares, Transylvania had no such laws. When they were finally proposed in 1846–47, the minima ranged from 2.25 to 5.75 hectares for top-quality arable land (plus a hectare or two of hayfields) to 8 hectares for poor-quality land (Baritĭu 1889: 648–649). The actual average sizes of serf holdings at the end of the eighteenth century varied greatly by region but tended to fall between 1.1 and 5.7 hectares (Botezan 1970*a*:156–157). Prodan gives a very low mean figure for the central Transylvanian plateau, 1.28 hectares per holding (Prodan 1944:95). This is not out of line with Botezan's finding that in 412 localities he investigated, over two-thirds (69 percent) of the serf holdings were under 2.85 hectares (Botezan n.d.:67–96). One must also remember that where two-field rotations were practiced, the effective surface area was halved. It is abundantly clear, then, that this was not a peasantry whose wealth and farm layout would support a landlord simply on rents or allow for much improvement. Given the prevailing crops and technology, it was a peasantry with barely enough for its own reproduction, over whose labor process the landlord therefore exercised tyrannical control.[20]

Although serfs did flee and there were years of famine that cut into their ranks, the problem with labor was less its scarcity than its productivity. This problem affected both peasant lands and lords' estates. During the eighteenth century the main crops sown were wheat, rye, and oats (Botezan n.d.:299). Maize cultivation was spreading by 1800 but was far from overtaking the others. Yet the ratio of yields to amounts sown averaged 3:1 or less for wheat, and scarcely more for rye and oats; it was highest of all for maize, sometimes reaching 30:1 (Botezan n.d.:266, 297–298).[21] These problems caused the state to press peasants to cultivate potatoes as a safeguard against famine. (And this, of course, would help to support higher population densities on smaller patches of land.)

Several things contributed to the low yields of the principal crops. First was the apathy of serfs doing forced labor, which encouraged resistance and low input—for example, covering the weeds with dirt when the master wasn't looking. Overuse and probable under-nourishment of both human and animal labor doubtless exacted their toll as well. Second was the rudimentary level of agricultural technology. At the end of the 1700s, two-field fallow systems prevailed in nearly half of 610 villages reported on by Botezan, and three-field systems in the other half (Botezan n.d.:276). The state was sufficiently concerned about this problem that its agents actively encouraged the switch from two- to three-field systems, ordering officials in Hunedoara County in 1771, for example, to report on progress in the spread of three-field tillage (Ionaş 1972:119 n. 6). (A few villages, such as Binţinţi through at least 1820, used a two-field system but reserved a small third field in which maize was planted every year.) Poor maintenance of the soil, inadequate implements, and the marginal health of draft oxen necessitated using multiple yoked teams to plow (four to six oxen or even more), which meant reducing either the efficiency or the number of plowings — especially on peasant lands, usually left uncultivated until after the oxen had been exhausted on the landlord's fields. Manuring was inadequate (Botezan n.d.: 266), probably because of poor pasturage and low cultivation of fodder.

A third source of low productivity was the fragmentation of both peasant lands and noble estates, which further impaired the efficiency of labor input. This subject deserves closer scrutiny than the others because of its historical roots and its implications for the modernization of agriculture. Though peasant holdings varied widely both in their size and in the degree of their fragmentation, one can get a glimpse of the problem's extent. Data examined by Botezan (1970a:156-157) show that peasant plots were divided into ten to twenty-five parcels. Breaking down some of his examples indicates that the average size per parcel ranged from 0.17 to 1.81 hectares, with most of the examples falling below 0.3 hectare per parcel (n.d.:106). The very limited evidence from my own data conforms to Botezan's ranges but shows a situation somewhat more favorable than his. In 1786 the estate of Imre Macskásy was inventoried for indebtedness, and the holdings of his seven (unusually rich) serfs broke down as follows:

	Arable Lands (i.e., excludes hayfields)		
Serf	Surface Area (ha)	No. Parcels	Average Parcel Size (ha)
Alexandru Iepura	3.99	9	.44
Gheorghe Borza	4.63	10	.46
David Teletyan	4.85	10	.48
Ion Hernya	5.91	14	.42
Apostol Tira	6.50	12	.54
Todor Iank	6.70	16	.42
Petru Borza	9.90	18	.55

(calculated from MC #2918)

Fragmentation of holdings was almost as extreme on landlords' estates as among the peasants and was a major impediment to improving agriculture, whether in feudal or capitalist terms. Except for the domains of churches and the Crown, large concentrated

estates were rare in Transylvania, far rarer than in Hungary. Botezan (n.d.:26) attributes this to the special status of Transylvania
under the Turks, whose involvement in the principality did not
entail, as it did in south and central Hungary, dispersing the nobility
and creating large open spaces to be filled later by Habsburg
ennoblements. Transylvania's nobility, in contrast, subdivided its
estates without interruption from at least the fifteenth century
onward. Since estates tended to be partible among offspring and
since many of the endless inheritance quarrels were resolved by
imposing complete and equal division among all heirs in all villages
where the deceased had owned land (Botezan n.d.:26), it is small
wonder that Transylvania's noble families had estates almost as
broken up as those of a backward peasantry. Nor is it surprising
that the nobles were on the average poorer than those of Hungary,
where subdivisions of estates had at least begun anew, and on a
larger land base, after 1700.

Fragmentation in Transylvania was worsened by the frequent
inclusion of sisters as well as brothers among rightful heirs to land.
It is clear from published genealogies that in Binţinţi, for example,
land was transmitted to women both with and without brothers.
This practice led to a high turnover of aristocratic surnames in the
village between 1700 and 1918, which turns out to indicate not
alienation of estates but continuity of family ownership as estates
moved through females.[22] This pattern was already established by
the mid-fourteenth century, in fact, when the lord of Binţinţi
secured transmission of part of his estate to his seven daughters in
the absence of male heirs (Zimmermann and Werner 1897:24-25).
Marriages of these daughters — and the ensuing squabbles recorded
in subsequent documents (Zimmermann and Werner 1897; Zimmermann and Müller 1902; Gündisch 1937) — began the fragmentation
of properties reflected in sources from the 1700s and after.

Just what did this fragmentation mean? At least three things: the
subdivision of a single village among several different lords, the
subdivision of the lands of each lord into many scattered pieces,
and impoverishment of the nobles. Data collected by Botezan (n.d.:
246) show that in 1820, 50 percent of the villages sampled in Alba
and Hunedoara Counties were divided among four or more nobles.
This retarded improvements such as consolidating field parcels and
switching from two- to three-field rotation or from open to enclosed
fields, for all landlords would have to agree among themselves on
the desirability of the changes before they could be implemented.
Binţinţi had at least eleven nobles for its population of 383 in the
1780s (Prodan 1979 I:339-340), fourteen serf-owning nobles for

about 273 peasants in 1820[23] (Cziráky conscription), and sixteen for a population of 600 in 1848 (Grimm 1863:pt. II). If the tone of the Macskásy documents is any indication, there is no reason to imagine that these nobles would readily agree upon anything.

As for the subdivision of their fields, lists from the Macskásy archives show the following ranges. In the early 1700s we find an 8-hectare estate in 18 pieces, with parcels averaging less than half a hectare, and a 50-hectare estate in 59 pieces, averaging about 0.9 hectare per parcel. For the late 1700s, two lists have parcels averaging 0.8 hectare (a 64-hectare estate in 81 fields, the largest piece being 3.5 hectares) and 0.9 hectare (a 48-hectare estate in 51 pieces, the largest being 5.75 hectares).[24] These figures match Botezan's data for estate fragmentation in Transylvania more generally. He finds that 80 to 85 percent of demesne lands in the period 1785–1820 were in parcels ranging from 0.25 to 5.75 hectares (Botezan n.d.:31–32). We can see the same effects a century later: when holdings were finally consolidated in 1882 in the village of Geoagiu near Binţinţi, Count István Kun — also a property owner in Binţinţi — owned in Geoagiu 350 hectares in 501 pieces, with an average field size of 0.7 hectare.[25] Figures like these reflect not only impediments to increased productivity through technological improvements but also a tremendous waste of serf labor, as serfs had to toil their way within a field's confines and then between that and countless other fields.

Finally, the partitions that produced such fragmented estates reduced the wealth of the nobility as a whole. If, as is generally agreed, Transylvania's nobles were on the average less wealthy than nobles in Hungary, a major reason was centuries of estate division. I cannot quote figures that would show exactly how impoverished these nobles were, but there are some indirect measures. First, in 1767, some 64 percent of the persons classed as nobles in the Counties were "nobles with one *sessio*," meaning that they had no more than a full serf holding (Csetri and Imreh 1972:204). Second, the ownership of serf-bearing lands as of 1848 — which excludes nobles who had no serfs — shows that 60 percent of the owners have ten or fewer serfs (figures to show this appear on the following page). Third, I can offer a wild estimate as to the maximal landholdings of this 60 percent. Using the uppermost of Botezan's figures for a serf holding (5.7 hectares), plus the information that Transylvanian estates tended to consist of two-thirds urbarial and one-third allodial land (Cherestesiu 1966:45), a ten-serf noble would have had a maximum of 85.5 hectares. This is not a stylish estate, and almost two-thirds of the serf-holding nobles would fall at or below that level.

Number of Full Serf Holdings Owned	Number of Estate-Owning Families	Percent of Families
1000 +	21	.6
500-1000	30	.8
100-500	192	5.3
50-100	230	6.4
10-50	961	26.6
1-10	2173	60.2
	3607	99.9

(Csetri and Imreh 1966*b*:110-111)

Thus, it is not surprising to learn that landlords had several different ways of rounding out their landholdings. In the Macskásy archives and other sources one finds four methods in addition to inheritance: usurpation of the village's communal pasture, confiscation of the possessions of a serf who has died, attempts to keep peasants ignorant of the actual size of their holdings, and loans of money or grain to peasants or to other nobles in exchange for pawns of land.

The usurpation of the communal pasture is recounted in preliminary hearings in 1736. While the event itself is not dated, internal evidence suggests that it probably occurred during the first decade or two of the 1700s.

10 ii and 10 v 1736
We serfs know that the field called "Bârceana" used to belong to the village in common and was used exclusively for peasants and nobles to pasture their cattle and horses. Then Mihály Olasz and his father-in-law Peter Macskásy, and later his brother-in-law János, plowed up and sowed as much of it as they wanted, and they prohibited everyone's animals from feeding there. The part that was not plowed was used by Ferencz Olasz and Ferencz Macskásy for secretly pasturing their horses, and now they allow no one's animals on it but theirs. (MC #2842, #2846)

This sort of episode is classic in the literature on the expansion of landlords' holdings at peasants' expense. The communal pasture reappears in a tax register from 1859-60 with a similarly classic manifestation: appended to the tax assessment is a note that the income for this community is unusually low because of the large payments required of the peasants for using the common pasture.[26] Thus, after usurping common lands, nobles returned them to peasant use — for a fee. Equally familiar to students of such matters is the testimony the serfs of Binţinţi gave in 1937, which described how after the death of Dumitru Hang, serf of the Macskásys, members of the gentry family Olasz burned down his house, occupied his arable lands and hayfields, and walked off with most of the hay and cereals on his property as well as with his five cattle (MC #2856).

The literature reports another tactic that helped landlords augment their fields with chunks from their peasants' holdings: keeping a serf (and the authorities) from knowing the precise amount of land to which he had use rights. Nobles reportedly connived with surveyors to record peasant declarations in very loose measures, when official conscriptions were ordered (Botezan 1970a:140). It is certain that most serfs did not know how large a "full serf holding" was supposed to be for their area, their village, or their lord, nor did they always know whether they had a full holding or only some fraction of one. In 1820 the Cziráky conscription tried to discover the extent of peasant informedness on these matters. The serfs of Binţinţi stood among the ignorant, responding to the questions "how much and what kind of land does a serf on a full holding have here?, and how much is that in *joch* or Viennese measures?": "We don't know how big a full holding is, and we don't know a thing about *jochs* or measures from Vienna" (Cziráky, Question 5). It is widely held that in this conscription, serfs declared even less than they had, believing their landlords' claim that their taxes would be less if they did so. Since these figures were the basis for impropriating peasants when serfdom was finally abolished in 1848, peasant ignorance and gullibility actually helped transfer their lands to their landlords.

Files of the Macskásys hint at other possible ways for nobles to acquire land. Between 1717 and 1736, thirty-seven peasants pawned land (in two cases, free peasants sold it outright) in exchange for loans—of cash, in four-fifths of the instances—and, between 1719 and 1766, eleven nobles pawned lands to other nobles, three-fourths of them for cash. According to L. Ursuţiu (1977), who finds increases of 350 percent in the arable surface and 390 percent in the hayfields pawned in his area between 1697 and 1715, most of these lands were pawned for money to pay taxes. There is no way of knowing, however, how many of the lands pawned remained in the hands of the noble money-lenders and how many were returned. Botezan claims that serfs seldom repossessed such lands (Botezan n.d.:336). The Macskásy archives show nothing one way or another as far as serf lands are concerned, beyond the notes of pawning, but they include several documents initiating—and taking to court —the repossession of lands pawned by other nobles.

After 1736 there are no more records of serfs pawning lands to the Macskásys for cash loans, but instead there are loans of wheat to be repaid at market value with labor as interest—a move from "collections" of land to mechanisms for "collecting" labor. Between 1754 and 1793 loans of this kind were made to twenty-one peasants (many not from Binţinţi) and to two villages collectively. The interest ranged from harvesting the equivalent of about 8 bushels of wheat (between two and three full days' labor) for each 3½ bushels borrowed, in 1760 (MC #376), to ten workdays of plowing for a loan of about 2⅔ bushels of wheat, in 1793 (MC #458). These documents lie among others that show the congruent interests of labor-hungry lords and impoverished peasants, as hitherto free peasants, contractual laborers, or gypsies enserfed themselves for loans and food.

9 February 1719

Cottar Găvrila Mihuţ of Mermezeu binds himself and his two sons and all their heirs in perpetuity as serfs of János Macskásy, in exchange for four florins and seventeen-and-a-half bushels of wheat valued at sixteen florins. (MC #316)

6 May 1755

Free gypsy Ion Lukács ties himself in perpetual servitude to General Farkas Macskásy for fifteen florins, a horse, three-and-a-half bushels of wheat, and four cups of wine. Four gypsy serfs stand as guarantors that he will not flee, and if he does they must pay 40 florins apiece [the value of about three oxen or twenty times the annual capitation tax of a serf]. (MC #2879)

This second document shows another feature of the labor economy of Transylvanian feudalism: that serfs were required to guarantee the continued presence and labor of new recruits and of other serfs who had fled and been returned, had assumed debts, or had been imprisoned and released on bail. In most cases the guarantors are recorded as promising a large sum of money, and they were occasionally summoned to pay it. But one document requiring restitutory labor rather than cash signals the possibility that so huge a cash sum was set with the intent of securing labor in its place from those whose friends jumped bail, defaulted, or fled. The effects of this peculiar institution of guarantorship (*chezăşie*) on village social relations can only be imagined, as evidence for its workings is very limited.

Landlords had a number of other ways of procuring labor besides as interest on loans. They created pretexts to charge labor, such as for the use of bridges or stud bulls, had labor "parties" with food and drink, and converted tithes into labor. They sought to extract dues from working adults in addition to the household head, and they pressed for subdivisions of serf holdings among sons, after which they would require the same amount of labor as before from each of the new families (Grimm 1863:22). This produced the result noted above: a tendency for labor to be assessed not by the size of each serf's holding but by the requirements of their particular lord. In addition, lords increasingly preferred to replace fines and corporal punishments with penalties exacted in labor (ibid.:14).

Finally, landlords began to create new categories of laborers. Their appetite for land made them uninterested in acquiring new serfs, for whom they would have to carve a new urbarial plot, vaguely commensurate with others, from their demesnes. Instead, they took to settling workers either on patches of land in their own courtyards, often very spacious—Farkas Macskásy refers to such a "courtyard serf" in a complaint in 1776 (MC #2908)—or on patches of their allodial lands *not* redefined as urbaria. Since allodia were tax exempt, these workers needed much less space than serfs, only enough to grow their food (and if the space proved inadequate they might be offered loans of food against payments in further labor). The trend toward creating these "allodial" or "irregular" serfs probably explains why there is no record in the Macskásy archives of anyone enserfing himself in the normal manner after 1755.[27]

It is difficult to chart the growth of this category from documents and official statistics. Although Kovács (1973:182) estimates them at 40 to 50 percent of the peasantry in Transylvania by 1848, he includes areas outside Transylvania proper (the Banat) where allodial serfs were especially numerous. In Binţinţi they must surely have formed a fair proportion of the population by 1820, yet because the Cziráky conscription left them out, one can only guess at their numbers from population figures before and after. Irregular serfs probably amounted to 35 percent or more of the population of Binţinţi in 1820,[28] an impressive figure even in the absence of earlier figures with which to compare it.[29]

Precisely why lords were creating irregular serfs is not entirely clear. Most scholars in Romania would interpret it as a process of building up a highly exploitable labor force, which implies that demesne production had become very rewarding and was being expanded over dues in kind paid by urbarial serfs. This is plausible and in some periods may have been true. However, if my conclusions about inelastic markets have any merit, expanded demesne production for market sale may not have been the chief motive for creating irregular serfs. Perhaps landlords were trying to minimize the agricultural surplus that went to taxes, for serfs settled on urbaria paid a much larger tax than the capitation fee for allo-dialists (see Pamlényi 1975:184, for a related proposal). This fits with the notion that landlords were struggling against reductions of income and incursions by the state, evident in spiraling taxes, and were reserving as much surplus product as possible for themselves. It is also compatible with the assumption that nobles would be increasingly interested in labor if only to extract more from it, though not necessarily for the market.

To learn about the economy practiced on large estates, specifi-cally in Binţinţi, let us first review the opportunities for market sale or for cash incomes among peasants in this particular village, which, given its location, was unusually well situated in both respects. First, Binţinţi was nine kilometers from Orăştie, a small enough town (3,200 persons in 1787) but at least a possible market, contain-ing an army garrison as well. A larger garrison was twenty-three kilometers away (Sebeş); it, however, was likely served by farming nearer by. Binţinţi lay at the rim of an extensive upland mining zone and may have helped to provision miners.

Second, concerning possible cash supplies with which peasants could purchase from the lords for whom they produced, the village was right at the western margin of the Saxon lands. This implies opportunities for day wage-labor, present also in not-too-distant small-scale vineyards. The village population contained a few peas-ants rich enough and close enough to market to sell some goods for cash (one document tells of how some rich peasants in 1767 carried off the cattle of another villager to market [MC #384]), as well as a number poor enough to require supplementary employ-ment, at least some of it for wages. The peasants of Binţinţi dis-closed their chances for cash income in their responses to the Cziráky conscription: "Some of us have enough extra hay to sell it, along with some cattails, sometimes we sell fish we catch in the lakes here, and because we are on the highway we can sometimes sell hay and oats to travelers. We also have good cabbage that we can sell. Those of us who want to work for money can do so in Orăştie, and some do" (Question 4). This catalogue should not be taken to imply too much, but that cash flowed in at least a trickle seems very clear. And these villagers were probably not unique among valley peasants around them.

As for what was being produced on the land, the evidence is thin but one can speculate. Outlines of the peasant economy as of the early 1700s appear from miscellaneous censuses and conscriptions[30] that list the amounts of various crops and animals pertaining to the serfs. Binṭinṭi villagers specialized in wheat and rye, with maize and oats being distinctly subordinate. They produced hay, raised animals (almost six head of cattle per full-serf household, a similar number of sheep and goats, and two to three pigs), and cultivated flax and hemp. Some of these items (it is not known exactly which) would have gone to the noble lord as dues. One important product on the census form is blank for this village: wine.

There is still less information concerning the large estates. An undated listing almost certainly from the late 1720s (MC #2821) tells that during the years 1724 to 1726, about two-thirds of the existing wheat on one estate—1,100 of 1,700 bushels—was sold, as was half of the existing 4,800 gallons of wine between 1725 and 1727.[31] If more of the wine had been sold—85 rather than 50 percent—the incomes from wine and wheat would have been equal. In Prodan's opinion (personal communication), however, this document probably does not reveal a normal state of affairs, since to market as much as two-thirds of wheat stocks in this era probably reflects financial distress. At best, one can conclude that money usually came from wine and wheat; and there is nothing listed but grain crops and hay, from which to draw income. A more detailed but no more conclusive picture is obtained from two documents of the 1790s. The first appears to list yields for crops planted in 1792: 190 bushels of clean wheat, 450 bushels of rye, 50 bushels of barley and *alak,* and 1,255 bushels of maize (MC #450). The second, a 1790 inventory of goods found in the courtyard of Ferencz Macskásy (MC #452), shows granary stocks of about 250 bushels each of rye and oats, not quite 100 pounds of (wheat) flour, and 1,670 bushels of maize. In addition, Macskásy had 33 head of cattle, mostly draft oxen except for "five red cows." This last item suggests possible cattle imports from Austria or Switzerland, not unknown in that period (Botezan n.d.:363). A large stable among an estate's buildings (see MC #2918) does not, however, necessarily imply anything but large stomachs among the residents. There is no indication of what was done with these grains and animals, especially with the huge amount of maize in comparison with other goods.[32]

While I cannot conclude firmly what these nobles were doing on their estates in Binṭinṭi or how they derived their income, I offer the following guesses. The nobles may have marketed some cereals locally to the purchasers hypothesized above, but they stockpiled the larger part of the harvest to use as payment for labor (not being cash, this payment was not considered a cost!) and probably for loans (see also Paget 1850 II:225). Much if not most of their local income derived from selling wine to the peasants for cash, as much as possible (see p. 154 above). Among the lords' feudal rights was a monopoly on making and selling spirits; scholars have noted the importance of tavern incomes over others (see, e.g., Prodan 1976: 76–78), and Imreh observes (1965:135) that for central Transylvania in the eighteenth century, evidence of commodity production appears earlier for wine than for cereals. In the summaries of damages after Horea's revolt in 1784, wine formed by far the largest category of losses for those claims that were itemized,[33] cereals following far behind. (Some of these wine supplies were doubtless intended for conspicuous consumption by nobles and not for sale to serfs.) The wine that swelled the incomes of Binţinţi nobles was not produced there so much as collected for debts from villages nearby where better wine was (and still is) produced. A document of 1779 shows 4,500 gallons of wine being called in for debts from three villages (MC #2914). From this, a pattern of exchange begins to emerge in which nobles sell some of their wheat on the market but lend more of it (or cash) to other villages, collect wine against or in payment of the debt, and sell it to Binţinţi serfs for cash.

A similar possibility is among the alternative explanations for the large stocks of maize noted above, which could have gone to one of two possible uses. Unusually high maize production in the 1780s and 1790s might have been a temporary change in the crop profile resulting from the Austro-Turkish war (see p. 153 above). Alternatively, the nobles could have been distilling alcohol. This industry generated significant incomes on many estates in the nineteenth century (Blum 1948:110; Boner 1865:182) but could reasonably have existed earlier, inasmuch as the Agricultural Society founded by the Court in 1769 included among its topics the manufacture of alcohol from maize (Surdu 1960:115). If Binţinţi proprietors were doing this, they also may have been engaging in the occupation that almost always accompanied it: raising cattle (or pigs) from the pulp that remains after the distilling process. In the 1800s, alcohol manufacture was the chief industry of northern Transylvania and was closely linked with cattle raising (Moga 1973:254–255). It is not wholly out of the question that the Macskásys could have been distilling alcohol in southern Transylvania in the 1790s, and feeding "five red cows" as a sideline. If they were, this together with wine sales would imply that the principal cash incomes of the nobility derived from producing intoxicants for the populace, rather than, as some would have it, food for a local or a more distant bourgeoisie. This suggestion provokes the thought that when serfs stole wine from their masters, as they often did, they were not just getting drunk: they were getting even.

As for other sources of income that nobles elsewhere were known to be exploring, the documents from Binţinţi tell us little. There is no mention of "manufactures," like the porcelain production begun in the 1700s on the not-too-distant estate of a noble with relatives in Binţinţi (Nalaczi) (see Surdu 1960:127-130). This silence is not surprising, however, for it was usually magnates rather than gentry like the Macskásys who took such steps. Moreover, the Macskásy documents break off at just the point when some of Transylvania's nobles moved tentatively toward agricultural modernization. Beginning with the 1800s, for example, landlords made some effort to improve varieties of sheep, for a wool export market directed towards Vienna (Botezan n.d.:363). This market was probably as short-lived as the wool boom in the Austro-Bohemian lands, which ended by the middle of the 1800s, but we know from Paget that at least some nobles of northern Transylvania had "recently" (as of the 1830s) introduced Merino sheep onto their estates for this purpose (Paget 1850 II:315).

The most renowned examples of economic modernization on Transylvania's noble estates, in the domains of both agriculture and industry, occurred well after 1800. A famous set of experiments took place in the northern Transylvanian village of Gîrbou, where in 1830 new heirs introduced the first industrial operation in that part of the region, a sugar factory for which the estate was to be chief supplier of sugar beets (see Báthory 1976). Machines were brought from London and Vienna, new crop patterns and rotations were instituted with new agricultural implements, and a special labor force of German colonists was imported. To this group of enterprises were later added distilleries and then silk-worm raising, with a factory for spinning and weaving silk. Yet alongside all the English machinery, serfs with *robot* obligations still labored one to three days per week, and their wives were still required to weave hemp. Another well-known case of agricultural improvement occurred at about the same time on the estate of Baron Miklós Wesselényi in Jibou, northern Transylvania. Wesselényi hired an expert administrator who planned to free the serfs on the estate in order to reorganize production, with sharecropping in place of *robot* as the principal form of working the allodia (see Csetri 1958-59). This estate, the most advanced in Transylvania, utilized improved plows, seeders, threshing machines, etc. — but not even there did one find truly advanced equipment or salaried labor.

By mid-century, agricultural modernization and agricultural industry were still rudimentary in Transylvania, well behind developments in Hungary. It was only in 1844 that a group of magnates formed the Transylvanian Agricultural Society to foster agricultural improvement, and institutions for agricultural education were founded even later (the first in 1869). As of 1848, estates that introduced sugar, vegetable oil, or alcohol production, or that sought to increase the effectiveness of labor input, were run by aristocrats who at their most liberal were less progressive than their counterparts in Hungary. While Hungary's nobles had become persuaded by the idea that efficient labor could be had only by emancipating the serfs, and therefore emancipated them during the Hungarian revolution of 1848, the Transylvanian Diet two years earlier had crashingly rejected any such notion. Even Baron Wesselényi, leader of the liberal faction, believed that emancipation was premature: he wanted little more than to make the serfs' lives a bit easier and to improve roads (Chereşteşiu 1966:95–96). The entrenchment of this oppressive system, in comparison with Hungary's, is all the more stark when contrasted with the concentrated capitalist production already evident in Transylvanian industry.

RECAPITULATION

The foregoing may seem very far from Transylvanian villagers of the present day, but it is not. Although for many peasants the structure of feudal relations described above was officially dismantled between 1848 and 1854, for many others a life of virtual bondage endured, as the following chapter will tell, until and even beyond the last laws issued concerning serfdom in 1896 — that is, into the lifetimes and recollections of my informants. The social and economic transformations the Binţinţi villagers have experienced in this century had, as prior conditions of their trajectory, the society and economy I have described. The mentality and perceptions of present-day villagers are rooted in a past unusual for its degree of oppression of these people's forebears. And this produced a life in which under-remunerated (and hence poorly motivated) toil was the chief reality, helplessness the chief fact of life, theft and cunning the chief forms of resistance except for the rare moments when a monarch's presumed sympathy encouraged them to something more ambitious.

(The relevance to current behavior is sobering.) If there was a single refrain that echoed most insistently through the unsolicited comments directed to me during my field research, it was this: "We used to be serfs, you know, we lived under the Magyars" (*Noi am fost iobagi, să știți, am fost sub ungurii*). They recognize that the experience exacted its price.

But their summaries of that experience do not do justice to its complexity. These people were not just serfs. They were serfs of an unusually reactionary nobility, one that was relatively poor and numerous (legacy, in part, of the principality's freedom under the Turks) and absolutely labor-hungry and status-conscious (product of their feudal history as strengthened by the agrarianization of the empire's eastern lands). This nobility played out its life on a stage occupied by many other actors besides their serfs and themselves. Their interlocutors included a Habsburg state that attempted to manipulate the conditions of everyone's existence in often contradictory ways; a segment of their own aristocratic status group bent on persuading the state to restrict industry to the western regions and leave the eastern lords agrarian; another aristocratic segment, their feudal counterparts in Hungary, whose interests they generally shared but whose chances at large-scale commodity production grew while those in Transylvania did not; an international merchant group including Armenian, Greek, Jewish, and Wallachian merchants active in the trade that linked Europe with the Ottoman and Asian lands; and a local Saxon bourgeoisie whose interests the nobles almost always opposed but whose power rested on the feudal privileges that were the unassailable foundation of existence for these nobles themselves.

The relations among these groups were complex and constantly shifting. Outcomes in one coalition sometimes crosscut and at other times reinforced outcomes of other coalitions. More than this, outcomes at the topmost level of the social system — imperial circles — constrained the possibilities for internal groups whose influence was less wide-ranging. The complex coalitions among groups through time, together with the hierarchical conditioning of possibilities for maneuver, produced the contours of Transylvania's economy as of 1848: indigenous manufacturing and mining had been stunted in several sectors, overtaken by larger-scale operations under the patronage of the Habsburg state or of nonindigenous merchant capitalists; these had not troubled with improving agricultural production and did little to stimulate local nobles in that direction, with the consequence that agriculture was barely transformed at all from its feudal form. We might briefly review how this came to pass.

At the topmost levels of policy, the Habsburgs faced competition in a Europe containing other economies more developed than their own. Because an improved imperial economy would facilitate more effective political interactions (especially more successful wars), state-builders looked to new and more lucrative economic forms. The state favored aristocrats who would convert to commerce and manufacturing; the aristocrats most ready for such conversion (the Austro-Bohemian magnates) feared adverse competition from tax-exempt Magyar nobles; the latter would not renounce their tax exemption; and the result was a coalition between state and industrialists that excluded manufacturing from Hungary. Transylvania's Magyar nobles participated in this outcome. Yet once it was accomplished, manufacturing in Transylvania would suffer also, both on noble estates and in Saxon towns. Internal agricultural markets would not expand, and feudal lords concerned to keep up with fashions would not have the option either of feudal manufactures or of increasing the commercialization of their estates. Thus, agriculture did not modernize but stood still, a situation the nobles had helped to produce. They aided it further with uncompromising partition of their estates, thanks to Turkish neglect. Also important were externalities not within their control, such as the ecological and locational endowments that suited Transylvania ill for exporting agricultural products (with the possible exception of extensive animal husbandry), for the region was not only more mountainous but also more distant from markets than were potential bread-baskets on either side. Indeed, one doubts that, under normal circumstances, the nobles would have stayed in agriculture for long but would instead have diversified into manufactures and commerce.

In all this we see the decisive negative effects of Transylvania's incorporation into the Habsburg Empire. The Transylvania of the late 1500s and early 1600s was thriving commercially, with excellent prospects for economic development. One can imagine a scenario in which Transylvanian princes succeeded in creating the greater kingdom (with Hungary or with Poland-Lithuania) they attempted to form in the 1500s, thereby fending off the Habsburg takeover, and in which the nobles developed their feudal mining and manufacturing for large internal markets. There was nothing inevitable in the eighteenth-century domination of Transylvania's feudal aristocrats: it was only the interaction of different groups in Hungary and Transylvania with the Habsburg state and the nobles of the western regions that reinforced this group's domination by restricting manufactures in the east. Influences from outside Transylvania also reinforced and rendered inevitable the exclusion of indigenes from commerce for most of this period. While local nobles had initiated the opposition to Saxon trading interests, the Habsburgs seconded it, preferring to deal with international merchants who could assure them access to Eastern raw materials and markets for Austro-Bohemian manufactures. This prevented domestic accumulations of merchant capital in Transylvania and necessitated measures to tie down the resources of foreign merchants somewhat. Such measures proved instrumental in developing the industries, especially in mining, that the Habsburgs found they wanted and could permit. Barred from significant local accumulations, however, Transylvanians could only sign onto outside enterprises; they could not initiate nor could they choose what developmental course would benefit their interests or even, perhaps, their regional economy, most.

Exogenously determined capital-intensive, export-oriented mining and manufacturing did not do much for Transylvania's internal market. Since there were no local interests concerned with this state of affairs who also had the power to alter it (as Saxons did not), the feudal agrarian sector was left to intensify. Peasant capacities for consumption would not be sufficiently bolstered even to create a rent-paying instead of a labor-paying peasant economy. The cash incomes of peasants would be adequate only to consume stupefacients as they toiled their way to work for a nobility whose appetites, underregulated from outside while noble expenses burgeoned, drove them to devise one of the most oppressive of labor regimens.

The ultimate villain in the piece, however, was political annexation (see also Hechter 1975). As Transylvania's sovereignty vanished under Habsburg expansionism, within the larger impetus of "Great Power" political competitions in Europe, the region entered a decidedly new milieu. Its interactions with other groups within the imperial framework froze tendencies that were, at that moment in Transylvanian history, unusually fluid and could have carved new channels rather than digging more deeply and narrowly into old ones. This freezing shows the point at which the internal development of a socioeconomic system becomes constrained by its contact with larger systems that encapsulate it, as one among several possible options becomes etched in stone under the hand of social actors with wider global reach. These changes, with such sobering consequences for the Transylvanian peasant, themselves originated in imperial policies explicitly crafted toward reducing the empire's position of disadvantage within Europe, toward insulating the empire from the vagaries of full participation in the world market by protecting its internal market and increasing its self-sufficiency. In short, although the Habsburg annexation set Transylvania on a downward course largely because of the empire's internal organization, this organization was itself an effort to buffer the empire from the world.

The chapter opened by observing that in this period a horizontal system of privilege was turned on its side. A form of society that had been portrayed as essentially a nonterritorial system of relations — lords on top and serfs on the bottom, without respect to their geographic locations on the land — gradually gave way to one in which that specific horizontal form of society was localized in the east, while privilege within the overall arrangement had moved from the upper, feudal "estate" to the western regions. The east's response to this arrangement and to the state centralization accompanying it was to aim for a new territorial *gemeinschaft,* based on ethnic ties. One possible consequence of such a *gemeinschaft* was that as serf labor was detached from the soil-in-general, in 1848, it would be reattached to the soil-in-particular through nationalist ideologies. Labor, so greatly desired at that time by developing industrial capitalism, would be nationalized (and further impeded, a century later, with an "iron curtain"). The next chapter will show how this nationalization unfolded, and with what effects.

PART III

THE CLIMAX OF NATIONALISM AND TRANSYLVANIA UNDER HUNGARIAN RULE

CHAPTER 4

"We've Been Here All Along": Nationalism and Socioeconomic Change, 1848 to World War I

They committed the crime . . . [of wanting] Romanians to be equal with Hungarians. (High Sheriff Pál Macskásy, on condemning two Romanian nationalists to death, 1848)[1]

On the occasion of the millennial celebration of the Hungarian Kingdom (1896), a Transylvanian Magyar was heard to ask a Romanian peasant, in a boasting tone, "And how about you? When will you people celebrate your millennium?" Came the reply, "Who, Us? No need, 'cuz we've been here all along."[2]

The preceding chapters have brought us to the mid-1800s, a period of turmoil and reorganization in Europe. Within the empire a shaky state had been emerging, one plagued with difficulties that forced it to be constantly attentive to the demands of Hungary's nobles, and one consolidated by recasting concern over privilege into concern over nationality. At the same time, economic transformation had produced a mongrel economy in which fairly advanced, capitalist industrial sectors coexisted with manorial estates, modern farms with subsistence peasant holdings, highly concentrated production with small-scale artisan shops. Both concomitant with and consequent upon the processes of state-building and capitalist penetration, the activities of and the relations among social groups had begun a process of profound change, accelerated by the revolutionary events of 1848.

The present chapter focuses on this transforming socioeconomic structure, particularly in Transylvania. Among the most important changes were those in the character of the peasantry, formally emancipated in 1854; the further development of capital-intensive industry and mining, controlled from outside, while the agricultural sector remained fairly retarded, especially when compared with capitalist agrarian development in Hungary; and the general reorien-

181

tation of the agrarian upper class, as many of its members turned their attention to bureaucratic employment and other activities. Shifts such as these contributed to expanding both the size and the heterogeneity of the middle strata, within a niche that had been chiefly a Saxon preserve until then. The new middle groups consisted of bureaucrats and intellectuals, bankers and merchants, a few manufacturers and a number of small tradesmen; they were disproportionately Magyars and Saxons, but Romanians were also entering these ranks at a rapid rate. Alongside this reshuffling of the class and ethnic statuses of Transylvania's peoples, nationalism became an ever more prevalent feature of daily life for all groups in society.

The intensification of nationalist concerns resulted from crises in Habsburg state-building (themselves related to inadequate economic and military performance), manifested most clearly in the Hungarian revolution of 1848 and the renegotiation of Hungary's status in the empire in 1867. As of 1867, Hungarians acquired their own statelike entity, which included Transylvania and thus became Transylvanians' new overlord. In producing this reorganization, Hungary's elite used a rhetoric of nationalist opposition to Habsburg "colonialism," protesting the imperial division of labor within which they saw Hungary's status as second-class. The elite appears to have found the idea of statehood attractive and were anxious to carve out a state of their own. It may have seemed to these groups that in a period of general economic stagnation (true of Europe ca. 1820-1850), they could hope to improve their economic situation only by participating as a state, in an interstate system whose most successful participants were other states.[3] Embedded in an empire they did not control, they easily saw the causes of economic downturn in the oppressive hegemony of Habsburg rule. This suggested that to remedy the effects of the downturn, they should take control of the state power mechanisms themselves.

This accomplished, the leadership of Hungary pursued the same priority as did the Habsburgs: industrial development. Alongside industry, however, capitalist agriculture also developed, and many lesser landowners found themselves pushed out of agriculture in an economy whose other sectors were inadequately advanced to support them all. Thus, employment in the new state bureaucracy was a lifeline for many Magyar nobles. They defended this resource, against both Habsburg bureaucrats and aspirants from Hungary's other nationalities, with increasingly rabid Magyar nationalism and the insistent magyarization of public life. This was not welcomed by non-Magyars in Transylvania, who possessed considerable nationalist awareness themselves. Because important groups in the Hungarian state legitimized nationalism as a basis for making claims within the new society, nationalist conflict permeated Transylvania's politics ever more intensely until World War I, setting the mentality within which peasants would perceive social struggle.

It would be unhelpful, however, to see nationalist rhetoric as a strategy purposely devised and adopted by rising bourgeoisies. These groups were merely speaking the language that had already been evolving, using the form of discourse that had emerged from the conjunction between Habsburg state-building efforts and aristocratic privilege within a system of feudal status groups. Preceding chapters have shown the conditions that created this discourse and the groups that developed it; we will now see how this discourse came to permeate its society so completely that its terms garbled the transformation of the socioeconomic order. From a feudal order that used a vocabulary of privilege, bondage, and obligation there had emerged a new vocabulary of nationality. As was true elsewhere in Europe, the groups who conversed in this vocabulary were very different from those of a prior era. As was not true in the West, however, the very process by which these new groups emerged was distorted by peculiarities inherent in the system's evolving discourse (itself the logical accompaniment of continuing peculiarities in the shape of the economy and the growth of the state). Groups in Hungary used nationalist rhetoric in struggling to create something statelike on the model of Western Europe, but their creation behaved differently from its models. Part of the difference consisted of this state's strong action in shaping an opportunity structure within which nationalist claims and national membership would sometimes have a role not found in West European states.

In the pivotal year 1848, this language, rehearsed since the 1790s, received its premiere public performance. The effect was dramatic and irreversible. To emphasize it, I will shed the terminology employed in previous chapters—coalitions, Habsburg state centralization, dominant group interests, and the intersection of local and world-economic events. Although developments after 1848 presuppose these processes and could be characterized with reference to them, I will remind the reader of reality's new cast by occasionally translating into the language of the participants, the language of nationalism.

THE REVOLUTIONS OF 1848 IN THE HABSBURG LANDS

The revolutionary year 1848 was as explosive in the Habsburg lands as anywhere in Europe; it both intensified and redirected several trends evident since the late 1700s. The events of 1848 shattered many of the constraints on economic change, in the eastern regions in particular, through a series of social reforms that abolished the jural supports of the feudal order and unfettered tendencies toward capitalist transformation of the economy. This year also inflamed already-existing nationalisms throughout the empire, not least of all in Hungary and Transylvania. Both the economic and the nationalist consequences of 1848 would have a tremendous impact on the Transylvanian peasantry, creating a new economic environment for them and new groups with authority over their lives and their perceived opportunities.

The revolution that began in Hungary[4] and inevitably spread to Transylvania broke out on March 15, 1848, two days after the Viennese urban middle classes and workers had taken to the streets. Giving voice to sentiments that had been swelling for some time, the Hungarian Diet voted extraordinary reforms tantamount to social revolution and to asserting Hungarian sovereignty within the imperial system. These rebellious constitutional enactments were the heart of what became a protracted and bloody civil and anti-imperial war. Its leaders were primarily Hungary's middle nobility, who successfully brokered both their own interests in economic modernization and the more radical desires of intellectuals concerned with Hungary's serfs. The nationalist facet of the revolt was the logical extension of the Magyar gentry reaction of the 1780s against Joseph II's reforms. Its social-reformist facet emerged from deepening aristocratic recognition of a crisis in the feudal organization of agriculture, which had to be transformed if the nobility were to retain a reasonable existence (Pamlényi 1975: 234-235). Many of the proposed reforms aimed to modernize both the antiquated agrarian structure and underdeveloped industry.

Reform and nationalism went hand in hand, but nationalism took pride of place, in part because the gentry instigators regarded sovereignty as a precondition to reform. This stemmed from their insistence on seeing Hungary's lopsided economy as the result of Habsburg oppression, to be ended only by forming an independent Hungary.[5] Gentry reformers did not argue that feudalism was a minor problem; they argued, rather, that its damaging effects could best be remedied by putting Hungary's house in the hands of its own masters. This argument emerged naturally enough from the historical meaning of *natio* and the assault on privilege that Habsburg state-building had entailed. It was also natural in that the best models for constructing an industrial economy were precisely those entities—states—that could tighten their own borders, make their own laws, and protect their own manufactures, as Hungary, lacking its own state machinery and economic policy-making apparatus, could not do. To create a Hungarian state would create a Hungarian employment structure and a Hungarian industrial matrix within which the existence of hard-pressed nobles could be ensured. Even Kossuth, the revolution's eventual hero, insisted that his program aimed to guarantee the continued political and economic ascendancy of the aristocrats (Deak 1979:98). Thus the peculiarity that what appears in many respects as a classic bourgeois reformist movement is led by nobles.

The revolution did not, of course, confine its effects to Hungary. Not only was the Magyar nobility of Transylvania drawn in, but urgent action followed on the part of Transylvania's other groups. As one might imagine from what has been said so far, however, the events of 1848 unfolded in Transylvania in a manner so chaotic and so rich in absurd ironies as to stagger the mind of an outside observer. Nowhere but in Transylvania, at the extreme end of a complex network of crosscutting interests, would one find contradictions of the following order. (1) Revolutionaries in Hungary proclaim a social revolution, free the serfs, guarantee equal rights for all citizens, and establish a separate Hungarian state within the empire; leaders of the Romanian national movement, for whom Magyar chauvinism had become the gravest concern, initially applaud. (2) Romanian national leaders then take up arms on the side of Habsburg absolutism (under the twin slogans of "We side with the emperor" and "Roman virtue revivified" [Cheresteşiu 1966: 431]) *against* the Hungarian revolutionaries, the one group in the empire actively fighting *for* the Romanian movement's two main objectives, national liberties and an end to serfdom (3) Among the Romanians' opponents are many of Transylvania's nobles, who, despite their complete lack of sympathy for the revolutionary goal of feudal abolition, are fighting on the side of Hungary's rebels. They fight against Habsburg absolutism and for Magyar supremacy, yet have serious misgivings about creating a Magyar state, into which Transylvania would be absorbed. (4) Other Transylvanian aristocrats remain pro-Habsburg, thereby breaking ranks with the group attempting to form a state that would guarantee the dominance of these very aristocrats, and thereby also becoming the very unnatural allies of Romanians, for whose political positions they have the utmost disdain. (5) The general of the Hungarian revolutionary forces in Transylvania, a Polish exile (Jozef Bem), holds strictly to the revolution's initial principles of national equality; Transylvania's Magyar-chauvinist nobles, fighting with him, are dismayed and alienated, and his Saxon and Romanian opponents become his open admirers (Deak 1979:271).

A few fragments from village life in this year will provide concrete images with which to sketch a picture of these confusing revolutionary events. Let us begin with the peasants.[6] Serfs in Binţinţi may have received with some bewilderment, two months after the outbreak of Hungary's revolt, the order from Romanian national leaders to send delegates to a mass meeting of Transylvania's Romanians (Blaj, 1848). One or two did go nevertheless, with others from other villages, believing their mission was to get rid of serfdom (Cherestesiu 1966:417). They returned from the thirty-five-kilometer trek with bleeding feet to announce that indeed the gathering had declared the end of serfdom. (It is not known whether they also announced the meeting's declaration of Romanian national independence.) The villagers' response was a jingle some still remember: "Iobăgia să se şteargă/Şi la domni să nu mai meargă" (Serfdom's ended now and so/To our lords no more we'll go).

Far more trying times were to come. Many serfs joined one or another group to fight against the Magyar revolutionaries and their leader, General Bem. The name of one Binţinţi villager, according to his great-granddaughter, appears on a monument because he carried the new Romanian national colors inside his tunic and flourished them at a critical moment to spur his comrades' fighting morale. Villagers recall having heard that some nobles poisoned the wine in their cellars—probably expecting anti-revolutionary forces to break in and drink, as indeed they did unless admonished by their leaders to beware. When Bem's troops retreated, his path ran directly through Binţinţi. First Bem scavenged and torched the village, to delay the imperial army chasing him, and then the imperial army destroyed what was left as they massed there for the night (Baritïu 1890:434). After Bem's rout, the random terrorist killings that occurred in nearby villages (ibid.:491) entered Binţinţi lore as "the time of fleeing," when "Romanians fled from their homes and hid in the weeds while Magyars came looking to shoot them without reason," in reprisal for peasant attacks on nobles and officials during the chaotic months before.

Binţinţi landowners took part in the revolution on both sides. There was, for example, Count Kálmán Lázár, whom we shall meet again below and who fought in 1848 as an officer of the revolution. He fled to Turkey with others after the revolutionaries' defeat, returned later to Binţinţi to write his memoirs, and for publishing them was imprisoned under the reassertion of centrist authority (Kenyeres 1969 II:45). On the other side we find Baron László Nopcsa, whose example is especially worth considering for the way in which his career refracts the intricacies of Transylvania's nationalist politics at this time. Nopcsa was High Sheriff of Hunedoara County and a landowner in Binţinţi, and like his cousin Elek, the Transylvanian Chancellor, he was among the conservative Magyar aristocrats. Romanians had long regarded him with hatred as their unusually cruel oppressor and as "one of the most retrograde" of the nobility (Chereşteşiu 1966:190, 470). In 1848, however, they were to see him opposing the revolt in Hungary and the oath to its new constitution. In so doing, he supported the Habsburg position — like many conservative, pro-dynasty Magyars — but also, ironically, the position of the Romanian national leaders, "natural" enemies of Magyar nobles. The Hungarian revolutionary forces put him under such pressure because of his reactionary stance that he finally resigned his public post.

Nopcsa next appeared at the same great meeting at Blaj that our village delegates attended, and here he participated — as a Romanian. Technically, this was quite possible, for many Hunedoara aristocrats had ancestors ennobled from Romanian ranks. It is likely that his switch of identity was opportunistic, enabling him to lend an eminent presence to Romanian objectives that opposed the Hungarian revolutionaries, and to gather intelligence. But the Romanians not only accepted him (as a Romanian) into their deliberations, they even elected him, after he had sworn with them the oath of allegiance to the Romanian nation, vice-president of the Romanian delegation that would present the Romanian demands to the emperor. For this was a time when Romanians were reclaiming all those who had earlier left their ranks in pursuit of the advantages of Magyar identity. One gains a glimpse into the mentality of those times by recognizing that the participants seem to have found nothing improbable in seeing an aristocrat whose own Romanian serfs had repeatedly cited him in court for cruelty, and who had set troops upon them, now standing with ungloved hand raised in allegiance to the Romanian nation, in support of reforms as damaging to the interests of agrarian nobles as was anything in the reformist constitution of Hungary's rebels.

The nationalist fervor of Hungary's revolution, however, with its echoes in Transylvania, initiated processes that would eventually eliminate performances like László Nopcsa's. By 1900, had he lived then, he would have considered no option but an inflamed speech in Magyar in Hungary's Diet. For the Hungarian revolution and its aftermath profoundly affected the course of subsequent ethnic relations in Transylvania. It did so most directly through a central proposition of the Hungarian rebels: the anticipated union of Transylvania with Hungary in a single Magyar national state. This proposal helped to win the allegiance of Transylvanian nobles otherwise unmoved by the revolution's social and economic reforms; and it aroused reciprocal nationalist concerns of Transylvania's Saxons and Romanians sufficiently to provoke their greater organization, which might not have occurred if local Magyar nobles had remained quiescent.

As chapter 3 has shown, social inequities were at least as marked in Transylvania as in Hungary. But Transylvania's nobles were more reactionary, seldom raising their voices either against serfdom or in favor of expanding industry and trade. They were, simply, not a revolutionary group (Makkai 1946:293). Many Transylvanian nobles outright feared the radicalism of the Hungarian revolutionary program and would not have supported it if the call to arms had not been made in the name of the Magyar "nation." Many even had doubts about Transylvania's absorption into Hungary, since they and their Hungarian confreres clearly did not share the same concerns. The Transylvanian nobility had one major concern, however, that had been mounting since Horea's revolt, through innumerable peasant disturbances and through the growth of an increasingly articulate national movement for Romanians' social rights. Being in the minority—a quarter of the population[7]—Magyars could not hope to retain their predominance in Transylvania if Romanian rights were won, a possibility that the various manifestoes of 1848 made increasingly real. For Transylvania's Magyars, therefore, the only hope was the union of Transylvania with Hungary. This proposal was thus at the heart of revolutionary support from Transylvanian nobles, and its importance to them helped them to ignore other revolutionary goals in which they were not interested, such as the abolition of serfdom.

Because in a united Hungary and Transylvania the Magyars still formed barely half of the population, high on the agenda of the proposed new state was a determined campaign to magyarize the remaining groups. It was this impulse in Hungarian revolutionary statehood that turned Saxons, Romanians, and other potential allies against the movement even as it won the sympathy of Transylvania's nobility. The Saxon and embryonic Romanian bourgeoisies would have fallen into line in support of modernizing the economy, but Magyar chauvinism touched their own raw nationalist nerve and made them fear for their legal existence as Saxons and Romanians within the new Magyar state. Kossuth himself heightened these worries when he said, "We must hasten to magyarize the Croats, Roumanians and Saxons, for otherwise we shall perish" (quoted in Seton-Watson 1963:276). As the Magyars raised their nationalist clamor, the other groups in Transylvania gave increasing attention to this issue. The Saxons retaliated with nationalism of their own, wearing their national emblem and later that of Austria,[8] opposing the union vociferously (and when the Diet voted it anyway, sending a petition of protest to Vienna with 17,000 signatures), arguing for inclusion of Romanians in the Diet, and otherwise displaying behavior fully pro-dynasty, antirevolutionary, and anti-Magyar. This did not endear them to Magyar Transylvanians.

Saxon forthrightness eased the way for similar expressions by the Romanian clergy and intellectuals who had been developing the Romanian national movement.[9] For a change they found sympathizers in their own environment. Intense activity followed: meetings among the movement's leaders, in which a program was drawn up that combined socioeconomic reforms with national liberation, and mass gatherings involving the leaders and huge numbers of peasants, to whom the program was explained. The degree of organization of the Romanian national movement increased exponentially in the extraordinary climate of these months—mellowed by the liberalized press and assembly laws that the larger revolution had produced, and invigorated by the threat of Magyar subjugation. In fact, the significance of 1848 for Romanians is precisely the crucial chance it offered for political socialization, for Romanian intellectuals and peasants. Leaders took from the mass meetings a new awareness of the possibilities for a broadly based social movement (Cherestesiu 1966:319–320). Peasants both saw that their social grievances were at last being taken seriously by important people—lawyers, bankers, gentlemen—and also perceived the importance of nationalist politics. Romanian intellectuals and peasants had certainly recognized these aspects of their situation before; but in 1848 they formulated for the first time a specific platform containing both nationalist and social-reformist planks, thereby uniting and systematizing in a single national movement objectives that different groups had been pursuing piecemeal.

It is obvious from the discussion so far that although the Hungarian revolution and Romanian nationalism emerged from the same conditions, spoke the same language, and matured partly in response to each other, they were movements of very different kinds. To try to understand this is to close in on the question of why Magyar and Romanian views on Transylvania have always differed so profoundly, and also to clarify the nationalist environment of the Romanian peasantry.

Some of the difference between the two movements lay in simple realities. The Romanians' collective economy and society were so rudimentary that the leaders were in no position to assess the benefits of being able to set economic and foreign policy, have their own army, etc., as Hungarians were proposing—and had successfully done for half a millennium before the Habsburgs came along. And this relates to differences in the historically generated organizational capacities of Hungarians and Romanians. Hungarians had organizational skills that Romanians did not, skills perfected during prior centuries of independence and more recent times of aristocratic anti-imperial resistance. Romanians not only lacked a tradition of political organization but were unschooled in *Realpolitik,* having been so long excluded from participation in Transylvania's political life. Reading through the records of their activities in 1848 and afterward (especially Barițiu 1890-91), one is continually struck by their submissiveness and by the naïveté of their trust that the Habsburgs would reward them for their loyalty by supporting them in return. Moreover, Romanian leaders were late in learning (during the 1700s) the vocabulary one had to use in discourse with the dynasty—the emphasis on constitutionality and legality—that Hungarians had mastered long before. Hungarians had had ample time to go even further, weaving constitutionality and nationalism together toward separatist ends, while Romanians had not yet had cause to see separatism as desirable. This was a difference in historically bred perceptions based in very different historical situations. It was rooted in the milieu from which Romanian nationalism grew, along with shifts in the meaning of natio. Having become primarily a jural and political concept by the 1600s, emphasizing privilege and nobility, natio retrieved and strengthened its ethnic—indeed, national—connotation during the eighteenth century, but with the idea of privilege still clinging to its edges.

Chapter 2 presented the essentials of this conceptual evolution, but a clearer understanding of Romanian nationalism requires more to be said. As the three natios of Transylvania—Saxon, Szekler, and noble/Magyar—had added ethnic connotations to their jural statuses, Romanians had been left out in the cold, with a position legally codified as inferior by the mid-1600s. For this they sought vindication by trying to achieve equal jural status with the other "nations" *as a "nation,"* the thrust of their movement from the time of the *Supplex Libellus* (1791) onward. The intellectual currents that nourished the Romanian movement all sprang from the idea of natio, rather than from social reformism. Romanian leaders were not out to change feudal institutions but to acquire a legitimate place within them, as a privileged estate like the others. When Romanian intellectuals encountered the Enlightenment doctrine of the natural rights of man—liberty, equality, fraternity—their first thought was to generalize this from natural rights of individuals to natural rights of entire "nations" (Hitchins 1977:40). In short, Romanians were preoccupied with the old terms of the equation— logically enough, given that for them, the equation had never been transformed. While elsewhere, advancing notions of citizenship meant equality and rights of *individuals*, Romanians fought to acquire citizenship for their *collectivity*, since that was what they had been denied. The meaning of natio had changed but not its salience; they bent their efforts toward making their now-ethnic "nation" jurally equal to others with whom it had not been equal when "nations" were jural. Their attention to collective (national) rights made it understandably difficult for them to accept at face value the Hungarian revolutionary promises that Romanians had nothing to fear in a new Hungarian state, where each individual would be the equal of every other citizen.

For these reasons, the Romanian national movement did not take the same political form as the Hungarian movement, even though rhetorically the two were tightly linked. While Hungarians created a separatist revolt that was at first parliamentary and then military, Romanian leaders talked about solidarity, counseled firmly against violence, and upheld the imperial system, seeing no advantages in statehood—in separatism—but preferring rather to gain acceptance into the established order. As the question of uniting Transylvania and Hungary became more inflamed and a kind of national exalta- tion took hold of Transylvania's aristocratic and bourgeois Magyars, some Romanian nationalists did raise the thought of going beyond local Romanian solidarity to create a Romanian state encompassing Transylvania's Romanians and the Romanian principalities. But this never became an articulated program—it would have required, in any case, their prior national recognition, the objective already being sought (Cheresteşiu 1966:124, 344, 351). If the idea of Romanian statehood was slow to take hold, it was because Romanians had not sprung themselves loose from the old dialogue with Transylvania's other "nations."

While Hungary and Austria argued, then, about *nation*hood — what kind of new Magyar state would be permitted to exist — Romanians joined the conversation with a proposal for Romanian *people*hood within the old order. To them, this made historical sense, and present sense as well, for the new Magyar state did not look like a promising place for Romanian people. Despite its comprehensibility, their proposal has an archaic ring, however, which can be accounted for only by seeing how groups differently placed in the social system were brought into the discourse of nationality at distinctive loci in their internal developments. The language used was the same: nationality, with hidden connotations of privilege and constitutionality as well as of ethnic community. But these notions meant something different for each group using them, because each interpreted their meaning from a different vantage point. Consequently, although it seemed as if they were conversing together, in fact they were talking past each other most of the time (and anyone who hears a Hungarian and a Romanian discussing Transylvania today will see that this is still the case).

For Transylvania's Romanians, the most signal aspect of these differences in vantage point was that they entered the new nationalist dialogue at a time in their internal development when national and class oppression were still tightly fused. Romanian national claims therefore always carried an element of social justice that Magyar nationalism never quite achieved — and this perhaps won Romanians a more sympathetic international hearing. The peace settlement of World War I was to award Transylvania to Romania, a judgment Hungarians would unforgivingly regard as a violation of their national sovereignty (and, by subtle implication, of their historical constitutional rights), while Romanians perceived it thankfully as the long-awaited realization of a morally just social order. Well before World War I, however, these irreconcilable positions had become hardened in deadly hostility to each other within a Hungarian state, the discussion of whose birth requires a brief retracing of our steps.

After the Hungarian revolution was quelled in 1849, the eastern lands were subjected to the most relentless imposition of centralized absolutism that they had ever known. The empire was to be homogenized under a single bureaucracy, a single set of laws; Vienna ruled

all parts of the empire directly without distinction among them—
as if by doing so, the Habsburgs could quench every flicker of the
newly stoked fires of Magyar nationalism and eradicate from Romanian memories all traces of their organizational achievements
and heightened national consciousness. Administrative boundaries
were redrawn; Diets and County administrations were disbanded
and replaced with a new centralized, germanized bureaucracy, a
unified tax system, and a law code that excluded special constitutional privileges. For Hungary this was a terribly humiliating defeat.
Although some Magyars participated willingly in the new system,
a large number engaged in one form or another of passive resistance
to absolutism. Nobles in Transylvania mounted the most active
resistance of all, organizing an armed conspiracy, which the government at length uncovered (Szabad 1977:51).

So extensive a system of armed force, repression, and censorship
as the state now exercised could be maintained only at exorbitant
cost. The repression combined with other financial woes to raise
imperial deficits; the state could no longer afford several of its
commercial ventures and therefore withdrew from them, turning
over the state railroad, for example, to a private consortium of
foreign capitalists. War in 1859 strained the situation unbearably
and convinced imperial circles that if the empire was not to forfeit
its Great-Power status, some readjustment would have to be made
with the Hungarians, who had been exhibiting constant, irrepres-
sible nationalism (Hanák 1975*b*:580). During the next several years,
and over the rabid protests of the radical gentry that compromise
was betrayal, Hungary's conservative magnates succeeded in re-
possessing for Hungary a number of the old privileges. These included the use of Magyar in many educational institutions, the
reestablishment of the chancelleries of Transylvania and Hungary
and of the old county boundaries (though not their administration),
and the right to appoint new functionaries in place of the German
bureaucrats imposed from the center.

The Court did not offer these concessions to Magyar historic pride
in blind desperation, however, but within a careful effort to find
the formula for a federated constitutional system of balanced national coalitions that might contain nationalist sentiment and keep
the empire together. Even while negotiations were proceeding with
Hungary's conservatives, Transylvania's autonomy from Hungary
was being carefully protected, and deputations and petitions were
received from Saxons and Romanians. In 1863 the Court instituted
new rules of franchise (they lasted a mere two years) that enabled
large numbers of Romanians to vote, for the first time, and stocked

the Transylvanian Diet with a substantial contingent of Romanian delegates.

Whether these ancillary courtships of other groups persuaded Magyars that they must go all the way with the Court, or whether, instead, setbacks in the mid-1860s convinced the Court to do everything necessary to win over that most powerful of its refractory constituencies, by 1867 the Hungarian revolution of 1848 had borne its revolutionary fruit. A year after Bismarck had excluded Austria from a greater unified German state and had then defeated the empire in the Austro-Prussian War, the Compromise of 1867 turned the Habsburg Empire into the Dual Monarchy. This entity had one monarch (emperor of Austria and king of Hungary) presiding over one great state within which coexisted two separate statelike beings. They made their decisions concerning war and foreign affairs jointly but in all other respects administered themselves separately via their separate parliaments and civil governments. As had been true a few years earlier, the Magyar architects of this arrangement were the great aristocracy (Szabad 1977; Baritïu 1891), but it is inaccurate to consider this a victory for the "feudal" segment, as did the Romanian leaders (Baritïu 1891:454). The magnate contributors to the Compromise included the most energetic opponents of feudal organization and supporters of commercial development. They were the new agrarian capitalists. It was no surprise that they, rather than the gentry, should have produced the Compromise, for not only were the magnates old allies of the Court, but the gentry had painted themselves into a corner with the extremes of their nationalist sentiment.

Yet, as is obvious from the outcome, the magnates negotiated from a separatist position also, even though years earlier most of them had been indifferent to it. Their change of attitude reflects in part the advantages now perceived in possessing something statelike that could be used for economic protectionism without always having to do battle with other interest groups in the imperial system. Hungary's magnates thus present an excellent example of how the increasing capitalization of the economy had begun to form new classes that organized themselves according to the prevailing formula of "nations." The new groups saw in the global economy opportunities that they wanted to obtain, and they imitated the organizational form most suited to seizing these opportunities, the form of the nation-state. It was a natural move, for groups who had matured in an environment saturated with nationalist discourse, to assume statehood by centralizing and homogenizing along nationalist lines; but this would make reciprocal nationalism from their internal minorities the paramount obstacle to further centralization. Moreover, since one of the acts of the new state apparatus would be to create a new opportunity structure for industrial development — new niches — nationalism would become an ineradicable part of these new niches and of aspirations to them. Let us look, then, at how the class structure and the economy changed in Hungary and Transylvania throughout the rest of the century under these nationalist rules, particularly as the Magyar gentry is ruined and a new, heterogeneous middle class takes shape, and see how the intensification of nationalism was part of "a manifold process by which the very foundations of society were being transformed" (Hitchins 1977:200).

DEVELOPMENTS IN HUNGARY

I will outline Hungary's social and economic development briefly, giving what is necessary to show the kind of system to which Transylvania was linked — a linkage that tightened after 1867 when the principality entered the Hungarian state within the new Dual Monarchy. The overall trend in Hungarian agriculture from 1848 to the early 1900s was for the great estates to be further capitalized and consolidated while gentry estates failed in growing numbers, their owners saved only by state employment once the new bureaucracy of the Hungarian state came to life. On large estates, grain production accelerated up to the 1870s, and capital accumulated in the hands of magnates, who were able to capitalize their estates further, as well as in the hands of Jewish merchants who managed the trade (Pamlényi 1975:295). This successful indigenous management of agricultural transformation freed the state to attend to the development of industry, a task it pursued with remarkable success. In the last two decades of the century, Hungary's industrialization proceeded at a rapid rate, chiefly around food processing and iron production. Eventually the development of food industries drew in the beneficiaries of capitalism in agriculture, uniting a diverse set of interests around the combination of capitalist farming and agrarian industry.

The development of agrarian capitalism presupposed that some estates would be winnowed out. This process began with the emancipation of the serfs in 1848 and was furthered by the state's relative inattention to making agriculture profitable for any farms but the largest. Following emancipation, nobles were to be compensated for the loss of their serfs' labor and services, the central government assuming the burden of payment. But compensation touched on only one aspect of the much more sweeping changes in agricultural relations, changes that hit the gentry much harder than the magnates. First, fewer gentry had begun capitalizing their estates before 1848; thus, the inevitable delays in the payment of indemnifications caused them difficulties in purchasing the necessary machinery and in hiring labor. A very weak credit infrastructure and high interest rates aggravated the difficulties — and one must recall that all nobles now had taxes to pay along with their other expenses. Second, because of differences in the composition of large and smaller estates' lands, many gentry lost proportionately more of their estates to emancipated serfs than did magnates.[10] Third, railway construction in the 1860s drove up wage costs, and during the 1870s conditions became even more dismal from bad harvests, cholera epidemics, and a drop in the price of grain, resulting from the entry of North American wheat onto European markets. And fourth, it is at least suspected that the government dragged its feet in compensating the gentry, to retaliate against them for their role in the revolution (Macartney 1934:172, 189–90). By 1870, bankruptcies among the gentry began to become epidemic, totalling 20,000 over the next twenty years, nearly all among the middle and small nobility (Macartney 1962:164). The victims entered state employment as functionaries (a domain they would protect nationalistically by insisting that as a Magyar state, Hungary must be run by Magyar bureaucrats).

The main beneficiaries of gentry misfortune and also of prompt government compensation were the magnates, whose share of Hungary's arable surface area doubled between 1867 and 1914 at the expense of middle-sized estates (Eddie 1967:297). They used some of the profits of their enterprises to acquire these new lands and some to mechanize production, especially harvesting machinery bought in response to harvest strikes (ibid.:308). They also began to diversify their activities, acquiring saw mills, paper mills, coal mines, and hotels (Taylor 1942:73–74). The power of this group in Hungary's economy and in the formation of economic policy for the Dual Monarchy is evident in one after another successful tariff battle to protect agricultural prices, against the opposition of imperial industrialists wanting inexpensive foodstuffs.

Although most estates continued to grow some cereals to market within the empire even after the grain crisis of the 1870s, changing price trends produced a shift to animal husbandry. This became the most important branch of Hungarian agriculture by the late 1880s (Gaál and Gunst 1977:29–30). The state took an active role in promoting new animal breeds for this shift, which entailed a switch from draft animals to meat and dairy cattle or triple-purpose breeds introduced from farther west[11] (ibid.:57). With the change to cattle-raising, there developed a symbiosis between peasant farms and the better-capitalized large estates: labor-rich peasant farming bred and reared young cattle that larger farms then purchased for fattening and export (ibid.: 31–32).

Where this symbiosis grew up, primarily in western Hungary, the rise of a capitalist export market in cattle reinforced peasant production of commodities. The state moved feebly to encourage this development, introducing a few peasant cooperatives—but not until the 1880s, and only in the dairy-farming regions, not in eastern Hungary, where grain-growing continued to predominate on large estates (which drew on peasant labor), or in Transylvania, less commercialized in its agriculture than anywhere else. Even where the state did attempt to foster commercial farming among peasants in cattle-farming regions, it encountered resistance from large-estate owners (ibid.:42–43). This was not a state that much assisted the transformation of serf farms toward petty-commodity production.

The transformation in which the Hungarian state most decidedly did assist, if not in agriculture,[12] was the development of industry. During the 1870s, as the agricultural depression deepened, the state assumed the role of entrepreneur with increasing vigor. It was able to do so with such success because of the benefits and constraints of the empire's new Dual structure, which eliminated from decision-making the outside groups that had formerly opposed Hungary's industrialization, and yet forced policy-makers to consider a wide range of actions to support industry, since Dualism precluded Hungarian customs protection against other industries inside the monarchy. The state adopted a number of measures designed expressly to boost Hungary's industrial growth. These included tax exemptions for founding new factories, railway rates that discriminated against products not manufactured on Hungarian territory (a move reinforced by nationalizing the railroad), and subsidies and interest-free loans (Berend and Ránki 1974*b*:55). In addition, the state became a major client of industry, consuming, for example, up to one-third of the output of machine-building (ibid.).

The most important of the state's actions was to create desirable conditions for the investment of foreign capital, which bore much of the burden of Hungary's industrialization. The manner in which this was accomplished is worth describing, for it is not quite the "colonialist" scenario of which some Hungarians (and, more generally, some analysts of economic underdevelopment) have complained. Hungary seduced foreign capital in part through direct loans to the state or the issuing of bonds and securities, all highly guaranteed so as to make investment in Hungary profitable and secure (ibid.:69–72). While some foreign capital was invested directly in Hungarian banks and industry, far more was mediated by the state itself, according to local policy-makers' own designs for the economy. These focused especially on laying down the transport and credit infrastructure considered essential to all further growth, as well as on setting up some industrial plants with highly capital-intensive technological endowments. By careful management, including the addition of profits from state enterprises into the pot of government funds that supported industrial development, state action was able to reduce the proportion of outside capital in accumulated capital stocks (Berend and Ránki 1974a:102–103). And because state-channeled foreign resources were providing basic infrastructure, nearly all indigenous accumulations of capital could go toward modernizing agriculture or setting up local manufactures (Pamlényi 1975:348; Hanák 1967:281). This division of investments helped ensure that many industrial profits would remain in Hungary.

Another subject deserving scrutiny, alongside the process of capital investment, is the source of Hungary's "foreign" capital. This subject leads us to consider more directly the Habsburg "colonialism" that Hungary's gentry and many subsequent Hungarian scholars have so often decried. During the last quarter of the 1800s, in particular, the bulk of "foreign" capital in Hungary came from sources internal to the empire, even if external to Hungary itself. Non-Hungarians in the empire held 61 percent of Hungary's state securities through the early 1890s, Hungarians held less than a fourth (Komlos 1978:189), and several of the enterprises opened in these years were Hungarian branches of Austrian and Bohemian manufactures. For Hungary to lure capital from such sources was easy, because capital flowed unconstrained within the empire's borders. Indeed, one analyst contends that not only was Hungary's unencumbered access to Austrian capital instrumental to Hungarian industrialization but it even hindered development in the empire's other regions (Komlos 1978, 1981). In any case, during the period's two depressions (1873–1883, 1906–1913) and to some extent in the early years of recovery (that is, 1883 to about 1896), capital flowed from the slumping industrial enterprises of the empire's western half into the more lucrative and secure Hungarian bonds, and both times the performances of Austrian and Hungarian industry reversed (Komlos 1981:26–27).

Such considerations have led several Hungarian historians to reconsider the orthodoxy that Hungary's connection with the empire was crippling, and impeded industrial development by prolonging an agrarian economy and depressing the accumulation of capital (see Berend and Ránki 1974a, 1974b; Hanák 1967, 1975a; Katus 1970). Instead, these scholars have proposed that, far from being an impediment, Hungary's inclusion in the empire after 1848 accelerated Hungarian industry, relative both to the empire's western half and to other East European economies. This can be seen more fully by taking a more integrated view not only of Hungary's relations to Austria but also of the relationship between the agrarian and industrial sectors of the Hungarian economy itself. Hungary's agricultural transformation, unlike its industrial one, took place primarily through individual initiative and without massive state assistance. Because the Hungarian economy was itself not very advanced overall, however, a necessary condition for the changes in agriculture was the development of textile and iron industries in the empire's western half (see, e.g., Gaál and Gunst 1977:21). Austro-Bohemian industrialization built up western food requirements and purchasing power. These capacities then enabled the empire to generate and absorb increasing food production from Hungary, a fact that proved crucial once North American grains began to undersell other cereals on the European market (the 1870s). Without the guaranteed and protected imperial market, Hungary's agrarian-export economy would then have gone under. Instead, imperial protection propped up Hungarian agricultural prices, allowing Hungarian estate owners to accumulate capital that modernized agriculture and spilled over into food processing.

The resultant transformation of Hungarian agriculture then combined with the transfer of capital, patents, technical processes, and other production factors from the empire's western regions—all these factors being freely mobile within the imperial common market—to generate Hungary's industrial growth. This in turn further contributed to the rise of food requirements and purchasing power within Hungary itself, improving the integration of sectors within its economy. To say that Hungary emerged a full industrial power by World War I is obviously to exaggerate. But even though agricultural products formed a large percentage of Hungary's exports as of 1910 (58 percent), many of them were processed goods rather than raw materials; and they coexisted with exports from timber industries, mining and metallurgy, machine construction, and paper and leather processing industries. Between 1870 and 1910 the agricultural portion of Hungary's population had dropped from 80.0 to 64.5 percent and the population in transport, trade, and industry had risen from 11.5 to 23.6 percent (Berend and Ránki 1974*b*:74), alongside an expanded service sector. It is likely that without Habsburg "colonialism" (doubtless in conjunction with developments in the larger world economy), these changes would have occurred more slowly, if at all. Their connection with the nationalism discussed above can be recapitulated in the following brief, if somewhat facile, way. Nationalist yearnings on the part of Hungary's nobles (yearnings deeply and complexly rooted in their history) fathered a Hungarian state whose economy was protected within the womb of the empire, yet from this milieu it diverted to itself sufficient nourishment for growth that was, in comparison with the economies of Europe farther east and south, abnormally healthy,[13] and one fostered less and less over time by foreign capital.

One might ask about the implications of this conclusion — that the imperial common market accelerated rather than retarded Hungary's growth — for Hungary's peasants, in particular for those in Transylvania. It is crucial to observe that because of the influx of Austro-Bohemian funds into Hungarian industry and the favorable prices for Hungary's protected agricultural goods, both resulting from the imperial connection, Hungary's industrial development did not require forced transfers of value from agriculture through low agricultural prices (Gaál and Gunst 1977:34). While not all cultivators benefited from the good agricultural incomes possible in these years — Transylvanians were among those who benefited less — to the extent that taxation drove peasants into marketing commodities, at least these were not grossly undervalued. Hungary's access to imperial capital made even its agricultural taxation comparatively light, until outside funds retreated between 1896 and 1906 (Komlos 1981:23). Thus, despite the political oppression of non-Magyars within the new Hungarian state, the economic situation of non-Magyar peasants in Transylvania was better than it would be after Transylvania passed (1918) from Hungary into a Romanian state that did not enjoy the advantages of Hungary's access to a more-developed imperial economic system.

This is not to say, however, that Transylvanian peasants within the nineteenth-century Hungarian state were in an enviable situation: to the contrary. The relatively encouraging picture painted of the economy of Hungary as a whole becomes grimmer when one focuses more narrowly on industry and the transformation of agriculture in Transylvania, where sectoral malintegration persisted and agriculture developed little.

THE ECONOMY OF TRANSYLVANIA, TO WORLD WAR I[14]

The general trends of Hungarian economic development were not simply echoed in Transylvania, for reasons having to do variously with geography, social composition, historical peculiarities, and the marginal role of Transylvanians in determining state policy. Overall, from 1848 to 1918, Transylvanian industry grew in a manner similar to Hungary's — which meant some changes in its previous pattern of economic development — but agriculture did not. This summary, given the last few paragraphs of the preceding discussion, suggests that the benefits and constraints of Dualism worked out rather differently for Transylvania, compared with Hungary. Transylvanian agriculture did not indigenously transform itself through access to imperial food markets, thereby feeding into the accumulation of local capital for industry. Instead, much of Transylvanian industry remained heavily dependent on capital from outside. Much of it was also both highly capital- (rather than labor-) intensive and aimed not at an internal market but at export into other parts of the empire. These tendencies significantly affected the integration of industry with agriculture. Although mining and industrial employment did draw in some of agriculture's excess workers and provide markets for produce, these opportunities did not expand greatly nor did internal food markets increase fast enough to raise the levels of commercialization and productivity in the agricultural sector. The external destination of many industrial products reinforced this by obviating any political interest in supporting rural purchasing power through assistance to agriculture.

Transylvanian Industry and Commerce within Hungary's Economy

As one would expect from section 3 of chapter 3, Transylvanian industry and mining were already advancing by 1848. They would become even more developed, in at least some sectors, by 1918. Although this development was retarded in comparison with industry elsewhere in the empire, it was nonetheless not insubstantial and was well ahead of other parts of southern and eastern Europe. One can see both parts of this comparative statement by first contrasting column *d* with columns *a* through *c* of table 4-1 below—which shows the overly agrarian characteristics of Transylvania and the lesser growth of its industry and commerce, relative to other areas of the Dual Monarchy in 1910—and then noting (column *e*) that twenty years later, the Kingdom of Romania (which by then included Transylvania) was even less industrialized and more agrarian than the Transylvania of 1910. To the extent that Transylvanian industrialization did advance prior to World War I, I postulate as its cause an extension of the process outlined above for the economy of Hungary. The waves of economic transformation that rippled from west to east across the empire, setting Hungary on the road to agricultural and economic development in the period 1867–1896 and again in a second brief surge of intraimperial "foreign" investment (1906–1913), impelled Transylvania in the same direction, though not as far.[15]

Transylvania's inclusion in the Hungarian state nonetheless did distort its industrialization to some extent, because its peripherality in the Hungarian economic plan handicapped some possibilities for its growth. The priorities in Hungary's plan only partially fit the existing activities and requirements of the Transylvanian economy. An idea of the Hungarian attitude to Transylvania can be obtained from the lower density of the railway network laid down under state initiative (map 4). It seems probable that factory locations often went preferentially to Hungary rather than to Transylvania, with the result that Transylvania became integrated into Hungary's industrialization as a supplier of raw materials (especially timber, coal, and iron ore) for industrial processing in the territory of Hungary proper. The preference for Hungarian locations probably stemmed from an amalgam of clear locational advantage and nationalist concerns on the part of Hungary's policymakers. As for Transylvania's indigenous manufacturing, it was now swamped in a much larger sea of agrarian interests than had lapped at its edges before, with consequences to be clarified below.

The external domination of Transylvania's economy, directed from Budapest in collaboration with Austrian financial interests, appeared most clearly in mining, especially of coal and iron ore, and in iron processing. These industries were already becoming concentrated and capital-intensive by the 1860s, worked by capital that was largely Austrian in association with other West European funds. Intensification in this sphere proceeded along with the building of the Transylvanian railroad—foreign monies going, in Transylvania as elsewhere in Hungary, into transport and other aspects

TABLE 4-1. Distribution of the Labor Force by Sector for Areas within the Dual Monarchy, 1910, Showing Relative Underindustrialization of Transylvania, and Comparing with Romania, 1930.

	a	b	c	d	e
			LOCATION		
Occupational sector	Czech provinces	Austrian provinces	Hungary (without Transylvania)	Transylvania	Romania 1930*
Agriculture	38%	42%	61%	72%	78%
Industry	34	25	19	14	7
Commerce/transport	11	14	7	4	5
Other	17	19	13	10	10

Source: Columns a, b: Nuţu and Egyed 1961: 279; Columns c, d: 1910 Hungarian Census; Column e: Berend and Ránki 1974a: 360.

*These figures for Romania include Transylvania.

MAP 4. Hungary's railway system (including tertiary lines) as of 1913, with Transylvanian boundary outlined.

of infrastructure (see Vajda 1965:77). The Austrian State Railroad Company had opened Transylvania's coal mines, and by 1867, 97 percent of all coal production emanated from that one corporation; two enterprises alone accounted for 71 percent of the production of iron foundries (Vajda 1967:173). Both coal and iron mining grew in significance throughout the century as Europe's economies competed for raw materials, especially coal. From 1876 to 1900, foreign capital in Transylvanian coal-mining quintupled; in the latter year, only 5 percent of coal production was in indigenous hands (Vajda 1972: 242, 252).

A fair proportion of these raw materials left Transylvania for use or processing elsewhere. For example, over 20 percent of the iron ore mined locally was sent to Austria for smelting, despite the existence of advanced techniques of iron production in Transylvania, and machine construction was almost wholly confined to Budapest (Berend and Ránki 1974b:95). Transylvania had some machine construction and other metal industry, but it remained weaker than other branches of processing and necessitated machinery imports for use in other industrial production (Egyed 1968:263).

As against the concentration of non-Transylvanian capital in heavy industry, indigenous capital tended, as in Hungary but to a lesser extent, toward investment in light industry — at least initially (Deutsch et al. 1964:220). Local merchants, together with some nobles who turned to industrial investments instead of to modernizing production on their estates (Surdu 1962:191-192), moved into processing in three areas especially: timber, alcohol production, and flour milling. Developments in the latter two were greatly assisted by the fact that the emancipation of 1848 had not revoked seignorial monopolies on milling and on alcohol sale. Local light industry of this sort suffered in two ways from Transylvania's inclusion in the larger Hungarian state. First, once some of these industrial branches achieved priority within the state development plan, new enterprises that operated as joint-stock companies (whose members included Transylvanians among larger numbers of outsiders) outcompeted their undercapitalized and, hence, undermechanized local forerunners. During the last decade of the century, outside capital initiated the majority of the largest ventures in light industry, including successful cellulose factories and industries based on forest exploitation, such as furniture making (see Egyed 1968). These were the branches in which industrial production in Transylvania had been "revolutionized" by 1910 — milling, alcohol, paper, timber, and mining (Egyed 1962:161) — and a large share of the developmental impetus came from capital that either was exclusively exogenous or was local but linked with larger amounts from outside.

Second, other local manufactures not directly challenged by non-Transylvanian or concentrated capital fell prey to the interests of Hungary's powerful capitalist farmers. This latter process climaxed with the Austro-Romanian tariff war of the 1880s and 1890s, in which a coalition of grain and cattle producers in Hungary and some Austro-Bohemian industrial interests succeeded in blocking imports upon which southern Transylvanian indigenous processing of leather, alcohol, and foods had depended. Each interest group in the coalition was responding to one or another threat in the larger continental economy, then in a period of stagnation and reasserted protectionism; the coalition responded, logically, with reciprocal protectionism and the reaffirmation of the empire's internal markets. As a result of the tariff war, Transylvania's southward export trade fell drastically, affecting both Saxon and Magyar trades and small industries such as leather, paper, flour milling, and beer production (see Mureşan 1969). On the whole, what died off was small-scale production. Large-scale enterprises emerged unscathed, and some middle-sized ones (particularly among textiles, dominated by the Saxons) responded successfully to the pressures to concentrate production and capital.

Transylvanian industry had therefore advanced noticeably in the decades around the turn of the century, but this process had been directed largely from outside the region. The priorities and strategies of economic development in Hungary, and the inattention of the Hungarian state to the needs of Transylvania's existing industrial groups, had shaped the niche that a manufacturing bourgeoisie in Transylvania could fill. Moreover, this niche allotted more space, a larger and more powerful role, to industrial interests from outside the region than to those within it. This, rather than any overt economic discrimination by Magyars against other groups, was the principal way in which the effects of nationalism ravaged the Transylvanian economy.

In the area of banking and credit one sees slight variations and somewhat greater detail on these same two themes: the mixture of indigenous and exogenous capital, with local bankers distributed differentially among the three national minorities; and the intrusion of nationalism into the workings of financial institutions (even though it did not in fact dominate their operation to the extent sometimes charged by various groups). The career of one Romanian banker, a member of the rising Romanian bourgeoisie, will help illustrate these themes.

Ioan Mihu (1854-1927)[16] was born in a south Transylvanian village near Binţinţi; his peasant parents had become wealthy through involvement in a timber-milling enterprise. Mihu was educated in non-Romanian schools—a Saxon lycée, the universities of Graz and Budapest—and earned a law degree with which he opened a practice in the city of Orăştie, in Hunedoara. (In all these respects he exemplified features typical of the Romanian bourgeoisie; most were from southern Transylvania, many from peasant backgrounds, and many emerged from Hungarian or German institutions with degrees in law.) Mihu was a man of no negligible fortune. In 1887, at the age of thirty-four, he ranked eleventh in wealth among the elite of Hunedoara County,[17] and his estate at his death included lands totaling 3,000 hectares.

Apparently finding his law practice insufficiently absorbing, Mihu founded a Romanian bank, the Ardeleana, in Orăştie in 1885. It was the town's third bank, following others opened in 1866 by Saxons and 1872 by Magyars. The three banks engaged in considerable competition, in which the Ardeleana emerged preeminent (Romania, Direcţia 1972:183). One can see a possible mechanism for this success — an appeal to national constituencies — in the announcement Mihu circulated when soliciting subscriptions to the new bank. His appeal wove together themes of national advancement and economic progress (see Mihu 1938: vii), linking the plight of Romanian merchants and tradesmen to foreign competition, foreign capital, and economic obstacles to progress. Among his guiding principles was a commitment to special subsidies for capital-poor Romanian tradesmen and merchants. He intended the Arde-leana to embody the Romanian national characteristics he saw as essential for institutions that would promote Romanian economic development. Aside from aiming specifically (although not exclusively) at a national clientele, he also emphasized the peasants: "Being the son of a peasant, I have given first priority to serving the interests of our peasantry, in setting up the 'Ardeleana' and conducting its affairs" (Mihu 1938:434). His policies were designed to facilitate land purchases by the peasantry at interest rates that, under his successor, were the lowest in the vicinity.

Mihu combined the themes of national progress and economic development in other ways. He set aside a part of the bank's reserves for donation to Romanian cultural institutions, and he participated actively in the political education of the peasants. At a meeting held in the village of Turdaş, near Binţinţi, he proclaimed, "I have come to this lovely community to recruit soldiers to fight for the cultural advance of our people . . . We can expect help from no quarter . . . all our work must be supported by the mass of our people, by our peasants" (Mihu 1938:ix). Moreover, he willed all his substantial properties to the explicit end of promoting agricultural science among Romanians: "My fortune for the good of the people" (ibid.:45).

Similar impulses appear in the biography of Mihu's Saxon contemporary, Karl Wolff (1849–1929).[18] Holder of a law degree with studies in Vienna and Heidelberg, Wolff served from 1885 on as president of a major Saxon financial institution (the Allgemeiner Sparkassaverein in Sibiu [Hermannstadt]). Through it he founded the first savings and loan institutions for Saxon peasants and pursued a number of schemes to benefit the Saxon community, including the construction of railway spurs into Saxon towns that lay off the main railroad line. He also developed a plan to redeem lands in three communities where sixteenth- and seventeenth-century Turkish wars had eliminated previously existing Saxon settlements (Anon. 1936:5). One of these communities was Binţinţi. Under Wolff's direction, his bank brought seventeen families of Swabian colonists from the Banat region and settled them in the village, at exceptionally favorable mortgage rates, on the bankrupt estates of two Magyar nobles whose mortgages the bank had acquired (Counts István Kun and Lajos Teleky). As did Mihu, Wolff often expressed his motivation as the desire to serve his people, the Saxons.

Both Wolff and Mihu were contributing to indigenes' share in a broad process of capital formation and deployment in Transylvania, a process in which Austrian and (especially) Hungarian financial sources also participated vigorously. Within the institutions controlled by Transylvanians, Saxons held a clear edge, in consequence of their historical specialization in commerce and trade. One can see in table 4-2 the rank-ordering of Transylvania's ethnic groups in financial management (lines 3 and 4), as well as the large amounts of nonindigenous capital administered within these local banks (line 2), as of 1915. Comparing the percentages in line 3 with population statistics (line 5) shows that the financial influence of the Saxons is wholly disproportionate to their numbers: less than ten percent of the populace, they manage almost half of all banking assets.

Although these financial institutions sometimes served nationalist objectives and sometimes relied on nationalist appeals—both evident in the two brief biographies above—the direct effects of nationalism on commercial practices do not seem to have exceeded these fairly modest limits. One might wonder whether the unusually large amount of foreign capital in Saxon banks came disproportionately from fellow Germans in Austria, but the more likely guess is that Saxons received disproportionate outside monies because they were more experienced financial managers. Wolff did

TABLE 4-2. Distribution of Financial Assets and Institutions in Transylvania, 1915, by Ethnic Group

	Management of financial institutions (including credit cooperatives)		
	Saxon	*Magyar*	*Romanian*
Number of banks	225	456	189
% of outside capital in total capital stocks	89.0	78.8	74.3
% of all Transylvania's banking assets	47.8	37.9	14.3
Average reserves per bank (million crowns)	1,982	775	708
% of the total population	8.7	34.3	55.0

(Calculated from Hungary 1920: 126, 135.)

indeed use his bank's resources to colonize German settlers; but that so successful a banker managed in all his term to colonize only three places in this way suggests that ethnic expansion was not a major goal in his work. No banker would do business solely on ethnic grounds. To look at it from the other end, Romanian peasants in Binţinţi had debts at all three banks—"anywhere you could get them to give you some money when you needed it," in one former debtor's words. Business might be intertwined with nationalism, but it was also, flatly, business.

Outside rather than inside their banks was where the nationalism of businessmen like these burned most brightly. Ioan Mihu, for example, became particularly visible when, acting as a citizen on behalf of the Romanian national movement in 1910, he negotiated with the Hungarian politician Count István Tisza toward solving the nationalist differences of Transylvania's Romanians and Magyars. Somewhat less publicly, within the general habit of parvenues like himself to use personal wealth for buying land, he seems to have made a specialty of buying the lands of non-Romanians (Moţa 1936:529). In Binţinţi he purchased over 300 hectares from Magyars, and it is rumored that he made an unsuccessful bid on the property of Count Kun, which fellow banker Wolff preferred instead to colonize with Swabians. Binţinţi peasants reveal his strong Romanian nationalist sentiments in several anecdotes. According to one, he bought a house from a local Magyar and then sold it to a Romanian peasant. Hearing a rumor (unfounded) that his buyer planned to resell to a Magyar, he accosted the peasant in the street during one of his frequent visits to Binţinţi and upbraided the man, "I snatched this property from the jaws of the wolf and you propose to hand it back?"

Another dramatic encounter occurred between Mihu and two Viennese tenants on his largest Binţinţi property. According to an informant whose family overheard the exchange from next door, the encounter led to the tenants' dismissal. The story goes that Mihu arrived in Binţinţi one day with his monocle and gold watch and chain, on the eve of a parliamentary election, and advised his tenants to present themselves at the polling place in support of the Romanian Nationalist candidate. For the tenants this posed a problem, since after 1867 Transylvania's Germans (and apparently Austrian Germans as well) invariably supported Magyar candidates. The two tenants arranged a sudden trip out of town. Following the election, which the Romanian candidate lost, Mihu stormed into the village, ordered the treacherous tenants off his property, and vowed that henceforth he would have no tenant but a Romanian. And so it was.

This last example confirms quite loudly a suspicion lurking at the edges of these remarks on Transylvania's commerce: to assess the growth of commercial establishments separately from processes occurring in agriculture is wholly artificial. Seeing bankers colonize settlers on mortgaged estates, lure peasant customers through low interest rates for land purchases, and evict tenants for unacceptable votes, one can no longer postpone inquiring into the fate of agriculture in the Transylvanian economy.

TRANSYLVANIA'S AGRICULTURE

There is currently no accessible synthesis of trends in Transylvanian agriculture during the Hungarian period, and such a synthesis is extremely difficult to achieve.[19] I intend to outline what I see as the overall tendency—the failure of capitalist agriculture to emerge—and to relate this schematically to developments in the agrarian sector and in the rest of Transylvania's economy. The discussion begins with anecdotal illustration of some of these larger processes from the vantage point of Binţinţi, which lay in an area more commercialized than average. In pursuing the question of agricultural transformation, my objective is to establish the economic environment of turn-of-the-century Binţinţi peasants, so as to direct attention fully to them in chapter 5 with the context of their action already understood. I preface the discussion, a fairly complex one, with a summary I hope will make it easier to follow.

Between 1867 and 1918, agriculture in Transylvania was transformed neither as rapidly nor in the same directions as agriculture in Hungary. Instead of capitalist production of agricultural commodities for export westward or for internal consumption, we see in Transylvania the bankruptcy of many properties larger than one hundred hectares (and some smaller), and the development primarily of rent capitalism or, especially, sharecropping on those large properties that remained intact. As before, there was some production for markets on properties with fair-sized surfaces, especially any farm larger than about ten hectares, the line below which 87 percent of farms fell by 1895. The markets were chiefly internal and did not begin expanding fast enough to revolutionize productive techniques until about 1900. But the brief growth begun then was interrupted by the war.

A major cause of the general stagnation of the domestic market for agricultural goods was that industry was capital-intensive, exogenously governed, and oriented to export rather than local consumption (see p. 202 above). Capital circulated through the agricultural sector in two forms—merchant profits from commodity sales, and mortgages on heavily indebted properties—but did not enter agricultural production to any great extent. Sectoral malintegration therefore contributed to making agriculture an unpropitious field for investment and retarded its capitalization. This in turn helped to perpetuate semiservile conditions for the peasantry, many of whom had been barely affected by the supposed emancipation (which occurred in Transylvania in 1854). These peasants, deprived of economic alternatives—because industry employed little labor and capitalist wage-work in agriculture was rare—entered land markets in desperation. It is unclear how this competition for small parcels might have affected the price of land or rentals, but it might have constituted a barrier to capitalist-minded tenants and might have encouraged owners to lease out parcels, as being ultimately more lucrative than working the land themselves (see Patnaik 1979: 400).

Let me begin exploring these trends by looking at specific careers from around the turn of the century. In considering these individuals, it is wise to remember that they participated in a zone of relatively high market development and therefore represent something of an extreme, not perfectly exemplifying the more general trends for Transylvania. They are useful, however, both as concrete illustrations and as representatives of some of the variation found within an agricultural economy that was, overall, underdeveloped.

Count István Kun (1843-1904), from a locally renowned family whose members founded a lycée in Orăştie and also an agricultural school (Transylvania's sixth, in 1891), had among his estates a farm of some 200 hectares in Binţinţi and two neighboring villages. It is not known how he ran his farm, only that the cultivators who soon acquired pieces of it said the soil was in dismal condition and clearly had not been properly worked in many years. This suggests at least that no profit-minded owner or administrator had attended to it and that it had either been sharecropped with rudimentary techniques or lain uncultivated. Despite his wealth—in 1887 he was the eighth wealthiest man in Hunedoara County[20]—Count Kun went bankrupt in the early 1890s. (Peasants say he lost his estate at cards, the nobility's favorite pastime, but despite his multiple marriages we have no evidence that Kun was a gambler.) The estate was either

ﬤ

purchased from creditors or possessed outright by a Saxon bank, the very one whose president was Karl Wolff, encountered above. As is already known, Wolff used this opportunity to bring in German colonists—thirteen families, in 1893. Their rough signatures are found on the property records of Binţinţi, on the deed by which they acquired lots ranging from nine to forty-five hectares.

Three years later, the same bank colonized another three families on another bankrupt estate. This time the lands belonged to one Lajos Kovács, who had administered a carting service until the railroad superseded it. Kovács had himself bought out a Count Lajos Teleky—also going bankrupt, it is rumored—in the 1870s, but he had used the 100-hectare estate in a casual manner, giving out much of it in sharecropping. After Kovács lost his estate to the Germans he turned to commerce, where he must have found greater success, for he was able to leave his son a shop in the city of Deva.[21]

Our most extended picture is of occupants of an estate containing three hundred hectares or more in nineteenth-century Binţinţi and a neighboring village. In 1800 the estate belonged to a branch of the great Bethlen family, whose daughter Maria in 1812 married Count Benedek Lázár, a captain in the cavalry and son of a wealthy Transylvanian family of titled aristocrats.[22] Settled on the estate in Binţinţi, Lázár divided his time between his farm and public office. He served as High Sheriff of Alba County and helped to save fellow nobles by calling in troops to crush an attempted peasant uprising in the 1830s (Lázár 1858:265; Tóth 1955:249). His son was Count Kálmán Lázár, whom we encountered above as an officer in the 1848 revolution.

As is clear from a letter to Transylvania's fiscal headquarters in 1860, Kálmán Lázár was among the irredeemable Magyar nationalists who refused to accept defeat:

Excellent Imperial Royal Vice-Regency Council for Transylvania!

Enclosed is a copy of a petition I submitted to the district office at Orăştie, written in Hungarian, together with the reply I received. In this petition I have asked to be availed of His Majesty's gracious dispensation concerning taxes, requesting that my assessed taxes not be collected until year's end. Unfortunately I do not know how this quite justified request was answered, for the reply was written in a language I do not know, in contravention of His Gracious Majesty's order of earlier this year that any petition to authorities must be answered in the language in which it is composed. Yet the District Officer, Mr. Novak, pointedly replied to my petition in German, which I do not understand, and I might add that this is characteristic of his disrespectful behavior towards me . . . I trust that you will help me resolve this urgent matter before it is too late.

Bentzentz, 12 August 1860   Count Kálmán Lázár[23]

It is quite doubtful that Count Lázár could not make his way through a note in German: he was a member of Parliament and of the Hungarian Academy of Sciences, an ornithologist renowned throughout Europe, and author of hundreds of scientific articles. His letter's real message is that in 1860 he was still fighting the revolution of 1848 against germanization and absolutism. It is likely that he was also seeing to his estate, for with the exception of a few brief periods, he was resident in Binţinţi until 1872. Tax assessments for Hunedoara County show him as the county's twentieth wealthiest inhabitant in 1871[24] (hence, he served on the county assembly). It is a fair guess that he gained some of this income from attention to his lands: he was knowledgeable enough, in any case, to be selected by the Hungarian Ministry of Agriculture as one of Hungary's representatives to the International Exposition and Congress of Agriculture in Vienna (Szinnyei 1900:915-920). Again, it is not known how this estate was farmed except that Lázár had a huge aviary and raised fish for his table in a large fishpond in the courtyard. Typically for aristocrats of these years, he ended his days in 1874 "burdened with material worries" (ibid.).[25]

The next occupant of Count Lázár's estate was József Graczik, a Jew who may well have been the Count's estate administrator and then bought him out. This pattern was not uncommon at the time, for Jews were often employed as administrators or tenants and had received in 1848, along with serfs, the right to own property. According to story, Graczik spoke poor Romanian and used to amuse his tardy workers by chiding them sternly, "You're coming too early to work," to which they would reply, "You mean too late, sir." One can make a guess at Graczik's agricultural activities on the basis of a partial inventory drawn up by Binţinţi's mayor when Graczik died in 1890. It shows large sums of money (double the annual salary of the village schoolteacher and more than the village's total yearly expenditures) taken in from the sale of hay that was standing on the estate at Graczik's death; market taxes for auctioning off animals; and wages paid to people who measured the estate's stocks of maize—which must have been substantial, for the work required three men's labor for three days. Either Graczik marketed maize or else he was a supplier for the alcohol factory that opened in 1866 in Orăştie; it appears likely that he also marketed cattle. I will return briefly to him below, to comment on his labor force.

Graczik's heirs leased the estate to a Jewish tenant, Isidor Mendel. This man does not seem to have had a serious interest in commercial production, for Hungary's 1895 agricultural census shows him as owning no sophisticated agricultural implements and as having only eighteen head of cattle on a tenancy totaling over 150 hectares (Hungary 1897–1900, vol. 2). He may well have given some of it out to sharecroppers. All anyone now remembers of Mendel is that on his property were the warehouses for the clover seed trade that began at about this time; the seed was stored in these warehouses until picked up by Jewish merchants. Because of the terrific prices paid for clover seed, it was a popular cultigen among peasant households that could afford the space. And peasant proceeds were doubled and trebled by the ingenuity of one peasant son, who managed to duplicate the keys to the warehouse using a wax cast of the lock, and would break in at night with his friends, to steal sacks for resale to Mendel on another day.

These tricks soon came to an end, when the estate was bought by the wealthy Romanian lawyer and banker Ioan Mihu (see preceding section). He leased it to two Viennese brothers surnamed Ulrichhofer, conscientious farmers who devoted their time, according to former neighbors, to growing grains and fattening cattle. The products were sent westward by rail, the railroad having been built very near Binţinţi. Neighbors recall that the Ulrichhofers went often to Vienna themselves and would buy goosefeathers from villagers, to sell on their trip. Otherwise, the brothers did not behave as merchants until after they were thrown out of their tenancy for not voting as landlord Mihu insisted (about 1915). One of them returned to Vienna and the other took up business in Orăştie.

Aside from these tenants, Binţinţi peasants remember only one proprietor, László Berivoy, who occupied himself seriously with commercial farming. Berivoy farmed about three hundred hectares, mostly in a village nearby, and used wage labor (poorly and infrequently paid) to grow huge amounts of sugar beets, which he sold to factories in central Hungary. The experiment seems to have been unrewarding, for he was forced to sell off increasing shares of his estate until he finally went out of business in the early 1900s— bought out by Mihu. Most of the Magyar landowners whom villagers recall from early in this century gave out the bulk of their land to be sharecropped, rather than troubling to farm it themselves (see chap. 5). Their farms were in the twenty- to fifty-hectare range.

Cheek by jowl with these larger farms, which at most numbered eight by the turn of the century, were a considerable number of peasant holdings, all but a couple of them small. Many among these were able to make ends meet on what they had inherited from the holdings granted their fathers and grandfathers after 1854. Take, as an extreme example, Toma Cristea, whose father had ranked ninth when village serfs declared their wealth in 1820. In 1890, when the common pasture was subdivided into individualized rights according to each household's wealth, Toma received the second-largest piece (4 percent of all shares allotted). His sons had inherited goodly portions and were buying houses and additional parcels that made them among the village's richer peasant families. Their holdings were not only bigger than average but probably of higher quality, for Toma was doubtless among those rich villagers who, in one informant's recollection, had benefited from the consolidation of village fields in 1880. As this woman tells the story, at the time of consolidation landlords and rich peasants collaborated to get themselves compact parcels in the most fertile soils of the village, leaving less productive land for the friendless poor (see also Suciu 1929:691).

Among the latter and at the opposite extreme from Toma Cristea there is Andrei Rusu, whose father had come into Binţinţi from a hill village looking for work as an agricultural servant. In 1900 Andrei and his wife Ioana had a scrap of land and worked as servants for the Ulrichhofers. According to their daughter, they augmented their income from their parcel and their servants' wage—chiefly in kind—in two ways. They fattened cattle for the Ulrichhofers for a monthly fee, caring for the animals and feeding them hay and fodder the bosses supplied. And Ioana had a Singer sewing machine bought from a peddler in 1900, with which she (along with two or three other very poor women) took in sewing from various villagers. The peddler had persuaded her to buy the machine, instead of the patch of land she was painfully saving toward, by telling her she would make more money with it than from a tiny parcel of soil.

Up the street from the Rusus lived another peasant couple who also had dealings with the Ulrichhofers. This couple, Vasile and Maria Cosma, were of poor status but, unlike the Rusus, were native to Binţinţi. Maria Cosma remembers working for the Ulrichhofers not as a servant or in the more usual sharecropping arrangement, in which peasants worked land and gave the landlord half or more of the harvest. Instead, Maria paid the Ulrichhofers a sum of money, two chickens, and ten eggs for the right to harvest a specific measure of maize; she did this as late as World War I. What Maria herself did not recount—and probably does not know—is that her great-grandfather was a serf of Count Benedek Lázár in 1820 and worked the same land that later descended, through inheritance, sale, and tenancy, to the Ulrichhofer brothers (Lázárs → Graczik → Mihu + Ulrichhofer), who a century later were collecting Maria's fee and products in exchange for her right to harvest maize from it. More striking still, among the obligations Maria's great-grandfather owed Count Lázár were labor (possibly later commuted to a sum of money), two chickens, and ten eggs. But had the serfs not been emancipated after 1848?

It seems that as late as 1875 or even after, many of them indeed had not been, at least not fully. In about that year, property registration was instituted in Binţinţi. Of the 125 households registered then, over one-third were listed in a manner indicating one or another form of continued dependence on landlords.[26] Well over half of these households occupied plots designated as "noble property" (*Curialisbirtok*), and many had specific obligations written down. Thus, some peasants owed their landlord set fees to redeem their labor obligations, and others owed actual labor: József Graczik had acquired the labor of several former serfs of the Lázár family, who owed him one day a week with four oxen, or one day's manual labor weekly, or twenty days per year; and Count Lajos Teleky (soon to be bankrupt) and Baroness Anna Macskásy were each entitled — amazingly — to three days per week of manual labor from several peasant families. All this, two to six decades after serfdom's supposed end! Subsequent entries show that some of these peasants had "their" land sold out from under them by the lord, others managed to acquire legal title on their own before World War I, and still others won their proprietorship only after the land reform of 1921. Seeing the recency of these entries, one begins to comprehend why elderly peasants often speak in the present of serfdom and its labor regime as if they themselves were familiar with it: for many of them, their parents were, veritably, still "serfs."

What is the larger context within which one can understand these vignettes? And what do they, in turn, suggest about the social system in which they occurred? My conclusion from the admittedly skimpy sources available is that the example of the Ulrichhofers (and possibly Graczik) notwithstanding, the context was a Transylvania in which agriculture remained much less developed and capitalized than in Hungary. Only in areas served by the railway or close to industrial centers, and not until near the turn of the century, did one find much commercial agriculture of the sort practiced by the Ulrichhofer brothers on Mihu's estate. Overall, it was a context in which owners of large and medium properties that had survived the difficult 1870s gave out their lands to tenants and sharecroppers, while shifting their attention to other sources of income. Those who attempted commercial farming, such as Berivoy with his sugar beets, did not meet with much success.

Few of them took the route of technological modernization. In the agricultural census of 1895, the ratio of agricultural machinery (e.g., steam-driven tractors, mechanical threshers and seeders) per farming household was in all cases lower in Transylvania than in Hungary, often by large gaps. For example, the total amount of steam-powered machinery per farm × 1000 was 1.7 for Transylvania, 9.3 for Hungary. Property concentration was less extreme in Transylvania, and it even diminished somewhat between 1895 and 1910.[27] Other indicators similarly suggest retarded agricultural development: Transylvania's productivity and export involvement were very low (Szabad 1977:29; Pamlényi 1975:354), and it was dependent on imports of some foodstuffs from Hungary (Gaál and Gunst 1977:95); its percentage of fallow land was the highest in all Hungary (Szuhay 1965:644); its schools for spreading agricultural information were very late in appearing; and the amount of credit extended to agriculture was less (visible in smaller amounts of outstanding mortgages) than in Hungary, probably reflecting lower levels of agricultural investment overall (Komlos, personal communication).

One should not overlook the few contrary indications. An Englishman, Charles Boner, traveled in Transylvania in the 1850s and 1860s and made numerous complimentary (though implicitly condescending) observations about the new spirit of enterprise among Transylvania's gentry. He noted their recent attention to careful management of their estates and their improved cultivation practices and implements (Boner 1865:71–72, 337–338, 553–554, 627). Many nobles were indeed pressed to introduce more efficient rotations, for emancipation had so reduced the size of their estates that they had to work each scrap more intensively than before. (But Boner also noted [p. 285] that often they did not follow the new rotations conscientiously.)

If any improvements were made, it was not — as in Hungary — with an eye to exporting cereals, for the ecological and locational reasons mentioned in chapter 3. Transylvania's high proportion of pasture and forest to arable lands, together with the poor transport facilities and the more proximate grain areas that separated it from export markets, meant that the only product likely to be exported was livestock. Specific evidence on this possibility is thin, however, for Hungarian statistical publications rarely disaggregate data on commodities to show regional origins. According to Mitrany (1930:

363), before the First World War, 10 percent of Transylvania's livestock production went to Vienna and Prague. In support of this, Boner observed (1865:287) that the Transylvania gentry "have begun doing what was never thought of before, fattening cattle." It is very possible, however, that this was just an ancillary activity to the more important one of alcohol manufacture, especially prevalent in the Transylvanian north (see Moga 1973:253-255). The economic historians Gaál and Gunst assert that Transylvania remained the most "traditional" area of Hungary as regards livestock production: older breeds were less rapidly replaced there than elsewhere; only there did no shift from draft animals to meat and milk production occur, oxen being still bred primarily for traction; and pasturage rather than stabled rearing prevailed (Gaál and Gunst 1977: 40-41). The main change was that Transylvanian draft oxen were now sometimes exported to farms in Hungary.

Thus, the market for agricultural products included a probable but poorly documented export of livestock (cattle from lowland areas, sheep from upland), an internal market that was not growing at a great rate, and some agrarian industry in the form of alcohol manufacture. The anecdotes above help to demonstrate that none of these activities presupposed increased capitalization of production. Cattle marketed from larger properties may have been raised "on consignment" in the barnyards and pastures of peasants or cared for by the labor of not-fully-emancipated irregular serfs. Owners of medium to large surfaces monopolized the internal grain market and alcohol production, yet this did not presume modernization of estates. Only part of the grain marketed internally was grown by extensive farming of large surfaces with agricultural laborers (some of them, again, having labor obligations): much of it was collected from sharecroppers, to be sold. Given that the Hungarian state had provided virtually no social overhead capital in the form of agricultural credit and cooperatives, and given that in many villages the fragmented fields of feudal times had not been consolidated, the most feasible use of fragmented properties was for the owner or tenant to sublet them, rather than work them with wage labor (see Forster 1970:1601-1602, 1608); and sharecropping was the main form such contracts took. To understand this better and to appreciate its significance for the condition of Transylvanian agriculture prior to World War I, we must review what happened to both property and labor in the wake of the emancipation, in 1854.

As of 1854, Transylvania's agrarian regime was, and would remain, the most confused in the empire (Grimm 1963:57). The emancipation of the serfs produced chaos there, particularly for the peasant population of the Counties.[28] A major source of confusion was that only one class of peasants—hereditary serfs settled on urbarial lands—was actually freed of obligations and given ownership rights to the properties they had worked. There were many other categories: workers settled in noble courtyards or on pieces of allodial land (an especially large category in Transylvania), who sharecropped or paid a fee for use of land, or whose obligations were contractual; and many individual peasants held tenures of more than one type. All these were, depending on their specific legal situation, either not freed of labor obligations or not given ownership of the property they worked, or both. A total of 173,781 peasant families received land, at an average of 5.3 hectares apiece (Maior 1906:227-228). They represented about 45 percent of the total Transylvanian population and brought to about 70 percent the number of legally free small-holders in Transylvania; many of these, however, while legally free, had too little land to function as independent, and they were therefore subject to the labor-procurement ploys of the nobility. About 15 percent of the population remained in one form or another of legal bondage and/or without legal title to any land at all.[29] Some received during the next several decades the legal conditions for purchasing their freedom, but it was an option not many were able to seize. All these considerations help to explain the baffling labor obligations noted on Binţinţi property records in the 1870s (see above).

Only full urbarial serfs were excused from paying for their emancipation. All who held a status other than urbarial serf, together with urbarial serfs who held additional lands or obligations of other kinds, were personally liable for their redemption. While the state assumed the burden of indemnifying landlords for their urbarial serfs, with money coming from provincial funds,[30] provincial funds proved inadequate and the shortfall was made up by surcharges on direct taxes, which came of course from peasant pockets. Peasants strapped for cash found little comfort in a region whose circulation of money was so low that, especially between 1848 and the 1860s, the principal medium of exchange was labor (Retegan 1978:200).

As for landlords, they did not fare much better. The high ratio of urbarial to allodial lands meant that many estates were reduced to a third of their former size, rendering them barely viable given their technological level. Fragmentation of these estates worsened the difficulties, and peasants usually opposed consolidation of village fields (with good reason for all but the rich, as we have seen). As the state did not take this matter firmly in hand, fragmentation continued to shackle agricultural production of many properties right up to World War I.

In addition to problems resulting from property structure, credit institutions were insufficient to the needs of the hundreds of noblemen whom emancipation had left with overindebted estates, labor shortages, and inadequate agricultural inventories. Dilatory indemnifications from the state served to aggravate the nobles' cash worries. The state's delay was not surprising (even if also retaliatory), given that Transylvania had the highest compensation burden of any land in the empire (Baritĭu 1891:269) and a sickly budget, but it further imperiled the solvency of aristocrats. Many nobles never even saw the compensations that were finally paid. Following a brief period of grace, from a moratorium on calling in debts to nobles (1848–1860), creditors holding old debts often received the compensation directly (Grimm 1863:iv).

All this combined with the poor markets for agricultural goods to create chronic distress for the nobility, too strapped for cash to modernize their production or hire laborers in place of the serfs they had lost. Relative to that in agriculture, opportunity was greater in the bureaucracy, in which the gentry cheerfully took up residence after 1867, and more favorable conditions for deploying capital existed in commerce and industry, where merchants and landowners increasingly invested their resources. These circumstances meant that no powerful voice survived to speak up on behalf of modernizing Transylvanian agriculture; agriculture thus got no help from the insistence of such a voice in the formation of state policy. The Hungarian state bent its efforts almost entirely in the direction of large-scale agriculture, agrarian industry, and commerce — not to creating viable middle-sized or small-peasant agriculture in Transylvania. We have already seen that the form of state-encouraged industrialization prevented it from redounding favorably upon agriculture.

During the process of shifting their attention from agriculture to other sources of livelihood, however, estate owners struggled to retain control over the labor supply without having to pay for it, access to semiservile labor being the only way they could keep afloat. By taking advantage of peasant ignorance about the legal niceties that classified the populace into so bewildering an array of categories, proprietors were able to keep many peasants in thrall who had in fact been freed. They also used their position of political supremacy to postpone resolution of the fates of irregular serfs: the final laws appeared only in 1896. Even then, litigation further protracted peasant bondage, as did the fact that many peasants could not afford what was necessary to purchase their holdings and their freedom. Thus, one finds peasants still occupying lands and houses in exchange for payments of workdays, on paper at least, as late as World War I (Pascu et al. 1964:54). Proprietors also took advantage of peasant destitution to hire labor on terms maximally favorable to themselves, engaging only workers who would throw extra unpaid days into the contract. Farming some of their lands in this manner and giving out the remainder to sharecroppers for one-half to two-thirds of the crop or to tenants who often did the same, large- and medium-property owners cushioned their transformation from a privileged agrarian elite into an administrative, professional, and business elite. In the process, they helped to keep Transylvania's peasants as subsistence-oriented semiproletarians.

The peasants contributed something to this result also. First, in those areas where they had resisted field consolidations, they had retarded the likelihood that compact estates susceptible to capital improvements would arise. Policies of the Hungarian state reinforced this effect. (One might say that in this manner, peasants had also retarded the rise of wage employments for themselves, but whether this is "bad" or "good" depends on one's point of view.) Second, in the absence of alternative earnings from agriculture or industry, they faced serious difficulties in their struggle to free themselves of the debts they had assumed to purchase their freedom, to pay rising provincial taxes (from surcharges that financed the state's share of compensation), and to acquire new means of production. Above all they purchased land, for which demand had risen owing to population increase and restricted opportunities for livelihood. How urgent this demand was becoming is clear from the fact that by 1895, half of the peasantry was landless or had less than the subsistence minimum of three hectares, and since 1870 the numbers of landless and land-poor had grown by 25 percent. The increase does not, of course, necessarily reflect proletarization and capitalist development but merely shows peasant pauperization.

To remedy their indebted and land-hungry plight, peasants looked increasingly to emigration. The numbers of emigrants rose toward the end of the 1800s, but after 1900 they reached epic magnitudes. Between 1901 and 1914 nearly 210,000 persons departed — in all, 10 percent of Transylvania's population of 2.5 million (see Hungary 1920:82). The principal destinations were the Romanian Kingdom and the United States, where emigrants worked, respectively, as agricultural proletarians on latifundia and as industrial proletarians in mines and factories. Those who left were disproportionately Romanians; Magyars were underrepresented.[31] Probably reflecting relative disadvantage, the discrepancy also indicates how insusceptible Romanians were to being bound in place by Magyar nationalism, at least over the short run. (For more on emigration, see chap. 6).

To put the same facts in a different way, Transylvanian feudalism decomposed in a manner that nourished a population of international proletarians. Some of them were temporary, their objective being to earn enough money to return home free of debts and bondage. Many others remained abroad, sending back remittances with which their families could become free. Most, however, were not proletarians in the strict sense of the term. They had left behind them minuscule bits of encumbered land, worked by families still partially bound to landlords in semiservile conditions, all symptomatic of capitalism's nonemergence within agricultural production.

Whether through the fruits of emigration or through inheritance or debts to banks such as Mihu's Ardeleana, the structure of property at the bottom of the scale changed greatly around the turn of the century. Between 1895 and 1915, peasant holdings under 2.9 hectares declined as a percentage of all farms, but their share of the agricultural surface area rose from 7 to 24 percent, suggesting an increased average size for very small holdings. Peasants owning between 2.9 and 5.8 hectares also increased their share of the surface (from 12 to 21 percent), while farms of between 5.8 and 58 hectares dropped from 49 to 25 percent of the arable surface (source as in note 27). This means that holdings just at or below the subsistence line had grown at the expense of capitalizable small and medium farms, forming an ever larger stratum of semiproletarized and noncommercially oriented peasants who would be perennial customers for supplementary income through sharecropping or wage labor. Chapters 5 and 6 will show which of these options they were able to seize.

NATIONALISM AND TRANSYLVANIA'S ECONOMIC DEVELOPMENT

The emancipation of the serfs in 1854 had laid the foundations not only for capitalist estate agriculture but also for a petty-commodity-producing peasantry supplemented by a sizable landless proletariat. In many parts of Hungary this was indeed the result, but not in Transylvania, where instead, "backward" landlords continued to place liens on the labor of their peasants, retarding the generalization of wages, the likelihood of marketable peasant surpluses, and the level of rural purchasing power. The majority of Transylvania's peasants remained semiproletarians and small-scale subsistence cultivators, constituting a backward sector up through and even beyond World War I. The cause of their backwardness was not the rise of capitalist export agriculture but, rather, capitalism's feeble entry into Transylvania's agrarian sphere.

Several factors contributed to this outcome: the historically determined property structure, with its fragmentation and its high ratios of urbarial lands; the paucity of credit (fixed partly by state action and largely by what capitalists found profitable and feasible in Transylvania, given the rest of the economy); the steady but not rapidly growing markets for agricultural goods; natural endowments; and locational and ecological constraints. Alongside these considerations, within the empire Transylvania had become a source of valuable raw materials and a locus of profitable investments in mining and industry. Because the products of Transylvanian mines and industries were exported for consumption within the empire— that is, because Transylvania lay inside a larger, industrially developing state—and did not depend on purchasing-power internal to Transylvania, state policy did not trouble itself with raising depressed purchasing-power by improvements in agriculture. Capital avoided Transylvania's agricultural production because there were more rewarding activities to which it could turn, including mortgages on properties that could not make a go of commercial farming.

What role was played in all this by the rise of nationalism, the subject with which the chapter began? Nationalism—more precisely, Magyar nationalism—shaped Transylvania's economy in several respects, not all immediately obvious. First, the whole chain of events recounted here began with the abolition of serfdom, a major reform demanded in Hungary's nationalist revolution of 1848. The revenue-pressed Hungarian nobility had come to require emancipation so as to take advantage of newly opening agricultural markets, and even though the revolution was defeated, this reform endured. What makes it a nationalist achievement is its underlying premise: that Magyars should have the right to determine the (national) development of their economy for themselves.

Second, once Magyars received the instrument enabling them to exercise that right—their own almost-independent state, in 1867— they used it to pursue priorities designed toward creating as independent a national economy as possible. The Hungarian state promoted industry, both capital-intensive heavy industry and light industries such as food processing, and also promoted large-scale capitalist agriculture. It did not provide institutional follow-up (credit, information, cooperatives, etc.) to make agriculture viable in smaller units, especially not in peasant-sized units. To phrase this somewhat differently, the group directly responsible for Hungarian state policy was the nobility, split into two distinct subgroups whose interests appear clearly from the direction state policy took: support of large-scale estate agriculture (magnates) and support of industry toward national independence (gentry).

These priorities did not always suit the existing economy of Transylvania very well. Their pursuit by state agents and by local and imperial capitalists served to undermine much of Transylvania's indigenous small-scale manufacturing and to concentrate and "rationalize" those (such as textiles) that remained, as described above. Because of this, concentrated capital-intensive industry came to prevail, often managed from and geared to the outside. In consequence, no groups having a vested interest in building up rural purchasing power for local manufactures survived to influence policy (nor did Hungary's industrialists yet concern themselves with the Transylvanian consumer), and potential urban markets for agricultural commodities failed to develop. Hence the stagnant domestic market that contributed so much to the flight of capital from Transylvania's agricultural production. The remainder of that flight arose from the small possibilities for export agriculture, given that cereal growers and cattle raisers in Hungary were already more advanced and better served by transport (itself state-influenced), and therefore could outcompete Transylvanian farmers.

Magyar nationalism contributed to the shape of things in Transylvania in yet a third way. The successful development of capitalist agriculture in Hungary had an often-met concomitant: large properties were concentrated and middle-sized ones that could not compete were eliminated (see Eddie 1967 for trends in Hungary's property structure). "Freed" from agriculture by the progress of capitalist farming, middle-estate owners moved into the bureaucracy — a logical choice, given that it was both a new, expanding niche and historically a preserve of lesser nobles, from their days in County administrations. The Hungarian national state thus became itself an economic resource, essential to livelihood, that required protecting. And an excellent vehicle for such protection was the claim that as a Magyar state, Hungary should be ruled by Magyars. Inasmuch as the state included Transylvania, where Magyars were a decided minority, this point of view would reverberate unpleasantly there and would produce increasingly vehement opposition to Magyar political dominance. Chapter 5 will suggest something of the village-level results of this nationalistically inspired distortion of the opportunity system.

Although Magyar nationalism did contaminate Transylvania's development, I hold that it was chiefly in this last sphere, of state employment (including the educational system) and related "white-collar" positions, that Magyar nationalism overtly influenced access to opportunity through outright nationalist discrimination; otherwise, its economic effects were fairly subtle and nondeliberate in character, of the sort I have argued above. Once freed from agriculture, the Magyar gentry turned to the only alternatives they considered desirable: political-administrative office, clerkships, and the professions; other Magyars, less often, looked to commerce or industry. Yet because, historically, position and privilege within Hungary and the empire had come to be defended in nationalist terms, Magyars' nationalist defense of political and administrative positions evoked similarly phrased counterarguments from Transylvania's other groups. Thus, nationalist rhetoric echoed throughout the society, making claims and charges as each group sought to fend off challenges from another or to move in on niches already occupied by another.

Magyars and Germans had specialties, rooted in their pasts, that they were particularly concerned to defend in this way: Magyars had administration and clerkships; Germans, commerce and industry. One can see these long-standing specialties in table 4-3, which shows how ethnic groups fell within the major occupations of the new elite strata that had been coalescing since 1848. Romanians, excluded from both political and economic specializations, were using nationalist claims to establish toeholds at the edges of both Magyar and German niches, as table 4-3 illustrates.

Nationalism served not only as a language for arguing with other groups but also as a way for elite members of each group to converse with their own masses. Part of the effect, if not the motive, of such conversations may have been to increase mass support for those who initiated the dialogue from above. An example is the way Romanian and Saxon bourgeoisies promoted "economic progress" among their respective peasants (as we have already seen in Mihu's exhortations to Romanian peasants, above). They founded agricultural newspapers and associations, disseminated agricultural calendars with tips for cultivation, held meetings in villages, encouraged cottage industry—particularly of national dress (see Dobrescu 1972; Jude

TABLE 4-3. Occupancy of the Commercial and Industrial Bourgeoisie, Clerkships, and State Employment, 1910. Areas circled show highest relative concentrations of each nationality.

	Ethnic Group		
Occupational sector	*Magyar*	*Saxon*	*Romanian*
Public administration	75%	13%	12%
Public justice	76	7	17
Functionaries in mines	80	15	5
Functionaries in agriculture	83	11	6
Functionaries in transport	91	6	3
Notaries (all levels)	63	13	24
Lawyers	65	9	26
Independent owners in industry	55	18	28
Independent owners in commerce	61	23	16
Functionaries in commerce	63	25	12
Functionaries in industry	62	35	3
Proportion in population overall	34	9	55

Source: Hungary 1912-16: vol. 56. Percentages exclude groups other than the three shown.

1974; Jude and Cordoş 1976)—while simultaneously increasing the nationalist and political education of the peasantry. The Romanian publications often gave information on the history of Romanians in Transylvania and across the mountains. The Romanian National Party, formed in 1881, both included in its platform some provisions for assisting Romanian peasant agriculture and aggressively sought peasant support. Romanian peasants therefore received information about "progress" laced with ideas about Transylvanian autonomy, more positions for Romanian functionaries, public use of Romanian, and the end of magyarization (Daicoviciu and Constantinescu 1965: 314-315).

Given this environment, one has a better sense of how participants must have seen the following career of a Binţinţi peasant family of modest means but unusual talents and ambitions. Dumitru Vlaicu (1852-1918) was not a wealthy villager—his grandfather had been among the poorer serfs in 1820—but he improved his status with several years' service in the Austrian army, where he made himself trilingually literate. Dumitru decided to send his son Aurel to school: Magyar schools in Orăştie, a Saxon gimnasium, the universities of Budapest and Munich, whence he emerged an engineer. No Binţinţi peasant before him had gone so far, and few Transylvanian peasants took his route, for the usual course of advanced study was law. In his case, his own special gifts, rather than the character of his society, determined his path.

Aurel's gifts had manifested themselves early, not only in his skill at making keys to steal clover seed from Isidor Mendel's warehouses but also in other technical inventions, which attracted the attention of politicians as World War I brewed. Approached by an influential Magyar in Orăştie, he was assured that resources appropriate to his talents would be put at his disposal if he would go to Budapest to pursue his work. But Aurel, like many Romanians, had passed through his magyarizing education determined to combat its nationalistic effects. He replied that his work would benefit no army but a Romanian one, and he went to Bucharest ([Ciura] 1920: 95-96). His work was no small matter, for Aurel Vlaicu was one of the greatest technical geniuses of Romanian nationality and built original airplanes fully on par with those of the Wright Brothers and others of his time.

In 1913, shortly before the outbreak of war, this restless Transylvanian peasant son climbed into his plane, north of Bucharest, to attempt yet another in a series of ambitious feats: to fly across the Carpathian Mountains. He envisioned this as not only a technical but a nationalist achievement, for it would link by air, for the first time, the Romanians of Transylvania and their compatriots in the Romanian Kingdom. Vlaicu died in the attempt, but Romania still celebrates his genius and his patriotism. After Transylvania was joined to Romania in 1920, the village of Binţinţi was renamed to honor him.

Aurel Vlaicu's career is one of those that prefigured the direction in which the social system was moving, rather than — like the career of Count István Kun, for example — showing what it had left in its wake. During the period between 1848 and World War I, the social structure of feudalism was passing out of existence, as educated professionals, bureaucrats, and entrepreneurs superseded the feudal nobility. Figure 4-1 captures one moment in that transformative process, one of Transylvania's last moments under the Hungarian state. The figure shows to what extent Romanians disproportionately bore the stigmata of the feudal order, being overrepresented in all categories of agriculture except the wealthiest, while Magyars and Germans disproportionately filled the more comfortable ranks of the new elite strata. Particularly striking is the exclusion of Romanians from positions as clerks and functionaries.[32] Yet throughout this period, despite serious obstacles from the Magyar upper classes, even Romanians were occasionally able to move

FIGURE 4-1. Transylvania's Occupational Composition in 1910, by Ethnic Group*,⁺

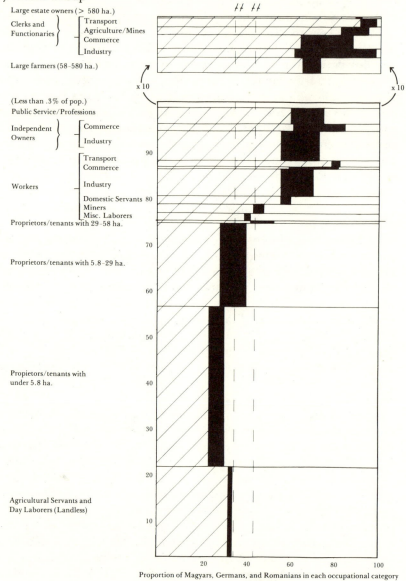

Proportion of Magyars, Germans, and Romanians in each occupational category

Magyars   Germans   Romanians

⁺⁺ Dashed vertical lines indicate the proportion of the three ethnic groups in the overall population.
* Percentages are calculated from the totals for these three groups *only.*
⁺ Excludes pensioners, army personnel, and unknown—4.8 of population.

upward in society, by attending the educational institutions of the other groups and financing this with the proceeds of forest exploitation, small trades like shoemaking, perhaps sometimes by cattle marketing, or, as in Dumitru Vlaicu's case, through bank debts (paid off by Aurel's aviation prizes). It was still difficult for Romanians to achieve elite status in Transylvanian society *as Romanians,* but it was less rare than it had been a century before, and after World War I it would grow common.

One should not make too much of the picture presented in figure 4-1, for it does no more than slice for an instant into a set of ongoing social processes. Visualizing this slice, however, helps to grasp the different life chances of groups in Transylvanian society at that moment in its history. In chapter 5, I will people more of the categories of this diagram with real human beings and will discuss their activities and their relations with one another up to World War I — that is, in the latter part of the period discussed in the present chapter. The outcome of the war overturned the power structure within which these groups pursued their existence. Chapter 6 will describe how this change radically reorganized the categories of figure 4-1, giving those who had "been here all along" in the most lowly conditions an unprecedented chance to turn themselves from peasants into gentlemen.

CHAPTER 5

Paying Like a German: Turn-of-the-Century Intergroup Relations in Binţinţi

Mielul blînd suge la doi oi.
(The docile lamb suckles from two ewes.)

Capul ce s-apleacă sabia nu-1 taie.
(The sword does not cut off a head that is bowed.)

— Romanian proverbs

Das Brot das Mann isst,
dass Lied muss Mann singen.
(You sing the song of the one who feeds you.)

— Saying from German informant

The three preceding chapters have broadly defined the historical environment that nurtured Transylvanian peasants of the early twentieth century, particularly peasants of a specific kind. They were peasants subjected to direct control by a feudal Magyar nobility; prime objects of courtship for any social group wishing to counter that nobility's power, prime victims of intensified feudal exploitation, and prime beneficiaries of emancipation; and eyewitnesses of a nationalist struggle among the various bourgeoisies during the economic and social transformations in the nineteenth century. Of this specific kind of peasantry the Romanian inhabitants of Binţinţi are fine examples. Their village was the sort in which the major structural changes of recent Habsburg, Hungarian, and Transylvanian history had an especially palpable existence, where the complex interplay of class and nationality was felt in daily experience, and where transformations in these structures met with, and were given life within, human action.

Although social groups have recognizable histories that can be written without disaggregating them into the experiences and perceptions of individuals or small communities, it is our tendency (whether bred of the Enlightenment tradition and the rise of individualism or merely of an imagination too irredeemably grounded in our own experience of the world) to empathize not with structures, systems, and collectivities but with the lives of communities and persons. We can comprehend the "lives" of social structures, but we tend to be more generous and understanding about the confusions of human beings than we are about the contradictions of systems. Although I have tried throughout my discussion to imply that the late Habsburg Empire was indeed inhabited by people, I will now shift my focus more fully to the inhabitants, as opposed to the empire and its parts, asking what these inhabitants show as effects of their residence in such a place.

More than simply wishing to show how these people's lives were grounded in history, however, I am also concerned with how they shaped their own conditions through their activities and their perceptions. History gave the peasants of Binţinţi an economic environment characterized by low capitalist development in agriculture; yet these peasant smallholders were the numerous participants of a residual sector that still reproduced and transformed itself in directions not entirely planned from above. History also gave this village — from very early in its existence, if not even from the time of its permanent settlement in the thirteenth century[1] — a population perpetually fragmented along many lines of social cleavage. Over the centuries there were serfs and resident masters, laborers and large landowners; speakers of Romanian, of Magyar, and of German;[2] adherents to Orthodox, Calvinist, Lutheran, Uniate, and Roman Catholic churches;[3] urbarial serfs and allodial serfs of different kinds; later, rich peasants and poor; persons born locally, immigrants, inmarriers, and even persons imported for their labor. Within this heritage some distinctions were perceived as more significant than others, some affected more spheres of behavior than others, and some were perpetuated more rigorously than others, not just by "the system" but by the persons who distinguished daily among one another in these terms.

The present chapter investigates the distinctions of nationality and class. Because intervening decades have filtered informants' recollections of the past, one cannot conclude decisively from their descriptions that at the turn of the century, nationality and class were the most significant categories of experience for the peasants of Binţinţi. So let me simply posit, from the evidence of chapter 4, that history gave the categories of nationality and class to this peasantry, and ask from there how the peasants infused them with life, and with life of what kind. A complete inquiry is impossible for in present-day Binţinţi there are no descendants of the original Magyar population, who might fill in our picture of them; and few, even, are the Romanians who remember something of how Magyars lived and were viewed. The discussion therefore centers on Romanians and Germans, necessarily if unfortunately underplaying the impact of Magyars on the ethnic and class organization of the community. I will describe the main organizational differences between Germans and Romanians in agriculture, inheritance, and the domestic sphere, and show how these differences both reflect diverse group histories and perpetuate different life chances and experiences. I will then tentatively approach the more elusive problem of intergroup perceptions, suggesting that although perceptions of ethnicity and class were tightly knitted together, when one looks at political behavior the problematic issues for Romanians appear to focus on distinctions of nationality, not on class. This proposal has several implications for how and where these peasants saw themselves oppressed and for their future relationships with Germans and with the state, subjects to be taken up in chapter 6.

GROUP DIFFERENCES IN THE ORGANIZATION OF AGRICULTURE

Let me begin with the central fact of life and source of daily experience for nearly all the residents of Binţinţi — agriculture. As of 1900, three broad patterns could be seen in agriculture: one associated modally with speakers of Magyar (and a few Romanians, such as nonresident members of the regional bourgeoisie); one with speakers of German; and one — more internally varied than the others — with the majority of Romanians. Each pattern reveals basic differences in the organization of agricultural production and of access to its means, although within each pattern there were farms that departed from the mode in one or another direction. I will describe the Magyar pattern summarily and concentrate on agriculture among Romanians and Germans.

The farm of Zsigmond Fogarassy (1850–1915) was about forty hectares in extent, toward the upper end of the village's Magyar enterprises (ranging from about 17 to about 50 hectares). According to the reports of elderly Romanian informants,[4] Fogarassy produced on this estate a mixture of crops and animals, for use and for sale, rather than specializing in a single market crop (as did one, and only one, of his fellow Magyars). The bulk of the land was farmed by administrators and resident agricultural servants, using the landlord's own implements and animals (he had no machinery); and the rest was given out to villagers in annual sharecropping contracts for 50 percent of the yield, making Fogarassy, like other Magyars, part farmer and part "rent capitalist." That far less of his land was sharecropped than was true of most other Magyars probably derives from his having, unlike most of them, no primary occupation outside agriculture, as notary, lawyer, or teacher. This meant that he relied solely on agricultural output for a living. When the farm passed to his daughter Erzsébet, married to a lawyer, the estate was given out entirely to sharecroppers and the owner raised only cattle. (One might add that Erzsébet's inheritance of the farm made her proprietress in the same manner by which all other then-resident Magyars had acquired their lands: through inheritance, and not through purchase. In her case, she acquired lands that had been transmitted directly, sometimes via women, from at least the 1670s.)

In the Magyar pattern, then, fair-sized estates were worked with the horses, oxen, and unmechanized implements of the owners or of chiefly Romanian sharecroppers; labor was provided by landless agricultural servants or land-poor peasants for a wage in kind or—at best—partly in cash (Negoescu 1919:58); owners never sold their labor except in professions external to agriculture; and they seem to have shown little concern with increasing labor's productivity. It was estates such as these that supplied most of Transylvania's internal markets, whether with their own or with sharecroppers' harvests. From a regional perspective, this mode of estate management was in part cause and in part effect of the continued stagnation of Transylvanian agriculture, evident in an apparent trend toward increased sharecropping and decreased direct farming of Magyar estates in Binţinţi. From the viewpoint of the Romanian tenants, this mode was one of the few factors that enabled them to continue in possession of their own marginal holdings.

The German and Romanian patterns contrasted both with the Magyar pattern and with each other, their distinctive features perhaps best summarized by labeling the former a "petty-commodity producing" economy and the latter a "peasant" economy, differing in the far greater proportion of Germans' than of Romanians' total efforts that went toward market production. Since commercialization of farms did vary both by wealth and through time, however, I am less concerned to distinguish two types than to sketch two general patterns of smallholder farming, one of which was as diverse internally as it was unlike the other. The main elements differentiating the typical German and Romanian enterprises were average farm size, machine inventories and types of draft animals, the use of cash labor (or receipt of cash wages) to supplement family labor (or family income), the prevalence of sharecropping and its place in the domestic cycle, and a disposition to produce for cash sale on the market. On all counts, most Germans in Binţinţi behaved more like commercial farmers than did most Romanians; and this difference, while it became progressively less true of Romanians in some respects, held well into the 1920s, if not beyond.

The German population of Binţinţi, amounting to 20 percent of the village in 1910, had arrived in the 1890s as colonists on the estates of two bankrupt Magyars (see chap. 4, p. 207). They acquired their farms, ranging in size from nine to forty-five hectares, on a 24-year mortgage at 5 percent interest and at very favorable prices, to be paid in biannual installments. From the very beginning, Jakob Pfeiffer, like all the Germans, worked his thirty-five-hectare farm with horses, rather than with the oxen or milk cows Romanians used as draft animals. By 1900 or shortly thereafter, he and several others began to acquire mechanical seeders and harvesters, and he and one of his neighbors purchased steam-driven threshers with which they threshed all grain produced in the village, for a fee of about 6 percent. Pfeiffer paid cash in full for his machines, as was the general preference, though his neighbor bought in installments. For Pfeiffer, these purchases were not just advisable and "rational" in the name of efficiency but were also encouraged by inadequate family labor power, for his several children were all still young.

Pfeiffer filled his remaining labor needs with day laborers from Binţinţi and two nearby villages, whom he paid in cash. In addition (and unlike many of his fellows), he employed a farm servant or two, in exchange for room and board and a small cash wage. His chief noncash expenditures for labor were at the wheat harvest, when he was obliged to supplement his inadequate household labor with other workers. Some of these workers were poor peasants from nearby, others—their numbers a function of the size of Pfeiffer's kinship network—were urban kinsmen who returned for the harvest. Both groups received about one in eleven parts of the yield, per worker. Aside from harvest labor, Pfeiffer and other Germans paid cash unless their workers specifically requested otherwise (which was rare), even in periods of inflation and most notably during the depression. One informant whom I pressed on the availability of cash in lean years rejoined, as if irritated at my denseness, "We *always* kept a capital reserve for this sort of expenditure." Hence the saying among Romanians that someone "pays like a German"— meaning both cash and on time.

The Germans had two and sometimes three principal sources of cash: sales of grain, primarily wheat (by far the largest source of income); weekly cash sales of eggs and dairy products to clients in town;[5] and wages earned by unmarried sons working for urban tradesmen (income for only a few families and of short duration). Most wheat was carted to the town of Orăştie (an old Saxon town, nine kilometers distant) on its weekly market day. Farmers who could afford to wait held onto their grain until prices rose, others marketed whenever they needed cash to make purchases or payments (for mortgages, new equipment, or settlement sums to noninheriting siblings, among other things). A few Germans with unusually large stocks, such as the miller and Jakob Pfeiffer with his thresher, whose services were paid in grain, unloaded some of it to villagers who came from elsewhere in search of food. Sometimes Jewish merchants drove into the village and bought up this grain in bulk for shipment on the railway that runs through Binţinţi. Unknown among Romanians, this manner of sale was reportedly infrequent, since better prices could be gotten by carting one's grain to town and selling it oneself. One can see from Germans' marketing and purchasing habits that aside from their mortgages, they preferred to avoid losing profits to merchants.

The Germans' cash concerns, machine inventories, and demographic characteristics all resulted in a very low availability of German-owned land to be worked by anyone else. Therefore, the sharecropping arrangements that typically bound Romanians to Magyars rarely occurred between Romanians and Germans. Moreover, when land was available it might as readily be rented as sharecropped. The few who gave out land in sharecropping were elderly or infirm Germans without offspring, who contracted 50-50 sharecropping schemes to save themselves a trip to market for their consumption needs. If the tenants were Romanian rather than German, it might be because no Germans were at that moment interested in extra land or because those interested had found rental arrangements, which they preferred to sharecropping. Germans did sometimes sharecrop, but when this occurred it was usually limited to a specific phase in the domestic cycle—the years between a man's maturity and his father's retirement—and even then was a feature of only some, not all, households.

In contrast, few Romanian households were fortunate enough to be able to dispense with sharecropping after a few years' time, and many lived with it as an integral part of the agricultural round for much of their lives—sometimes turning it around in their old age, becoming to other peasants "rent capitalists," like the Magyar and Romanian gentlemen they themselves had served. Informants estimated that in general, no peasant family with less than 3 hectares, and few with less than 4.5 hectares, could subsist adequately without obtaining extra income from wage labor, sharecropping, or other supplementary activities. Lacking property figures from before the war, I can only hint at the magnitude of this stratum: in a list of village properties in the late 1930s — after a major land reform that rescued many peasants from the brink of disaster — about half the properties fall below 3 hectares and about three-fourths below 4.5 hectares. It is improbable that the situation was better in the early 1900s. Sharecropping was therefore likely to have been a permanent part of many Romanian household economies throughout most of their lifetimes.

Year after year from the time of his marriage, Ion Stoian supplemented his two-hectare holding with small pieces of one to two hectares, sharecropped from the locally resident owners. Like most in his situation, Stoian got this supplement for a 50-50 division of the harvest; it was rare to find a Romanian acquiring extra land for a fixed rent, whether in cash or in kind. Stoian's "landlords" included a German, some of the Magyars, and a number of his fellow Romanians: the village priest, two Romanian lawyers from elsewhere, several widows or elderly couples without children, some families temporarily absent in the army or abroad on labor migration, a few wealthier peasants whose health or labor reserves were inadequate for working the whole of their possessions. Stoian's sister-in-law was very explicit about the reasons for sharecropping: "We sharecropped so we wouldn't have to leave." From the way this woman and other informants spoke, there seems to have been a preference for sharecropping over cash day-labor. This preference may bespeak an unfavorable relationship between agricultural wages and the price of produce, or a desire to avoid market transactions by sharecropping for subsistence; but it may also reflect status notions from earlier times, when persons working land (serfs) were superior to those imported as landless laborers. It does seem that villagers who resorted to day labor were mainly the despised poor who lacked animals or sufficient implements for cultivation. These people were employed by other Romanians rarely, sometimes by Magyars, and most often by Germans.

What of those Romanians with less meager holdings, whose lands afforded them a livelihood without recourse to supplements? Did wealthier Romanians, not at subsistence margin, organize more modern farms along the lines of the Germans? "Wealthy" must be properly understood: the richest Romanian peasant in 1900 had less than thirty hectares of land (the priest had thirty-five hectares) and most of those whom others classified as rich had no more than about ten hectares, that is, scarcely more than the most modest of the German farms in this period. Take as an example Iosif Bogdan, who farmed nine hectares, and most decidedly did not run his enterprise in the German manner.

To begin with, neither Bogdan nor any other Romanian acquired agricultural machinery until well after World War I. His inventory consisted of oxen, cart, plow, harrow, and hoe. He worked with oxen (those who could not afford to keep oxen worked with cows), sowed and harvested by hand, and threshed by hand as well until Germans brought in threshing machines. German informants report with amusement that like most Romanians, Bogdan sowed grain by walking along the plowed furrows carrying a plank, against which his wife threw the seeds to scatter them. To Germans this exemplified the backward and irrational technology and work habits of the Romanians, for as a sowing procedure it was more wasteful of seed than a mechanical seeder (hence it cut into the consumable or salable yield), and it produced not neat, easy-to-weed rows of maize but a chaotic jumble—the sort of jumble, a Romanian observed to me, within which peasants of earlier days were sufficiently hidden from view as to "cover the weeds with dirt, for the master isn't looking" (p. 126 above).

Despite their critical stance (and one doubts that their fathers were more tolerant), German informants recognize that even for a peasant of Bogdan's resources, much less for poorer Romanians, small farm size gave Romanians less reason than Germans to experiment with labor-saving devices. Modest resources, however, still do not excuse other aspects of what Germans saw as irrational farming, particularly practices connected with religion. Bogdan was no exception among Romanians for his deference to the saints of the Orthodox church, whose numerous holidays he observed by refraining from all agricultural work. As a consequence, heavy rains, hailstorms, or early frosts often caught his ripe crops still sitting out in the fields while he socialized with the saints—a habit perhaps quite rational in earlier days, when those crops were mostly not his own. Such disastrous losses rarely befell his efficient German neighbors, if we are to believe their reports; but Romanians have a fund of tales recounting the misfortunes of nonbelievers who worked on religious holidays, angering saints who apparently stood on the Romanian side of the class struggle.

Another major difference between Romanian farms like Bogdan's and that of, say, Jakob Pfeiffer, was that although both imported labor, Bogdan almost never paid wages but secured extra labor in one of three nonmonetary ways. First, he exchanged labor in cooperative arrangements with neighbors and kinsmen, all working to hoe or weed the crops of one household on a given day and moving the next day to those of the next person. In this his work arrangements were not unlike those of peasants with somewhat less land, such as Gheorghe Pera, who could work his fields adequately with family labor but often engaged in labor exchanges anyway. The principal difference between Bogdan and Pera, if data collected for a later period are valid for earlier years as well, is that the Bogdans of the village tended to associate somewhat more with kinsmen and less with (nonkin) neighbors, the Peras more with neighbors, reflecting Bogdan's use of kinship ties to counter the inequitable labor demands at which his poorer neighbors might balk.

Second, Bogdan was among those wealthiest of Romanian peasants who completed their labor needs by holding an occasional "work party" (*clacă*). For periodic weeding or other tasks, he would provide a day's food and drink in exchange for the labor of a number of others, often his ritual kinsmen, for as a rich peasant Bogdan was frequently asked to sponsor other villagers' marriages and baptisms. His diffuse obligations as sponsor (*naş*), such as actual or potential backing in money matters or local politics, won in return a sense of willing obligation on the part of the person he sponsored (*fin*), which often meant extra labor for him. This arrangement was completely absent among Germans, who did not utilize ritual kinship as a social institution.

Third, at harvest time Bogdan, like most Romanians with more than five hectares of land, would import teams of workers from upland villages, providing them with food and lodging and paying them between one-tenth and one-thirteenth of the harvest. Differences in altitude between Binţinţi and upland villages meant that uplanders were free for this sort of work, since their own crops did not require maximal labor inputs until about three weeks later, and ecological differences made them eager for these arrangements since most of them could not grow enough wheat and maize on their mountain farms to sustain them throughout the year.

All three of these ways of obtaining labor without paying cash — labor exchanges, work parties, and upland imports — had antecedents in the feudal economy. In those times, different serf households associated to work with one another if neither had sufficient oxen for plowing their own or the lord's fields; indeed, in the Cziráky conscription of 1820, some nobles specified that serfs with too few animals *must* associate to fulfill their *robot* obligations.[6] One can imagine bailiffs encouraging peasant cooperation further so as to provide adequate labor without inefficient delays, and the peasants themselves may have found such arrangements beneficial for their own tillage. The feudal economy also saw many work parties, organized both by the landlord for his serfs (Imreh 1965:145) and also by the richest serfs to secure necessary additional labor. Since ritual kinship was rarely practiced across religious lines, its moral ideology probably did little to mitigate the exploitative overtones of work parties held by landlords (though it surely did within the serf population), but notions of the landlord as patron might have salved relations somewhat. Finally, a third important feature of labor organization on feudal estates was that laborers were moved around from one part of the estate to another according to seasonal changes in the need for labor (ibid.). The major landlords in nineteenth century Binţinţi had serfs in upland villages as well (see Grimm 1863, list I), whom they could easily have brought down for lowland harvests in the manner later used by rich Romanian peasants. In addition, it is clear that even in feudal times landlords sometimes imported upland labor with payment in kind: a late eighteenth-century document in the Macskásy collection lists large amounts of wheat paid to residents of three upland villages (and smaller amounts of hay to some lowland villagers) in exchange for labor in Binţinţi (MC #471).

My reason for mentioning the feudal antecedents of noncash labor arrangements is to suggest the very different historical and environmental contexts of "rationality" for Romanians as compared with Germans. For Germans, commercial farming was not a novelty in Transylvania but the normal state of affairs, given that they had migrated from an area farther west where their ancestors and their own families had been heavily involved for at least a century in grain exports for Viennese consumers. This tendency was reinforced by two features of their situation once they arrived in Transylvania. First, having purchased rather than inherited their large farms, they had mortgages to pay, which necessitated at least some cash income. Second, close to a town of moderate size but constant growth (Orăştie increased by 10 to 11 percent per decade between 1890 and 1910) and surrounded by a poor rural population much of which relied on grain purchases in a relatively grain-poor Transylvanian economy, they enjoyed steady markets for the grains they produced. Thus, their unflagging — and successful — cash orientation was amply rooted in both their history and their contemporary environment.

The Romanians' situation was different in many respects, despite apparent similarities in the environments of the two groups. Romanians were heirs to a long-standing social system characterized by the constant movement of upland peasants into lowland estates, over several centuries, for acquiring loans, temporary employment, and food, as well as sometimes for fulfilling feudal obligations to low-land masters some uplanders served. This pattern of labor move-ment and this mode of acquiring labor were part of the history "given" to Romanian peasants of 1900; they constituted, along with labor exchanges and work parties, time-worn procedures for aug-menting household labor supplies without spending cash. One sees a shadow of the different rationality to which this contributed, in the following statements from Romanian informants in the 1970s: "We didn't need machines, since we had uplanders." "We didn't need horses, since we could cooperate with others who had cattle." "We would *never* pay for labor if we could bring it in without paying."

Romanian agricultural practices also had as part of their history decades of heavy feudal exactions, consisting of labor on the demesne rather than feudal rents, which curtailed the possibilities for com-modity production and market involvement for all but the wealthiest and largest peasant families. Once serfdom was abolished, condi-tions changed somewhat but not enough, given the legacy of land fragmentation and the tiny plots inherited by the serfs. If feudal "rationality" perdured long after feudalism, it was precisely because so few of the larger parameters of economic organization changed, as problematic property structures went unameliorated and Tran-sylvanian agriculture continued to stagnate despite the successes of a few German farmers. Trapped between the more efficient cereal-raising economies of Hungary and Romania, to west and southeast, Transylvanian grains still moved chiefly toward internal markets (and chiefly from larger farms), which were not expanding fast enough to transform peasant agricultural habits very rapidly. In-dustry was growing, yet too slowly to generate numerous urban consumers for peasants products: between 1890 and 1910, Transyl-vania's rate of urbanization increased by only 2 percent, from 10.7 to 12.5 percent of the population.

Insofar as there was any export demand for a Transylvanian agricultural product, that product was livestock, which appears to have been raised for sale on both large estates and (some) peasant holdings. Informants do remember a few villagers, both rich and poor, who marketed some cattle; and from these recollections it seems that the poorer may have done so on the example of landlords who employed them as agricultural servants. There is no evidence, however, that this export market was large or engaged many villag-ers. The general economic context explains not only Romanians' relative undercommercialization but also their reliance on share-cropping: with inadequate wage labor in industry or agriculture to permit marginal peasants to buy the food they could not grow, sharecropping kept alive on the land a population that would otherwise have emigrated or starved, given the contours of the regional economy.

Any interest Binţinţi peasants might have had in cash transactions was further retarded by those with whom they regularly interacted. First, it is said that imported seasonal workers actually preferred payment in kind because it saved them from having to take their wages and displace themselves still farther afield to buy food at the market. The direct payment obviated two trips to market and was mutually convenient. Second, a large number of the goods villagers required were supplied through exchanges in kind with peasants from elsewhere rather than via the market. Peasants came from other ecological environments with necessary firewood, fruits, wine and brandy, storage barrels, ceramics and other items, which they preferred to exchange for grain rather than cash, further reinforcing the "cash-laziness" of Binţinţi villagers. Third, even within the village, local tradesmen who made shoes, carts, and plows often accepted or even preferred payments in kind, since all of them had taken on these trades because they could not adequately subsist on their own lands. These encouragements made it perfectly reasonable for most Romanians to avoid the market; and with this, they— like Germans— avoided the merchant's cut. One can even argue that their environment (and what was rational within it) was not the same as the Germans' at all.

Let me summarize the contrasting German and Romanian patterns that prevailed between the 1890s and World War I. In the German pattern, medium-sized farms fully adequate for subsistence were worked with horses and agricultural machinery belonging to the owners of the land; family members and hired Romanian workers paid largely in cash were the chief providers of labor; persons rarely resorted to selling their own labor except perhaps as tenants or sharecroppers during a brief period in early adulthood; and high market involvement in grain growing entailed great concern with productivity, marketability and profit. The Romanian pattern shows a range of farms at least half of which were inadequate for subsistence, worked with cattle and no mechanization other than the use of German-owned threshing machines; much of the land actively worked by Romanians at any given time was not owned by the workers but sharecropped, and Romanians were also found working as day laborers; family members, kinsmen, and neighbors provided labor on most farms aside from the largest, where ritual kinsmen and imported uplanders supplemented these sources, all without cash outlays; and market involvement was low, centering (such as there was) upon cattle rather than grains.

It would be erroneous to picture Romanian peasants as completely or uniformly insulated from the market, for *all* peasants needed cash for taxes, and a number of peasants, mainly some among the wealthier but a few poorer as well, wanted cash to pay for land purchases, which appear on the property registers during this period. Nonetheless, I believe it is fair to represent the Romanian population of Binţinţi as generally much less commercialized than the German population and to link this with differences in the organization of their agricultural enterprises. Both of these were linked, in turn, to different economic rationalities with divergent historical antecedents, in the feudal relationship between Romanians and Magyars, on the one hand, and in the prior commercial agriculture and continued cash imperatives of the German colonists on the other. A couple of my German informants expressed something like this view themselves when, after describing at length the backward and irrational agricultural practices of Romanians, they added, as if uncomfortable at this display of criticism, "But what else could you expect? The Romanians were serfs, after all, and it wasn't their fault if centuries of oppression kept them from advancing."

COMMERCIALIZATION, CLASS POSITIONS, AND INTERACTIONS BETWEEN GROUPS

Analysts accustomed to a structuralist view of class, rather than the historical and contextual view employed here, might argue that to explain differential commercialization one need not resort to history and environment but only to look at the different rural class positions of the two groups. In fact, some of my native "analysts" also understood the situation in this way ("The Romanians didn't need horses and machines, their farms were too small"). This would make ethnically linked "rationalities" merely the cultural form of position in the rural stratificational order. Although the association of German ethnic identity with the rural upper strata and Romanian identity with the lower positions clearly contributed to their separate views of the world, it would be inappropriate to reduce the differences in German-Romanian farming patterns to nothing but rural class structure, as is obvious from the fact that the dissimilar histories of the two groups and differences in their perception of what was relevant in the environment were as important as rural class position.

Even those who remain adamant structuralists, however, must recognize that the different behaviors of Germans and Romanians were conditioned far beyond their local structural positions. Their two rationalities were products of their participation in a regional class system, with the bulk of Germans situated above the bulk of Romanians both in agriculture and in commerce and trade (see fig. 4–1). From the moment that the German "upper class" of Binţinţi established connections with the Transylvanian Saxon bourgeoisie — a connection established even though the Swabian colonists and the Saxon bourgeoisie themselves had no history in common except their inclusion in an empire in which nationality had become the decisive factor — German-Romanian relations in Binţinţi became a microcosm for Transylvania's historical and territorial division between the commercializing Saxon areas and the feudal Magyar Counties (see chap. 3). It was not merely their rural class position but this linkage to a region-wide German ethnic group, with a specific history and in a time of nationalist ferment, that determined the rationality of Binţinţi's Germans.

These two factors together, the Germans' rural class position and their relationship to the solidary Saxon community of the region, also laid the foundations for an almost complete self-isolation of Germans within the local community, which aggravated their cultural differences from Romanians. The primary institutional vehicle for separating Germans from Romanians in Binţinţi was religion. The two groups shared almost no social events, for most of their festivities were organized around their two distinctive faiths. The noncongruence of the Lutheran and Orthodox religious calendars meant that their separate celebrations of even the major religious holidays (Christmas, Easter) occurred on the same day only once in seven years. The centrality of religion in the lives of both groups separated them from childhood onward, since children of each group attended confessional schools. Social events connected with the life cycle (baptisms, weddings) and other organized social functions like village dances were also segregated, as differences in language reinforced those of religion.

Social relations were segregated in other ways also. Between 1896 and 1918 there were two interethnic marriages, both involving a spouse from outside. The one of these couples that remained in Binţinţi did not create affinal networks between the two groups, since the kin of the German groom lived in another community. Kinship ties were further restricted by religious differences that prevented networks of fictive kinship, so common among Romanians, from binding the two groups together. I have little information concerning the existence of close friendships across the ethnic boundaries in this period; as for visiting patterns, the Germans lived in residential clusters separate from most Romanians, and this would have kept casual visiting—not exaggerated even in the present—to a minimum.

Formal institutions did not make up for the lack of informal ties. The village council, itself not a vital community organ, contained a token German whose role and participation appear to have been nominal. Germans studiously avoided creating or contributing to controversy in village life; this member's chief duty was to report to other Germans any important decisions, of which there were few. The token councilman was the only formal role to imply that Germans and Romanians might constitute a single community.

Another point of potential contact was villagers' use of the several resident craftsmen and purveyors of local services. Many of the certified specialists in the village were Germans, and German villagers manifested great disdain for the abilities of the few Romanians who professed a skill. Where there was only one practitioner of a certain trade, he was usually a German and had clients from both groups; this was the case with the village barber, roofer, and miller. Germans sometimes used the village cobbler, who was first a Magyar and later a Romanian (the only Romanian workman whose talents they applauded) but more often they had shoes made in Orăştie. All the village wheelwrights were Romanians; Germans took their business to urban specialists. Village midwives were also Romanian; a few German women used them, but more brought in midwives from town. Where there were both Romanian and German practitioners of a trade, as with the village smiths, each ethnic group tended to go to the practitioner of its own group, although not exclusively. There was a succession of small village stores throughout the period, patronized mainly by Romanians; Germans bought their wares in a large German store in Orăştie when they went to market each week. Of the two village taverns, one had been opened by a German near the German section of Binţinţi and was frequented by Germans; several of the richer Romanians also preferred it, making it the most regular locus of the simultaneous presence of German and Romanian men—who nonetheless tended to socialize separately. In sum, the provision of services in the village gave an opportunity for a few German specialists to serve Romanian clients, but custom in the reverse direction was almost nil.

The only remaining context in which some Germans had regular, if periodic, interaction with Romanians was when they hired wage laborers or arranged sharecropping contracts. Because their fields lay against the borders of two neighboring villages, many of the Germans' Romanian day laborers were not from Binținți; and sharecropping, as already mentioned, tied Romanian tenants to Germans infrequently. Therefore the Germans of Binținți managed to avoid the appearance of exploiting their Romanian covillagers while still occasionally providing them with desirable occasions for cash wages.

Alongside the few relations that lay like fragile one-way bridges across the yawning chasm between Romanians and Germans in the village, between the upper and the lower strata, there was one more relationship that neatly captures the contrasting rationalities, systemic linkages, and social trajectories of these two groups. Shortly after 1900, a small store appeared in the village, opened by Frau Müller, whose husband had recently transmitted the farm to their son and retired from its responsibilities. Frau Müller sold matches, tobacco, candy, sugar, lamp oil, and a few other items to Romanian clients (Germans bought them cheaper in town), taking as payment either cash or two kinds of produce: maize and eggs. She herself marketed the maize she accumulated in this manner; the eggs were carefully packed into large crates and sold to Jewish merchants for sale in cities, reportedly as far away as Budapest.[7]

From the Romanian point of view, Frau Müller was a bargain: those who had no cash could still pick up what they needed, and she was very obliging, as well. From the point of view of Hungarian tobacco growers and sugar refineries farther west, she helped expand the internal market. From Frau Müller's point of view, retirement proved unexpectedly lucrative. She made a good profit on her inflated prices, and gold she (inexplicably) received from her Jewish merchants accumulated so rapidly during the terrific inflation around World War I—egg prices in Budapest increased 1,106 percent between 1910 and 1918[8]—that her children were soon able to purchase sizable chunks of land. In this way Frau Müller, faithfully representing the commercially-minded Saxon community of Transylvania, helped keep her numerous German offspring wealthy farmers by bartering a few lumps of sugar for a few eggs from market-shy Romanians.

INHERITANCE, HOUSEHOLD FORM, AND DOMESTIC RELATIONS

Frau Müller's method for reproducing her class position through time was unusual for Binținți. The more common mechanism by which Romanians and Germans perpetuated their positions in the

rural stratification system was inheritance, whose norms and practices differed between the two groups in precisely the direction that
would reinforce the contrasts described above. Linked with inheritance were differences in household organization, patterns of migration, and consequent patterns of region-wide class recruitment. In
the present section I will turn from divergent patterns in the social
organization of agriculture to these further social-organizational
contrasts between Romanians and Germans, focusing particularly
on inheritance and domestic life. I pursue four objectives at once
in this discussion, expanding upon themes already evident: to speculate about the historical origins of organizational disparities between
Binţinţi's Germans and Romanians; to underscore the importance
of interactions between the village-level forms of these disparities
and the structural positions of the two groups in Transylvanian
society; to investigate how what is historically given is nonetheless
also perpetuated and modified by the patterned behavior of individuals; and to convey a sense of the texture of individuals' daily
lives as they are affected by these group-specific behavioral differences.

Romanian peasants selected their marriage partners under the
guidance but not the absolute authority of their parents, who (if
nothing else) might register strong disapproval by threatening, and
occasionally delivering, a reduced dowry. Marriage negotiations
consisted principally of agreeing on just how much land of what
quality would be transferred at marriage and where the couple
would reside. At marriage each offspring received a portion of the
parental holdings, which were subdivided into N more or less
equivalent pieces for each of the N offspring, plus an additional
piece that was reserved for the parents. (This extra portion sometimes went to the child who remained at marriage and cared for
the parents in their old age; the share allotted this child was in any
case larger than that of his siblings.)

Forms of postmarital residence were governed by several ideal
conceptions that often conflicted: to marry all offspring into a
house (whether their spouse's, the parents', or one built or purchased
for them), to avoid uxorilocal marriages if possible, and to keep the
youngest child at home. In practice, offspring who remained with
their parents often were men at or near the end of the sibling set,
some men did marry into their wives' households, and many couples
took up neolocal residence. About half of all Romanian marriages
in this century led to virilocal residence, the proportion remaining
more or less constant over time; of the remaining half, neolocal
residence was more common than uxorilocal early in the century,

although even so about a fifth of all residence choices were uxori-local. As for the place or origin of the spouses, between 1895 and 1920 over two-thirds of all marriage partners contracted endoga-mous unions, while far more women than men departed the village through marriage.[9]

Inheritance among Romanians was often a two-step process, as I have implied above: offspring received a part of their inheritance at marriage and the rest when their parents died or became too old to work it. The two essential rules governing inheritance were endowment of a portion at marriage and approximately equal division of assets among offspring (except perhaps for the one left at home), but actual practices varied widely. For example, if a woman married virilocally and her husband's family were very well off, she might receive only a small amount at marriage since the initial viability of her farm was not at stake. Departures from equal division might occur if one child could win an especially desirable match only through a disproportionate dowry, if a suitor of one sibling did not press for an equitable share, or if the parents were at odds with a child and penalized him with less. Among very poor families, offspring who migrated to cities might forego their share altogether, or one or two offspring might be given a patch of land and the others nothing. I suspect, but do not have the data to prove, that women received a share less often than men among families of few means and that women may in general have received less than an equal share. Nonetheless, informants claim equality as the rule, and unequal division has caused several conflicts and even court cases among siblings.

On almost every point mentioned above, German practice differed from that of Romanians. Inheritance was what I call quasi-impartible, estates were not carved up until the dotage of the parents, the heir in the household was an elder rather than younger child and was invariably male unless there were no surviving sons, and defiance of definitive spouse selection by one's parents was almost impossible, usually achieved only through elopement and departure. Germans resembled Romanians in residing virilocally about half the time, but they differed in almost never marrying into the wife's household (marriages that were not virilocal were neolocal).

The inheritance rule of the Swabian colonists in Austria-Hungary — the parent population of Binţinţi's Germans — was impartible inheritance, usually by an eldest son, with cash payments to the other offspring. Germans in Binţinţi modified this somewhat by giving a disproportionately large share to one or sometimes two offspring, always males and generally among the elder; younger sons were apprenticed in the towns and became urban tradesmen, and they along with their sisters received very small portions of land. Rarely was any land transmitted before the marriage of the last child or the father's decision that he would retire.

Because in the first generation German families were larger than Romanian ones (most had between five and nine adult survivors, as against two to six among Romanians), quasi impartibility reduced farm size more than would have occurred if farms had passed intact to one offspring who paid all the others cash. This departure from impartibility may have been an adaptation to the relative under-development of Transylvanian urbanism, which precluded sure live-lihood for urban tradesmen (whose small plots at home helped cushion their incomes) and also reduced markets sufficiently to make it difficult for farm heirs to come up with cash payments for each of many siblings (cf. Mayhew 1973:133). Several strategies helped mitigate the fragmenting effects of quasi impartibility. Some outmarrying siblings—especially the numerous outmarrying sisters —opted for cash in place of their smaller share of land. Endogamous marriages consolidated some shares into more viable holdings.[10] And some Germans resorted to first-cousin marriages and sibling exchanges; in one case, three pairs of step-siblings married from a combined sibset of fifteen. These examples still cause excitement among Romanians, whom the Orthodox church prohibits from marrying within the range of second cousins or close affines.

As among Romanians, marriage and the eventual designation of an heir produced a household of stem form, but while Romanians preferred a younger child Germans preferred an elder. If an eldest son tired of waiting, the position devolved on his next-younger brother, a circumstance that occurred more often than not. The frequent defection of eldest sons resulted from their fathers' low average age at marriage (about twenty-four years) coupled with very late transmission of the property. An eldest son might reach age forty and still be the equivalent of his father's agricultural servant (taking in land on the side), while younger brothers were well into commercial careers. He might finally weary of abasement to his father's continual demands and strike out on his own.

Table 5-1 compares German and Romanian heirs to the parental home—what I call "stem heirs," who were also in both groups the offspring inheriting the most land. The table shows all possible sib-ling positions, for sibsets of three or more containing both sexes. Because the major points to be made do not require a detailed breakdown for female heirs, these are lumped together in the top row of the table. Each cell shows a percentage representing the number of heirs in a given sibling position divided by all persons who occupy that position in the sample (that is, for example, how many heirs were there among all elder-born sons); actual totals appear in parentheses. A strong male bias is evident for both groups, stronger for Germans than for Romanians; Germans show a much greater preference for elder sons (see row 3) and Romanians for younger sons (see row 5). If the figures for German elder sons are disaggregated (not shown), one finds more heirs among second-born than among first-born sons. In general, the results confirm Germans' normative statements in favor of primogeniture and Romanians' in favor of ultimogeniture, while also indicating Romanians' somewhat greater willingness to live with a son-in-law as farm manager rather than with a son. The patterns exhibited are constant over time with one important exception, which explains

TABLE 5-1. Heirs to Parental Homesteads, Binţinţi Germans and Romanians. All mixed-sex offspring sets containing three or more adult offspring. Number of heirs in sample: 18 Germans, 66 Romanians.

Sibling position[a]	Germans		Romanians	
	Percent who are heirs, among all occupants of a given sibling position			
Daughter — all sibling positions[b]	2	$\left(\frac{1}{59}\right)$	9	$\left(\frac{14}{151}\right)$
Only son (with 2 or more sisters)	83	$\left(\frac{5}{6}\right)$	65	$\left(\frac{15}{23}\right)$
First- or second-born son with younger brothers (plus 1 or more sisters)	41	$\left(\frac{9}{22}\right)$	14	$\left(\frac{9}{25}\right)$
Middle-born son	0	$\left(\frac{0}{14}\right)$	18	$\left(\frac{3}{17}\right)$
Last-born son	25	$\left(\frac{3}{12}\right)$	58	$\left(\frac{25}{43}\right)$

[a] Where there are only two sons, they appear as first-born and last-born. The category "middle-born sons" includes only those men having two or more elder and one or more younger brothers, as well as elder and/or younger sisters. The distribution of sisters seems irrelevant to the outcome for male heirs.

[b] Among Romanians, half of the female heirs are the last-born child in their family; 30% are the family's only daughter.

an otherwise puzzling irregularity in the table: deaths and emigrations of elder brothers during World War II produced unprecedented youngest-son heirs (as well as the one female heir) among the Germans.

Before asking about the significance of these differences, one might speculate as to their origins. Whether or not the German norm of impartibility antedated their departure from their Swabian homeland toward their eighteenth-century colonies in southern Hungary (whence they migrated to Binţinţi in the 1890s), as obedient citizens of the Austrian Military Border they were under strong legal pressure not to divide their farms. Their postponed estate transfer and preference for elder-son heirs might be rooted, I hypothesize, in the labor requirements of peasant farms competing with the more highly capitalized and rapidly commercializing estates of the Hungarian gentry in their midst. Given that nonheirs would depart once the heir were selected, mobilizing an adequate labor pool meant postponing transfer of the estate, retaining as many offspring as possible in a subservient role. Hungarian demographic research shows for the early 1800s a correlation of precisely the factors that defined the situation of these Germans at the time: large households among free peasants developing along capitalist lines in conditions of manpower shortage and relatively abundant land (Andorka 1979:24). That the heir would more often be an elder than a younger son followed naturally from the earlier maturation of his offspring, who could begin replacing the labor of departing nonheirs sooner than anyone else's children. This would also make the eldest son the logical heir in the event of a father's premature death. Should an eldest son tire of waiting, the benefits of patience would tend to devolve upon his next-younger brother for the same reason (see Cole and Wolf 1974:242).

The Romanian inheritance and household patterns are probably rooted at least to some extent in feudal history, given the power of landlords to affect peasant inheritance practices and household forms as well as possible counterstrategies by the peasants (see, e.g., Kula 1972, Plakans 1975), but precisely how partibility and ultimogeniture emerged from this is not clear. Several things might have caused younger rather than elder sons to remain in the parental house. In late feudal times, from 1700 on, when landlords were hungry for extra labor, one of their principal stratagems was to try to subdivide existing peasant households so as to create new ones, and to exact labor obligations from the several new household heads. The peasants' interest, in contrast, was to keep together as large a unit as possible, so as to lose as little as possible of their total labor power to *robot* (M. Ursuţiu 1979:234-236). Many hands made prosperous serf households, a connection that shows up often in the statistical preponderance of large extended families among the richer serfs (Stys 1957, for Poland; Andorka 1979:20-21, for Hungary 1770-1820). If peasants could keep their households large, they could shield themselves from the economic change and land scarcities that pressed many toward proletarian status, by devoting more labor to the care of animals and to producing small marketable surpluses (Andorka 1979:25).

Given the minuscule size of most serf holdings (see p. 162, above), even serf families who saw the benefits of extended-family collaboration might still exceed the carrying capacity of their small parcels. In this situation they were very vulnerable when the landlord's agents came and urged them to "marry and set up new families" (M. Ursuţiu 1979:235), on subdivisions of the original holding or often on new lands the master might himself provide.[11] By the mid-1700s there were no longer tax incentives to keep households from dividing, since taxes were figured not by "portals" but by the number of animals and working adults in each household unit. These circumstances made it likely that if a holding could not support an extended household, offspring would depart the parental home more or less in order, at or after their marriages, perhaps as the increasing requirements of their growing families began to tax household resources and provoke discord, and certainly as the offspring of elder siblings became capable of rendering the field assistance that would make a new household viable. In this way the stem heirs would tend to be children near the end of the offspring set, last to marry and last subjected to the exhortations of the landlord's agents. They were likely to be sons rather than daughters even if daughters were younger, given the male-female differential in age at marriage and given a probable male bias (evident in Hungarian inheritance notions, at least).[12] This set of speculations suggests that Romanian household form, like that of the Germans, was the result of interactions between external environments and peasant households trying to secure an adequate labor force; but the outcome differed for the two ethnic groups because the external environmental constraints were of very different kinds.

Understanding Romanian inheritance practices involves even more guesswork than does household form. There was very little specific legislation concerning inheritance among serfs in Hungary and Transylvania; these were matters regulated more by manorial custom and private law than by national legal codes (Király 1975: 50 n. 20). Research on these manorial customs and their actual execution is still in its infancy. Among the few certainties are that the sons of a serf had a (theoretical) right to divide his holding (Botezan n.d.:49), but lords could refuse this and also had great discretion in disposing of a dead serf's movable property, the widow receiving no more than a third of the animals and implements while the rest reverted to the lord (Prodan 1971:99). It is plausible that serfs might have sought to avoid this by a premortem division of movable property, as a safeguard against its repossession.[13] Given low life expectancies,[14] endowment of each child's portion at marriage (rather than later) may have provided the greatest security. At the same time, however, dispersal of property at marriage fed directly into the designs of the landlord by creating the conditions for early independence of constituent households, and it was precisely in the number of his independent households that the lord's chief assets lay. By dividing the estate before fathers could become patriarchs presiding over households of grown sons, this custom reduced paternal authority and, with it, the chance that powerful peasant households would arise to challenge the landlord's social position.

Although serfs had no inviolable provisions for transmitting their feudal plots, it seems that lords in Hungary and perhaps also in Transylvania tended to allow offspring of a serf to divide his holdings (Andorka 1976:340) and even encouraged this as long as the resulting households were not incapable of supplying the manual and draft labor the lord required. Where unviability threatened, some of the heirs could be settled on new plots — perhaps an allodial plot, or that of a serf who had died without heirs, or of one who had died with children still so young that the lord threw the whole family out and replaced it (Barițiu 1889:387), or a holding freed by the marriage of a widow and widower hoping to escape jeopardy to their families and belongings (Kula 1972).[15]

One can easily imagine such considerations determining inheritance outcomes through 1848 (and on into the late 1800s for allodial serfs still subject to lordly control), as landlords encouraged the subdivision of some serf tenures and "dowered" other serfs with new portions at marriage. One can also imagine serfs and their families being uninterested in preventing the equal division of property among offspring when division of the household finally became necessary: it was no concern of theirs if a new household had inadequate oxen for the lord's *robot*, especially since they could continue to associate among themselves for their own needs. How these historical conditions became converted into the rustic "traditions" of partibility and ultimogeniture found in the twentieth century is, of course, a separate question, and one that I will not belabor.[16]

Let us turn to some of the effects or correlates of the German and Romanian inheritance systems. First is the consequence noted at the beginning of this discussion: the different inheritance customs reproduced through time the rural class differences that were intertwined with Romanian-German ethnic differences.[17] A wealthier population of Germans transmitting its farms primarily in one or two large chunks, with some attrition around the edges, would tend to maintain a more favorable property structure than a poorer Romanian population dividing its farms among all heirs in each generation. Germans would retain an adequate property base for commercial farming while Romanians stayed closer to the subsistence margin, reversing the situation only by a radical drop in fertility or by initiating other strategies to keep Romanian farms intact. Something of these strategies will be seen in the next chapter. Through World War I, however, the relative economic positions of locally resident Germans and Romanians were neatly maintained.[18]

Second, German impartibility tended to expel labor from rural areas while Romanian partibility kept laborers in agriculture (even though they had to sharecrop and work for wages so they "wouldn't have to leave"). This supported the tendency for these Germans, like Transylvania's Germans as a group, to be more urbanized than Romanians, and it also fed into the region-wide differentiation between an urban petite bourgeoisie that was largely German and a marginal peasantry and rural (and international) proletariat that was largely Romanian. Thus, local inheritance practices funneled the people of Binţinţi into Transylvania's more and less advantaged ethno-class positions, apparent in figure 4-1. Moreover, a partible inheritance custom that kept a large labor surplus in agriculture would not have been disagreeable to cash-poor and labor-hungry estate owners, who therefore would not have been likely to legislate it away by making inheritance impartible (one thinks of the benefits of partibility for the pre-Famine lords of Ireland). One might see partibility as playing directly into estate-owners' hands, eminently suited to the residual agricultural sector dominated by its postfeudal nobility, just as the impartibility of Binţinţi Germans suited their position in the urban economy of Transylvania's Saxons.

Inheritance also affected the continuity of social status within the two ethnic communities and had major implications—not necessarily realized—for the maintenance of kinship ties across status gaps within each of them. Cole and Wolf, as part of their masterly discussion of the correlates between inheritance systems (ideology and practices) and other aspects of social life (1974: chaps. 8, 11), observe that inheritance creates conditions for recruiting a village's

core population. Binţinţi Germans recruited their core population
in an authoritarian manner that expelled some offspring and tended
to maintain the lineal continuity of a few families in elite positions,
as differences in property — an important basis of status — were transmitted with some faithfulness. Romanian partibility, in contrast,
tended toward recruitment by chance, since obtaining respectable
property qualifications was largely a function of demography in
this era of low commercial involvement and relatively closed land
markets. I found, in a crude tabulation of the mobility rates of
Romanians prior to World War I, that the principal determinant
of upward or downward movement in socioeconomic status between
1880 and 1920 was not mere wealth but the combination of wealth
and sibset size.[19] Given that in this period rich and poor peasants
tended to have larger sibsets than did middle peasants, fertility had
democratizing effects, since epidemics and famines would kill more
offspring of the poor than of the rich, reducing partition of dwarf
farms while larger ones continued to be divided. The result was that
although rich peasants were likely to be more successful than poorer
ones in expanding their estates within the constraints of the economy, in order to counter the downward trajectories of their larger
offspring sets, in each generation the Romanian village elite had a
slightly different composition from the previous generation. The
composition of the village poor changed similarly, as, with the help
of demography, some families' fortunes declined while others
climbed, and a few poor lines disappeared altogether, evident in
the fact that of families present in the 1890s but absent in 1920 the
large majority are from the ranks of the poor.

The German and Romanian inheritance systems thus provide two
models for recruiting the village population. In one, families represented in the village are stable over time and roughly the same lines
are poor and rich in each generation. In the other, the community
constantly percolates with potential elites and outcasts. The authority inherent in the father's position is greater in one than in the
other, as well. A status order of stability and continuity is juxtaposed
to one characterized by fluidity and uncertainty — and possibility.
In all likelihood, "possibility" was not, however, viewed as "opportunity," for one might speculate that in the German system people
would be prone to see their fate as managed by personal forces —
the father's will, the tenacity of elder brothers — while in the Romanian
system the determinants would seem impersonal — accidental death,
the number of children God sends. Whatever the perceptions, in

one a hierarchical authority structure in the family pushes nonheirs out, while in the other a network of kinsmen spreads its web across the community, inherently eliminating very few.

This last statement should not lead us to think, however, that the labor-expelling German system necessarily entailed the rupture of kin ties while the Romanian system preserved them. One might expect impartibility to drive a wedge into the ethnic solidarity of Binţinţi Germans in their rural and urban occupations, but this seems not to have been true.[20] Part of the reason, ironically, may have been the underdeveloped state of Transylvania's economy. If impartibility tended to separate rural heirs from their migrant siblings, what reduced the social distance between these groups was kinship — not the simple existence of rural-urban networks but the use of kinship to solve problems of both urban and rural kinsmen. German farmers in Binţinţi had large enough farms to require labor at peak periods, and urban Germans were pressed by Transylvania's low urbanization to rely on rural relatives for a portion of their year's supply of food. At harvest each year, those village Germans with urban kinsmen enjoyed the extra labor of carpenters, glaziers, smiths, and tailors, who left their urban workshops to help bring in the harvest. Like other harvest workers they were paid a percentage of the yield, important to their household economies, but unlike other workers they were first hired and last fired because, as kinsmen and Germans, they were regarded as the most reliable and efficient workers. At a time when ethnic feeling was high, as Transylvania's Romanians and Magyars sought entry into the traditional German strongholds with increasing insistence, kin ties helped ethnic sentiment to bridge the gap between Germans' urban and rural occupations.

The bridging of such gaps was less problematic for Romanians, who were more uniformly rural in their occupations than Germans and whose inheritance practices produced less marked differentiation within their kin groups. There were, surely, potential sources of friction within the Romanian population, such as tensions among siblings over equality of inheritance, or possible antagonisms between richer and poorer peasants (subjects for which information is now almost impossible to recover). But although differences of wealth and occupation were doubtless significant to Binţinţi Romanians and would soon become even more so, there is good reason to suspect that these paled beside the ethnic differences so pervasive in their social environment. The sphere in which nationality proved especially divisive between groups and especially cohesive within them, uniting not only village Romanians but Romanian peasants with members of the new Romanian bourgeoisie, was politics.

INTERGROUP PERCEPTIONS AND VILLAGE-LEVEL POLITICS

It is always easier to describe behavioral patterns than it is to grasp the perceptual and attitudinal dispositions that accompany them. This is particularly true of a retrospective interpretation, in which the external checks on remembered information are much more abundant for organizational and behavioral matters (family sizes, dates of purchase, heirships, migrations) than for cognitive ones, especially when the cognition one ideally wants is not the informant's but that of his parents or grandparents. It is nonetheless important to pursue the matter, if for no other reason than that human action emerges from the understandings within which people assess their situations, and these assessments and understandings often do not conform to what an analytic rendering of the "objective" situation might predict. Concerning the Romanian population at the turn of the century, it is my view that even though differences of class were glaringly apparent in their daily environment, as they came into frequent contact not only with richer German peasants and Magyar landowners but also with their own parents' and grandparents' memories of serfdom, the inclination of these peasants was to perceive the ethnic face of the class/ethnic cluster simultaneously with, and perhaps even prior to, its class face. I do not mean to assume that people carry in their heads rigid perceptual frameworks that shape their perceptions in one specific way all the time; perceptions of one or another feature in an environment will always differ from person to person and across contexts. I do believe, however, that Romanian peasants tended, on the whole—particularly in recalling past relations with Magyar landowners and offering views about the justness of those days—to see ethnic rather than class differences as the greater source of what was irksome or unjust, even though the two sources were superimposed and were equally real to the participants.

If this interpretation is correct, then I would explain it by referring to the nationalism that had become so rampant throughout the empire and had penetrated down into its local communities, as described in chapter 4. Arguing thus would enable me to specify and perhaps refine, with reference to ethnicity, the currently popular views of E. P. Thompson on the nature of social consciousness, namely, that class consciousness is the product of how people experience their history at particular times and places: "Class is defined by men as they live their own history, and, in the end, this is its only definition" (1963:11). This argument, in the form in which it is often quoted and discussed, begs the issue of how the definition of social reality evolves within a social system and shapes the very terms in which people conceive of, and therefore live, their experience. In his own magisterial work, Thompson implicitly provides many of the systemic parameters of men "living their history" in class terms; yet it is worth making explicit the connections among these parameters, experience, and how experience is defined. To avoid speaking of "class" for Transylvanian society in the Habsburg social system simply because what surfaces first are ethnic perceptions, is to skirt the very complex issue of the larger social reality encompassing and, indeed, defining these perceptions, a larger reality produced by the interactions of groups and regions in the empire and of the empire with others in the world. It was, in fact, precisely the systemic ideological constraints on perception, generated by such larger interactions, that pulled informants' understandings toward construing reality in primarily ethnic terms. This was not, however, to deny the other realities, which would soon make their appearance in cognition once the systemic context of action changed.

Insofar as I can support my position with the evidence at my disposal, the better vehicle is Romanians' perceptions not of the Germans with whom they have been juxtaposed for most of this chapter but of the Magyars so glaringly absent from it. After World War I only one Magyar couple (Erzsébet Fogarassy and her husband) remained in Binţinţi to continue in daily interaction with Romanian villagers. This couple left a vivid and nasty impression on villagers' minds, but because they were only two they gave Romanians no cause to reperceive Magyars. In contrast, I believe Romanians learned to reconsider the Germans, with whom they have now been in continuous and increasing contact for more than sixty years in a Romanian Transylvania. Thus, those Romanians who remember stories or actual encounters with Magyars are recalling something closer to a reality crystallized in the form suited to my purposes than is true of how they remember earlier days with Germans. I will briefly touch on Romanian-German attitudes, to round out the picture given so far, and will extend this sketch further in chapter 6; but I will devote more space here to the Magyars.

At least some of the attitudes and stereotypes held by Germans and Romanians concerning each other in the present (discussed in chapter 1) are probably of sufficient longevity to apply to the period before World War I. These consist of value differences that fit with uncommon ease the two different organizations of farming already discussed. Germans, pursuing commercialized agriculture with hired labor and little interhousehold cooperation, might be expected to constitute competitively autarkic single family enterprises striving for success on the basis of efficiency and rationality. Romanians, oriented more to subsistence than to market and relying on high intragroup cooperation, would be enmeshed in dense social networks with sociability and cooperativeness as prime values. Two contrasting value orientations are indeed evident, and probably were in 1900, in the way Germans and Romanians talk about the world and each other: one set emphasizes calculation and rationality, the other harmony and sociability.

Although with reluctance, Germans will admit to what were almost certainly their views of Romanians in the past: a backward, childlike, unsophisticated, irrational people (even when the irrationality is excused as the legacy of serfdom), prone to superstitions and wasteful of good time and resources in observing these, not wholly trustworthy, liable to thievery, sneaky rather than courageous, bright but undisciplined and disorganized. From the Romanian side, on the other hand, Germans have long been regarded — even more in the past than in the present — as wholly deficient in life's important matters, having to do with hospitality, generosity, and emotional warmth, despite their also being a "civilized" and hardworking people with many virtues. The reciprocal negative stereotypes are evident in two vignettes, both from the 1920s. The first is told by Germans, the second by Romanians.

The lands of an elderly German, Herr Bauer, were for a time jointly sharecropped by three Romanians. Bauer would on occasion go out into the fields to see how his tenants were doing. Seeing that they were not plowing deep enough, he would adjust the plowshare downward, saying, "No, no deeper; you must do the basic executions properly, and God will take care of the rest — and you needn't assure this by taking tomorrow off to celebrate St. John." As soon as he was out of sight, the three Romanians would readjust the plowshare upward (to ease the burden on their much-overworked oxen, one of them told me). A few hours later the scenario would be repeated. The next day when the tenants failed to show up, Bauer could find them drinking and visiting happily in careful observance of St. John's day.

Pl. 3. Romanian women enjoying a sociable evening
in honor of a saint's day.

The second vignette shows us Avram Stoian, a Romanian in his late teens, who went at dawn one day to earn some extra cash by working for the Pfeiffers. Christina Pfeiffer worked ahead of him and constantly complained about his pace and work habits (she was a horse of a woman, Avram said, and could outwork most men). At dusk when, exhausted, he announced that having completed his day's work he must go home to cart his family's wheat, she docked his wage ten lei because he hadn't finished "what was expected." Several days later Christina's father saw Avram at the pub and asked, "Well, boy, need some money? Next time maybe you'll work until you're through and then you'll get paid," ignoring Avram's protests that he had worked the agreed-upon length of time. Avram determined to get even. The following day (a German holiday), he sneaked off to a distant corner of Pfeiffer's fields, picked corn, and piled it carefully; and that night he went with his cart and loaded it full of corn (at least fifteen times the value of his unpaid wages, if not more), which he squirreled away in his barn, over his brother's protest. Avram finished this story to me, "So I got back at that stingy German for the ten lei he found it so hard to part with."

There remains, however, the other facet of Romanian attitudes, which admires Germans as a people more civilized and advanced than themselves. One might detect here traces of the historical mission of Romanian nationalism: to acquire the same privileges as other nationalities, rather than to draw an exclusive boundary that would keep others out (as with the tendency of German and Magyar nationalism). A number of my Romanian informants spontaneously attributed to the Germans' presence the rapid modernization of their own agricultural practices after World War I, saying "We Romanians in Binţinţi were way ahead of Romanian villages around us by 1940, and it's all because of the example of these Germans."[21] A few behavioral indications, some from before and some from just after the war, suggest that Romanians held this same grudging admiration in the early 1900s as well as in the present. First, some Romanian houses built before World War I, and even more in the 1920s, imitate German house architecture, with several rooms and outbuildings going straight back from the street in a line and with a corridor the length of the structure. This was distinct from the older Romanian house form, as well as from both the Magyar house architecture (a subdivided rectangle facing onto the street) and the form Romanians began adopting in the 1940s. A second piece of imitative behavior, from immediately after World War I, bears the same message. During the 1920s Romanians in the village finally began to abandon peasant dress and take up what all older Romanians still refer to as "German clothing" (*haine nemţeşti*): — the standard urban costume of purchased dark trousers and work shirts, as opposed to homespun white shirts and linen breeches. Third, by the late 1920s the largest tavern was divided into two rooms; in one, Romanian peasants danced traditional peasant dances and in the other those Romanians who were pursuing higher education danced the waltzes, tangoes, and polkas seen at all German festivities. All three of these examples show that Romanians had determined to become "civilized" like the other nationalities, and they knew they had had a ready model at hand for several decades.

These examples might lead one to conclude that Romanian identity was something easily shed, as Romanians attempted to "pass" into the higher-status nationalities. This conclusion would be inappropriate because it takes a context in which ethnic differences were unimportant and generalizes from that across all contexts. For Romanians, to imitate German houses, clothing, and dance styles was not a significant statement about *ethnic* identity, it concerned only mobility aspirations. One could even see similar imitative behavior (as Germans do) in the inclination of rich Romanian peasants to hire uplanders for field labor and then sit back like Magyar gentlemen to watch while others did the work. Imitations of this kind were not statements of ethnic identity but of social status. Moreover, they were politically neutral.

Other kinds of statements with ethnic overtones were not politically neutral at all, and few Romanians made them. These included behaviors that would symbolize the political order in which Romanians perceived nationality and oppression most intensely. In particular, they included the behaviors that Hungary's government singled out in its campaign to magyarize its subjects: changing one's name to Magyar form, abandoning Orthodoxy for Roman Catholicism, and adopting Magyar speech. Any Romanian who hoped to attend university or be employed in public service (including the railroad, on which peasants sometimes worked) was expected to conform to these Magyar standards as part of the privilege of his new position. But the small number of villagers who aspired to such positions adopted Magyar standards only pro forma, as temporary — and clever — expedients dictated by necessity and by Magyar political domination. Those who did this did not regard the changes as a form of "passing" but only as a short-term requirement for which there was no alternative, and they did not think of themselves as abandoning their ethnic community with these changes. Still, most peasants preferred to avoid making them at all. Peasants might casually imitate German dress or even Magyar gentryhood, but no such casual imitation was possible when nationalist domination in the political sphere came into focus. In that sphere, one found Romanian peasants stubbornly insisting, after years of exposure to Magyar in school, that they did not know Magyar. I will seek to show this more concretely by examining how Romanians recall Magyars and feudal times and then by discussing the interaction of groups in village politics.

My picture of Magyar-Romanian relations comes from several unstructured interviews with six Romanian informants born in the 1880s and 1890s, mostly of middle-to-poor peasant backgrounds. To remind the reader of the dubious foundations of my analysis and to convey something of the quality of these people's recollections, the several themes that emerged most often are presented as a composite interview, with much of the wording my informants used. Readers can thus better appraise the suitability of my interpretation.

Q: Let's talk about what you know of the old days, what you remember hearing about serfdom, about the Magyars who used to be here.

A: Well, not *all* of them were bad, it was just that we had to work for them, and we had no rights. Three days for the lord (*domn*) and three at home, that's how it was. They were the lords (*domni*) and we had to do what we were told. And a lot of them really were nasty. Their cattle would go out to pasture before Romanians' cattle, and if one of ours strayed into their area we would be dragged off and beaten until the blood flowed. I heard stories from my father-in-law when I was young, telling how the *domni* would mistreat the Romanians—how they would yoke a man together with an ox if they hadn't enough oxen to plow; how women would be tied up just out of reach of their babies so the babies' hunger cries would drive the mothers nuts; how they would hitch a bunch of Romanians together with a big rope and line them up near the river and push them in, so they all drowned; how they would make us go after firewood three times a week in the dead of winter, when it was so cold that the breath froze on the noses of man and beast alike; how the gendarmes ordered Ioan the son of Nicolae to stop playing his [Romanian] flute and when he didn't they beat him with sticks. These were Magyars, you know, we had Magyars here then. And we had no rights. If we went to court we always got fined, no matter who was really to blame. We had no right to vote—you couldn't vote unless you had a lot of land, and most of us didn't have much. We couldn't even talk our own language, that was the worst thing. This was Magyarland then. I remember going to the notary for a permit to travel to see my husband at the beginning of the War, and when I got to the village hall and told him in Romanian what I wanted, all he would reply in was Magyar, until I gave up and went home empty-handed. Oh sure, they made us learn Magyar in school, but no one really did learn.

What else of the *domni*? They had all they wanted, while we were starving. They did themselves in with high living and fancy things, and they gambled more than you could believe. They were always playing cards, these Magyars here. Why, did you know they'd gamble away a field of two hectares in an evening, as if it was a kernel of corn [two hectares represented the lifetime acquisitions of some of these informants]? The worst of the lot was Jigoaia [žigwaya—Erzsébet Fogarassy], you know, the one who lived where the collective farm is now. We always say, the place was a mess before, and it still is today. Well, it's said that she nearly ruined her father with her high living in Budapest, parading around with officers and other fancy people. And when she moved back here, she behaved like something not even human. Her neighbors used to say she slept in the same bed with her dogs and ate off the same plate with them. People would work for her, and when they went for their pay she'd laugh in their faces. One of her maidservants died, and later the body was dug up and it was proved she'd been beaten to death. Worthless, disgusting woman.

Q: If they were such nasty people, why didn't Romanians do something about it — rise up and throw them out?

A: Well, we did a couple of times, you know, with Horea's revolt and with Avram Iancu in 1848. But mostly we were afraid, because we knew if we did anything they'd beat us even worse. My grandmother used to say, "Heaven keep us from the *domni*'s rage, 'cuz then there'll be real trouble." As it was, they beat us up all the time over nothing. We were afraid. What could we do against them with our pitchforks and rakes? You know those old proverbs: "The sword does not cut off a head that is bowed," and "A docile lamb suckles at two ewes," and "Sit tight and shut up if you want to survive." That was us.

Then too, we tricked them a lot. We'd get as much as we could when they weren't looking. I remember hearing about how my grandmother used to go to work for the *domn* wearing huge leggings under her skirt, and while she worked she would stick grain into her leggings through a pocket, then three or four times a day she'd say she had to go home to feed her kids and she'd empty those leggings so she could fill them up again. I also heard that the *domn* would take his cart to the village wheelwright, who was a Romanian, and instead of fixing it the wheelwright would take all the good wheels off and put on worn ones. We'd steal chickens and pigs from their courtyards when we were leaving for home, and sometimes at night we'd even steal their gates off the hinges. Then they'd really get mad, but by that time there were fewer of them and they were afraid to beat us up so much.

Still, we had to hide our Romanian customs from them or they would beat us up anyway. When I was in school [ca. 1899], the teacher would sometimes decide to put on a show with some Romanian songs and dances, and he'd rehearse us far away from the center of the village, out by the railroad, to keep the Magyars from finding out. We weren't allowed to wear Romanian colors then or do Romanian dances, but sometimes young men would dress Romanian and see if they could dance through the village and escape without getting caught. They were real heroes, those fellows. And one day around 1917, I dressed my little boy up in Romanian costume, national colors and all, and when no one was looking — fsshhtt! — I shoved him into the courtyard of the gendarmerie and then I waited with my friends out in the street to see what would happen. The gendarmes were nice enough to him, but they ordered me to take him home at once and change him or I'd be sorry. If I'd done that maybe ten years earlier, they'd have beaten me to a pulp, I'm sure, but by then there were fewer of them and a lot of us, so they weren't quite so mean.

But you know, we beat up on them some too. I remember when I was young and one of Jigoaia's parents died [1915–16], they opened up the crypt on the hill to bury that Magyar and some other kids and I hung around to watch. Well, inside the crypt were a lot of skeletons of Magyars, and the Romanians who were supposed to deposit the body there went in with sticks and beat all those old bones and skulls to dust. I saw the name on one of them, it was that guy Kodar who built the high school in Orăştie [Kocsard Kun]. There were statues of him and his brother in the high school, but in 1918 the Romanians threw them all out. You know, when Jigoaia died after World War II they wanted to open that crypt up again, but Relu Todea—he owned the land it's on—said he didn't want anyone opening up any crypt and burying any stinking Magyars in *his* garden, so they buried her in town.[22]

Several things seem worthy of remark in these stories. First is that when serfdom per se is the subject, informants most often use the words *domni* and *Români*—lords and Romanians. Otherwise, the words *domni* and *Unguri* (Magyars) are used more or less inter-changeably, "Magyar" occurring more often when the issue involves politics, questions of rights, etc. The category-mixing pair *domni* and *Români* suggests the interlocking and undifferentiated cluster-ing of class and ethnic position in this system; the association of "Magyar" with political issues will be taken up in a moment. Second, I was struck in these conversations by how matter-of-factly the rela-tionship of landlord to serf was presented, as if there was nothing questionable in it: working for the lord was simply accepted. "We worked three days for the *domn* and three at home" was a refrain I heard from many informants beyond the six with whom I worked most closely on this subject. When I probed for details, it emerged that many peasants now think the serfs held their portion "at home" as *owners*.[23] Third, it seemed to me, given the poor-peasant origins of my principal informants, that these people would be, if anything, more likely than others to think in terms of exploitative class rela-tions. Instead, however, indignation appeared primarily in the repeated emphasis on the willful cruelty and inhumanity of land-lords in their treatment of serfs, which was presented as an aspect of Romanians' having no rights—to their language, customs, even their lives and humanity. This indignation was visible in the words of my informants but even more so in their tone. The frequent repetition of the ideas that Romanians would get beaten up, espe-cially for displays of nationality, and that their principal disposition in return was not rebellion but fear (and theft), suggests to me that they perceived oppression primarily in their political subordination to a Magyar state rather than in an inequitable economic order.

If this was indeed their perception, it probably owes a lot to the activities of the late nineteenth- and early twentieth-century Romanian politicians and leaders of the Romanian national movement. Chapter 4 has already shown that although Romanian politicians did pay some attention to the problems of peasant agriculture, for the most part they were (justifiably) concerned with Romanian political and civil rights and with resisting the Hungarians' implacable will to magyarize the non-Magyar populations in Transylvania. The politics of the Hungarian state, pursued in an environment hypersensitive to nationalist questions, had provoked a Romanian response that pushed national concerns to the fore at the expense of class concerns, for all Romanians.

It was precisely around politics and the implications of politics for national rights that antagonisms between Romanians and Germans flared also in Binţinţi, and these disagreements came to a head around elections for deputies to Parliament. The right to vote was not broadly distributed in Transylvania in the early 1900s, requiring a property or income qualification that effectively disenfranchised all but a few, Romanians being disenfranchised disproportionately. In 1915, in the whole of Transylvania 3.4 percent of the population was eligible to vote (Popa and Istrate 1915:184); in Binţinţi, the male heads of about 15 percent of Romanian households had voting rights,[24] while nearly all among the Germans did. Those Romanians who did vote felt fully the unpleasant fact of their lowly status in Magyardom; for voting was not secret, and several informants described being intimidated, bribed, or outright chased away from the polls if, as the day wore on, the Magyar candidate began falling behind.[25]

On the eve of an election, interethnic sparks flew in Binţinţi. Since most of Transylvania's Romanian voters were villagers, candidates of the Romanian National Party generally campaigned in rural areas, hammering home Romanian dissatisfactions with Magyar rule and even declaring that any pro-Magyar vote amounted to a vote for Romanian destruction. If the candidate did not himself stop in Binţinţi, his part would be taken by the village priest and by local property owners of the Romanian bourgeoisie, such as lawyer Mihu (see p. 206). The real source of heat, however, was that the Germans always voted pro-Magyar in these elections (from 1867 on), to the fury of Romanians, who often believed that their candidate would have won if only the Germans had voted otherwise. Before the election even the children of Romanians and Germans could be heard hurling slogans at each other in support of the Romanian and Magyar candidates. Germans aver that pro-Magyar voting had been imposed upon them by their superiors in the Saxon hierarchy, a policy one of my informants justified with the saying, "You sing the song of the one who feeds you." But they paid for this tune, for whenever the Magyar candidate won, Germans returning from the polls were greeted by jeers, rock-throwing, and ready Romanian fists.

One might be surprised that a community of largely disenfranchised ex-serfs would be so enthusiastic about politics, until one recalls how highly the atmosphere had been politicized by the Romanian national movement of the previous century. These effects were particularly marked in villages around the towns and cities that had seen the early growth of the Romanian movement, including the town of Orăştie near Binţinţi. I have already touched on the public activities of Binţinţi's own Romanian nationalist landowner, Ioan Mihu, who doubtless had a strong impact on villagers' national consciousness. It is also a fair guess that political energies were fiercer in multiethnic villages than in monoethnic ones, as pro-Magyar German and Magyar voters rubbed shoulders with Romanians, especially when the Romanians included among their number such politically ardent citizens and patriots as village son and aviator Aurel Vlaicu (1881–1913; see p. 227).

In 1918 the Central powers of World War I were defeated, among them Austria-Hungary. Many thousands of Romanians, the majority population of Transylvania, responded to President Woodrow Wilson's declared principle of "self-determination of peoples" by determining in a mass meeting (attended by peasants from Binţinţi) to sever Transylvania from Hungary and unite with the Romanian Kingdom. This decision was supported by troop movements from Romania through Transylvania into Hungary, by the vote of the Saxons (who perceived that a new hand was about to feed them), and by the Allied powers at the Paris Peace Conference. Hungary's wartime alliance had done what 150 years of Romanian political activity in Transylvania had amply prepared but not yet accomplished: removed Transylvania's Romanians from Magyar political control and decimated the ranks and power of the Magyar upper class.

Even before the transfer was effected, Binţinţi joined many other Transylvanian villages in setting up a local branch of the Romanian National Committee to smooth the transition. The records of the Binţinţi branch — an unusually active one (Frăţilă and Ionaş 1979:

469), which is not surprising, given what we know by now of this village's history—still sit in the village church. Their opening lines attest to the earnestness of these Romanian villagers and the seriousness with which they viewed the occasion:

> The commune of Binţinţi, being informed by its superiors concerning the organization of Romanians in all of Hungary and Transylvania, hastens despite its small numbers to give a sign of life and organizes itself in the following manner. First, a Romanian National Committee has been elected, under the presidency of Ion Vlaicu [the aviator's brother] with twelve other members. . . , and this Committee chose the following persons to form a Civil Guard . . .

This register meticulously records, over the next several months, matters concerning the management of village affairs: what to do with libelous and threatening circulars being disseminated by Magyars; provisions for restituting goods with which the pro-Magyar village notary had absconded when he fled; temporary arrangements for pasturing animals until the agrarian reform could be implemented; etc. Sensitized for years to be aware of and to despise their powerlessness, these Romanians were more than ready to take part in an orderly transition to a new era.

Their response illustrates the prominence of nationality issues, both in the minds of these peasants and in their environment. The durability of these habits of mind appears again in postwar voting patterns in a datum that could easily be misunderstood. For a decade or more, Binţinţi Romanians tenaciously cast their votes for the National Peasant Party (again differing from Germans, who voted, predictably, with whatever party was already in power). One might uncritically think this represents a sudden discovery of class consciousness on the peasants' part or even see it as evidence for their having perceived the importance of class issues all along. But for Transylvanian peasants, in fact, the National Peasant Party was just the continuation of the Romanian National Party (now fused with a peasant party from the Romanian Kingdom) that they had loyally supported all along. While their perception of this party gradually changed during the 1930s, their initial support for it shows how deeply ingrained was their habit of seeing nationality as the chief issue in politics.

Indeed, conversations with several informants imply the possibility that once Magyar political dominance ended, peasants ceased for a time to perceive oppression in their environment at all, even though they were well aware of class differences and continued to interact (often to their detriment) with representatives of banks and of a now-Romanian state. I will return to this issue in chapter 6. For the moment, it is enough to note that when I questioned informants on what was thought to be unjust (*nedrept*) before World War I, they usually replied with remarks about Romanians being without rights in a Hungarian state; yet for the same question applied to the interwar period, they could think of nothing. Another informant offered her view on the injustices of poverty and nationality thus:

> [After the war] if a man had nothing to inherit, if his parents had nothing to give him, or if there were so many kids that they all got only a scrap, then he was poor and it wasn't unjust or anyone's fault, that's just the way it was. It was unfortunate. If you worked hard and were lucky, you managed; if not . . . Injustice? After Transylvania went over to Romania there wasn't any more injustice: we were no longer under the Magyars.

Another informant offers a story that shows both how enmity continued between Magyars and Romanians and how times had changed. Avram Stoian, the same fellow who tangled with the Pfeiffers over a day's wage, tells of a similar contretemps with Mr. Janó, the husband of the Magyar Jigoaia. One day in the late 1920s Janó called Avram in and demanded 500 lei to get back one of the Stoians's lambs, which had strayed into Janó's property and eaten some grass. Avram, stunned by so immense a sum, proposed simply leaving the lamb (worth at most 100 lei) with Janó, or calling in someone to assess the damages. Janó, a lawyer, refused. Avram saw no alternative to paying the sum, a tremendous hardship for his very poor family, but he swore to Janó's face that he would get even. Some time later, as the village herd was being driven to pasture by a patch of Avram's land, he opened his fence, shooed in four of Janó's cows, and sent word demanding 500 lei apiece for damages. In the old Transylvania, Avram would never have won that case in court, but Janó too knew that things were different now. Furious, he paid up—but it was not to be the last time he would regret having thrown his Magyar weight around with this simple Romanian peasant.

For Romanian peasants at the end of World War I the main source of injustice—national discrimination—had been wiped out. What they had seen as the major evils were no more. Transylvanian Romanians became citizens of a Romanian state; Magyar schools, Magyar privileges, and magyarization were ended; the Romanian language, traditions, and national colors were no longer suppressed; Romanians' rights were won, making them the equals—indeed, the superiors—of the other groups. With so many decades of subjection to a discriminatory class/ethnic system in which the main inequities were seen as concomitants of ethnically-based political exclusion, it would be a while after the end of national discrimination before peasants would come to question the necessity of their lowly class position.

When they did come to question it, they would once again find the class issues knotted up with ethnic difference. This discovery is foreshadowed in the opinion of an outspoken German who assessed the interwar period thus: "It was class war here, between Germans and Romanians, that's what it was. The Romanians were all envy and ambition because we had more than they." Uncovering his meaning requires learning how the massive alteration of Transylvanian society after 1918 set the village-level conditions for the transformation described more generally in the previous chapter: while at the regional level the Romanian bourgeoisie had already been making serious inroads into the bourgeois niches of Saxondom, in the village economy it was only after 1918 that Germans and Romanians came into direct competition within a single economic niche. In the next chapter I will examine the consequences of 1918 for the economy and social structure of Transylvania and Binţinţi and will explore the changed character of ethnic relations that accompanied these.

PART IV

TRANSYLVANIAN PEASANTS IN PRE-COMMUNIST ROMANIA

CHAPTER 6

Peasants into Gentlemen, and a Liking for Cattle: The Transylvanian "Revolution" of 1918 and the Interwar Village Community

Boii ară, caii mănîncă.
(The oxen plow, the horses eat.)

La pomul lăudat să nu mergi cu sacul mare.
(Don't take a big sack to the tree everyone is praising.)

— Proverbs

During the present century the peasants of Binținți experienced not one but two major revolutions, one in the wake of each world war. Although both transformed the lives and environments of these peasants significantly, the closing paragraphs of chapter 5 would imply that the "revolution" of 1918 was in some ways the more far-reaching. In many respects it set trends that the second revolution in 1945 would merely continue. The changes wrought in 1918 were multidimensional both for the agrarian structure, radically altered by a massive land reform, and for the complex of nationality, class, and political privilege that were Transylvania's hallmark.

The peasants of Binținți were fully aware of these multiple dimensions. One informant, when asked about changes in the village after World War I, scarcely knew where to begin: "What *didn't* change? Everything changed" — political rights, ownership of arable land, unharassed entry into Romanian schools and outside jobs, access to pasture that enabled more people to keep oxen. The land reform was unusually extensive in Binținți and gave rise to new behaviors in several realms, including new patterns of migration, fertility, and marriage. Even the village's fundamental identification changed: a place known for centuries as "Binținți" was rechristened "Aurel Vlaicu" by the Romanian government, in proud nationalistic recognition of the accomplishments of this village son. Thus Binținți —

"the people of Benchench," a Szekler noble settled by feudal donation in a conquered land — became Vlaiceni, the people of a Romanian of humble serf origins, remarkable talents, and great patriotic
achievements. The switch aptly symbolized the expanded horizons
of Romanians in the new era.

Revolutionary effects and expanded horizons notwithstanding,
some things remained too much the same, although the parameters
of their continuity had changed. Chief among these was that capitalism made scarcely any more headway in Transylvanian agriculture during this thirty-odd-year period than it had before the war.
There was change, to be sure, but one might call it commercialization without development. A major cause of both the revolutionary
changes and the continuities was another piece of continuity: the
widely ramifying effects of nationalism and its relation to social
structure. For Transylvanians, incorporation into a Romanian state
served decisively to overturn the discriminatory distribution of the
different national groups in society; for all peasants, the terms of
existence were set by a program of nationalist industrialization that
retarded agriculture by milking it to nurse a new Romanian industry. Issues of nationality thus continued as before to color life for
Binţinţeni, although in novel ways.

This chapter will trace what happened to peasants in Binţinţi
during the interwar period, with particular attention to the village's
Romanians. Its Germans had not disappeared, however, as will be
evident when we consider agricultural practices and interethnic
relations. The discussion overlaps with the time period of the preceding chapter, for interwar changes in patterns of migration, fertility, and marriage are best seen when compared with data from
before the war. Like the preceding chapter, this one attempts to
show not only how policies from above constrained what was possible for the peasants but also how people's daily behavior gave life
to the policies and pressed their consequences in directions not
entirely intended by policymakers. A preliminary discussion of the
interwar Romanian state and its development strategy therefore
interrupts the narrative of events in twentieth-century Binţinţi.

For those too impatient to pursue a tale for its own sake, I offer
a highly schematic overview of this story's structure and external
parameters. The interwar period was one of global economic stagnation. Industrial states unable to market their wares sought to
improve unhealthy trade balances by reducing imports of foodstuffs
(i.e., to reagrarianize their own economies), which in turn harmed

the agricultural export economies geared to them. Structurally speaking, one remedy for such a state of affairs is to expand the purchasing power in areas of the world, such as "backward" sectors within national economies, not yet fully integrated into the global economy as consumers of manufactured goods (see Wallerstein 1979:124-125). A large fraction of Romania's elite during these years was not interested, however, in merely padding agricultural incomes so peasants could buy manufactures produced elsewhere: rather, this fraction aimed to develop the industry of Romania for its consumers. Thus, interwar Romania was the scene of a conflict between a national bourgeoisie and Western capitalists, and internally between nascent manufacturing interests and supporters of the agricultural population. The forces favoring national industry won out locally but did not prevail in the longer run. Again speaking structurally rather than motivationally, the most crucial early developments were Romania's decision to block foreign investment and the implementation of an agrarian reform, which at one stroke divested large landowners of a sector of the economy that was becoming unprofitable, undercut peasant rebellion, and increased the potential purchasing power of the rural masses. The Romanian state then embarked on autarkic industrialization that was to rest on a prosperous middle peasantry, implicitly capitalist smallholders set in place by the proletarization of many reform-land recipients. Among the factors conditioning this outcome were tax policy and other mechanisms that changed the peasants' relationship to the economy, as integration through the market and through indebtedness became even more widely generalized means of surplus extraction than before, and rents declined. Through policies such as these, during these years the state increasingly became the prime determinant of everything in peasants' lives, to a degree not achieved before.

Despite these imposing forces, many peasants insistently refused to become proletarized. Their resistance employed several social instruments and was reinforced by the land reform and by other state measures taken during the depression. Both consequence and continued cause of this resistance to proletarization was their growing participation in an international livestock market, directed into this area precisely because the persistence of marginal peasant holdings kept livestock cheap — a result in which the state also collaborated. The export marketing of Binţinţi cattle betrayed Romania's inability to alter its structural position as an agrarian exporter in the world economic periphery and aptly captures the many-layered connections between individual behavior and world-system processes.

THE INTERWAR ROMANIAN STATE AND ITS ECONOMIC POLICIES

The new postwar Romania that emerged from the Treaty of Versailles, with pieces from Soviet Russia and from a dismembered Austria-Hungary, had more than doubled both its population and its territory and was now the second largest East European state, after Poland. Its grain-exporting neocolonial economy (see Chirot 1976) was augmented by the more industrialized regions of Transylvania and the Banat,[1] creating an economic unit that might, if further developed, serve as its own producer and consumer of both agricultural products and manufactured goods. Sitting atop this possibility was the Romanian state, with its bureaucratic civil service, organizational roster, and other organizational instruments whose exercise would determine the direction of the economy by whatever political party or clique was in temporary control.

In several respects the Romanian state resembled the Hungarian state of the nineteenth century, described in chapter 4. Transylvania's passage between the Romanian and Hungarian kingdoms therefore did not subject it to an entirely new sort of governing entity. The state of interwar Romania had two particularly important features. First, its bureaucracy was manned by a group similar to the one that was the mainstay of the bureaucracy in Hungary: small gentry landowners and intellectuals rather than great aristocrats. This bureaucracy would manifest, more than Hungary's, a strong tendency toward involutional and hypertrophic growth (Roberts 1951:338) beyond the sustaining capacities of its sources of revenue. Second, as in Hungary, the Romanian state was used by different parties to perform the leading entrepreneurial role in economic development (ibid.:341; see also Berend and Ránki 1974a), for interwar Romania shared with nineteenth-century Hungary the notable lack of a strong native bourgeoisie to lead economic development as it had in the West. As the leading entrepreneur, the Romanian state acquired property of its own—banks and corporations—that during the 1930s became central to industrialization, ahead even of private banks and corporations operating with government supports (Roberts 1951:196). It is not inapt to see in this state role, one held by several other East European states of the past one hundred years (Berend and Ránki 1974*a*), a precursor of the state capitalism that in some analysts' view characterizes East European socialist regimes since 1945.

The extent to which the state was the chief industrial actor and was synonymous with powerful manufacturing interests at any given time depended on which of Romania's innumerable political parties were in office. Without surveying the plethora of these parties and political currents, I must nonetheless mention the most important: the Liberal and National Peasant parties, which alternated in power until the mid-1930s, to be succeeded first by a royal dictatorship[2] and then by a quasi-fascist military one. (For extended discussion of these developments, see Henry Roberts's outstanding analysis [1951], on which the present summary rests.)

The Liberals generally represented the fusion of the bureaucracy, small landowners from prewar Romania (the "Regat"), and commercial interests. Despite Parisian training they were strong nationalists. Their policies tended, more than those of other parties, toward corporatism and use of the state as the instrument of industrialization. The National Peasant Party was a peculiar amalgam of radical agrarian interests from the Regat with the Romanian Nationalist Party of Transylvania, whose constituents were both peasants and middle classes. Their policies were consequently less uniform than those of the Liberals: sometimes internationalist, sometimes proagrarian, sometimes proindustry. The National Peasants came to oppose not the industrialization program of the Liberals but their corporatism, financial oligarchy, and strict administrative centralization, which were anathemas to politicians from the newly incorporated territories. It was the misfortune of the National Peasants to be in power when the depression struck, and their political effectiveness was damaged irreparably.

A third major current, much less organized but with considerable popular support during these years, was the growth of various fascist groups, the most important of which was the Legion of the Archangel Michael. Romanian fascism, an indigenous product, differed from its Italian and German counterparts in not seeking alliances with industry, the army, or a corporatist state (Roberts 1951:346). Romantic, proagrarian, and nationalist, it lacked a positive political program and was defined largely by its oppositions: to industry, to capitalism, to communism, and to the Jews. While the leaders were most often students, unemployed intellectuals and civil servants, and other marginal urbanites, fascism appealed to many sectors of the population, including many peasants, and would have captured a larger share of power had elections been fair. Even so, it grew in organization and appeal through the 1930s, briefly exercising state power in the early 1940s.

The new era began auspiciously enough, from the peasant point of view, with the most radical land reform in Eastern Europe. Scholars generally agree that this reform, which had been broached even before the war, was enacted out of fear for the life of the state (and in anxious recollection of the 1907 peasant revolt), to pacify land-starved Romanian peasant troops on the Russian front who were infected by the radical promises of the Russian revolution (Roberts 1951:23–24; Mitrany 1930:99–100). This explanation may adequately represent the immediate perceptions of the Romanian elite, although they must have seen the threat to the state as unprecedentedly grave to be induced to legislate away the basis of their livelihood. An important effect of this decision, whether or not it was consciously motivated, was to divest the latifundists of holdings in a stagnating agricultural export market that overseas competition and falling rates of return were rendering unprofitable. The compensation to be paid, while not overly generous, would assist their move into other sectors where they might expect higher rates of profit, leaving the troublesome agrarian sector to be managed by the peasants and the state (Yambert MS:6). If managed successfully, the reform might foster capitalist development in agriculture and thereby increase rural purchasing power enough to spur the industry that its new efficiency would feed. Thus, a second effect of the reform was to redistribute income, implying the possibility of renewed expansion. These potential benefits notwithstanding, the reform itself was in all likelihood seen as a social necessity rather than as an integral part of the program of economic development.

Despite differences in the four laws implemented in 1921 in each of Romania's four major regions (Transylvania, the Regat, Bessarabia, and Bukovina), a universal, stated objective of the reform was to enable self-sufficient farming on plots of minimally three to five hectares, provided to as many households as possible. A number of peasants received no land, a function of whether or not there were expropriable estates in areas of high need, but villagers fortunate enough to live near large estates fared very well. The reform not only granted portions of arable land but provided wherever possible for the expansion of communal pastures and woodlands— a great boon to many villagers. A major shortcoming of the reform, however, was that adequate measures were not taken to consolidate existing farms and to ensure that new ones would not be rendered unviable through sale or subdivision. As will be seen shortly, the consequences implicit in this were important to government designs.

The issue of compensation for reform lands created problems that brought others in their wake. It proved difficult to arrive at figures neither exorbitant nor too low, and continued depreciation of the currency necessitated revision even of the solutions that were developed. The state shouldered about half the burden of these compensations (nevertheless financed partly by taxing the peasants). Currency depreciation did not work to the peasants' advantage as it might have, for although in theory peasants had twenty years to pay their share, they were pressed to pay in full as soon as possible and many strove to do so. Their promptness caused them misfortunes, as compensations were paid at precisely the time when peasants most needed their cash to replenish or acquire animals and tools, without which they could not work their newly acquired lands (Mitrany 1930:321), and declining agricultural prices together with high tariffs soon made farm implements very costly. Since the state failed to provide sufficient credit to make these necessary purchases, the level of peasant indebtedness began to rise (Şandru 1975:266). Some peasants resorted to selling pieces of their new properties as a way out of the impasse, a subject to which I will return below.

The agrarian reform spawned much debate as to its successes and its effects (see Mitrany 1930 and Roberts 1951 for good discussions of the issues). I do not intend to assess its consequences fully but will mention the ones most important for the analysis to follow. First, the reform effected a major transformation of the property structure. In Transylvania, it raised from 24 to 56 percent the proportion of arable land in holdings of less than 10 hectares and decreased the holdings of over 100 hectares from 37 to 15 percent of the total (Macartney 1937:350). It reduced the number of landless families and permitted thousands of peasant households previously unable to feed themselves to do so. Circulation of property in the land market shot up, enlivened not only by sales of some parcels granted to poorer peasants but also by the addition of large amounts of land not previously circulated as private property, such as lands belonging to various churches (Mitrany 1930:213). The amount of land in sharecropping fell sharply—in Transylvania this had been about 16 percent of the total arable surface, one of the highest tenancy rates in all Romania (ibid.:244)—and many of these lands were transferred to tenants who had been working them. If productivity declined after the reform[3] and rational cultivation practices failed to develop as expected, at least people were eating better (Şandru 1975:324) — for the time being.

With this land reform, an entirely different Romania was constituted from the one of prewar days, and it contemplated its position in the world economy from a new vantage point. Formerly an exporter of grains, it now held greater potential for industrial growth. The land reform had reduced the obstacles a landed nobility might raise against commercial expansion. During the next two decades this agrarian periphery made a serious bid to develop its backward economy rather than to continue as a market and source of raw materials for Western industrial production. In a series of debates remarkably similar to those raised concerning economic development in the Third World in the 1980s (see Chirot 1978a, and 1978b), many Romanian theoreticians argued that Romania's underdevelopment was the product of exploitation by the West, that the international division of labor amounted to imperialism, and that Romania would develop only by barring imports of both Western manufactures and foreign investment and by accepting, at most, foreign loans made for use at the state's discretion. It was the Liberal Party, in power from 1922 to 1928, that carried these arguments into practice in a program of autarkic nationalist industrialization. The reagrarianization of Western industrial economies during the depression deepened Romania's neomercantilist tendencies: as price scissors reduced the value of agricultural exports and as markets for these exports dried up, it became clearer than ever to Romania's leaders that agrarian countries were at the mercy of more powerful states and must change their situation. They were not alone in this assessment, which was being made by other East European states with similarly stagnating agricultural economies (see Berend and Ránki 1974a).

The course Romania had chosen was fraught with difficulties, however, for the initial refusal to import foreign capital created serious hardships in generating the resources necessary to economic development. Indeed, the options faced by interwar governments constituted a long series of Hobson's choices. It is not surprising that the consequent trends were contradictory and that peasants suffered. International conditions posed crippling constraints, in the form of ruinously low world prices for agricultural products, high foreign debts incurred for Romania's participation in the war, and the eventual foreign loan secured to stabilize the currency, at a cost of 9 percent. Within such strict limits, the government was forced into making highly selective investment decisions, especially stringent before the policy shift (1929) that invited in foreign capital. How could a capital-poor economy afford inexpensive credit to peasants and high investment in agriculture, which would divert vital support from industry and finance? Yet to ignore agricultural improvement was to relegate that crucial sector to further stagnation and hamper industry in the long run. Given the low level of internal demand, the best way to accumulate domestic capital was through agricultural exports (Berend and Ránki 1974a:179); yet North American grain was crowding Eastern European producers out of foreign markets, further diminished by global depression. Only some animal and vegetable products (decidedly secondary in Romania's economy) had favorable markets abroad. But to build capital by exporting agricultural products ran counter to the government's wish to encourage an abundant and inexpensive food supply for the urban population it intended to create. The resulting policy was one of heavy export taxes on agricultural products, which generated revenues while producing a tremendous drop in agricultural exports and in internal grain prices; and this retarded the rural purchasing power that was an important term in the overall development equation. To raise agricultural prices would increase agricultural incomes and feed consumer industries but would also make the program more costly and risk its failure.

In 1928 the National Peasants took over from the Liberals, and one of their first moves was to ease the capital crisis by inviting foreign investment. Predictably, these investments went into export industries such as petroleum rather than into developing local capital stocks. From 1931 on, however, outside capital ceased to be so readily available (Roberts 1951:177), forcing Romania to build its own finance capital as best it could through local banks that had survived the crisis and through other means (Axenciuc 1966:13; Iovanelli 1975:64–66). The depression years undeniably helped Romania's industrialization, as local production of many consumer items covered for the import reductions necessitated by a 73-percent drop in receipts from cereal exports (Berend and Ránki 1974a: 247–248). Between 1929 and 1938 Romania's industrial production increased 55 percent (Mellor 1975:195) at a growth rate above that for world manufacturing as a whole (Roberts 1951:68–69). The structure of imports and exports changed significantly: raw-material imports increased while imports of semi-processed and manufactured goods fell off (Madgearu 1940:253).

Impressive as these results were, signs of poor health abounded. Capital and production were excessively concentrated, enjoying a monopoly position (Berend and Ránki 1974a:311); the state rather than the populace had become the major customer, and the disproportionate development of large-scale capital-goods industries relating to foreign interests or state demand was accomplished at the expense of the rural population. Many analysts conclude that Romania's interwar industrialization occurred to agriculture's detriment, reducing rather than building purchasing power in the countryside (Madgearu 1940:254–259; Roberts 1951:68, 336). Against the 55-percent increase in the index of industrialization, purchasing power dropped by 60 percent between 1927 and 1942 (Larionescu 1980:7). Internal prices for all but agricultural goods were so high that agricultural incomes were inadequate for necessities, and agricultural production itself was hobbled. Logical opportunities for domestic processing, such as agricultural industries, went unexplored. Urban industrial concentrations did little to absorb the huge excess rural population.

In sum, there was industrial development but it was not integrated with the rest of the economy. Foreign loans had been spent in enlarging the state apparatus and army and in other nonproductive investments; in consequence, continued protectionism rather than local industrial performance was Romania's response to foreign competition, and loans were still required (Berend and Ránki 1974a:230, 237). The country remained an exporter of raw materials, its economic structure had not decisively changed, and its goal of an independent national economy went unrealized (ibid.: 308). Roberts offered this homely assessment: "In general, one receives the impression that the Rumanian economy in attempting to lift itself by its bootstraps had merely driven the feet through the soles" (1951:83).

Success was even less eye-catching in agriculture. To begin with, agrarian problems were too often not addressed in their own terms, as most of the interwar parties were generally agreed that the agrarian question was best solved by developing industry (ibid.:64). In consequence, the outstanding and intractable problems in agriculture—absolute overpopulation,[4] continued extensive rather than intensive cultivation, low productivity, and inadequate capital or credit to improve it—persisted, despite occasional measures designed to alleviate them. The problem of credit is especially telling and is widely seen as the major cause of continued low productivity and "irrational" farming (Frunzănescu 1939:168; Roberts 1951:64): allocations of credit stood at about 3 percent of their prewar level (Mitrany 1930:245) and were not compensated for by other investments in agriculture, which received barely 2 percent of the state budget during the late 1920s and early 1930s (while France, Italy, and Bulgaria gave 12 to 13 percent of their budgets to agricultural improvement [Şandru 1975:328]). A few cooperatives were set up but on insecure footing; there were some, but not enough, model farms dispensing select varieties of seed; some efforts to promote special crops like soybeans and to subsidize the improvement of live-stock breeds; and some attempts to motivate better agricultural techniques by offering prizes for outstanding peasant production (Cristea 1929:426-427). Such efforts intensified on the eve of World War II, for which high agricultural performance was vital (see Zago-roff et al. 1955).

These measures were not enough, however, to break the vicious circle in which agriculture was such a poor field for investment that peasants could not get credit, which went instead to industry, and which would continue to do so until agricultural productivity was raised, unlikely without investment (Roberts 1951:83). Low invest-ment was not the only source of difficulty for agricultural produc-tion; it was also aggravated by the low prices that were a conscious element in the industrial program. Peasants were therefore unable to accumulate enough income to modernize their farm inventories or pay off debts incurred for land purchases and implements (Şandru 1975:342). High tariffs on imports of agricultural machinery further hampered acquisition of these items.

These hindrances on agricultural improvements played into an-other aspect of government strategy in a complicated manner. All the major interwar parties agreed on the desirability of consolidating a prosperous stratum of "middle peasants" to support industrial growth (Göllner and Ştirban 1971: Şandru 1975:254-256), although there was disagreement on how large a "middle peasant" holding was: National Peasants spoke of holdings in the 10- to 50-hectare range, Conservatives of 25- to 100-hectare farms, and Liberals of "middle" farms of 250 to 500 hectares. Whatever figures were used, it is obvious that this objective ran wholly counter to the aim of the agrarian reform — to create a self-supporting peasantry on farms of 3 to 5 hectares — and that realization of the new objective would have entailed proletarizing much of the rural populace, over three-fourths of whom were on plots of less than 5 hectares. It was expected that consolidation and (implicit) proletarization would occur hand in hand, a crucial instrument being the free circulation of proper-ties. This was assured in 1929 by removing restrictions on the aliena-tion of lands received in the reform. Enterprising farms were then expected to expand with what weak ones sold off, the enterprising ones were to modernize their equipment, and a prosperous middle peasantry was to arise, ready to support industry. Although low agricultural prices inhibited this prosperous middle peasant's capacity to modernize his farm, aggregate statistics showed that indeed the reform's initial leveling of rural differences in wealth gave way to increasing inequalities, as holdings were sold and divided far more by recipients of reform land than by nonrecipients (Golopenţia and Georgescu 1941). Analysts who decry the low level of purchasing power and the lack of credit seem to forget that at least some consequences of these facts were very congenial to government intentions.

Only when catastrophe threatened were trends revised. Between 1929 and 1932 the per-capita income was almost halved (Roberts 1951:176), making emergency measures essential — in part, one guesses, because peasant reversion to subsistence farming (Mitrany 1951:108) sorely hindered the industrial opportunities inherent in the crisis (see p. 281 above). Policies were gradually altered beginning in 1929: agricultural export taxes were replaced with import tariffs, tariffs on imported agricultural machinery were reduced, and the state supported wheat prices (albeit not at inspiring levels) and subsidized livestock exports into countries where the trade balance was negative, such as Italy, Greece, and Palestine (Madgearu 1940:244). By 1932 the problem of rural indebtedness had to be faced. Debts left over from the 1920s and those more recently incurred for consumption (because of insufficient agricultural earnings) had reached such high levels and interest rates had climbed so steeply that the countryside was near chaos. In that year the government ordered a conversion of debts, which were halved and given a 34-year repayment term at 3 percent interest. Variable provisions introduced later increased the debt forgiven, in exchange for more prompt repayment. This measure saved thousands of peasants from foreclosure and dispossession. It also, coincidentally, worked against the process of proletarization (Roberts 1951:210–211), and helped to retain an excess of people on the land.

It is well to remember at this point that those analysts who despaired at the trends in agriculture mostly did so from a particular position: one that regarded as "backward" anything but rational, efficient, capitalist cultivation, one that favored the multiplication of farmers who would consume the manufactured tools and machines and other products of nascent Romanian industry — in short, the position of the manufacturing bourgeoisie. The peasants did not entirely share this perspective. For many of them, what was presented as rational cultivation was often not very rational, and therefore obstacles to it were not a serious problem. What did it matter if tractors cost a fortune? Who would buy a tractor to plow four hectares? Arguments about low market prices must have sounded peculiar to many of them, who were glad that they had a place to sell an ox when it came time to pay taxes. What could it mean to say that because of low prices, "peasants lost money by raising animals" (Frunzănescu 1939:164) — how could a sale be a loss of money, and what had it "cost" to raise the animal when labor had no price?[5] Even the term "depression" is biased. Many peasants fared better in the depression than either before or after it, once the conversion of debts took place, since the lack of market sales left them with more "surplus" to eat (Mitrany 1951:109). For society's oxen, plowing while its horses ate, work was work rather than some sort of fancy "profitable" activity. The main objective was to keep from losing the farm, and if you had to you worked harder, fattened another pig, worked a season in construction, not noticing that if the plow seemed heavier these days this was because all of Romanian industrialization was loaded onto it.

At the dawn of the interwar period, the state had launched a program aimed at producing national self-sufficiency in industry without the use of foreign capital, and had hoped to bring into being a prosperous middle peasantry farming rationally to feed the industrial population and to be an internal market for its products. By the eve of World War II, industrial production had increased but not by enough to produce exports other than the previous ones, namely, cereals and livestock and petroleum destined for the markets of the industrial states; and too much manufacturing was concentrated in heavy industries to which peasant purchasing power was irrelevant. Rural purchasing power had in any event remained low until the very end of the 1930s, when Romania capitulated to Germany's economic penetration of the Balkans. In their new partnership, Romania provided grains, minerals, petroleum, fodder crops, soybeans, and oil-bearing seeds (Berend and Ránki 1974*a*: 274, 283) while Germany paid higher prices than any other buyer would have paid. Thus Romanian dependency was reaffirmed, Germany's war machine was oiled, and peasant incomes briefly improved.

It is not clear how much progress was made toward consolidating the prosperous "middle peasantry" during the interwar years, but it is certain that the complementary process of proletarization had received two major setbacks, first from the land reform and then from the conversion of debts. The 1941 agricultural census showed that 83 percent of all farms were cultivated exclusively with family labor; 94 percent of all properties were smaller than ten hectares (58 percent were smaller than three hectares, thus largely subsistence plots) — hardly a prosperous "middle peasantry" by even the most modest of government proposals.

Romania had passed through the interwar global economic contraction without changing its structural position in the world economy and indeed more subservient than ever to the powerful economy of Germany. The national bourgeoisie had made some progress in creating a more profitable sector of economic activity, in industry, but was still in the thrall of international capital, with at least 70 percent of industrial capital belonging to foreigners (Jowitt 1971:91). Not only had capitalist agriculture failed to emerge in the countryside, but a marginal peasantry had been reconstituted and its dissolution retarded. Despite the high taxation that brought these peasants into the market, they had shown no consistent trend toward modernization: the result was commercialization without development. By keeping prices low enough to support cheap industrialization until very late in the period, the state had also kept food inexpensive for international markets as well, while at the same time helping to limit the accumulation of capital in the countryside and to assure that capital would flee to the area of the state's priority: capitalist industrialization toward national autonomy. These restraints on agricultural capital provided room at least temporarily for the survival of the peasants constituted by the agrarian reform (see Warman 1980: 258–259).

From the point of view of national capitalist manufacture and of those desiring a rounded capitalist development of the Romanian economy, the peasants were backward and the economy was in trouble. From the point of view of international capital, Romanian autarky had, happily, failed and prospects were good. From the point of view of the peasants, things were both bad and good: although people worked at least as hard as ever, there were new opportunities to explore and people had more land, which did not require costly purchases of machinery or fertilizer to farm well.[6] Surely their opinion — and not only government bungling — contributed something to the outcome.

THE NEW REGIME AND TRANSYLVANIA

Because of major historical differences between Transylvania and the old Romanian Kingdom, many of the policies just described had a slightly different impact when applied to the former region. Three subjects merit a quick summary as preparation for the data to be considered below. First, the most acute of the revolutionary effects of 1918 in Transylvania was that Romanians had new access to positions formerly dominated by other ethnic groups, and this new access went hand in hand with the decisive loss of such positions by others, the Magyars in particular. Second, Transylvania figured centrally in the nationalist industrialization policy of the state, owing to its history of greater industrial development, and this provoked some discord between Transylvanians and political and financial interests from the Regat. Third, the trends in agricultural development moved, more than they did elsewhere, in the direction of the "more rational" animal husbandry and mixed farming, displacing cerealism and perhaps easing the problem of overpopulation.

Changes in the relationship between nationality and occupation or class position were the most significant and far-reaching consequences of the new regime in the interwar period. I will not address arguments about Romania's possible reverse discrimination against Transylvania's Magyars and Germans (see Macartney 1937, where some of these arguments are reviewed), but it is important to mention the major areas in which Romanian control reverberated throughout Transylvania. The effects were greatest upon Magyars. To begin with, because Magyars had owned large estates disproportionately, the agrarian reform inevitably expropriated Magyars and gave to Romanians. Land totaling 1,664,000 hectares from about 9,000 estates, the bulk of them Magyar, passed into peasant lands, leaving their owners to turn compensations toward other uses.

Many of the owners did not stay to do so: 197,000, or about one-fifth of the entire Magyar population of Transylvania, repatriated to Hungary between 1918 and 1924 (Macartney 1937:253n). This egress itself left holes to be filled; and although it is not known from which occupations the exodus was greatest, it is a fair guess that the largest holes were left in traditional Magyar strongholds such as the professions, civil service, and administration (see fig. 4-1). A radical shift in the ethnic composition of the bureaucracy was unavoidable, even though at least initially the non-Romanian administrators were encouraged to remain. New openings for Romanians were not restricted to the administration per se but extended to the strategically vital army and transportation system, especially the railway, as well as to positions in what had been Hungarian government monopolies before the war.

A result of the change of administration, then, was that the chief sector of employment valued by the Magyars was lost to them and opened to Romanians (whose presence in it before had been limited), and the Magyars were left with few options outside private employment.[7] Germans in general fared better, often moving ahead in preference over Magyars (as when a Swabian rather than the customary Magyar was made Roman Catholic bishop), but they were in no wise preferred to Romanians and they suffered, as Magyars did, from some of the new regulations concerning the use of language. Macartney observes that in consequence, "A Roumanian middle class is beginning to grow up side by side with the minorities. There are far more Roumanian banks, Roumanian shops, Roumanian doctors, lawyers, and journalists than there were fifteen years ago" (Macartney 1937:323). In short, the mobility perspectives of the average Romanian in Transylvania were now infinitely greater than they had ever been, as new slots in an expanding bureaucracy and economy were coupled with a proliferation of Romanian educational institutions.

It should not be imagined from the fact of Romanian nationality that relations between Transylvanians and people from the Regat were entirely cozy. Despite the improved access to positions of influence and wealth, Transylvanians discovered drawbacks to their transfer from the industrializing Habsburg Empire into the agrarian Romanian Kingdom, whose aspiring industrial elite looked covetously on the resources that Transylvania had already developed. From the beginning, there was evident tension between the centralism of Regat politicians and the decentralization espoused by political leaders from Transylvania and the other new territories (see Helin 1967). Centralism clearly carried the day in the new constitution of 1923 (Roberts 1951:98). It seems evident that budding industrialists from the Regat gained many advantages from a policy that treated Transylvania firmly as an integral part of the kingdom. The victory of centralism went together with political dominance by the Liberals, who enjoyed very little support in Transylvania and ran the government for the first several years.

An important sphere of activity for people from the Regat was Transylvanian industries, newly nationalized according to provisions in the peace settlements. Hungarian and Austrian capital interests in Transylvania were largely displaced in two different directions: many of them were bought out by Romanians, and others were clandestinely transferred to outside capitalists not subject to the nationalizations, such as British, French, and Czech concerns (Berend and Ránki 1974*a*:193–196). These clandestine transfers worried the Liberals, anxious to exclude foreign capital in any form other than loans, and probably contributed to the tendency for Romanians to buy out capital interests in Transylvania at exorbitant prices (Mitrany 1930:447). It is a reasonable guess that this massive transfer of foreign capital into the hands of a Romanian bourgeoisie involved Romanians from the Regat disproportionately, given that for historical reasons fewer Romanians from Transylvania would be capable of making such large investments. If so, it would have been a major cause of Transylvanians' complaining, as Macartney reports they did (1937:331–332), at being treated like a colony by Regat taxation policy and financial interests. Transylvania did in any case contribute more than other areas to Romania's industrialization, for more than half of the total industrial production generated by the six main industrial sectors in interwar Romania came from Transylvania — which had about a third of the national territory and population (Mellor 1975:196).

The combination of the land reform and a policy that gave industry top national priority made less attractive than ever the prospects for large-scale capitalist agriculture in Transylvania, and chapter 4 has shown that the prospects had never been marvelous. From 1918 on, it was clear that at least the short-term future of agriculture was in petty-commodity-producing small farms. This future was perhaps more promising in Transylvania than in the Regat. Despite poorer soils, Transylvania had a generally higher level of agricultural technique: more widespread rotation of crops, greater diversification and more livestock-raising alongside cereals, higher productivity per hectare, and the highest per capita output in Romania (Madgearu 1940:30; Roberts 1951:44). Ecological conditions made the supply of locally produced cereals scarcely equal to the demand, in contrast with excess supply in the Regat, and grain prices were consequently somewhat higher in Transylvania (see, e.g., Romania 1936:40, 46). Therefore, although state policy kept agricultural prices universally low, their level in Transylvania permitted peasants slightly better earnings from agriculture there. On the other hand, it is suggested that Transylvanian peasants were hungrier than others for credit (Ciomac 1931:85). And while earnings in agriculture may have been better in Transylvania compared with the Regat, compared with agriculture in prewar Transylvania the situation may have been worse, owing to differences in the levels of agricultural protection and, consequently, in prices between pre-war Austria-Hungary and postwar Romania (Klein 1929:573).

This latter comparison probably bore on the development of more "rational" cultivation in Transylvania, winning those peasants the approval of pro-development agronomists. Even though Transylvanians were also cerealists like other Romanian peasants, they used their cereals less and less for direct sale than for fattening pigs and cattle, from which they derived proportionately more of their income than did others. In 1935, 19 percent of the total raw income of Transylvania (excluding the Banat) came from cattle, compared with 10 percent for the Regat; and 16 percent came from pigs, compared with 8 percent for the Regat (Gusti et al. 1938, III:317). These figures are in spite of state export restrictions that hit Transylvania especially hard; restrictions and wartime depletion of livestock notwithstanding, livestock exports from Transylvania had been high even between 1919 and 1928 (Cristea 1929:434). Livestock raising was encouraged by several different factors: ecology, market conditions—including increased meat consumption in postwar Austria and Czechoslovakia (ibid.; Ciomac 1931:69)—and the fact that the agrarian reform had endowed Transylvania with an average of only 1.5 hectares of arable land per recipient (compared with 3.25 hectares in the Regat) but larger amounts of communal grazing land had been created there (from Roberts 1951:app., p. 367).

Specifics of the situation in Transylvania, then, imply minor departures from the general picture presented in the preceding section. The somewhat higher prices and level of industrialization provided a slightly more promising market environment for the much vaunted "middle peasant." In contrast to this trend, however, the prevalence of livestock farming somewhat reduced the size of the farm on which a peasant family could continue to subsist without dispossession, and to this brake on pauperization was added the possibility of occasional work in industry for at least a few more people than in the Regat. The greater potential tenacity of marginal peasants may have slowed the accumulation of land by the wealthier despite other trends in their favor; one might expect that the impetus to mechanize would have been consequently depressed and that some of these peasants would have found other uses for their earnings. When one recalls the new chances for upward mobility on the part of Romanians, one can guess what the other uses might have included. The net effect of all these factors was that Transylvanian agriculture probably would have manifested the same commercialization without development as did the rest of Romania. Given the concentration of capital in industry, one is no better advised to look for the effects of capitalist development in Transylvanian agriculture than in other parts of the country.

This summary emphasizes what will be a central theme in the continuing tale of Binţinţi: that of processes promoting and inhibiting social differentiation within this group of peasants. The theme has preoccupied Romanian scholars in both the interwar period and the present (e.g., Golopenţia and Georgescu 1941; Madgearu 1940; Şandru 1975), who usually start with the agrarian reform, asking whether it advanced or retarded the development of capitalist relations in agriculture and seeking to clarify the problem with evidence of social differentiation within the peasantry. My familiarity with Binţinţi does not enable me to join this argument authoritatively, since I lack figures on changes in property distribution during this period; and in any case the time span is too short to permit decisive conclusions. The theme is nonetheless a very suitable one for this narrative, whose objective will be to show the countervailing processes at work rather than to demonstrate a particular outcome. One moral of the story is that the progress of social differentiation in the countryside owed much to forces not directly governed by the putative development of capitalist relations and therefore cannot be taken as evidence for the growth of capitalism in agriculture.

BINŢINŢI BETWEEN THE TWO WORLD WARS: CHANGING PATTERNS OF MIGRATION, FERTILITY, AND MARRIAGE

Among the young men returning to Binţinţi after the war was one Petru (in local pronunciation the *e* rhymes with the *u* in "but"), born in 1894 to a family of near-landless agricultural laborers. Filling his evenings with tales of how he had seen the Russian Revolution firsthand as a prisoner of war and craftily capitalized upon the greater prestige of being "Austrian" rather than Romanian to gain special deference from the Russians, Petru settled down to farming in the new Transylvania. At his marriage that year to a village girl from a wealthy family—she brought a dowry of 2.5 hectares—his father gave him two fine oxen but almost no land, since there was little to be given. (Petru's uncle had even "become Hungarian," changing his name to work on the railway and help keep the family from starving.) It was unusual, although not unheard of, for two villagers of such disparate means to marry, and while Petru's personal qualities were and have remained unsurpassable, his suit was perhaps advanced by the wartime decimation of the pool of eligible bachelors and by the promise of land in the reform (he received a hectare-and-a-half). Together they bore five children, of whom three survived. An exceptionally diligent worker, Petru managed to purchase 2.5 hectares more during the next thirty-five years, by renting land from what was left of a local Magyar estate after expropriation and by sharecropping from one or another villager whenever he could. His two daughters were able to marry village peasants of good families, and after the next war his son would bring in a wife from nearby. Although Petru grew both maize and wheat on his lands, he usually fed them to cattle instead of taking the grain to market, and most of his income for land purchases was earned in this way. He had always liked cattle, and it is still said that he raised some of the finest.

Almost of an age with Petru was Adam, one of six children from a family of well-to-do peasants (by village standards),[8] whose marriage portion of 3 hectares was enlarged by a dowry from his wife and later by small purchases and an additional hectare's inheritance. Married before the war, they had a son in the old Transylvania and a daughter in the new. Both children survived, but they did not marry into good village families, for the son was sent to school and moved to the city to practice his profession in law, and the daughter married a man from outside the village, who moved into the family farm. The money Adam made by fattening cattle and by selling cabbage and wheat (sometimes paying these directly to the high school in lieu of fees) went not to purchasing more land or machinery but to the education of his son. The amount of land and number of implements he would eventually donate to the collective farm were almost identical with those of his poorer fellow veteran, Petru. Even so, to educate a son in those days of unpredictable markets was a costly undertaking, one made just a bit more feasible because the state, in its eagerness for new functionaries, made law the only profession for which one could prepare without full-time university attendance, as Adam's son explains. He was therefore able to study partly at home and reduce the expenses of his education.

These two careers together illustrate one very visible pair of trends in the behavior of Binţinţi peasants between the wars: poor peasants turned with vigor to village agriculture and ceased to resort to the external environment as often as before, while a number of wealthier peasants proceeded in exactly the opposite fashion, using village agriculture as a springboard upward into the larger environment.

The immediate causes of this reciprocal shift in strategies were the agrarian reform, which retarded processes of impoverishment among the poorest strata and permitted them to remain peasants, and the nationalization of the bureauracy, professions, and educational system, which enabled richer peasants to turn their children into gentlemen. Both of these trends had their nationalist facet. Thanks to the village's location, nationalist industry gave some of its poorer members temporary jobs and regular markets for items like eggs and fowl, helping them to keep afloat; and nationalist exhortations by the Romanian elite in Transylvania were largely responsible for pushing the sons of well-to-do peasants upwards into the educational system (Binţinţi Germans of equivalent and greater wealth followed no such route). Tendencies for the poor to turn inward while the rich turned outward are visible in several aspects of village life but appear most clearly in patterns of migration from the village through time.

It is reasonable to assume that without the land reform (along with the irregular acquisition of a rich wife), Petru's three children would not all have remained in Binţinţi. Without the early deaths of two of his own three siblings, Petru himself might very well have followed a path taken by many of the village's poor peasants at the turn of the century: migration. One frequently encounters in the family histories of poorer peasants the departure of one or more siblings, aunts, or uncles for "the city": "What else could they do? They were poor, and there was nothing for them here, so they went to the city. That's what poor people did." Most of them became domestic servants (especially the women), unskilled workers, or apprentices to a trade; most were either poor or from middling families with large numbers of children; and most never returned. These migrants seem to have gone far more often to cities in the Romanian Kingdom than to Transylvanian ones, perhaps reflecting a preference of Transylvanian urbanites for Magyar rather than Romanian servants or the de facto exclusion of Romanians from many Transylvanian cities.[9] Of the many persons who appear in the land registers or parish records from the 1870s and 1880s but leave no further trace, the majority are from poor families[10] and migration was in all likelihood their fate.[11]

There was also a very distinct stream of prewar migration that included some persons who were neither poor nor intent on staying away permanently. These were persons who left for work in the mines and industries of the United States, during the massive emigration from Austria-Hungary to America in the late 1890s and early 1900s. The emigrants were not restricted to the poorest strata (though, again, many were of middle families with large offspring sets), and many of them returned to invest their earnings in land or to pay off debts. Unlike the migrants to Romanian cities, who left agriculture to fend for themselves, most of these emigrants went so as to be able to remain in agriculture, and the emigrants who did not themselves return continued to send money back to improve conditions for their families still on the land. That the stream included destitute as well as propertied peasants was due to agents who recruited the workers with specific contracts, often advancing money for the fare, and to the collaboration of American shipping companies, which sometimes arranged with employers to have a man's fare taken from his subsequent wage (Puskás 1975: 69–70). Some peasants borrowed the money from banks or from other villagers (who were not always repaid, they hasten to complain). The phenomenal level of American wages compared with local ones, and of the dollar when converted to local currency, made this form of emigration a tremendously efficient strategy for improving or at least holding onto a marginal position in agriculture. According to informants' stories, many more would have gone before the United States restricted immigration had it not been for fears of the ocean or objections from their wives.

Of the thirty prewar migrants from Binținți concerning whom I have some information, all but one[12] were of these two types: needy peasants seeking unskilled jobs either in Romanian cities or in the United States. Only one was of the sort that would begin to be more prevalent after the war, and that one was the aviator and inventor Aurel Vlaicu, who left the village to acquire his engineering degree and, subsequently, his fame (see end of chap. 4). After the war the migrant stream began to diversify, first with recruits into the new Romanian army—largely peasants who had served in the war and been invited to remain—and the railway; then, by the late 1920s, with more and more village children treading the path beaten by Aurel Vlaicu, going to university to become lawyers and teachers for the newly Romanian Transylvania. Table 6–1 shows these changes in the migrant stream from 1890 to 1944;[13] arrows direct attention to the period in which each kind of migration is concentrated relative to the others. (The wartime period is extended to 1926, when the land reform was completed in Binținți and the outflow into unskilled jobs began to diminish. Within the next six years this flow would come almost to an end.) Table 6–2 shows that

TABLE 6-1. Migration from Binţinţi, 1890-1944,
According to Migrants' Occupational Destination

Year	Unskilled Urban Labor (including US)		Railway/ Army		Univerity/ Professions		T
	#	%	#	%	#	%	
1890-1914	29	97	0	0	1	3	30
1915-1926	14	64	8	36	0	0	22
1927-1944	11	32	2	6	21	62	34
	54	63	10	12	22	25	86

$\chi^2 = 55.0$, p $<$ .001

TABLE 6-2. Migration from Binţinţi, 1890-1944, According
to Economic Standing of Migrants' Family

Year	Top Quartile		Lower Three Quartiles		T
	#	%	#	%	
1890-1914	5	16	25	84	30
1915-1926	6	27	16	71	22
1927-1944	18	53	16*	47	34
	29	34	57	66	86

$\chi^2 = 9.9$, p $<$ .01

* The depression accounted for a large number of these migrations.

the prewar emigration was associated with middle and poorer peasants and dropped off, relatively speaking, after the reform, while the postwar migrants come from wealthier families and their numbers go up sharply in comparison with before.[14] The contrast exemplifies the peasantization of the poor and the outward strivings of the well-to-do.

The movement of peasant children into the professions deserves a closer look because of its connections with Romanian nationalism and with village property structure. The history of this migration is closely tied to the history of Romanian national oppression, and the education of these peasant sons is still seen as a crucial step in the collective uplifting of the Romanian people. Witness the following extract from a sermon delivered in Binṭinṭi in 1979, at the funeral of one such village intellectual, who had been among the village's interwar students of law:

> We are gathered today to commemorate the passing of an intellectual of this place, one whose dying words were, "I wish to be buried in my native village." We are reminded of when our great village son Aurel Vlaicu won his first aviation prize, and his chief thought was not for himself but for his village, for he gave a large donation to our church in honor of its importance to him and to the Romanian nationality that he knew so well how to celebrate. Like Aurel Vlaicu, today's esteemed departed saved his most important thought for his village despite the education and culture he had achieved. He kept close to his heart the soil that nourished him and fed his faith, and the faith of his ancestors, against centuries of oppression and enserfment when the Romanian church was all that kept the Romanian nation alive. The departed kept company with great men of our nation, men of distinction like himself; and like many other sons of this village who went to school and became intellectuals after World War I, he contributed to the glory of our people.

The emphases of this oration are not peculiar to the 1970s.

Some light is thrown on the superficially puzzling connection between education and nationalism — and on why this village population turned so quickly to exploit the new opportunities around it, which many peasants might not have noticed — when one learns of the role of the village schoolteachers after the war. In 1924 there arrived in Binṭinṭi the first schoolteacher who could be openly Romanian and was not obliged to tout the Magyar state. Like so many Romanians educated in prewar Transylvania, he was an ardent nationalist. One of his associates described thus the views this man propagated passionately in Binṭinṭi: the only way for a people to raise itself up and to escape the domination of others is through becoming educated, and Romanians have been so long oppressed by Magyars because they have been kept in a state of ignorance, which it is now their responsibility to cast off. During his eight or more years in Binṭinṭi, this teacher created a rich educational environment for villagers, outside the classroom as well as in it, organizing periodic conferences with villagers and friends who were at university and discussing everything from the state of agriculture to jural institutions. Despite his elevated status, he appeared on Sundays and holidays in Romanian national (peasant) costume. From his first year he could be seen buttonholing the skeptical parents of his sharpest pupils, exhorting them to send the children on for further schooling, regardless of the cost, and helping to secure scholarships for some of them. His insistence produced a steady trickle of educated migrants that his successor continued to encourage.

It was precisely this flow, of course, that gave rise to the "academic proletariat of lawyers and classicists" spewing forth in constantly greater numbers from Romania's interwar universities, and making Bucharest a city with more lawyers than Paris (Rothschild 1974:320). To ponder the aggregate trends makes the Binţinţi peasant seem insignificant indeed. The shape of this entire social system was what made careers in law less costly for peasant sons than careers in agronomy, paralleling the connection between bureaucratic hypertrophy and agricultural stagnation; it was inherent in the system that the proliferation of parties made a national pastime of recruiting partisans by creating official posts for all degree-holders in law and the arts (Mitrany 1930:532-533), and inherent in the system that these legions of officeholders turned to fascism when their party was out of office and their posts reassigned. One cannot say that Adam of Binţinţi produced all this. Yet he did decide to take his income and send his son to school, rather than buying a mower, "so as to have a gentleman or two in the family and not be all just peasants." Informants recall clearly that this was the era when the old parental complaint, "We're not making you priests and teachers! Get out to the barn!" was replaced (by those who could afford it) with "I'm going to make my son a gentleman." It had not taken much — a change of regime, a patriotic schoolteacher, and (perhaps) conditions that made land hard to accumulate and mechanization therefore irrational — for some Binţinţi peasants to swell the hypertrophic bureaucracy and the ranks of proliferating parties, including the fascists, leaving agriculture to move imperceptibly forward without them.

The migration of offspring from some families of well-to-do villagers had two important consequences for the property structure of Binţinţi. First, families supporting one or more children through school were not among the contenders for land that came up for sale, which gave poorer and middle peasants something more of an opportunity to accumulate property. This is not to say that all wealthy peasants sent their children to school, leaving a clear field for the others: of the seven Romanian households who would have made it (just barely) into the government's "middle peasantry" in

1939, having about ten hectares of land each (the richest had thirteen), two sent children to university, and two sent daughters and one a son to high school but not beyond; one would have schooled his son if the child had had any aptitude, and one was childless (and both were busily accumulating land). There were still many families below these, however, who exhausted their resources with schooling and bought little or no land. Thus, the retarded proletarization of the poor and the migration of the rich went hand in glove.

Second, those peasants who sent children to university were at the same time creating an impartible holding for the child who remained, and this heir received a farm that was doubtless bigger, failures of acquisition notwithstanding, than the portion he would have received as a coheir. The education of village offspring was one face of a coin whose other face was accumulation of land over a longer run. It was tantamount to a new inheritance rule, operating under the genial surface of egalitarian partibility, and it boded well for the government's prosperous "middle peasant" if a bit behind schedule. But the result was not to be achieved as the state had envisioned it — through the free circulation of land, the pauperization of the weak, and acquisitions of their properties by the enterprising. These well-to-do peasants were not budding capitalist farmers but country gentlemen. Perhaps their behavior reflects how difficult it was to accumulate land with such low prices and inadequate credit, with so little extra land to rent or even buy, with such a tenacious poor peasantry.

This conclusion suggests a more general way of phrasing the relationship between the reciprocally changing strategies of rich and poor peasants. In the previous chapter I argued that across generations, Binţinţi Romanians reproduced their lowly class position, in Transylvanian society as well as in the village, through partible inheritance, which ensured that they would always be found on tiny plots (or in the urban proletariat) while Germans occupied somewhat larger holdings (or urban enterprises). The significance of 1918 was that it changed the parameters of Romanian peasant strategies. Poor peasants were given a chance to cease reproducing their pauperization and rich peasants to cease reproducing peasanthood, without changing the mechanism (the inheritance rule) of earlier days. The poor could now produce more peasants while the rich could produce city and country gentlemen.

In an apt example of the Matthew principle, however — to those that have, more will be given — the "revolution" gave better instruments to the wealthy peasants than to the poor. The export of surplus offspring through education would reliably reproduce several generations of gentlemen, but the pursuit of peasant agriculture on expanded holdings with larger pasture would gradually reproduce marginality again as long as partibility remained the rule. No matter that Binţinţi was remarkably favored in the land reform, with both arable and pasture lands; the eventual result was still inevitable. Or so it seemed.

Many families, however, were determined to avoid this result — and richer families were among them too — by limiting their offspring. After World War I a greater degree of fertility control appears among all sectors of the village population, as can be seen by examining changes in the size of offspring sets before and after the war. Civil and parish registers of births and deaths provide the basis for reconstructing all offspring born to marriages after 1870, as well as for determining the ages of death for children who did not survive to maturity. On the assumption that any conscious family planning by these peasants would take into account the all-too-obvious reality of child deaths, I counted family sizes as consisting of only those children who survived to age fifteen. The offspring sets[15] were arrayed chronologically by the date of birth of the last child to each marriage (whether or not the child survived, since its birth indicated that as of that time, parents had not chosen to prevent additional births). Inspection of the results showed a visible break in family sizes around World War I; hence that date is used in table 6-3, showing changes in family size.

This table shows that of all the families that could be reliably included in this approximately seventy-five year period, 38 percent consisted of zero to one child and 20 percent of four or more children; but whereas fully a third of all families completed before the war had four or more children and smaller families each took less than a fourth of the total, after the war more than half of all families consisted of zero to one child, another fourth of two children, and only one-fifth of three children or more. To avoid an inaccurate impression I should note that the mean family size (survivors only) for the prewar period is 2.74[16] — that is, not as large as table 6-3 might imply — but the rapid drop to a mean size of 1.64 after the war, and the statistical significance of the table, clearly suggest family limitation.

This conclusion is strengthened when one observes that declining offspring-set size was being achieved against a decline in child mortality. Mortality trends may be very roughly captured as follows: at least 45 percent of all children born to couples married before 1890 did not survive to age fifteen;[17] couples married between 1890

TABLE 6–3. Changes in Family Size, Binjinji, Around World War I

Number of Children Surviving to Age 15

Offspring sets Completed Between	0–1*		2		3		4 or more		T
	#	%	#	%	#	%	#	%	
1870s and 1917	40	24	41	24	30	18	53	33	164
1918 and 1944	76	54	37	26	19	14	8	6	140
	116	38	78	26	49	16	61	20	304

$\chi^2 = 45.7$, p < .001

*These are combined on the assumption, borne out in fieldwork, that childless couples did not plan childlessness. Many adopted the child of a relative.

and 1915 saw 37 percent of their children die before age fifteen;[18] and couples married between the two wars lost only 21 percent of their children before age fifteen—still a high rate (one in five) but considerably below the nearly one in two of a few decades earlier. The huge drop in infant mortality in the interwar years may well reflect improved standards of consumption, both after the land reform and during the depression, when peasants ate more because markets were so poor (Zagoroff et al. 1955:264). If, in the face of this, offspring-set size nonetheless declined, the impetus to limit families must have been serious indeed.

It would be improvident to adduce a village-specific explanation for this phenomenon when the demographic transition is still sweeping across the globe, and in one sense the fact of fertility control in Binţinţi is more significant than its explanation.[19] My objective in further exploring the fertility behavior of these peasants is to suggest some of the things that may have contributed to it[20] whether or not they were consciously realized, and to provide a sense of how these peasants themselves thought about the issues.

Binţinţeni offer a variety of motives for family limitation. Few are old enough to remember clearly the attitudes and habits prevailing both before and after the war, but several believe that something did change then ("after the Hungarians"). The cause they most often mentioned was that people became more concerned not to divide their farms. Some added, "People got prouder. Before, it was all right to have a brood of kids dressed in rags and pigskin shoes (*opinci*) but after the war people laughed at you if your kids weren't freshly turned out in new clothes and shoes, and so you couldn't afford so many any more." Others said that peasants didn't know as much before, and maybe more would have limited families earlier if they had known how. (Perhaps a more appropriate wording is that after the war there appeared techniques less potentially fatal than the "old wives'" remedies that peasants had clearly known about all along;[21] these were replaced with medical abortions, whose cost restricted them to the wealthier families; with more consistent resort to abstinence and coitus interruptus; and, for some, with use of condoms, which seem not to have been known about at all before the war.) Finally, "People started to see that having many children was a pain in the neck and a misfortune, and that all the large families were poor."

In fact, historically it was not true that all large families were poor, for in earlier days large family size was, if anything, more prevalent among the rich, being a sign of their wealth. To associate fertility with poverty did have some basis nonetheless. Not only could poor families ill afford doctors' abortion fees, but two informants' stories suggest that they (at least, among poor families from before the war) did not think of fertility as something over which one exercised control: "However many children God sends, and He will also send the means to feed them." In addition, these informants imply that poor families earlier in the century may not have considered family limitation because they did not regard themselves as responsible for the fates of their children, as did other peasants who limited so as to avoid dividing the inheritance: "We had as many as God gave, and we never expected them to stay here with us since we had no land; we counted on their finding whatever they could for themselves." A passive and individualistic attitude toward fertility is consistent with being at the mercy of others and having no collective estate, and both of these became less true of poor peasants after the land reform, when they limited fertility just like others, than before it. A final impetus toward controlling fertility may have come from the same urban elite who urged that children be educated so as to uplift the Romanian people. Given the widespread opinion among sophisticates that peasant hyperreproduction was the cause of the backwardness of agriculture (Roberts 1951:205), it is likely that urbanites preached to peasants about fertility and poverty, urging restraint through example and ridicule.

There is a further notion not mentioned by informants but related to their idea of not dividing the inheritance. This notion involves the effects of the land reform, and links reduced fertility to current arguments in historical demography concerning premodern population increases (see, e.g., papers in Tilly 1978*b*; Levine 1977). Several scholars propose that the great population increase accompanying the industrial revolution in Europe resulted from rural by-employments that permitted a denser population than did simple peasant farming. These studies show that purely agricultural populations had lower fertility than did proletarians or peasants involved in cottage industry (e.g., Braun 1978). Turning this argument around suggests an association between declining fertility and declining rural opportunities for income supplements (Tilly 1978*b*:37). For Transylvania the crucial shift was not the replacement of cottage industry with factory production; it was the expropriation of large estates, which had offered income supplements through some wage labor but, more importantly, also through sharecropping, which had enabled Chayanovian peasants to adjust the supply of land to the size of their families.[22] In other words, the land reform reconstituted a peasantry in two ways, by retarding proletarization with grants of land and by reducing the nonpeasant roles of sharecropper and wage laborer that many had occupied simultaneously with their peasant status. Sharecropping did not disappear entirely after the reform; peasants (such as Petru) continued to rent from the few local estate owners not vulnerable to expropriation, as well as from elderly couples or emigrants whose lands were temporarily available to be worked. Nonetheless, income supplements from agriculture appear to have contracted after the war. Some supplements from industry provided a small counterweight to this trend, and some Binţinţi peasants took advantage of them, but they did not become available until the early 1930s when fertility control was well underway.

The consequences of this reduction of births are clear: by ceasing to fragment their estates among so many offspring, at least some peasant families added to their own life on the land and that of their heirs, resisting pauperization. And depending on their position in the social structure, they either forwarded or resisted social differentiation: rich peasants who kept farms intact were helping to create a "middle peasantry," and poorer peasants who reduced subdivision were determinedly remaining peasants and postponing their elimination from the rural scene.

Although data on wealth are insufficiently reliable to warrant tabulating fertility by socioeconomic group, the trends from a rough calculation are enlightening. After the war, richer peasants ceased to be the ones with the largest families and dropped significantly to about two children. Peasants in the middle ranks displayed two patterns: many of them had just one child, but a goodly number (several of them with families started before the war) had three children or more, and they did so more than richer or poorer peasants. Most poorer families, like the rich, began having consistently smaller families than before, though a few still had three or more children. Overeager to reduce their offspring, proportionately more poor peasants ended childless (though not sterile); many had only one child.

The middle and poor families with one child thus assured their place on the land, as did the rich with two, one of whom was likely to become a "gentleman." Zero- and one-child families tended to occur a bit more among middle and poor peasants, two-child families among the rich, with their additional strategy for reducing farm fragmentation. Still, almost a fifth of all families had three children or more, and inasmuch as they tended to be among the less wealthy, their future looked grim.

Both migration and fertility control exemplify behavioral responses to the altered postwar circumstances that also influenced the course of social differentiation. A third such change was in marriage patterns, although here the effects on differentiation are a bit less clear, probably because marriage is a much more multivalent social phenomenon than the other two. I restrict my discussion to fairly mechanical aspects of it: endogamy and exogamy, and their relevance to acquiring land. The most striking change in marriage patterns around the war was a sharp drop in the general rate of village endogamy for all, explainable by the effects of the land reform. This change can be seen in table 6-4, based on official marriage records and interview data. The table summarizes marriage patterns for men and women between 1890 and 1945, combining all marriages between 1890 and 1917 and from 1918 to 1945, since the patterns within remain fairly consistent. As is apparent, endogamy was much more frequent for both sexes before the war than after it, when increasing numbers of spouses were brought in from elsewhere. One also sees how much more common outmarriage was for women than for men, reflecting a preference to keep sons close at hand.

The decline in endogamy is best understood as a consequence of the land reform, together with various state measures to increase the circulation of land. These loosened the very tight prewar land market in rural areas (Eddie 1967:297) and made it possible for some villagers to marry peasants from elsewhere, sell their more-distant dowry, and buy property closer to home—the only catch being to find Binţinţi properties for purchase. Romania's interwar sociological researchers (Golopenţia and Georgescu 1941:35) found especially brisk circulation of lands, through both dowry and sales, in plains villages where large amounts of land had been transferred in the reform. This was a perfect description of Binţinţi, where about 350 hectares were expropriated; about 100 hectares of it went to the communal pasture, and most of the rest (arable and hayfields) was distributed to approximately 125 households in varying amounts.[23] The average distributed plot was larger in Binţinţi than in any of the villages around it. Their unique good fortune made Binţinţi peasants the most marriageable ones in the area, surely evident in the much larger number of inmarrying spouses than before, as good soils, healthy-sized plots, and extensive common pastures lured prospective partners to the village and gave Binţinţeni the upper hand

TABLE 6–4. Changes in Marriage Patterns of Binṭinṭi Men and Women, 1890–1945

		Type of Marriage Made						
		Endogamous		Spouse Moves In		Local Moves Out		T
		#	%	#	%	#	%	
Men's Marriages*	1890–1917	92	79	16	14	9	8	117
	1918–1945	75	58	48	37	6	5	129
		167	68	64	26	15	6	246
Women's Marriages†	1890–1917	92	67	16	11	29	21	137
	1918–1945	75	48	40	25	43	27	158
		167	57	56	19	72	24	295[a]

*χ^2 = 17.8, p < .001

†χ^2 = 13.3, p < .01

[a] The total number of marriages is higher for women than for men because more women remained in the village until marriage; more men emigrated or died in the war.

in negotiating postmarital residence. (From their comments, villagers clearly preferred remaining in the village to marrying out.)

Changing marriage patterns and the new land market affected social differentiation in several ways. Because of the favorable situation of Binţinţeni, poorer peasants who previously might have either married out to less desirable locations or made unsatisfactory — perhaps undowered — endogamous marriages could now hold out for a better match, acquiring property one way or another. This helped to cushion their descent into landlessness through subdivided inheritances. Champions of the poorer peasants will note with glee how peasants used the free circulation of land, intended to produce the capitalist "middle peasant," to bargain instead for better semi-proletarian marriages. Best of all was to marry endogamously, which assured easy access to both partners' fields and eliminated the risk that no village land would be up for purchase when distant dowry lands were sold. Rich peasants had long monopolized this most desirable option. After World War I, however, there were shifts within the roughly 50 percent of marriages that were still endogamous (thus, the marriages of Petru and Adam were typical), and the shifts gave more endogamous marriages than before to middle and poorer peasants, partly because more daughters of richer peasants were marrying upwardly mobile urban migrants.

This survey of migration, fertility, and marriage patterns has uncovered several tendencies relevant to processes of social differentiation among Binţinţi peasants. The trends overall worked more to the advantage of richer peasants than poorer ones, as richer families stemmed the division of their holdings not only by reducing the number of their children to about two but also by making some children into gentlemen, who would lay no claim to a piece of the farm. Some richer peasants consolidated their village properties through favorable endogamous marriages, while others searched beyond the village for the ever-better marital arrangement. Among middle and poorer peasants, many did not remain defenseless against the forces working for their impoverishment but took some steps to retard that process, having only one or two children and more often acquiring property through the optimal marriage form, endogamy. Some of the poorer, however, along with some middle peasants — who tended to be the ones with the largest families — were in a precarious situation. They continued to subdivide property through inheritance, and they ceased to export as many of their number as they had done before. Given the uncertain development of industry, these people's children might have ended in desperate straits.

Because the wealthier peasants had more effective means at their disposal, in the greater resources that enabled them to export off-spring into socially desirable employment, social differentiation did proceed within this population. Nonetheless, the mechanisms for it were not chiefly those of a capitalist economic system; rather, they combined social traditions (inheritance) with newly available resources in the broader social structure. Insofar as differentiation was slowed, it was primarily by manipulating fertility and marriage within a stagnant agrarian economy. The next section will show that the most important social divisions were not those inherent in wealth differences among Romanians but—still—those separating Romanians and Germans.

ECONOMIC RELATIONS AND AGRICULTURAL PRACTICES IN BINŢINŢI BETWEEN THE TWO WORLD WARS

During the interwar period the majority of Romanian peasants in Binţinţi came to be integrated into the economy chiefly through petty-commodity production for market, rather than through rents or occasional wage labor; the mechanisms permitting this increased market orientation were the land reform, increased urbanization, and taxes. Well before the war a number of these peasants had been involved in some market production but they were far from being the majority, most of whom had been primarily involved in subsistence farming, while only the Germans were conscientious market farmers. When more Romanians began increasing their production of marketable commodities after the war, the position of Romanian peasants as a group more closely came to resemble that of the Germans. Differences in their situations, however, were as salient as the similarities: the Romanians' market activities were more often mediated by merchants than was true of Germans, and Romanians were becoming entangled in new debts just as Germans finally were paying off the last of their mortgages and were becoming more or less independent of commercial capital.

The forces that pulled Romanians ever more fully into the market were of several kinds, all of them facilitated by ownership of land. First were the necessary cash expenditures most often referred to by informants: firewood and taxes. Although these had been perennial peasant obligations (with firewood often being bartered for rather than bought with cash), there is some suggestion that the tax bite increased after the war. Taxes were fairly low in the first few years of the new regime, and government revenues from agriculture came primarily from import and export duties. When these were revised in 1927, however, taxes were trebled to compensate (Mitrany 1930: 43). The government take may have remained the same with this move, but more of it was now coming directly from the peasant's pocket; and with depressed agricultural prices, this meant more marketing and more work. The primary contribution to peasants' integration into the market, then, was probably the conjuncture between taxation levels and prices set by the state.

Other things contributed as well, chief among them new levels of indebtedness. Some recipients of reform land had indebted themselves, less to pay the required compensation than to purchase implements and draft animals. Their debts forced them into marketing so as to pay interest and principal. While the persons most likely to borrow for these items were poorer peasants, borrowing was widespread among peasants of all stripes during these years — for new plows, for building or modernizing houses and sheds, for buying land, and, when the economic situation became increasingly grave, even for basic consumption needs. In the absence of credit institutions, peasants borrowed from banks, a possibility open to anyone who could find two respected persons to stand as guarantors and easier still for those having land as collateral. From informants' stories, it appears that some very poor peasants had trouble securing loans, but others found it less difficult to get money than to find someone willing to sell them a piece of land when they were ready to buy. It is a nice piece of irony that the landowner whose expropriation enriched so many Binţinţeni was the very same lawyer Mihu (see chap. 4) who had founded the bank now being enriched by the interest on these peasants' debts.

The increase in postwar marketing for taxes and debts was accompanied by increased consumption, a further indication of larger cash incomes.[24] While informants are not very articulate about the process — at best, they attribute it to "city influence" — more and more of them began to purchase urban work clothes ("German clothing") and shoes instead of wearing home-woven peasant costume. One imagines that city influence might have come from public servants, teachers, and priests, serving as unconscious sales agents for industry while consciously promoting civilization and progress for Romanians (see Warman 1980:89). The changes were reportedly first taken up by the wealthier peasants and then generalized to the rest. Many informants speak of a new competitive and acquisitive spirit, which led everyone suddenly to become interested in building nicer houses in place of straw-covered huts, getting better cattle, becoming better off, being ahead of their neighbors. One woman reported how she fell in love with her husband-to-be in the mid-1930s when he went from Binţinţi to her village, finely dressed in a leather jacket and gloves such as she had never seen on a peasant before. Among other indications of increased consumption is that Romanians picked up the custom of making cakes and preserves, which suggests increased use of sugar. Except for the changes in clothing, which began right after the war, informants do not date these changes precisely, and it is probable that much of the increased consumption dates only from the price rises of the late 1930s.

What were some of the sources of cash earnings? A few of them remained the same as before the war. There was day wage-labor for Germans, which may have gone up slightly in these years as the birth rate among Germans dropped almost as low as the Romanians' and from a much higher original rate (see note 16). There were the few local trades, such as shoemaking, carpentering, and smithing, which had allowed several families to subsist in the village on sub-marginal holdings. There were a few poorer women with sewing machines—Singer models, bought from traveling merchants in the early 1900s—on which they did repairs for cash.

There also developed during these years a small number of possibilities that had not existed before. In the nearby towns of Orăştie and Cugir the interwar industrial drive saw the founding and expansion of a few factories, which, although they absorbed very little Binţinţi labor on a regular basis, provided a source of occasional income either in construction of the facilities or in factory work itself. There were small chemical and leatherworking installations in Orăştie, an iron- and steel-processing plant at Cugir, and for a time a timber mill in a village down the road. Most informants who spoke of temporary employment in one or another of these places (all of them from poor families) worked there during the 1930s, when the effects of the depression on agricultural markets made cash very difficult to find.

These factory jobs were crucial supports for peasants at the margin; they could also, on rare occasion, be a way of moving up from marginal to more comfortable status, as in the following story. Avram Stoian, whose exploits with German farmer Pfeiffer and Magyar lawyer Janó were encountered in the preceding chapter, was one of only two or three Binţinţeni regularly employed in a factory. One day in the late 1930s he was approached by a doctor who owned some land in the village and from whom Avram's cousin sharecropped. The doctor, desperate for money with which to gamble at a fancy resort outing that weekend, proposed selling his extra house to Avram for 100,000 lei ready cash. When Avram's brother and cousin finished revising the proposal, what changed hands was not a house but two-and-three-fourths hectares of land with the crops standing on it, in exchange for 120,000 lei — by Avram's reckoning, his salary for two years, which he had stashed behind a brick toward buying a house of his own.

The end of the story required the last and most common of all sources of cash, the marketing of agricultural commodities, through which Avram's brother and cousin repaid him the loan that enabled them to take advantage of such a rare opportunity. Increased opportunities for sale of produce may have begun with the war: Petru reports that his father had two cows in 1914 and had worked up to nine head of cattle when Petru returned from the war in 1921. But the marketing of agricultural products doubtless received further impetus from the very urban and industrial growth that provided Avram Stoian his job. Between the 1930 and 1941 censuses, Orăştie and Cugir grew by 33 and 65 percent, respectively. Although this meant absolute increases of only 2,500 to 3,000 people each, it was nonetheless an expanding market for agricultural produce at a time when more peasants had the wherewithal to provide these and the cash needs to motivate them. There were further opportunities — more important ones — in the export market for livestock, to be discussed below.

Several kinds of commodities moved from Binţinţi farms into these various markets: cabbage, butter, eggs and chickens, wheat, maize, pigs, cattle, clover seed, and later some soybeans and sunflower seeds (in response to Germany's demand for these items). The products tended to divide complementarily, some coming from some kinds of farms and others from other kinds of farms, with a few areas of overlap. The two kinds of farms were German ones — marketing primarily butter, cereals, and eventually pigs — and Romanian ones — concentrating on cabbage and cattle, with some marketing of grains and pigs but less so than the Germans.

Many features of the organization of agriculture on German and Romanian farms were set out in the preceding chapter, and these were not much changed in the interwar period. Germans continued to pay primarily cash wages while Romanians exchanged labor or imported it seasonally for pay in kind. While sharecropping was much reduced for both groups, at one time or another there were always some households with land to give out — widows or aged couples, the priest, persons absent from the village—and sharecropping at fifty-fifty remained the norm, with Romanians its principal tenants. German farms continued to have more diverse agricultural inventories and more mechanization than Romanian ones and to be worked with horses or tractors, while Romanians still plowed with cows or oxen, except for a few well-to-do farmers who switched to horses in the 1930s.

The difference in inventories and working habits was still justified partly by reference to the continuing difference between the farm sizes of Germans and Romanians, which a property register from 1939 illustrates clearly.[25] Table 6-5 shows that Romanians were underrepresented in all farm sizes except the smallest (primarily subsistence holdings), and Germans were overrepresented in larger farms, especially those over ten hectares. The different labor densities on these farms accounted in large part for the differences in commodities marketed from them.

Ecological differences explain only one of the complementarities in products from these farms: Germans did not grow much cabbage because it required wet growing conditions that did not obtain on their lands, as on some Romanians' lands. The other complementarities are matters of strategy and scale. For example, Germans made butter—using separators, bought in the early 1930s precisely as government protection of dairy products drove up prices and butter production (Madgearu 1940:244)—and marketed it directly to private clients in town. Their farms were large enough to keep several milk cows, making the trip and the investment in separators reasonable; butter provided them a small but constant flow of cash. Romanians did not begin using separators and marketing butter

TABLE 6-5. Property Distribution in Binţinţi, 1939, by Ethnic Groups

Size of Farm (ha)	Germans	(%)	Romanians	(%)
0–2.99	7[a]	6.0	110[b]	94.0
3.0–9.99	14	18.2	63	81.8
10.0–14.99	5	41.7	7	58.3
15.0 +	3	100.0	0	0.0
	29	13.9	180	86.1

[a] All are widows or persons whose principal profession is a trade.

[b] About one-fourth are widows or elderly couples with offspring in the village.

directly until after World War II, following the expropriation of
German farms. Throughout the interwar period their only dairy
revenue, from the one or two cows their farms could support, came
from a milk merchant who moved into Binţinţi in 1928. He purchased milk directly from Romanians, turned it into butter and
cheese, and marketed these in distant cities. Paying 1.2 lei/kg for
milk—as opposed to 40 lei/kg for the butter alone—this merchant
skimmed off a considerable profit. (Realization of this may have
eventually prompted Romanians to switch, which in turn caused
the merchant to leave, in 1946.) Thus Germans marketed dairy
products directly, while Romanians were entangled with merchants
because their dairy enterprises were too small to make direct marketing feasible, in an economy that nevertheless required cash
income.

Dairy products provided small change. Far more important were
Romanian-German differences in their principal cash crops: for
Germans, wheat, and for Romanians, fattened cattle. Some Romanians with larger holdings also marketed a bit of grain, but
nearly all Romanians paid off their debts and purchases of land or
of implements by fattening cattle, which Germans never did. During
the 1930s, when grain prices hit an all-time low, Germans were
persuaded to depart from their traditional cerealism and move
toward animal-raising, but even then they more often raised and
sold pigs than cattle, and they continued to market cereals as well.
Informants of admirable loquacity on other topics are laconically
matter-of-fact on this, and the explanations they give for the difference leave something to be desired: "Why? We were attached to the
idea of wheat, and were proud to see carts loaded with grain."
"Germans didn't like cattle and we liked them a lot." "Cows are a
better deal than pigs because cows eat other things besides cereals."
"We fattened cattle because this village is great for grains." "Romanians plowed with cattle and we used horses." "Germans had
more land, that's why." One soon realizes that neither the issue of
the different commodities nor rigorous logic concerning it is a gnaw-
ing preoccupation for these people.[26] The explanation gradually
pieced together rests on both property structure and history.

When Romanians insist (and some Germans even agree) that
grain brought a better price if fed to animals and marketed thus
than if sold directly as cereals, strictly speaking they are correct
(Mitrany 1930:364), but only by ignoring the question of how much
labor is available to carry out the various activities. At every point,

Pl. 4. Petru and his son cart hay for the cattle they still like to raise.

Romanians made more labor-intensive choices than did Germans, producing more maize than wheat, more livestock than cereals, more cattle than pigs. For their small farms, too small to earn a reasonable income from selling grain directly, these were rational choices, since 80 percent of the Romanians were living on farms of five hectares or less—well within the range of what informants say could be worked by a husband and wife without importing labor. Their farms were for the most part labor-rich; having minimal opportunities for expanding their cultivated surface and absorbing labor through sharecropping or renting, they intensified their use of labor by growing relatively more maize and fodder beets (as well as other fodder crops) and by raising cattle. One of the very few Romanian exceptions to this pattern was the wheelwright, whose planting and livestock pattern was closer to that of the Germans because, as he himself observed, his time was taken up with his trade and he had little available labor. Germans, with their much larger farms, could never have intensified the labor at their disposal both to grow cereals and to raise the number of livestock their output would feed. Their farm sizes were sufficient to provide a reasonable income through mechanized extensive grain-farming. Only when grain prices plunged were they moved to alter the ratio of their activities.

The initial divergence in strategies was reinforced because Romanians entered commodity production in larger numbers after World War I, precisely as grain prices began to slide relative to livestock prices (Ciomac 1931:69; Cristea 1929:434), the export taxes of the 1920s notwithstanding. When the maximal crisis of cash hit in the 1930s, drawing even more peasants into marketing, livestock prices continued to be the more inviting because the state actively encouraged livestock exports. One informant saw these macro tendencies clearly from her barnyard: "We sold cattle because there was no one buying grain and the state was wanting people to contract oxen for export." Meanwhile Germans, after decades of dedicated grain farming, suffered a few years of terrible grain prices. Then they began shifting to more dairy farming and pig-keeping, but government support of wheat prices from the mid-thirties on made continued grain production feasible, with animals kept on the side for increased security.

As for why Germans turned more to pigs than to fattening cattle, they say first that fattening cattle was more work and second that they had excess grain they could not sell so they gave it to pigs, where it acquired value. The second statement is particularly significant. Germans gave excess, unsalable and unconsumable grain — something few Romanians had — to marketable pigs, which compete with people for food but take less labor away from cultivating grains. In contrast, most Romanians squeezed every possible resource to feed themselves and to keep cattle; the animals might be worked with first (hence the comments about plowing), and pastured on common lands some of the time, which reduced by a bit the surface area necessary for fodder; they were fed grains that would not bring adequate income if marketed, fodders that were often put on marginal lands with no other productive use, and hay from otherwise unproductive natural hayfields especially abundant in the Romanian part of the village. Pigs for Germans were an extra, cattle for Romanians a necessity. For the poorer Romanians, in particular, whose strategy is the one I have just described, cattle permitted them to utilize every corner of their ecological niche and to survive in it.[27]

Their survival depended in part on the communal pasture, a resource that was historically distributed unevenly both between Germans and Romanians and within the Romanian population. In the late 1880s, village pasture lands had been divided up and portions assigned to those residents who had cattle (including most of the former urbarial serfs but excluding many peasants without animals, i.e., some former irregular serfs and also all immigrants into the village). From that time, anyone without rights could pasture animals only by purchasing rights or paying a stiff fee. Germans entering the village in the 1890s received almost no natural pasturage in the properties they acquired. Only as of the land reform, when the pasture was enlarged and individual rights abolished in favor of the collectivity, did Germans and the remaining poor Romanians receive access to this important resource. While the shift at this late date did little to German farming patterns, it was important in enabling a milk cow to be kept by some poor peasants who might otherwise not have managed to feed it year-round off their own small plots, and in assisting others to feed a pair of work oxen that might eventually be fattened for sale.[28] The pasture provided a small but vital margin of safety for marginal peasants, helping to retard their proletarization.

There is one final point to be made about German wheat and Romanian cattle, to put these patterns and their consequences fully into their context in history. The twentieth-century niche of Romanian cattle-rearing had been created directly by eighteenth- and nineteenth-century feudalism. Landlords on large estates had cornered the internal cereal market,[29] partly by pressing serfs onto ever smaller plots from which marketing of cereals was both difficult and unprofitable. Germans were able to move into the internal cereal market precisely because they replaced those same landlords, on holdings large enough for cereal cultivation. Romanians had little choice but to raise cattle if they raised anything, for two reasons. First, they were restricted to tiny parcels in a tight land market under conditions that obviated their significantly expanding their holdings to farm grain. Second, densely packed in the countryside because of the labor-hunger of feudal production, they had plenty of labor to intensify and could survive only by doing so. Even in the 1800s some Romanians raised cattle for sale, but mostly they raised cattle to maintain the wherewithal for cultivation on their own and the landlord's fields. (One even imagines that serfs whose cattle were their only real property understandably "liked" them and found in this sentiment justification for their work.) These necessities of history produced, in the twentieth century, a commodity that made viable for occupation small holdings otherwise inadequate to sustain a peasantry at such a level of indebtedness, expenditure, and taxation.

The same historical necessities entailed additional, less benign consequences. Germans and Romanians did not just market different commodities; they were also tied into significantly different networks of exchange, networks differentiated by the destination of the product and by the role of merchant capital in them. Germans on rare occasions sold their wheat to Jewish middlemen for local and long-distance trade (see chap. 5), but most often they sold it themselves directly to consumers in the market—upland peasants, urbanites, or land-poor lowlanders—or, less often, to villagers from nearby who came into Binţinţi to buy grain from them. And they aver that such direct sales got a better price than sales to merchants. Even when Germans diversified into raising pigs, they were only sometimes implicated in a longer chain of exchange, since, they believe, the pigs sold in Hunedoara County were less often exported (owing to propitious conditions farther west) than consumed locally as fresh meat or salami. Romanians, in contrast, although they did market such products as eggs and fowl directly to consumers without the intervention of middlemen, nearly always sold their fattened cattle in the market to Jewish merchants—one in particular, who sent the best animals off into international export and processed the rest into meat products in his factory in the city of Deva, for subsequent local sale or export. The poorer a Romanian was, the more likely he was to participate only in these longer chains, for the Romanians directly marketing some grains or cabbage were usually those with larger amounts of land (who, nevertheless, also marketed cattle).

Thus, there were Germans producing wheat for direct internal marketing to consumers and Romanians producing cattle for an international export market mediated by merchants. However, only a history like that of Romanians would have brought the international market to them, as well as them to the market.[30] Marginalized by feudal lords, held in place by capital's disdain for Transylvanian agriculture, integrated into a national economy through debts and taxes, they provided cattle that were cheap. Moreover, the Romanian state collaborated in keeping it that way by putting a price ceiling on meat so workers could be cheaply fed. Cattle raising was consequently not a very profitable activity (Frunzănescu 1939:164; Mitrany 1930:364), except to the merchants who mediated the trade. The state's role makes especially poignant one Romanian's proud if self-serving recital concerning his hard work in raising six to eight cattle for export per year: "Our country needed these cattle so we could get things from other countries. We sent cattle to Italy, Palestine, Greece [cf. p. 284, lines 22–23] and they sent us things we needed in exchange. I was glad to raise cattle for my country's needs."

Many forces conspired, then, to engage Romanian producers in a circuit of trade that took profits beyond the Romanian border and that subjected Binţinţi peasants to the determinative effects of international capital. Villagers themselves tell stories, possibly apocryphal, that illustrate this in a strikingly evocative image. The changes of 1918 erected a national frontier between Transylvania and Hungary, informants say, creating a problem for Jewish merchants. Having amassed much gold from their trade in cattle, clover seed, fruit, nuts, and other local commodities for export, the merchants now had trouble getting their gold out. So they loaded it into the stomachs of cattle bound for export and directed their agents across the border to paw through the dung and retrieve their profits. Romanians who chortle with delight at this idea seem not to have considered that some of the gold would have been lifted from their own pockets.

If on the one hand Romanians became subjected to international merchant capital through fattening cattle for export, on the other hand they were subject to national merchant capital through their indebtedness to banks (and again the state was a collaborator because of its failure to supply adequate credit). Since borrowers were both rich and poor, one cannot say that this connection with capital worked more to the disadvantage of the poor (as did the export connection) except insofar as other economic conditions made it more difficult for them to free themselves of debt. In any event, all peasants fared better in relation to national than international merchant capital. Some might say they were even briefly victorious over it, and the reason was the grudging alliance of the state. When interest rates climbed, according to informants, from the usual 15 percent to 30 percent or more during the depression, the state had finally to step in and rescue peasants from their creditors (and itself from almost certain rural rebellion) by converting debts. Otherwise, many peasants' connection with national merchant capital would have resulted in their losing their means of production and becoming a landless proletariat (see Roseberry 1978).

As it was, informants say that some poorer families had already sold land before the conversion, unable to meet the interest payments, while among the more numerous middle- and rich-peasant debtors many had managed to survive that long on their income reserves and had not yet had to sell property when the conversion took place. Even though poorer peasants may have lost more, however, it was not only they who would have ceased to survive as peasants without the debt conversion. Among the names informants mention as debtors during these years, there were as many middle and well-to-do Romanian peasants as poor ones, all indebted for building houses, for schooling their offspring, and for purchasing land, and all candidates for elimination had the conversion not intervened.

There were a few names conspicuously absent from the verbal lists of debtors saved by the conversion; these were the names of Germans. It was not that they never borrowed: one did for a tractor, another when the motor of his mill blew up in 1937. Rather, as German informants present it, they had finally freed themselves from the toils of their 24-year mortgage debts and, at least for the time being, assiduously avoided borrowing money. When they wished to purchase lands or implements, they did it insofar as possible with ready cash. They were so well insulated from debts, both as borrowers and as lenders, that the depression scarcely touched them except to reduce their incomes. They were also insulated from savings, which were spent on new equipment rather than saved in banks. Only one German lost a large amount of money in savings during the crisis. The rest weathered it fairly well, so well that one otherwise astute informant kept having to be reminded of what "crisis" (their word) we were talking about.

Here—at last—was the state's prosperous "middle peasant," alive and well in small German numbers in Binţinţi. A quarter of Binţinţi's German farms (but only one twenty-fifth of Romanian ones) had ten or more hectares as the state said they should, fully a half (but only one-fifth of Romanians) were above the five hectares that assured full commodity production and sale. This peasant conscientiously bought land whenever its free circulation put it within his reach,[31] instead of making it a resource for better marriages. He did not fritter away his income on educating sons for an overstuffed bureaucracy but kept his farm intact by apprenticing sons inexpensively to urban trades. He enterprisingly purchased machinery— seeders, mowers, tractors, threshers—even in 1927 when tariffs made the prices outrageous, and he therefore gave goodly sums into state coffers. He diversified ("rationally") from his beloved cereals into mixed cereal and livestock farming and, shortly before the Second World War, made tentative experiments with chemical fertilizers. He religiously studied the technical manual *Der Pflug,* published each year by the Saxon organization (Romanians regularly received no such publication), which gave detailed suggestions for improving agricultural productivity. And with his production he obligingly fed urban populations for national industry, despite

sometimes-abysmal grain prices. He did not do all the things prosperous peasants sometimes do — for example, he did not lend money
much nor expand from his farm into petty commerce, but rather he
kept his capital in agriculture. His commitment to agriculture was
beyond dispute and his position in it secure. Had the state made
room for more people like him, the situation in agriculture might
have been very different.

The state's only problem with this prosperous German "middle
peasant" was in making him consume in the local market for which
he produced, and this meant developing the industries that would
enable him to buy a Romanian tractor instead of a German or
American one. In this respect alone was the German peasant spon-
soring the gains of international capital rather than supporting the
national plan (and even here one could argue that he had no choice).
It was to obtain this peasant's business that the state kept his as well
as Romanian peasants' incomes depressingly low, placing on them
both a disproportionate share of the burden of economic development. Both groups of peasants suffered from this burden, although
one suspects that the German peasant was in a somewhat better
position to bear it without permanent injury. (His position of advantage was soon to crumble.)

One might wonder why German farmers found investment in
agriculture worthwhile when so few others did. It is only part of the
answer that their larger farms made it rational to invest in machinery
to compensate for departing nonheirs and smaller families. Part of
it is that spending habits and local marketing patterns kept them
relatively independent of merchants and middlemen, leaving a
greater part of their products' earnings in their own hands. Perhaps
even more important than this, however, was the serious erosion of
the historic "bourgeois" monopoly of Germans in Transylvania. The
region's integration into a new Romanian state produced an expanded
Romanian middle class and a national industry into which Regat
financial interests were quick to move. One need not look for overt
discrimination to see that these new developments in the polity and
economy would swamp Germans in a sea of Romanian middle-class
interests. Germans might remain bourgeois, but they were no longer
the bourgeoisie.

Contributing further to this erosion of their niche was the severe
blow dealt to Saxon communal strength by the land reform's expropriation of 20,000 hectares from their corporate properties. Shorn
of collective resources that had helped sustain the Saxon organization through centuries of often-inimical rule, this community would

be supported henceforth by its individual members. It remained a solidary community but it now lacked its corporational infrastructure. If Germans in Binţinţi took interwar agriculture seriously despite the obstacles that made many others abandon it, perhaps the reason was that they no longer had automatic and privileged entry into more lucrative spheres of endeavor.[32] This change is yet another aspect of the Transylvanian revolution of 1918.

INTERETHNIC RELATIONS AND SOCIAL DIFFERENTIATION

The earlier discussion of processes furthering and impeding social differentiation within the Romanian segment of the village concluded that some of the wealthier Romanian families were on their way to becoming "middle peasants." The possible instruments at their disposal were family limitation, the schooling of children, and (for some) endogamy. In the ten richest Romanian families of the 1930s, each having eight or more hectares of land, one sees all these instruments at work: excluding the one farmer who was an outsider, none of these families had more than two children, in those with two children one was being given at least some schooling, and all but one had made endogamous marriages. In the face of this juggernaut the village's *real* "middle peasants," the Germans, might have begun to be alarmed. Not only would just the richer Romanians have concerned them, these people being more likely to compete with them in marketing some grains, but all villagers, including the poorer, were in the market for land. Speaking more generally, one would expect that the reversal of fortunes for Transylvania's Germans and Romanians and the increasing movement of Romanians into commodity production during a time of economic crisis would have brought the two groups into direct competition within the same niche for the first time. And one might expect this confrontation to have been reflected in more acerbic relations between them. This conclusion was foreshadowed at the end of chapter 5, where a German villager was heard voicing his opinion about the "class war" between Romanians and Germans in the interwar period.

The kind of social analysis encouraged by the present government has probably influenced this German's wording. In somewhat less dramatic terms, however, other Germans have confirmed his opinion, although with some discomfort, since they are reluctant to disturb the calm of today's peaceable interethnic relations with references to the rancors of the past. Several recalled episodes of rock-throwing and name-calling by Romanians; one proclaimed that when Romanians received political rights in 1918 they suddenly became very full of themselves, and Germans felt the difference. Some blame the spitefulness of Romanians on "wealth hatred" (*ura de avere*) and jealousy. Some also regretfully blame themselves and the chauvinism of the Nazi era, when many Transylvanian Germans enlisted in support of the Reich and held themselves very superior. (Concerning this, a few Romanians recall, "During the second war Germans used to spit at us, and if we were on foot and they passed us in a cart going to market, they wouldn't stop to pick us up.")

The diverse explanations merely underscore the agreement among German informants that relations between the two groups were more strained during the interwar period than at any other time. Two hints of evidence bear out these opinions. First, although marriages between Germans and Romanians had not been frequent before World War I, in the interwar period these fell to one case, in 1935, and the parties to the marriage found village life so unpleasant that they left, abandoning to their families the taunts and gossip that had been aimed at them. Table 6-6 shows changes in patterns of intermarriage, using all marriages made by Germans as a base and including those of recent years to dramatize the interwar drop. Second, a small example illustrates one specific way in which Romanians and Germans came into confrontation over critical resources. After rights to village pasture were extended to the whole community in 1918, Germans went on the advice of the notary to pasture their cattle in the now-common pasture, only to be driven off by Romanians and advised not to return. One German decided to take their case to court; after several encounters, Romanians finally began to desist and Germans could pasture undisturbed.

Although Romanians, like Germans, are hasty to tell stories that show pleasant dealings between the two groups in these years, they

TABLE 6-6. Intermarriages Involving Binţinţi Germans, 1893-1979

Year of Marriage	No. of Marriages Made by Germans	No. Made with Non-Germans		%	
1893–1918	45	5	{2 Romanian {3 Hungarian	11.1	{4.4 {6.7
1919–1944	58	1	(Romanian)	1.7	
1945–1979	56	18	(Romanian)	32.1	

too hint of trouble. A number of Romanian informants (n = 33) were asked in interviews a question about the most significant differences between themselves and Germans in the past; half of them responded not with the expected ethnic traits but with the rejoinder, "Wealth. They were richer than we were." Many others gave a similar reply in more veiled terms.[33] The responses suggested, at the very least, jealousy.

While retrospective readings of social attitudes are risky, I believe it is more accurate to call the attitude of Romanians "jealousy" than to look beyond that for "resentment" or actual "class war." For some Romanians, to be sure — the very poorest, who could become heated in speaking of how the rich unjustly monopolized land so poor people could not buy it — "resentment" may be apt. But among the rest there prevails an ambivalence that makes one hesitate. The Germans' economic edge is referred to their greater degree of civilization and is not just envied but admired as well. Countless times one hears from Romanian informants, "These Germans civilized us, they taught us how to farm, without them we'd be as backward as those upland hillbillies." The comments can only refer to the interwar period, for after 1945 Germans had nothing with which to set such an example. The attitude underscores how the history of intertwined ethnicity and class in Transylvania shaped the perceptions of both class differences and ethnic characteristics; it also exposes the persistent tendency of Transylvania's Romanians to strive for inclusion and for equality with more privileged nationalities, sometimes even to emulate them.

This history of viewing differences among the nationalities may have been one factor among several that dampened the emergence of real class war. Objectively speaking, the bulk of the two groups were indeed in different classes. Any Romanians who did wage labor were likely to be doing it for Germans; large numbers of Romanians had more problematic access than did Germans to adequate means of production; Germans had much more of everything; Germans retained more control over their labor, its products, and the survival of their enterprises than did Romanians, linked with international commodity circuits by the pressure of taxes and debts. Yet these different classes were linked by few class *relations,* and to those Romanians who worked for Germans, the opportunity was a boon, retarding their proletarization. Moreover, both groups were subject to other processes that kept them from being progressively polarized. Germans as well as Romanians were victims of the state's low agricultural prices. The land reform had restricted for both Germans and Romanians the possibility of renting additional lands for greater production. Romanians purport to have been a bit more willing to sell land to a Romanian than to a German, thereby somewhat inhibiting Germans' acquisition of new means of production. Against these forces that prevented Germans and rich Romanians from concentrating their properties at a rapid rate were forces retarding the pauperization of the poorest Romanians—temporary employment in industry, fertility trends, and communal pasture and livestock raising, which in other historical circumstances have worked against proletarization (see Spufford 1974:pt. 1).

Also important in buffering relations between the extremes was the fact that the better-off among Romanian peasants did not amalgamate with the Germans to form a single group of wealthy peasants opposing the mass of poorer Romanians. Whether or not they would have wanted to, they were not in a position to do so; at most, they sometimes stood as guarantors for German (as well as Romanian) bank loans. In addition to the restrictions set by taxes, prices, and the unavailability of lands to rent, even the wealthier Romanians were still held back by farms not quite large enough to merit investments for machinery, especially since the labor-richness of Romanian agriculture inhibited modernizations that would displace labor having no other use. A look at the characteristics of the well-to-do Romanian farms as late as 1948 (the date of a detailed agricultural census) shows how far they were from taking on the trappings of German farmers. According to the 1948 census, 56 Romanian households, or about one-fourth of the total, engaged extra-household labor either permanently, seasonally, or by the day; but only 5 of them (none having more than 7 hectares) paid their workers any cash at all, usually mixed with wages in kind.[34] The rest were still bringing in uplanders for payment in produce. Agricultural inventories show a similar result: only 10 of 207 Romanian households have additional implements beyond the basic plow, harrow, and hoes, and none of the additions is a major item. There are two seeders, six mincing machines for fodder, three spray pumps, two sifters, and a winnowing machine. The one major acquisition— a thresher bought jointly by three Romanians in the 1930s with a bank loan—had been sold shortly thereafter because its owners decided it was not worth the trouble. This is not to suggest that Romanian farms were capital-poor; they had a higher ratio of capital per hectare, in the form of cattle, than did Germans. The difference nonetheless underscores the point.

Well-to-do Romanian peasants in Binţinţi were not exactly the leading edge in rural society, in many senses. They did not turn to usury, as do some rural bourgeois (and it seems the Germans did not either).[35] It was often not wealthy peasants but Romanians of more modest means—those having in the range of three to four hectares —who initiated innovations. These included two of the three who experimented with the thresher and the two Romanians who, along with two or three Germans, first took advantage of state subsidies to buy pure-blood Simmenthaler cattle to improve their stock. From this middle peasant stratum came the two Romanians (having two-and-one-half to four hectares) who briefly ran the tavern. This stratum provided the only villager during the period (to my knowledge) to take on an activity often associated with the rural bourgeoisie: petty trading. The villager in question, from a family owning 3.5 hectares in 1939, involved himself in petty commerce with grains in an effort to find new routes to accumulating land. Taking advantage of re-duced railway fares that his father enjoyed as a railway employee, he periodically traveled to and from the Regat, where he bought grain at the cheaper prices prevailing there and resold them more expensively at Transylvanian prices. Only for a short time during World War I had a few villagers (again, not the richest) taken simi-lar advantage of price differentials to make some extra money. Such petty commerce was otherwise not found among Binţinţi peasants, although poor peasants from nearby villages sometimes engaged in it. After the unrepeated experiment of Frau Müller (chap. 5, p. 245), not even Germans pursued small-scale commerce. In fact, in a neat reversal of what we might expect, our model German entre-preneurs *sold* some of their grains to petty-trading poor Romanians from other villages who came around looking for bulk to break. For these outsiders, petty commerce was yet another instrument to avoid pauperization, not the mark of a rising bourgeoisie; and when asked why Binţinţeni did not do the same, informants replied haughtily, "We didn't have to. Ours was a *rich* village."

All this evidence indicates what we have concluded independently about the condition of agriculture in interwar Romania. Some peas-ants did accumulate means of production in the form of land, but under prevailing conditions this did not imply capitalist practices as much as a greater cushion of comfort and of security against debt. The only peasants who took on bourgeois activities did so as a temporary expedient designed to facilitate their acquiring this cushion of land. Everyone was involved in an extraordinary intensi-fication of effort aimed primarily at staying in place, with a few investments in education on the side. Those farmers who intensified capital—mainly Germans—were engaged in a holding pattern (as one German said, "We didn't move ahead at all in those years. Without markets, who could move ahead?"). The same was true of Romanians, although they intensified labor more than capital. These intensifications must have been remarkable, if informants' reports are to be believed, for against a 1935 national average yield of 7.6 quintals per hectare of wheat and 10.4 quintals per hectare of maize (Madgearu 1940:30), Binţinţi peasants of both groups obtained wheat yields ranging between 10 and 25 quintals per hectare and maize yields from 25 quintals per hectare on up.

The way the Romanian economy thwarted such intensive efforts helps to explain the ambiguous character of interethnic relations between the wars: rancorous yet not inflamed, filled with both envy and admiring emulation. On the one hand, Germans and Romanians competed with one another directly in a contracting economic niche that frustrated forward movement. Despite some complementarity in their marketing patterns, both groups strove to buy land to boost their paltry agricultural incomes. On the other hand, this same frustration prevented the gap between rich Germans and poor Romanians from becoming a chasm, and held firmly in place a middle group between the divergent extremes. The fact that the community did not polarize into two distinctive rural classes, on one side a biethnic amalgam of rich Romanians and Germans and on the other a mass of poor Romanians, allowed the overall class difference between Germans and Romanians to be softened somewhat by Romanians' inclination to see the "civilized" nationalities not just as enemies[36] but also as models. They became enemies mainly in the same arena as before, the arena in which most of the name-calling and rock-throwing probably occurred: village politics. Even there, inflammation was less severe than before 1918.

INTERWAR VILLAGE POLITICS

As previous chapters have shown, this Romanian population had been given powerful exposure to the politicizing influence of Transylvania's Romanian nationalist elite. The peasants of Binţinţi had thrown their weight vigorously behind the Romanian Nationalist Party in prewar elections, and they had taken an active part in the administrative transition to a new Romanian state (see chap. 5, p. 267). Their political ardor did not evaporate after their party's main objectives were achieved. Although there was a small crack in the solidarity of Romanian voting in Binţinţi — as two or three rich peasants voted for the Liberals ("They were bought," scoff others) — most Romanian villagers staunchly backed the National Peasant Party.

Their support was not casual. Informants recall fights launched against those few who imprudently argued for the Liberals, and even more exciting were the occasions when Liberal partisans came from outside to persuade villagers to their causes. Here is Petru's account of such times:

> There was one General Moişoi who came to get us to vote Liberal, and he promised us more land if we'd vote for him. Well, Iosif Bogdan's grandfather — he was a big Nationalist — shouted back at him, "And how do you propose to do that? We already had a land reform and there's nothing more to give away." General Moişoi said to him, "We'll cut it from the moon if we have to, so as to give you more." And everyone roared with laughter at him, and the women threw rotten eggs at him and chased him out of the village hollering, "Down with the Liberals! Down with the Liberals!" The women always got more het up about these things than the men, I don't know why.
>
> But you know, it was true that if the Liberals promised something to buy your vote, they delivered. So I'd heard, and once I decided to give it a try. It was when the interest rates at the bank had gone sky high and I couldn't even pay the interest much less touch the principal. I wrote my problems down on a piece of paper and put it in an envelope, and when Mitiţa Constantinescu came around to give a speech — he was the Liberal deputy from Geoagi' [and the very man who had defined his party's "middle peasant" as one owning 250 to 500 hectares of land (Şandru 1975:256)] — I put the envelope in his hand and promised him my vote if he'd help me, and he agreed. Well, the Liberals won, as usual, and a few weeks later a man came from the county finance office and erased all my debts for that year. After that I used to argue with people sometimes, telling them we should all vote Liberal and get a new school, like those hill villages always did. But I always got into trouble for it. Folks would get all high and mighty at the very idea and say, "*We* don't sell ourselves."

With this attitude, Romanian Binţinţeni must not have had much patience with the voting habits of Germans, who — obedient to their orders from the Saxon hierarchy — voted unfailingly with whatever party was in power. Since the party in power was more often the Liberals than the National Peasants, their obedience set them at odds with Romanian villagers more often than not. Germans sought to defuse the issue by keeping a low profile at election time and avoiding discussions of politics. It was not easy in those days to be a minority trying to assure survival in a new and unpredictable political environment.

What were these Romanian peasants so determinedly supporting? Initially, they were giving their vote to the Nationalist party that had pressed their interests as Romanians in a Hungarian state. In the new Greater Romania, this amounted to voting for invitations to foreign capital and for decentralization and Transylvanian autonomy within an increasingly powerful Romanian state (a platform that would not have excited them even though many were suffering from the state's power and from the exclusion of foreign capital). It also meant voting for somewhat more investment in agriculture (a platform that would have excited them except none seem to have realized it was the National Peasant position!). They thought of themselves as simply supporting the party of Romanians and peasants, the party that had given them the land reform — which it had, along with the other parties, including the Liberals.

As the 1920s progressed, and as the National Peasant coalition between Romanian Nationalists and Regat agrarianists was more firmly cemented, villagers' perceptions of the National Peasant Party shifted somewhat, in accordance with its own slogans. They now remember it less as the party of Romanians than as the party of peasants against the "landlords" (*boieri*) and big money, a perception that suits perfectly the image presented by Madgearu when, as a leader of the National Peasants, he advocated opposing the Liberals not on their program of industrialization (the *real* opponent of these peasants) but as the party of financial oligarchy and despotism (Jackson 1966:242). The women who pelted General "Moişoi" and others with rotten eggs were making known their views on landlords (an old concern) and people who controlled banks (a new one, but common to many smallholding systems and reflecting expensive credit and susceptibility to debts [see Stinchcombe 1961:172]).

In discussing villagers' voting habits and their perceptions of the major parties, one or two informants said baldly, "Most people didn't really know much about what the parties stood for. People had heard that the Liberals were the bankers' party; we also heard that they were thieves, that they were all rich because they stole money from the banks, but for all we knew that was just a rumor someone started and all of a sudden everyone believed it. All the rumors were against the Liberals." This perception of the Liberals as the party of big money was used to explain why the National Peasants were so unsuccessful in power: "The National Peasants weren't very rich, they could only govern for a year or two and then they had to stop. When they won an election, the Liberals would boycott them and they would fall. Look what happened in 1929, the Liberals closed all the banks! How could the National Peasants run the country after that?"

Regardless of how they understood the issues, these peasants' political positions were apt enough. Their perception of "big money" as their opponent was accurate in more ways than they could realize at the time. Even though some analysts might say that Romania's continued dependency in the world economy was sealed when the National Peasants invited in foreign capital — intended to augment the resources available for developing industry and agriculture at the same time — in a peculiar way it made sense for peasants surviving on an international export product to support the internationalist National Peasants. The party did inaugurate policies that improved conditions somewhat for cultivators and might have done so more had the depression not forced them from office. If the National Peasants doomed their peasant constituents to continued struggle by failing to oppose the plan for national industrialization, it was the fault of the party's Transylvanian history, in which peasant and bourgeois interests had been mixed from the beginning.

Early in the interwar period villagers enjoyed much excitement from their vigorous participation in politics, but this was to disappear gradually, from the mid-1930s on, first with the constant succession of new coalition governments, uninformed by popular elections, and then with the royal and military dictatorships. Villagers who had fought about their views and registered these views with votes — never mind if the army would often come in the middle of the night, empty the voting urns, destroy the ballots, and replace them with new ones — now became accustomed to seeing village mayors change overnight with no one's say-so. With each new government coalition, word would come to Binţinţi from Orăştie that Mayor Q representing Party X was to step down and Mayor R representing Party Y was to assume office. The succession of marionette mayors exemplifies how closely village life was subject to constraints from outside. Yet villagers developed their own reaction to this too, a reaction that would prove to be a rehearsal for their political behavior after the next war: apathy. If nothing else, the change had a calming effect on interethnic relations.

CONCLUSION

At the end of World War I the Romanian state set itself the task of pulling away from its dependent position in the global economy and creating a strong national industry. Given the relatively low level of capital accumulation in the country, this process would have to be managed as cheaply as possible. Therefore, yoked to the industrial strategy was the plan of withholding a portion of agricultural production from export in order to feed the anticipated industrial population, and to do so at low cost. This strategy was thought to be furthered by encouraging the development of middle peasant farms, whose creation implied the dislocation of unprosperous poor peasants (destined for industrial labor) and a general rise in rural purchasing power to sustain the industrial program. It was an ambitious plan, and it was to be tried again in a new guise after 1945, for it failed in its first run.

For the peasants of Binţinţi, entering the new era as Romanian citizens, the interwar years brought changes in abundance. First came the distribution of land in the reform, which entailed a number of alterations in life. More peasants could keep cattle; peasants could marry farther away to make better matches; poor peasants no longer had to send so many children out into the world to make their own way. Rich and poor peasants alike adjusted themselves to living off their own properties by limiting the size of their families. Then there were new demands as well as new possibilities offered by the state. Taxes drove people into market, and rich peasants had unprecedented opportunities to educate their children and thereby keep their farms intact. For the village's Germans, the changes were mostly for the worse: smaller agricultural incomes, fewer options for renting extra lands, the necessity for diversifying production beyond the staple wheat crop. There was also greater confrontation between Germans and Romanians than there had been before, and both groups felt a rise in the temperature of their relations.

The most noteworthy of the interwar processes, however, were the ones from which change was absent. Capitalist relations did not progress far in agriculture, and peasants remained peasants. Any headway made by capitalist relations had occurred largely in industry, where capital had settled, leaving agriculture to reproduce itself as a residual sector just as it had done before the war, though now under different rules. The industry to be upheld by the development of agriculture continued throughout these years to suck commodities from an undercapitalized sector whose purchasing power declined as the period wore on. Because this industry was capital-intensive heavy industry, financed from abroad, it did not create enough jobs to absorb marginalized peasants and change their status. The rarity of capitalist agricultural enterprise also precluded their becoming rural proletarians. Social differentiation did proceed among the rural populace, but it was not from capitalism in agriculture. Rather, it was because the state failed to permit enough investment to keep population increase from creating a mass of rural paupers.

These events were played out in a number of theaters. First, there were the reciprocal interactions of richer and poorer peasants in Binţinţi. Sometimes their strategies complemented one another — for example, German wheat and Romanian cattle, or the rich peasants' children who went to school while middle and poorer peasants bought land. The strategies sometimes echoed one another on different scales, such as the further development of marketing among all sectors of the peasantry; they sometimes involved one another in potential or actual conflict, such as Romanians' wage labor for Germans, or arguments over politics; and sometimes they simply replicated one another, although perhaps with variations in the frequencies, such as with strategies of marriage and family limitation. The theater for all these encounters was not just interwar Binţinţi but the whole Transylvanian plateau, with the characteristics peculiar to it: the high ratios of pasture to arable land, of livestock to cereals, and the complex ethnic and feudal history that distinguished it from other parts of Romania.

Second, there was the ever more intense dialogue developing between peasants and the Romanian state. In some cases the dialogue was reasonably friendly, as between the state and its protégé middle peasants, the Germans (who nonetheless grumbled, out of earshot, about the low prices). In other cases the exchange entailed resistance, mixed signals, and sudden changes of mind, as well as mutual benefit. The peasantry reconstituted by the land reform clung to its peasant status partly on its own and partly because of the treatment the state accorded it. Peasants stayed peasants because they were unable to consolidate and modernize their farms as much as had been hoped; but this came from their inability to earn enough in an agriculture whose prices the state depressed to support industry and whose possibilities the state neglected by not setting up cooperatives. Peasants acquired cash for the minor developments they were able to make (mainly purchasing land and iron plows) because they had begun to market more; the state created the conditions for this by expanding urban markets, by taxation, and by granting so little credit that peasants had to acquire bank debts, which encouraged further marketing. Peasants also stayed peasants because every now and then they could purchase land—usually by indebting themselves—whose free circulation was a product of the state's agrarian reform and of continued measures to keep land markets active. The cycle of land circulation, low credit, and high debt was on its way to proletarizing many peasants when the depression struck, forcing the state to come to their rescue.

Since not all states rescued their farmers in those years (American small farmers being a prime example), we might wonder why Romania did. The most probable reasons are political: the size of the affected population, and the more-radical solutions some politicians were voicing. Opposition from banks could not prevail against the fearsome consequences of taking no action. (And government assistance to banks was precluded by objections from foreign creditors to whom Romania was by then itself heavily indebted.) Thus, the state reversed the process of "natural selection" by which the countryside was to have been vitalized (Roberts 1951:343) and helped its peasants to stay on the land.

They were helped to do so in other ways as well, by further resources and opportunities the state provided. They served temporarily in its industry, sent children into its bureaucracy and professions, reduced families in the land reform's wake (thereby helping with the seemingly insoluble problem of rural overpopulation), and kept land in circulation through exogamous marriages that might bring a better dowry than a local marriage would. These gifts from the state—land from the reform, chances for upward mobility—were the major elements of the Transylvanian revolution of 1918. They enabled at least some peasants to cease reproducing the proletarian and lower-class status that had been their lot before the war. In the revolution of 1918, the Romanian state had given its peasants the means to resist, and it strengthened those means by the conversion of debts.

Third, there were the national and international theaters within which different capitals vied with one another and Romanian cattle ambled from Binținți farms to stomachs in Prague to help peasants remain peasants. Within the Romanian economy there had been relative unanimity among sectors of capital investment: all local capital fled agriculture for industry and commerce, the best sign of this being the latifundists' divestiture of their agricultural holdings. The exception of Binţinţi Germans upholds the rule. It shows that only where some concentration of capital and modernization of agriculture had already occurred, for historical reasons set out in preceding chapters, was there any sign of continued development; and this was in part the result precisely of the Germans' new *marginalization* in Transylvania's economy. It was the internal harmony of capital interests that had diverted credits to industry (and thus given local commercial capital its peasant debtors) and set agricultural prices so low as to force peasants to remain peasants.

They were not just forced, however, but also enabled to remain peasants, because international merchant capital smelled profits in Romanian livestock. While international industrial interests kept a concerned eye on Romania's insolent industrialization, international commercial capital won the day over national commercial capital, symbolically defeated by the conversion of debts. With the conversion, Romanian bankers managing Romanian capital (along with others building up local accumulations) were prevented from dispossessing their innumerable endangered debtors and had to swallow terrible losses. (Many did not survive, which shows how Romania's foreign creditors aided in concentrating the country's finance capital, much of it also foreign.) Meanwhile, the international livestock market could continue to draw cheap cattle from the marginal peasant farms that had been allowed to survive at the expense of Romanian banks. And by giving these peasants a source of income from such small holdings, it kept them alive to resist the encroachments of the state, if not also to be its supporters.

Capitalism had not developed *within* Romanian agriculture, but this did not prevent its working from without on a peasantry already marginalized by prior historical developments. The action of capitalism in the Romanian countryside had served not to make its peasants proletarians but to keep them peasants. Through the conversion of debts, there was retained on the land a group of persons working under a different rationality from that prevailing elsewhere in the economy: noncapitalist peasants operating chiefly in terms of use values, not calculating their ever-intensifying labor as a cost, and exploitable by those who controlled and mediated the circuits of exchange,[37] namely, international cattle merchants and the Romanian state.

The peasants of Binţinţi were oblivious to the magnitude of this drama. They were probably also unaware that their tenacious hold on their peasant status was advantageous to international merchants and international creditors, and hindered the more national plan for a "middle peasantry" supporting industry, just as their votes favored invitations to foreign capital against the nationalist autarky of the Liberals. The outcome presents ironic symmetries: nationalistic Romanian peasants stayed peasants through the actions of their state and international financial interests, while German farmers, whose behavior implicitly supported the national plan, pursued an increasingly unprofitable livelihood in an agriculture that was contracting thanks to the very plan they supported. Compensation lay only in the fact that Germans kept a greater portion of their product's value, while the state and the merchants took increasing proportions of the intensified labor of Romanians.

Yet the costs to these peasants went largely unperceived. None but the very poorest — and not even all of them — seem to have recognized obstacles in the environment.[38] As they saw things, anyone who worked hard during those years could get along fine, as long as there weren't too many children. Petru, despite his successful debt cancellation after he voted for the Liberal Mitiţa Constantinescu, had to sell a house he had bought or he would have been dispossessed. Had he waited another six months the conversion of debts would have saved him, but he could not have paid another week's interest. Yet in discussing this with me he said, "It wasn't the banker's fault. I wouldn't have lent more money to me either if I'd been in his shoes; he'd have to be a fool to risk his capital on a poor man." Then I asked, later in the conversation, "Let's talk about a word I see a lot here in your books and newspapers, 'exploitation.' Can you tell me what it means?" He replied, "Someone's taken something from someone, and he didn't have a right to. [Pause]. Nothing like that was happening here then."

EPILOGUE: ON THE THRESHOLD

In 1940, on the eve of Romania's entry with Hitler into war against the Soviet Union, Binţinţi peasants could not possibly have anticipated the changes they would soon face. They approached the threshold of revolutionary takeover unwittingly, toiling their way to market with their carts or alongside their fattened cattle. Some of them had less to sell than they had hoped, because of government wartime requisitions throughout the countryside. Some had less available labor than they had expected (but also fewer mouths to feed), as hundreds of thousands of peasants were enlisted in the armed forces, leaving agricultural work to the womenfolk (a good rehearsal for the role these women were to assume after 1959). Temporary jobs on the railroad and in Cugir's munitions factory, however, cushioned these reductions and departures, and the need for provisioning led to intensified peasant cultivation. There was continuity also in the tensions between Germans and Romanians, especially in spheres beyond the village. Romania began World War II as Hitler's ally, and until the alliance was broken Romania's citizen Germans were given a choice between fighting in the Romanian army or with Hitler's forces; but Germans who preferred the army of Romania say that military life was made unpleasantly tense for them, causing them to switch to the more hospitable German troops.[39] It was a choice they would come to regret a thousandfold, when their lands were later confiscated for this collaboration.

We have now come full circle to the events and organizational forms described in chapter 1, whose context is finally complete. Of the changes that were to follow 1945, some marked a radical break with the previous era, some were the climax of tendencies already apparent, and some were direct continuations of earlier trends and policies. The concluding chapter will summarize the major trends and changes for the period covered in this book. It would help, however, to be reminded briefly here of what chapter 1 has already presented as the situation that came to prevail after World War II.

The peasant community of the interwar period was soon to see a repetition, at slightly smaller amplitude, of the same sequence that occurred after the 1921 land reform: the land reform of 1945 once again saved the poorest peasants from being eliminated from agriculture and provided the basis for expanded commodity production among them. (This production took place, of course, at the expense of the more "efficient" German agriculture, which the reform swept away.) These villagers would face compulsory deliveries of produce, in place of "free" marketing induced by debts and taxes. Then they would endure collectivization, a more radical change than anything since 1854. Wealthy peasants—some to be named *chiaburi*—would come under attack as a class of rural exploiters (although, if I am correct in arguing that agriculture was a field for retarded differentiation and stunted capitalist development, the treatment accorded the rural rich was rather less than perfect Leninism). They would no longer be able to afford sending their children to school—much less modernizing their farms—and would be educationally overtaken by the children of middle peasants; and then, as the entire educational process became fully state-supported, peasants of all ranks would go on to university to "become gentlemen."

Under the Communists, three of the major mechanisms by which these peasants reproduced their differential social standing would be gradually removed from their hands: education would be generalized, eliminating differential wealth as a basis for educational attainment;[40] land would be collectivized, eliminating the reproduction of peasant status—whether rich or poor—through inheritance; and control over fertility would at first be facilitated for all, so even poor peasants could afford abortions, and then withdrawn altogether for everyone, in the antiabortion decree of 1967. Each of these underscored the irrelevance of interwar peasant adaptations to the new national plan for economic development. This point would be hammered home when collectivization effectively rendered all peasants proletarians, apt for, if not at once incorporated into, industrial labor. The proletarian status, that poor peasants in particular had struggled to avoid, became the lot of all, and after decades of partial proletarization, the process was made complete.

As peasant conceptions of mobility changed and industry at last expanded, "worker" status came to mark an improvement over peasanthood and to constitute a new upward mobility, accessible to peasants of all ranks, as the new upward mobility after 1918 had not been. Like that earlier one, though, the new mobility of 1945 was based on the sudden opening of holes in the social structure, holes created before by the transfer of sovereignty over Transylvania and now by the new and underinhabited industrial edifice of Communist development policy. Although the Communists generated their proletariat in a very radical manner, the policy was nonetheless fully consistent with government strategies from before: like its interwar predecessor, the Communist regime intended to create an industrialized Romania, through a more advanced version of autarky and protectionism and a more stringent support of industry by agriculture. As before, agriculture would be milked for surpluses to feed industry. Conditions would be so unpropitious for the accumulation of earnings in the countryside that no investments would be diverted from industrial growth; and peasants would even, under the revised incentives of the mid-1970s (see chap 1, p. 46), be prevented from earning amounts in excess of industrial wages, so as to ensure a permanent industrial labor force.

Thus, peasants were consigned to a role with which they were already all too familiar, but now they would play it with greater intensity. Whereas incomes had still been marginally supplemented with sharecropping before 1945, afterwards sharecropping would be eliminated entirely except in the form of the the usufruct plot. Whereas the interwar state had helped keep alive on the land a large sector that operated according to a noncapitalist rationality, feeding industry cheaply, the socialist state would greatly homogenize the rationalities within its purview, leaving a much restricted sphere (the usufruct plot, and perhaps the "portion") to principles of accounting different from those practiced in the system as a whole. Whereas peasants had occasionally used industrial employment to remain in agriculture, they would come to use agriculture as a supplement to industrial wages. And whereas formerly they had had difficulty accumulating the income to expand and then modernize their holdings as peasants, they would now have difficulty finding uses for the income they accumulated as peasant-workers. Their increased purchasing power (increased by industry, not by agriculture) would go to buying products made within Romania, rather than to products imported from outside. Gradually, the efficiency and "rationality" of agriculture would be improved, but largely without using the peasants as intermediaries in the process, as interwar governments had intended to do.

One could simplify the overall contrast between the interwar and socialist economic environments of these peasants thus: an agricultural sector characterized by increased commercialization with minimal development gave way to one characterized by development with minimal commercialization. The difference lay in the degree of industrial growth and in the state strategies linking agriculture to the strengthening industrial sector. The difference is crucial. Both the interwar and socialist regimes intended to build an industrial economy upon an agriculture inadequate to sustain it. Both would render large numbers of peasants proletarians as part of the requirements of supporting industry with food (as well as with workers). But the interwar government opted — was pressed by world circumstance? — to pursue capital-intensive industrialization that gave these marginal peasants no place to go, whereas the socialist government, by excluding Western capital, would force itself into a labor-intensive industrialization that would absorb proletarized peasants and accumulate sufficient resources to reinvest in improved living standards, even — eventually — for workers in agriculture. The interwar advances in agriculture and in drawing peasants into market doubtless helped the socialist plan; but it is doubtful that more years of the interwar policy would have raised villagers to the living standards of the 1970s.

In the sphere of interethnic relations, villagers would see the frictions of interwar days disappear into relative harmony in the postwar era. The expropriation of Germans' properties would clinch their dislodgement from the Transylvanian bourgeoisie, a process begun by the loss of their church lands in the 1921 land reform and by the interwar growth of a Romanian middle class. Emigrations and deaths connected with their deportation would diminish the size of the German community both in Romania and in Binţinţi, further undermining the competitiveness of their relations with Romanians. More important, the fact that both Germans (after their expropriation) and Romanians (after collectivization) were to enter an expanding industrial employment sector meant a reversal of the interwar situation in which relations had become so tense: instead of competing for similar resources within a contracting economic niche, they would now jointly utilize a new niche whose phenomenal expansion would preclude competitive interactions over economic opportunities.

After 1945, few differences would remain to serve as bases of invidious comparison and differentiation: Binţinţi Germans' slightly larger pensions, slightly higher overall levels of skill, and slightly lower representation in the CAP. The sole exception is that as of the 1970s, Germans would have increasing possibilities to emigrate (Romanian spouses with them, should they intermarry). This would put a premium on maintenance of the German language and give village Romanians reason to gripe, as they wonder what else Germans could possibly want when so many opportunities abound in modern Romania. With emigration, Germans have become "internationalists," having long been staunch supporters of the Transylvanian homeland and Romanian government policy (albeit often unintentionally), as chapter 6 has shown.

The immediate agent of all these changes was the installation of a new regime in the same Romanian state with which peasants had been engaged in intensifying dialogue throughout the interwar period. This change of regime itself had, like so many other things affecting these peasants' lives, international causes, in the increasing power of the Soviet Union and its extension of control over Eastern European states. But what peasants felt most keenly was the state, headed by the Communist Party, and now the chief determinant of nearly all their life circumstances. Always a central fact in peasants' existence, their relationship with the state had taken a decisive turn.

Conclusion:
That's How
It's Always Been

Hey John! Did you hear we've made a deal with the Americans to get hold of the bomb?
—Good Heavens! What equivalent deadly weapon could we
possibly be giving them in exchange?
Our system for organizing labor.

What's the difference between an optimist and a pessimist?
—An optimist says, "Things can't possibly get worse,"
a pessimist says, "Oh yes they can."

—Jokes from 1980

Din cîine nu se face slănina.
(You can't make bacon from a dog.)

—Proverb

In the feudal conscription of 1820, ordered by the Habsburg Emperor Francis as part of the monarchy's assault on the relations
among state, lords, and peasants, serfs were asked a number of
questions about the extent of their feudal labor dues and the times
when these had been instituted. Their reply to these questions was
often, "*Aşa am pomenit,*" or "That's how it's always been," as if
these things could have no beginning and could know no change.
In my interviews of the 1970s, undertaken as part of an assault on
the relations among state, economy, and peasants, I asked villagers
many questions about how things used to be and why they were
thus. The reply to these questions was often, "*Aşa e,*" or "That's
just how it is," as if these things were incomprehensible.

Coming from a world very different from that of these respon-
dents, I do not think of these things as either changelessly continuous or incomprehensible, even though it may prove elusive to render
the changes and their interpretation clearly. It is time to make such
an attempt.[1] Because so many problems have been raised throughout the course of this exposition and so many devices used to link
one part with another, this summary will necessarily leave loose
ends. I will concentrate on weaving together the main threads of
the story—state-building, economic change, and ethnicity—and
will do so by moving back and forth across them, sometimes repeti-
tively, making an effort to show not just their relations to one another but their effects on villagers. Implicitly, in a few places, I will

338

defend my having given this interpretation an international context rather than something less.

THE STATE AND THE PEASANTS

One fundamental secular trend manifested during the two-and-a-half centuries covered here has been a tremendous increase in the state's power over villagers[2] and a concomitant extension of its presence in their lives. A simple formulation will help to illustrate this assertion. If power is a relationship, and is the reciprocal of relations of dependency (Emerson 1962), then the state's power over its peasants rises in inverse proportion to the degree of its dependence over them. Focusing on the revenues on which the state depends, the trend is clear. For the eighteenth-century Habsburg state, the foundation of revenues was peasant taxes—a fact the Habsburgs set about determinedly to alter. For the twentieth-century socialist state, the budgetary foundation is now public manufacturing industry, supplemented by agricultural production and the manipulation of agricultural prices. The Habsburg state bent its efforts to "protecting" its peasants from ruinous exploitation by others; the socialist regime is making a bid to do without its peasants altogether. The difference speaks eloquently of the relative degrees of power these two states have had over their rural population.

This trend is not unique to Eastern Europe. Many analysts see the growing dominance of state organizations within their territories, and with respect to other collective actors in society, as a general characteristic of the modern era (Chase-Dunn and Rubinson 1979: 280; Boli-Bennett 1980; D. Smith 1978; Warman 1980). Nor has it progressed in our Eastern European examples in an unbroken line. The Habsburg state both centralized its bureaucracy and developed its economy in fits and starts. Building through the eighteenth century, it regressed at that century's end; its next rise stumbled over the Hungarian revolution in 1848 but was also facilitated by the social and economic reforms of that year. The supersession of the empire by a Dual Monarchy with Hungary in 1867, however, was proof to all that Habsburg state centralization had failed—in part because its economic diversity and development had not grown enough to sustain the growth of the state. In the new Hungarian state the rhythm of centralization and economic development was different. It did not ebb and flow with the waning and waxing of the global economy as it had for the Habsburgs, probably because of the way mercantilism and the empire's economic unity cushioned and supported Hungary's industrial takeoff (see pp. 198–200), which reduced the state's dependence on peasant agriculture and thus enhanced state power. With the switch from the Hungarian state to Romania, in 1918, peasants encountered a state more dependent on them (hence of diminished power) because of Romania's lesser industrial capacity, relative to Hungary's. The dependence was symbolized by the 1921 agrarian reform. The depression and Romania's attempt to industrialize, however, entailing severely exploitative use of agriculture, saw the power balance fluctuate, to become a linear progression under the socialist regime. The state's dependence on peasant production has dropped as decisively as its bureaucracy has centralized. This represents exceptional power felt in countless ways, from extensive policing to unparalleled social benefits to the unprecedented integration of peasants and state through collective agriculture.[3]

The means by which these states exercised their dominance over the peasantry varied through time, in correspondence to the state's increasing centralization. Overall, one can discern three main patterns. In the first, from the early 1700s into the mid-1800s, agents of the state tried to manipulate other social groups and organizations in the environment, especially the nobility and the church, to achieve greater control over the products of peasants' labor and greater ideological commitment from the peasantry as the state's ally. This set of strategies gradually gave way to the next, applied in some measure even before but exercised with ever-increasing sophistication through the mid-1900s. In this second pattern, the state manipulated the social environment less than the economic parameters of peasant production. These manipulations took primarily indirect forms: pricing policies, taxation, and allocations of credit and sectoral investments, which left room for other social groups, particularly merchants, to intervene in the process of surplus extraction. The third pattern is that of the socialist state, in which indirect (pricing and investment) manipulations are but a supplement to direct extraction, eliminating merchant intervention and upping the stringency by means of which surpluses are delivered. Direct extraction of surpluses occurred first in an ad hoc manner, through forced deliveries, and then institutionally, through collectivization. This institutionalized form works best for extensive cultivation, which the state in effect took over; cadres are left with the job of trying to pry surpluses from the intensive cultivation left to peasants (dairy products, meat, and the more labor-intensive crops), without making the mailed fist so apparent as to squash producers' initiative altogether. Chapter 1 showed some of the tactics adopted toward this end.

Peasants have thus been witness to a very long-term shift, in which the total surplus extracted from them, which under early feudalism went entirely to lords, now goes entirely to the state. The shift commenced as agents of the state began to vie with other societal groups for revenues (efforts not only to compete for sources of revenue but to diversify them will be taken up shortly). The state's prime adversary in this contest was the nobility, evidence for which goes back to even before the era of Habsburg domination. In early Hungarian and Transylvanian statecraft, sovereigns sought to reduce the weight of the nobility in the military wing of their administrations by replacing feudal levies with mercenary troops (Hungary's King Matyás, 1458–1490, and Transylvania's Prince Gábor Bethlen, 1613–1629). This culminated in the Habsburgs' creation of a standing army, in the early 1700s. The changes accompanied fundamental modifications in the feudal order, for feudal lords no longer acquired kingly grants of new means of production (land) in exchange for military service. Henceforth, feudal properties were reproduced through legal institutions of a public character that regulated inheritance and proscribed the alienation of noble lands. As long as the nobility continued to monopolize the judicial and executive apparatus for these laws, their hold would remain secure; but part of state-building was to create a loyal administration without such auxiliary interests (Weber 1946[1918]), and thus state and nobles clashed in yet another quarter.

The contest between state and nobles was won by the state. Its aristocratic opponents gravitated or were pushed into new sectors of activity where their interests and those of the state seemed more complementary. In tandem with this victory, peasants were slowly becoming less subject to arbitrary exactions from nobles. This did not mean, however, that claims on the peasant product were relaxed, nor that struggles over it diminished. The competition between landlords and revenue-hungry Habsburg tax collectors gave way to competition among weakened nobles, a Magyar state, and profit-hungry merchants, succeeded in turn by demands from a Romanian state in partial collusion with merchants. Finally, under socialism, extractors' claims have achieved greater unity, but conflicts remain over the distribution of the spoils among the bureaucracy's various levels.

Only at the beginning of the process did peasants have tactical room for maneuver, in which to protest being universally used as no more than a source of wealth. Only when nobles and state were squared off against each other was there space for peasants to play the role of *tertius gaudens:* to refuse catholicization throughout the 1700s, to rise up in 1784, and to choose sides in the revolutions of 1848. As the interests of claimants on peasant surplus gradually approached greater harmony, peasants had ever less room. This is evident in the relative ease with which Communist cadres effected collectivization despite massive resistance, whereas the Habsburgs had not even managed to convert peasants to a new faith. The long-term trend, then, is not precisely toward an ever more antagonistic relationship between peasants and state but toward dialectical simplification of the social field within which both parties operate, a simplification that has worked to the state's advantage and left peasants relatively more powerless. In the present, the stage is set for further simplification of the field by eliminating the peasants themselves.

ECONOMY

If in their political environment peasants saw a gradually intensifying opposition between themselves and an ever stronger state in a social field cleansed of other serious competitors, their economic environment was marked by greater continuity: Transylvanian agriculture remained a perpetually backward and marginal sphere of activity. One can perceive small increments in agricultural development, but more conspicuous is the absence of significant change. The sequel to periods of small forward movement was often the reassertion of anterior conditions. During these two-and-a-half centuries, small-scale feudal commodity production under very poor technical conditions yielded to a postfeudal agriculture that scarcely modernized its technique on either the aristocratic estates or the new peasant small holdings. The growth of industry in the late nineteenth century somewhat enhanced commodity markets, chiefly for large estates, but these commercial possibilities were met without substantially modernizing production (chap. 4). The very same sequence ensued after the next agrarian reform (1921): smallholding expanded, industry grew, and commodity markets were supplied through commercialization — this time by peasants rather than large proprietors — without development (chap. 6).

Indeed, the striking similarities between the agrarian situation after the reforms of 1854 and 1921 extend beyond this. In both reforms, properties passed to smallholders under circumstances that indebted most of the recipients and jeopardized their successful proprietorship. The financial status of owners — landlords after 1854, and peasants after both — precluded capital investments for modernizing. And moratoria on debts — first for nobles, in the 1850s, then for peasants, in the 1930s — prevented the elimination of many "noncompetitive" firms that might have been absorbed into larger, more "rationally" farmed capitalist ones. The pattern was only partially repeated with the land reform of 1945, since initial plans for compensation were scrapped; but even so it remained true that forced deliveries prevented the accumulation of capital to modernize agriculture. Collectivization fundamentally transformed the elements of this long-standing situation, yet without reversing the stagnation of agriculture relative to industry.

Together with the continuities in agriculture's marginal status were continuities in the position of peasants. Throughout, the majority of peasants were either semiproletarians or sharecroppers or both, barely able to subsist on their holdings: first as serfs on tiny feudal plots; next on small holdings they sweated to buy from expropriated feudal lords, to whom they continued to give what should have been paid labor but too often was not; then and later, increasingly supplementing the production from their own plots with lands sharecropped from unmodernized large estates; and after World War I, reducing their tenancy but maintaining a hold on subsistence only through cattle sales and fertility control. For a brief moment after World War II, tenancy and marginal status evaporated; with collectivization, the peasants are proletarians whose exodus is restrained by the "semiproletarizing" effects of the private plot. Although it is important that the mechanisms producing this marginal position differ for each period, in formal and structural terms this position has remained more or less the same.

The continued marginality of both agriculture and the peasantry has an additional concomitant: from 1700 to 1980, the villagers of Binţinţi have seen a steady intensification of their labor, which only in recent years has shown signs of abating. This perpetual intensity of labor had several causes, but first among them has been the failure of integrated sectoral development in the economy, which might have gradually reduced the extraction of absolute surplus labor from agriculture. Alongside this constant tendency were

internal trends varying it. Competition among aspirants to peasant
surplus probably contributed to breaking peasant backs. This would
have worsened as competitors perfected their techniques or upped
their requirements. For example, a deepening revenue crisis on
Transylvania's feudal estates toward the end of the eighteenth century intensified the demand for serf labor, precisely as Habsburg
reforms of the tax structure were being perfected. The abolition of
serfdom freed from the labor trap only those peasants who did not
have to pay compensations; the rest, including the irregular serfs
still bound to capital-poor landlords whose labor-hunger was even
greater than before, saw no letup in the intensive extraction of their
labor, to be turned into value for someone else. Labor intensification persisted under the interwar Romanian regime, with its debased
agricultural prices and high taxes — only then, peasants worked even
harder because there were no landlords for whom they could loaf,
"covering the weeds with dirt." The same situation prevailed through
the early years of the socialist government, with its continued depression of agricultural prices and its forced deliveries. Only as
these villagers have become industrial workers (who nonetheless still
often work in agriculture after factory hours) have they seen the
possibility of not having to work *"all the time"* (see p. 63); and only
with the recent rise in industrial wages has their labor ceased, for the
first time in generations, to be other than woefully underremuner-
ated. For those who work chiefly in the cooperative farm, that age-
old pattern still obtains.

The reasons that Transylvania's agricultural backwardness persisted, with its attendant peasant marginality and labor intensity,
are not wholly uniform through time and will be recapitulated
below. Here it is sufficient to note two things. Consistently through
time, conditions prevailed in which capital avoided agricultural
production in favor of the more lucrative opportunities in industry
and commerce. Consistently through time also, partible inheritance
exacerbated the situation, fragmenting properties and making them
ever less susceptible to rational farming. It was not just peasants
who contributed to this result but the nobles as well; tiny numbers
of Germans attempting something different could scarcely influence
this trend. It was slowed only after World War I, through fertility
control (prompted by the decline in sharecropping after the agrarian
reform) and through peasant migration into the middle class (facilitated by the ethnic consequences of Transylvania's new Romanian
state). It ceased altogether, of course, when collectivization eliminated the inheritance of agricultural land. As shown in earlier

chapters, however, these were far from the only causes of the long-standing "traditionalism" of Transylvanian peasants.

ETHNICITY AND NATIONALISM

In looking at ethnic and national identifications one must separate the long-term trends for the phenomenon as a whole from trends specific to each group, and within the latter one must also distinguish between the structural supports for ethnic identifications and such evidence as can be gleaned of tendencies in actual ethnic consciousness. Overall, ethnic identification greatly changed its significance for the members of this social system, a change most visible if one begins tracing it in fifteenth-century Transylvania. In those early times, ethnic identification was far less salient than was noble or nonnoble status. Ethnic "cultures" tended to be associated with the different status groups and sometimes with different territories, and nationalism was in no way the central issue in Transylvania's intergroup relations that it was to become. Persons who entered the privileged estates, especially Romanians who were freed or ennobled, automatically assumed the (Magyar) trappings of nobility without any sense of deprivation. Groups coexisted in relative peace, in complementary social and economic niches.

This fluidity of self-conception began to erode during the sixteenth and seventeenth centuries, as the idea of *natio* (privileged feudal estate) evolved toward explicit congruence with the idea of "nationality," and as struggles for national sovereignties and recognition spread throughout the empire. By the early nineteenth century, the rigidification of national identities and their strong association with different social classes in Transylvania was complete, and ethnicity was fast becoming individuals' most salient attribute. The dissolution of feudal status groups and the centralization of polities tended to individualize ethnicity, a process furthered after 1848 by the incorporation of individuals, rather than of collectivities, into state citizenship. Thus, the principal unit within which ethnicity inhered passed from groups to individuals identifying with those groups. In Transylvania, the main change thereafter was the continual undermining of the social-structural foundations with which group difference had been associated: the inclusion of large numbers of non-Germans in the middle classes, from the mid-1800s on, and the removal of Magyars from political power, in

1918. Under Communist policy, identities that remain are minimally attached to social-structural supports, and they draw impetus
largely from international events and from the historical meanings
of those identities in the present context. Let me briefly review the
specific trends for German (Saxon)[4] and Romanian identifications.

Transylvania's Germans have witnessed a nearly unbroken decline,
from 1500 to the present, in the structural supports for their collective solidarity. The only support that has not diminished is an international one, namely, the difference in degrees of economic development between Romania and West Germany, these people's most
important reference population. If developments in the world
economy should see Romania catching up with West Germany, even
this support would vanish — and with it, perhaps, the benefits to be
had from maintaining a separate ethnic identity from the Romanians with whom Germans increasingly intermarry. Germans today
comprise a loose aggregate of individuals whose formal differences
from Romanians consist, at most, of slight statistical deviations from
the norms of skill, CAP membership, and income.

But it has not always been so. Germans were once a distinct
feudal status group different from Romanians on every imaginable
count; their identity had formidable structural underpinnings,
based in their collective incorporation as a privileged but recogniz-
ably separate and territorially segregated estate in Transylvania's
feudal charter of 1437. This foundation in feudal privilege enabled
them to develop and protect an economy very different from that
prevailing elsewhere in Transylvania. The protection included
restricting guild membership and urban residence to Saxons, and
(usually unsuccessful) appeals to the Habsburg dynasty, based in
their common germanity.

With feudalism's decline, however, with the rise of Magyar nationalism in the empire, and with the individualization of state citizenship, the structural reinforcements of Saxon identity began to
weaken. First (1790) their representation in Transylvania's Diet
went from sectional to proportional, reducing their say in internal
affairs from one in three to about one in twelve. After 1848, feudal
privilege ceased to justify the autonomous corporate existence that
had protected Saxon trade and industry; economically, the growth
of large-scale industry with nonindigenous capital swamped much
of Saxon manufacturing. Throughout the second half of that century, members of other ethnic groups slowly infiltrated the bourgeois
ranks that had been a Saxon monopoly. In 1867 the Hungarian

state violated centuries-old precedent by abolishing the special office of Count of the Saxons, and magyarization threatened German educational institutions as it did Romanian ones. After World War I, corporate Saxon landholdings were expropriated, and Romanian interests flooded the manufacturing and commercial spheres. The Saxon community had become a corporate collectivity in little more than name. Germans differed (in structural terms) from Romanians chiefly by their disproportions in more lucrative activities and occupations, and by their near-absence from society's lower classes. Hitler's transnational helping-hand briefly reinvigorated the Saxon organization and German identity, but the price was the definitive end to Germans' superior class position: expropriation of their lands and nationalization of their enterprises in 1945. Germans were at last proletarians in all senses of the word, detached atoms amid the Romanian masses. Radical though this change was, however, it was merely the culmination of a long process in which their membership in Transylvanian society was moving from collective incorporation, as a privileged group within a feudal status system, to singular incorporation as individual representatives of their nationality and citizens in a modern nation-state.

Concerning German ethnic consciousness, it is important to recall that Saxons were probably the first of Transylvania's groups to manifest ethnically defined solidarity, in response to changes in the economy. Saxon ethnicity emerged from their involvement in precocious mercantile capitalism, as they built local manufacturing and short-distance trade on the back of long-distance trade that fortuitous changes in global trade routes had cast into their territories. The Saxon economy had never been identical to that of the other privileged estates, since Saxons excluded servile relations from their lands while refeudalization settled into the rest of Transylvanian society. The differences became more significant, however, with Saxons' new mercantile pursuits. But the remaining privileged estates proved unenthusiastic in their support of their Saxon brethren, denying them monopoly trading rights and favoring foreign merchants instead—Greeks, Armenians, Wallachians, and Jews. As Saxons competed with these outsiders by closing ranks qua Saxons, they effectively created a permanent breach within the noble Transylvanian estates. With their en-bloc conversion to Lutheranism later, their separation was further cemented, and the protection of the Saxon niche thenceforth had an inevitable ethnic character.

It is difficult to chart the rise and fall of German ethnic consciousness after this, except to remark on its upsurge during the inflamed revolutionary and nationalist period of the 1840s to 1860s. This era nonetheless produced a schism, as some Saxons took up the idea of a Magyar national state and others sided with Romanian nationalists against it. German ethnic awareness seems to have crested again in the twentieth century, between the wars, although one cannot tell to what extent the increase was a result chiefly of Nazi influence and what from the widened competition between Germans and Romanians in the economy. In the present, German ethnic consciousness appears relatively quiescent, owing such life as it exhibits, in part, to chances to emigrate. This makes it an international rather than a local phenomenon.

It would be incorrect to generalize the progressive individualization and decline of German identity to Romania's other minorities, however. There is some evidence of high ethnic consciousness among Romanian Magyars, and although one can adduce several arguments to explain this, perhaps the most powerful is the different historical positions of these two groups in Transylvania's political economy (see Verdery 1978). Germans, as the system's middle class, never held or hoped to capture political power; Magyars did, and they show signs of not being reconciled to its loss. One can carry this argument to its extreme by observing that German identity continues to serve, as it has over the past three-and-a-half centuries, to protect and expand economic opportunities (rather than political and administrative control, the perennial Magyar concern), which constitutes their principal motive for emigrating to West Germany in the present.[5]

If the trend for German ethnicity has been a linear one towards its structural disintegration and individualization, with cyclical awareness expressed locally toward events that often originate outside, the trend for Romanians has been almost the reverse. Romanian nationalism had no corporate resources, based in feudal privilege, with which to defend itself. Romanian ethnicity was defined largely by exclusion from privilege: Romanians were not a natio, and their religion was not recognized. They were a residual category. Before the decline in the monarchical grants and ennoblements that had underlain the feudal system, "Romanians" could change their identity with ease as they changed their social status, assuming lands, privilege, Magyar language, Roman Catholicism, political citizenship, conspicuous display. Thus, many Transylvanian nobles (like László Nopcsa, chap. 4) could say they were "of Romanian origin."

By the time some nobles were using this argument to justify their opinion that Romanians were not oppressed, however, Romanian ethnicity had become something very different, and nationality in general much more rigid. Upward mobility had become nearly impossible for most Romanians, making their nationality the equivalent of a caste alongside their status as serfs. Beginning with no structural support but this association between their nationality and class status, Romanian nationalism later gained one institution, given by the Habsburgs in the form of the Uniate church, in the 1690s. This institution sustained over the next century the climactic manifestation of Romanian ethnic consciousness. Responding to Magyar nobles, who were responding in turn to the dynasty, Romanian nationalism confronted Transylvania's feudal natios in a bid to achieve collective gains for Romanians. The timing was unfortunate: hopes for collective benefits were ill-fated in an era newly won to Enlightenment ideas about the rights and citizenship of men qua individuals. Thus, the modest institutional support provided by the Uniate church was not further augmented, in social-structural terms, until Transylvania passed into the Romanian polity in 1918, empowering Romanians nationally as never before.

These two main structural facts of Romanian nationalism — the lack of an institutional base parallel to that of Saxons and Magyars in the feudal system, and the strong association between Romanian ethnicity and low class position — gave Romanian national attitudes their most distinctive stamp. In combination, they set the tone of the Romanian movement: to achieve political and social rights for Romanians equivalent to those of Transylvania's other ethnonations, thereby permitting an improvement in their disadvantageous class situation. Unlike Magyars and Germans, who from at least 1800 on were using ethnic identification to *exclude* others and protect privileges, Romanians built into theirs a yearning for *inclusion,* for equality and dignity, that implied admiration as well as resentment of those with whom they interacted. I believe one can still discern a shadow of this cast of mind, in Romania's present concern with respect for its sovereignty and integrity and with its autarkic efforts to become the economic equal of the world's more privileged nations.

Ethnic consciousness among Romanians has had a different rhythm from that of Germans. If the early 1600s were the epoch of

the rise of German nationalism, Romanian nationalism's epoch was
the later 1700s. The two nationalisms grew in direct response to
different kinds of stimuli and emerged from very different environmental conditions. The formative milieu for Saxon ethnicity was the
autonomous Transylvanian quasi state of the sixteenth and seventeenth centuries; for Romanian nationalism, the whole imperial
formation, with its arguments between monarchs and Magyar
nobles as well as the Habsburg-created Uniate church. Both groups,
particularly the Romanians, operated at a high level of self-aware-
ness from around 1848 onward. Later, as the Hungarian government took aggressive action to create a homogeneous Magyar state,
the nationalism of Transylvania's Romanians (against whom the
actions were especially aimed) was kept at fever pitch. At its apogee
in 1918, it accomplished the incorporation of the region into Romania, after which we can no longer easily chart the course of
Romanian ethnicity except in local settings, for it became trans-
muted in its enlarged national context. (Thus, the present excess
of chauvinism in Romania cannot be adequately explained by the
information presented in this book.)

These are the broad lines of Romanian and German ethnic
sentiments. Manifestations of such sentiment at the village level,
and the consequent tone of ethnic relations, did not necessarily
move in lockstep with these larger trends, although the two tended
to be linked. The linkage was especially close for village Germans,
directly tied through priest and teacher to the center of the Saxon
organization. This connection was likely to have its effect not just on
village Germans but on Romanians with whom they resided in
villages like Binținți. One suspects that the nationalist concerns of
Romanians in monoethnic settlements would have gradually sub-
sided after 1918, but not in Binținți, where Romanians continued
to rub shoulders with Nazi-inspired Germans wary of Romanian
competition in the German economic niche. That this was a time of
unusual ethnic friction in the village has already been seen. The
socialist period has synchronized a reduction in ethnic antagonisms
from both sides by simultaneously eliminating the different class
positions historically given to these two ethnic groups as well as
the niche within which they were competing, and also by taking
measures that made Romanian peasants more "civilized" than they
have ever been (something Germans note with respect). Insofar as
some village Germans still look upon Romanians with disdain, this is
in large part the legacy of the attitude their ancestors entertained

for centuries toward the backward, uncivilized, and childlike Romanian serfs.

To link changes in ethnic consciousness with changes in social structure is not to deny that German and Romanian experiences of the world differ greatly, and in all likelihood will continue to, in consequence of the ethnic cultures they inherit with their socialization as Germans and Romanians. Nor do I mean to suggest that the present state of calm between these groups is necessarily permanent or that Germans are slated for assimilation. Changing circumstances could revivify notions of ethnic difference; for it is only historically, and not of theoretical necessity, that ethnic group membership was joined to class in Transylvania and derived much of its social significance as well as its content from this conjunction. As that historical connection has receded, other meanings have arisen: the internationalization of germanness, first through Saxon partnership with the Nazis and now through emigration, for example; and the present attempt at further historicizing Romanian identity, legitimating it with new, admirable, and ancient claims, whose audience is not just in Transylvania's past but in the international present.

STATE AND ETHNICITY, STATE AND ECONOMY, AND EMPIRICAL SYNTHESIS

Since the attempt to treat this study's three themes in isolation was already faltering at the end of the previous section, I will encourage the threads to become further entangled, continuing on with the connections between the state and ethnicity or nationalism. Recent social science literature posits some explicit relationships between the state and ethnicity, especially when ethnicity takes the form of organized political action or separatist movements. For example, Coulon and Morin (1979) argue that in general, the strengthening of states invigorates separatist sentiments, as the modern state's direct incorporation of local citizens bypasses the elites of ethnically differentiated regions. This idea might help to account for the present restiveness of Romania's Magyars, whose elites have been deprived of crucial intermediary functions by the centralization of the Romanian polity. Others propose (e.g., R. Cohen 1978) that with its increasing strength the modern state acquires ever more critical importance as a dispenser of scarce and valued goods (jobs, development programs, access to education, welfare, etc.), and that when this occurs in the context of prior ethnic inequalities, it threatens to perpetuate discrimination unless ethnic groups mobilize to compete for their proper share. Somewhat modified, this would be one way of interpreting the conflicts among regionally differentiated groups in the Habsburg Empire, who struggled for influence or control over the policy-setting apparatus so as to benefit their own national territories (Verdery 1979:392). It also aptly summarizes the ethnic effects of some policies of the Romanian state both before and after 1945. The interwar Romanian government often dispensed sweets to Romanians and bitter pills to Germans and Magyars, a pattern of which Magyars accused the state after the 1921 agrarian and bureaucratic reforms and also in the present, while Germans voiced similar grievances in the years immediately after 1944.

These proposals, and others one could offer, suggest how state actions may inspire or aggravate ethnic and national difference, especially under current conditions. All of them, however, presuppose the prior existence of ethnic difference as an issue. In the central chapters of this book I have shown how that issue arose historically. Even in this history, however, "the state" — whether actual Habsburg, Hungarian, or Romanian states, or the ideal state that some nationalisms strove to create for themselves — has played its part. I have shown how Magyar nationalism had its roots in the thirteenth-century pact between Hungary's king and nobility, defining the rights of the noble "nation" against monarchical usurpation. Under usurpations by Habsburg monarchs — especially the efforts of Joseph II to centralize the state — this tradition of rights combined with the Herderian variant of Enlightenment ideas about "nation" to kindle Magyar gentry nationalism. Thus, Hungarian nationalism was the state-provoked eighteenth-century transformation of a much older relationship between monarch and nobility. This nationalism also infected the Magyar nobility of Transylvania, ensconced in county administration like their fellows in Hungary and yoked with them in opposition to a single Habsburg state; the two groups formed a united noble front that defended aspirations to a greater Hungarian state (consisting of Hungary and Transylvania). Their sentiments were further inflamed by what they came to see as a state-supported bias, favoring industrial magnates from Austria and Bohemia and obstructing the industrialization of Hungary, which was left as an agrarian "colony" within the empire.

Romanian nationalism too was a product of Habsburg state-building. From the base provided by the Uniate church (symbol par excellence of Habsburg centralization) and encouraged by other state-generated improvements in the condition of Romanians, this nationalism erupted in reaction to the antistate Magyars, who intended to nullify Romanian gains by reversing centralization and rescinding the emperor's liberal edicts. Romanian nationalism aimed to rectify social grievances of Romanians within Transylvania; thus, its audience was a provincial one, like Saxon nationalism before it. The theatre within which it played, however, was empire-wide, and the scene had been set by developments in the state and by other groups' response to them.

The wording of these summaries suggests a brief digression on the character of nationalism (and ethnicity) as a form of ideology. One frequently encounters the view that these ideologies are a form of mystification, serving to obscure class differences within the ethnic group in the interests of goals sought by the ethnic elite for themselves. In all three ethnic ideologies in Transylvania, one can identify one segment of the population in question—the Saxon traders (there were also Saxon farmers and artisans), the Magyar gentry (there were also Magyar serfs and magnates), and the Romanian clergy (there were also Romanian serfs)—that benefited most directly from the nationalist idiom employed. One can readily leap to the conclusion that the leaders created this form of ideological statement precisely to obscure their position of advantage within their ethnic group and win the support of all its members, thereby gaining further advantages for themselves.

The ideology of nationalism may have come to function in this way, but it did not begin so. Rather, it began as a way of describing difficult problems, as understood by those who wanted to argue about them with others, regarded as the problems' cause. Ethnic ideologies were perfectly reasonable formulations of how the interlocutors saw themselves *in relationship to one another*—the Magyar gentry in relation to the dynasty, Saxon traders in relation to other traders, Romanian clergy in relation to Transylvania's estates— rather than in relation to their own lower classes. The relationships among these elites were of greater moment to them than was their relationship to their own masses, and in this struggle among class fractions, territorial and occupational differences were most concisely expressed within different nationalist ideologies.

It may seem puzzling why this formulation, rather than some other, was the one that seemed reasonable. The reason relates to the imperial striving for self-sufficiency, the regional division of labor that evolved (with state assistance) among its territories, and the late demise of feudalism under a noble estate. One must recall that the empire comprised a multitude of entities, each having a prior independent history and each having been governed by aristocratic elites, some of whom would later clash with the Court. Thus, the Western idea of the internally homogeneous, centralized nation-state was spread to a multinational empire in which such hopes were unrealizable. It was not the empire but some of its constituent "nationalities" who would use this idea to try to create their own state organizations, so as to withdraw from the imperial division of labor and build new, more diversified economies (while creating problems for their own internal minorities). Nationalism, against one centralizing state and for another, wrought this change for the Magyars. By a complex route, so also for the Romanians, whose nationalism crossed into Ottoman territory and helped to midwife the birth of a Romanian Kingdom. Romania has been withdrawing from larger divisions of labor and trying to build new, more diversified economies ever since, often with explicitly nationalist rhetoric — and with very powerful effects on its peasants.

Thus, fractions of elite groups, transformed in relation to a centralizing multinational state and a changing economy, used national idioms apt for the objective of influencing state power, or even of acquiring it to create centralized states and new economies of their own. With this one is led to ask further about the relationship between state-building and economic transformation. There are several ways of approaching this, but as before, I will concentrate on the state's quest for revenue, thus emphasizing the possibility that states may act from motives not identical with those of bourgeoisies whose interests they may appear to foster.

The concern for revenues comes into focus with the reminder that as of about 1700, the Habsburg emperor and the king of France administered territories and populations of nearly equal size, yet the French king disposed of revenues five times greater than those of his Habsburg rival, whose pretensions were no less grand. Some of the Habsburgs' devices for increasing revenues have been discussed or hinted at in chapters 2 and 4: controlling the salt trade, regulating serf-lord relations to draw more taxes from the peasants, acquiring mines, and so forth. Perhaps the most significant device was the encouragement of manufacturing — more broadly, of capitalism. These new economic forms would generate greater tax and customs revenues and assist, inter alia, with the important matters of state centralization: expanding and feeding the bureaucracy and the army — so often displayed during these years (and useful in quelling tax revolts, also) — as well as gradually building institutions like education, so important in creating a homogeneous national citizenry. To encourage capitalist economic activities meant encouraging a more efficient system of extracting surplus. This need not necessarily have taken the form of fostering industry — capitalist agriculture might have served reasonably well[6] — but manufacturing was already more developed than agriculture in some parts of the realm. This probably gave industry an appeal that won the monarchs' hearts and bought for Austrian and Bohemian manufacturers a monopoly of seats on the imperial Economic Council.

Habsburg state-builders' general interest in promoting (and controlling) the production of commodities, especially of industrial commodities, is apparent in their consistent mercantilistic concern with self-sufficiency; in their restrictions on the entry of foreign goods that might have competed with internal production; and in their explicit hindrances to the production of items in some parts of the empire — most notably, Transylvania — that might have competed with the empire's more advanced western centers of manufacture. Habsburg mercantilism set a precedent applied by every overlord of Transylvania from that era into the present. After protective imperial tariffs came the mercantilistic protectionism of the Romanian Kingdom and then the Communists' even more severe restrictions on foreign imports, all designed to spur local industry. (For states seeking to alter their position in the world economy, it is a matter of *plus ça change.* . . .) The main difference for Transylvanian peasants, and it is a significant one, is the role each of these mercantilistic regimes assigned Transylvania. Only the two Romanian regimes have hoped that Transylvanian villagers would become an internal market, consuming for protected industries; and only the Communists have actively sought to improve the standard of living enough to make that possible.

The Habsburg and subsequent states did more than merely encourage industry: they all, increasingly, undertook economic activities of their own. All of these states have acted as their own entrepreneurs,[7] taking over the role of a bourgeoisie in economies from which a strong native bourgeoisie was absent. Indeed, what distinguished early industrialization in Eastern Europe from that in the West was precisely the degree of direct state involvement in stimulating industry and promoting capital accumulation, through active inducements to foreign capital to compensate for inadequate domestic accumulation by either landlords or local bourgeois groups (Berend and Ránki 1974a:92; Katus 1970:84). The Habsburgs bought mines, supplied funds for the necessary infrastructure (especially railways and water transport), and founded state enterprises. Hungary created state bonds to attract capital that was then used according to the state's own development plan. The interwar Romanian state did many of the same things, adding to them the manipulation of prices to ensure the transfer of surplus value from agriculture to industry, which was accomplished also by the credit conditions set for various sectors of the economy. The Romanian state further served, as had its predecessors, as one of industry's major customers, particularly for military equipment. The Romanian socialist regime has carried this process to its limits. Not content to control the process of circulation, it has moved directly into production (like merchant capital in some times and places) in both industrial and agrarian sectors. The socialist state has become the primary accumulator and manufacturer in its own right.[8]

Because of the economic priorities set by all these states, from the Habsburgs to the Communists, industry has been preferred to agriculture. Each successive state reasserted the conditions for perpetuating the backwardness of Transylvania's agriculture, and it was this, more than the aggravations of partible inheritance, that contributed to the constant marginality and labor intensity of Transylvanian peasants. Decade after decade, each state ensured preferential conditions for capital accumulation elsewhere in the economy, by consistently favoring large-scale capital-goods manufacture, while agriculture stagnated. With the ascendancy of the poorly industrialized Romanian state after 1918, the state turned from neglecting agriculture to actively underdeveloping it. This would not have been necessary had not the state insisted on rapidly industrializing, in my view an insistence motivated by nationalistic designs to diversify the economy using protectionist methods, in order to avoid what were considered the detrimental effects of monocrop export dependency. The choice to industrialize dictated the retardation of agriculture, because of the low levels of capital accumulation within each of these enterprising states—the Hungarian less than the two Romanian ones. The deficiency required stratagems to build industry through very stringent surplus transfers from agriculture. In other words, the high cost borne by agriculture was a historically specific product of the relative underdevelopment of these areas within a world economy containing developed capitalist industrialist states. This trend has only just shown tentative signs of being redirected.

These developments had myriad consequences for the peasants. First, once the state yoked itself to the engine of industry, its power over peasants began an exponential rise, producing the trend, noted at the beginning of this chapter, toward increased state dominance over the lives of its peasants. Second, given its priorities, the state set nearly all the parameters of the economy within which these peasants labored, and set them largely to the peasants' detriment. By determining the conditions for marginal agriculture, the state determined their perpetual traditionalism.[9] Only with the arrival of a state that intended to use these villagers as industrial consumers was tradition effaced — again, primarily through state action. But those peasants who have not entered the industrial work force and limp along on diminutive rural incomes have a long pedigree: they come from an unbroken line of stepchildren to the state's economic plan.

State actions did more, however, than craft backward peasant agriculture and conjure up labor intensification. They were instrumental in keeping a semiproletarized peasant population on the land at all, rather than letting them become entirely "free." One can see this as early as the first intrusions of Habsburg state enterprise into Transylvania.[10] The Habsburg approach to state-directed economic growth had the important effect of breaking down the unity of a multifaceted feudal production, in which some feudal nobles farmed domains, worked mines, and produced rudimentary manufactures, all with serf labor. They interdigitated these various activities to spread labor demands throughout the year (see Prodan 1958-59) and to draw uniformly, if demandingly, upon the available labor supply. When the state began acquiring Transylvanian mines and setting up industries, with the support of merchants enriched by imperial trade (see chaps. 3 and 4), this disaggregated the various sectors of economic activity and laid conflicting and multiple claims to the labor supply.

One result was clashes between state and nobles over the obligations of serfs, but another was the long-term consequences these different sectors of activity had upon peasant production. Latifundism tends to eliminate peasant smallholding and peasant commodity production, while mining and manufacturing tend to reinforce them, both by encouraging peasant production of commodities to feed workers and by not competing with peasants for agricultural lands. Had events promoted agrarian capitalism in Transylvania, the peasants would have been pushed aside; but the enduring failure of agricultural development,[11] plus the mining and manufacturing preferences of the Habsburg and subsequent states, helped keep the peasant population on the land rather than fully proletarized. The large estates produced (inefficiently) for modest internal markets, keeping peasants in subsistence. Once the estates disappeared, industry enjoyed the benefits of low-cost peasant production, and the state increased it through reconstituting further peasants. Communist policy followed suit. Throughout, intensive labor has been the peasants' lot, but at least it has been agricultural labor partly for themselves rather than full wage labor from the outset, and this has helped them to survive economic downturns.

That peasants were alive (if not completely well) in Transylvania throughout this period, then, was due in large part to the actions of one or another state: preferences for manufacturing, agrarian reforms, conversions of debts, delayed compensations to cash-poor nobles who thus could not modernize estates, bureaucratic expansions that absorbed some nobles. While the states were thus helping to reproduce a traditional peasantry, peasants were doing their part by dividing farms and emigrating temporarily to the United States, so as to retain their hold on traditional livelihood.

But one must not forget the even larger environment: the interstate system, and global economic processes. To the extent that the Habsburg, Hungarian, and Romanian states took strong action in shaping their internal economies, the motive was to gain ascendancy not just in relation to their internal field but also internationally, in relation to other states. This is especially visible in the Habsburg case, where a desperate quest for resources was conducted partly to sustain frequent, ambitious, and costly wars abroad. For all these states, greater internal and international strength often entailed efforts to improve their underdeveloped economies, within a world economy characterized by unequal development. The Habsburg state sought to reduce its financial dependence on foreign loans and to maintain internal self-sufficiency in order to reduce the drain of revenues. Similarly, Hungarian state-makers aspired to economic parity with Austria (they could not wage separate war); and interwar and socialist Romania too have pursued development and greater self-sufficiency, with constant attention to military budgets.

Even these direct actions of states were constrained by international economic events beyond their control. The persistence of Transylvanian peasants owed much not only to state policies but to such things as the world economic downturn of the 1870s, which moved capital from the western to the eastern part of the empire and accelerated the industrial growth Hungary's rulers so eagerly sought. One might speculate that because of this, Hungary demanded less of its agricultural population than it might have, and that the low commercialization of Binținți Romanians before 1918 reflects this distant capital flow. Again, the 1930s depression boosted Romania's industrial development, but this time the internal economic situation meant paying for the opportunity by severely exploiting the peasants. The recent growth of Romania's socialist economy is hindered by global inflations and recessions that distort its planned balance of trade. The possible consequences for villagers include a further prolongation of backward agriculture, in which they are trapped if industry does not expand at the anticipated rate to absorb them, and more determined incursions into the products of their usufruct plots.

The more one considers the various elements of this discussion — state, peasants, nationalism, internal political and economic environment, international environment — the more impossible it seems to separate them. Such separation is further inhibited by the growing slipperiness of the concepts themselves, a reminder that the objects of scrutiny are changing form and meaning throughout. "The state" is increasingly more of a formal organization and increasingly "bourgeois" in its behavior; by the time one reaches the socialist epoch, it can almost be said that the state is not simply a "bourgeois" committee but *is itself* the bourgeoisie, with no division at all between accumulators of capital and managers of the state.[12] The concept of "peasant" is fortunately so vague that changes in its meaning need not be marked. I might merely note that in the socialist present, it is arguable whether peasants exist at all: divorced both from the individual means of production and from effective control over collective means of production, in a system noted for extreme centralism and very little democratic decision-making, cooperative farm members are surely not peasants. "Feudalism" has changed from a system based on kingly donations and military service to one held together through laws of entail; the "peripheral capitalist" systems discussed have shifted from agrarian-export to industrializing economies. "Nationality" has lost its fluid character, become trapped in the struggles for control over states, been individualized and then internationalized — and all along it has meant something different for Romanians than for others. The global environment develops ever stronger states and ever changing forms of capitalism. Because of this, even "underdevelopment" no longer implies what it did two centuries ago.

With these changes in mind, I might return for a moment to a puzzle posed in the epilogue to chapter 1: the formal similarities between CAP members today and serfs of the eighteenth and nineteenth centuries. These forms have different meanings, within changing contexts described and summarized at length. Despite long-term continuities in labor intensification and economic backwardness, the differences are overwhelming: a weak versus a strong state, a stagnant versus a developing economy, nobles who exclude manufacturing versus cadres who create it. The surplus product of the serf with his tiny plot went to a noble who used it to support the foreign manufacture of luxury items, and with these and the remaining surplus product he reinforced his dominance and powers of exploitation over his serfs. From 1700, anyway, this noble redistributed the surplus product only in times of severe need, and then often as loans that procured him more land or labor. The surplus product of the CAP member with his tiny plot goes to a state that invests it in local manufacture of consumer and capital goods; although the success of these manufactures reinforces the state's dominance over the "peasant," the trend has been toward self-generating accumulation, not toward increasing "peasant" exploitation but toward redistributing much of the product in the form of social services. From this come the opinions of Binţinţi peasants that "things were never so good before as now" and "you don't see a poor person anywhere."

The serf and the CAP member differ profoundly in the extent to which their "state," or some significant group in their society, has found it necessary, desirable, and possible to include them in a process of development that has entailed creating an internal market, of which they have formed a part. Their situation as consumers — and not just their purchasing power but also their level of welfare — has improved, while their exploitation as producers has, one hopes, passed its zenith.[13] Even if the present-day form of socialism proves to be just another way of accumulating profit in a capitalist world (see Chase-Dunn 1980), at least the profits are concentrating in new hands, and the path between these hands and their pockets is somewhat obstructed, if not by a redistributive social ideology then by the necessity of keeping internal purchasing power high enough to fuel Romanian industry.

STATE, ECONOMY, AND ETHNICITY:
THEORETICAL SYNTHESIS

A final pass of the shuttle will show how these three themes might be woven together in a single form of argument. Although the argument will not be fully finished, one can at least contemplate its design.

Scholars interested in the encounter between capitalist and non-capitalist economic forms, a problem mentioned in the introductory chapter, have understood this encounter in several ways (see Foster-Carter 1978). Capitalism is thought in some cases to break down other forms of economy, transforming and assimilating them into the forms and relations of capitalism. Sometimes it appears to rein-force preexisting economies and to preserve them, keeping down the costs of capitalism (to express the notion in terms of effects rather than intentions) by draining other economies of labor, raw materials, and the like, which are differently valued in those other systems. Sometimes these traditional systems put up a struggle against the intruder and hold it off, at least for a while. Sometimes the encounter creates new economic systems that are neither capi-talist nor traditional, and these too may either assist capitalism or resist it. Sometimes the various possibilities are seen as a historical sequence: capitalism encounters noncapitalist forms, reinforces these or creates new ones, thus quickens the process of "primitive accumulation," and then, at a certain point in capitalism's maturity, it destroys or assimilates the other forms. In all likelihood, some version of each of these is a way of describing real outcomes in different empirical situations at different times.

Upon inspection, one begins to see that very similar arguments occur in the literature on the rise and decline of ethnic conscious-ness, especially of nationalist or separatist movements. The entire structure-functional school in sociology, for example, took it as axiomatic that "modernization" (meaning both economic develop-ment and nation-state formation) would destroy ethnic residua, wiping out "tribalisms" and causing the assimilation of different cultural groups into the mainstream. Other scholars argued to the contrary: that the contact of ethnic groups with political moderniza-tion or with economic development (Geertz 1963; Gellner 1969; Collier 1975; Hechter 1975) would produce an increase in the salience of ethnic or national differences, that is, would reinforce separate identities, just as advancing capitalism is seen by some to reinforce noncapitalist economies. Still others have proposed that ethnicity may actually be created by the spread of "modernity," often in the form of imperialism (Levine and Campbell 1972; Fried 1968). Still others discuss the possibility of sequences: first created or reinforced ethnicities, then gradual if sometimes only partial assimilation (Geertz 1963; Ragin 1979). Interestingly, paral-lel theories for the two subjects—capitalist and noncapitalist encounters, and ethnic politics—appeared in Western social science literature at roughly the same time and were sometimes combined, as in Hechter's (1975) blending of a form of dependency theory— internal colonialism (capitalism creates or reinforces different modes of production that support it)—with a theory about ethnicity (ethnic reaction occurs because processes of unequal political and economic development reinforce ethnic difference). In all cases it is easy to read for "development and modernization," the terms most frequently used in writings on ethnicity, the spread of industrial capitalism with its inevitable accompaniment, the modern nation-state.

The similarities in the form of these arguments suggest a unified conceptualization that, if not applicable to all instances of economic and ethnic change, at least appropriately recapitulates the processes this book has examined. To unify the discussion's several themes, I must point, as does Warman (1980), to a crucial function of states, as the organizations coordinating society: to set the conditions for the coexistence of different forms of economy. The Habsburg, Hungarian, and, especially, Romanian states, like Warman's Mexico, set with increasing authority the conditions for the coexistence of industrial capitalist production (fostered partly by direct state action) with a peasant economy, operating according to its own rationale rather than to the rationality of capitalism. By consistently encouraging capital flows into the preferred mercantile and manu-facturing sectors, with generally retarding effects on Transylvanian agriculture, each of these states has reinforced a peasant economy, which they have actively shored up by emancipations, land reforms, etcetera. This peasant economy has then contributed to the develop-ment of industrial capitalism through a transfer of value, as items produced for use in the peasant economy are converted to cash in order to pay debts and taxes. Crucial in this process is that those who mediate the conversion—merchants and, increasingly, the state —set interest rates and prices very differently from the values that the land, labor, and agricultural products being converted would have for most in the peasant economy (see Warman 1980: chap. 6). It is therefore critical that these different forms of economy be separated by a boundary, and that the state help to hold this boun-dary in place.

This phrasing is reminiscent of Fredrik Barth's ground-breaking work on ethnicity (Barth 1969). Barth saw ethnic groups as sepa-rated by boundaries, which compartmentalize the different value and evaluation systems specific to different ethnic groups and also maintain the integrity of these separate systems through conventions for behavior at their interface. Barth saw the possibility of "converting" across these different systems of values — manipulating and changing identity, often in pursuit of advantage — and some of his colleagues (Eidheim 1968) have written of how political "entrepreneurs" can "capitalize" on such value differences by converting across the boundaries between them, much as merchants do for peasants and capitalism. Justly considered the most original and influential contribution to anthropological studies of ethnicity, Barth's work has been criticized for (inter alia) inadequate attention to societal distributions of power and to the embedded cultural meanings of ethnicity. To place ethnic relations in the context of economic and political development and to trace ethnicity's historical meanings, as the present study has done, enables one to build fruitfully upon Barth's insights.

Both the ethnic systems of value discussed by Barth and the value systems proper to coexisting forms of economy can be subsumed under the broader notion of different cultural systems, or more subtly, of different intentionalities and perceptions, systematically varying according to their placement in the social system and in contexts within that system. Anthropologists long ago abandoned the assumption of homogeneous and unitary relations between "a culture" and "a society." It is thus possible to speak of interacting ethnic groups and conjoined economic systems as *in some cases* referring to the coexistence of different systems of intentionality and perception, entailing different notions of value both in the sense of the worth and utility (or "price") of culturally embedded objects and relations, and in the sense of how "peoplehood" and behavior are assigned different ethnic meanings and categorizations. I believe such a formulation makes sense for the cases investigated in this book, where for historically specific reasons, groups placed differently in the system of production (both within the territory of the Habsburg empire and within Transylvania) came to be identified as different "nationalities" or culturally different ethnic groups.

This association emerged simultaneously with several circumstances: the growth of states, conjoining groups and activities that had previously interacted and unfolded in a more decentralized way; the increasing penetration of mercantile and capitalist forms; and the shift of the feudal idea of natio from "estate" to "people," or "nationality." In Transylvania, this began with the precocious mercantilism of an autonomous Transylvanian quasi state (soon swallowed up in a Habsburg state) with its Saxon traders who, as a result of their struggle to control trade, affirmed their separateness as an ethnic group, thus propelling the idea of natio on its national-ist trajectory. How can these and subsequent events be linked more specifically with the state as articulator of ethnic and economic values?

I have already observed that the historical meaning of ethnicity before this early period of social change in Transylvania was other than what it was to become. With this period, however, I believe we can discern (oversimplifying a bit) the intensification of three distinctive systems of value already present to a degree, associated with the feudal (Magyar and magyarizing Szekler) nobility, the Saxons, and the (mostly Romanian) serfs. The global shift in trade routes and the rise of Saxon crafts and trade produced a more complete association between Saxons and values associated with exchange, for the growth of towns on trade routes meant not just crafts and trade but rural commodity production to feed town dwellers. This set of values within the Saxon economy contrasted with those predominating among the serf population, who were producing for subsistence on holdings too small for much commer-cialization, and also with what I would call the display values proper to the nobility, that is, the conversion of goods into symbolic capital through conspicuous consumption. Looking at a single item, food-stuffs, one can see that it has different meanings for noble, Saxon, and serf. Each of these differences was embedded in cultural sys-tems that differed in other respects as well.

Although this brush with capitalism sharpened identities (at least, for the Saxons), relations among Transylvania's ethnic groups still did not take on the highly competitive coloring they would acquire by the eighteenth century. What made the difference, I suggest, was the process of Habsburg state centralization, in which the state became the proponent of a subset of the values available within the society. State partisanship of particular economic forms affected the empire's different cultural groups by infringing on their different cultural notions of value, which jeopardized the groups' very per-petuation, while at the same time seeking to maintain some of the economic compartments that accompanied such notions of value. The fact that agents of the state were also in a position to manipu-late the terms of conversions from one sphere to another—increas-ingly, as state strength grew—made control of the state machinery, qua apparatus of such conversions, ever more desirable to the lead-ers of some national movements. In promoting capitalist industry, the state not only brought different modes of production into sustained conjunction, it also reinforced ethnic difference and created nationalism.[14]

I am not suggesting simply that new economic processes cause hitherto compartmentalized groups to begin competing with one another for a set of "scarce resources." Because of the coexistence of different cultural as well as economic systems, the situation is more complex than the skirmish for resources so often emphasized in writings on ethnicity. I will illustrate this with the nationalism of Magyars against the dynasty, which, although it does not involve two ethnic groups, will show the role played by different notions of value within different systems of cultural and political intention. The example aims to demonstrate that it is not just the spread of capitalism that fortifies or intensifies ethnic conflict (*pace* Cole 1981), but the spread of capitalism in conjunction with the growth of states.

Habsburg state centralization entailed at least two major emphases that collided head-on with the cultural system of Magyars: state-building itself threatened the historically valued rights of nobles, against sovereigns and for the autonomous administration of their counties; and state partisanship of capitalism — of exchange values, to oversimplify — threatened the display values of the nobles' social economy. I have already explored the first of these at sufficient length to show why centralization would provoke Magyar nationalism, as a state rationalizing its bureaucracy threatened the administrative offices of gentry, for whom office had become essential to noble status. Thus, the same basic item (administrative office) had different values for the state and for the Magyars, and the state seemed to be in a stronger position to impose its system, thereby controlling the destiny of both the item and the gentry. (It drew some of this strength from its growing association with capitalist manufacturing.)

A similar dynamic is apparent in the conflict between exchange and display values. One aspect of the state plan for industrial development was high tariffs on luxury imports, which were viewed as commodities subject to manipulations of their exchange value, toward encouraging domestic production of commodities like them. Because of this, the cost of luxury items for noble consumption soared. But nobles did not see luxuries as commodities (nor, for that matter, as replaceable with domestic goods): luxuries were essential to the maintenance of noble life-styles (see also Schneider 1977).

Nobles also did not see their own estates as the source of commodities whose production could be increased, or made more efficient, to generate more value through exchange in order to pay the increased prices. The treatment and the value accorded to "luxuries" therefore differed absolutely, in the views of the state and the nobility. To take a second example, when the state sought to regulate feudal relations and increase its revenues from the peasants (simultaneously jeopardizing noble incomes), a conflict again arose between discrepant evaluations of a single good: grains, having use value for the peasants, had exchange value for the state, as the vehicle for taxes; but the nobles saw grain stockpiles as fundamental to their style of life, and insofar as grain had an exchange value, this mattered less than the destination of the income in noble display. The crisis produced was not a crisis of income per se but of the meaning of income for different groups in the system. By laying conflicting claims to those who supplied the sources of value for both groups—the peasants—the state was not merely reducing incomes for nobles, it was whittling away at their very nobility.

This was not a circumstance permitting accommodation. Therefore, the conflict between different systems of meaning, including different notions of value, reinforced and even created a nationalism in which Magyars asserted their lack of enthusiasm for the values held by the state and their reluctance to be modernized, homogenized, and assimilated out of existence. It is possible that initially, Magyar nationalists wanted to *insulate* their territories from the values promoted by the Habsburgs. Later, however, the conceptions and values of Magyars had changed sufficiently, under the press of economic and political circumstance, to make them shoot to capture their own state machinery so as to direct the accumulation of exchange values more to their own advantage.

The subsequent histories of the Hungarian and Romanian states exhibit intensifications and variations of this same process. Each successive capture of a state machinery entailed a more rigorous alliance with values promoting industrial capitalism, necessarily bringing it into conflict with noncapitalist systems of value and meaning in the countryside. Each capture altered the configuration of values incorporated into state priorities; Hungarians, for example, championed industrial development but also retained their valuable political autonomy and control. Each alliance with economic development also increased the state's ability to set the conditions conjoining and compartmentalizing different systems of value, funneling capitalism into industry and withholding it from the economy of (Romanian) peasants. This contributed to retaining both the peasants' traditional economy and their cultural separation from other groups having different relationships to the values of the state. Because different groups (Germans and Romanians) *continued* to have different relations to the systems of value fostered by the state, separate cultural identities persisted even after 1918, as the state policy kept alive a compartment for use values as against exchange values and mediated the conversion to the benefit of the latter, which was more consonant with German than with Romanian ethnic history.

I will not further illustrate this set of arguments with extended recasting of the ethnic and economic histories that have already been recapitulated at length. But I wish to remark upon the importance of "local response" (see Introduction) in relation to the views just presented. While the state can and does strongly influence the conditions for coexistence of the economic and cultural systems within its bounds, the systems thus conjoined do not always play precisely the role, maintain the continuities, or adopt the transformations envisioned for them. For example, the Habsburg state tried to create religious uniformity and to promote the production of use values by Transylvanian serfs so as to convert those to state ends; thus the Uniate church and improvements in the situations of serfs (and of Romanians, by implication). Agents of the state did not bank on the possibility that from these efforts would come Romanian nationalist and peasant uprisings, which would inflame internal relations and raise rather than lower obstacles to political centrality. The examples investigated in this account might suggest that as states centralize and increase their power, there is diminishing room for the resistance of forms other than those it promotes. But this conclusion is not a necessary one; it is merely the outcome in these examples.

Any coherence in the above discussion derives largely from my premises about "the state" and my unwillingness to see it as a mere extension of global capitalism, an integral element in the single logic by which global accumulation occurs. I have dramatized these premises by overemphasizing the autonomy of the state, assisted by the reification inherent in our use of the word. I cannot marshal theoretical arguments to support this position, which amounts to a gamble that messiness, rather than parsimony, prevails in the unfolding of human affairs. Although there appears to have been a historical tendency for states to promote capitalism within their borders, I do not see this connection as imperative. It is precisely through investigating the socialist states of Eastern Europe (and elsewhere) that one may eventually be able to assess this gamble, for much of the present wide disagreement concerning the nature of these states (see Chase-Dunn 1980:512–513 n. 9) is about the extent to which they guide the production of use values, rather than exchange values, marking a reverse over the previous situation. If these socialist states increasingly demonstrate that they are *not* merely an alternative way of pursuing capitalism, but are instead promoting the spread of something other than exchange values, and are less concerned with increased efficiency of extraction and profit than with increased redistribution, this would encourage us to separate conceptually the state from capitalist expansion and would strengthen a view of the state as the grand articulator of internal economic and cultural systems.

THE GREAT AND THE SMALL: IN DEFENSE OF ANTHROPOLOGY[15]

It would be inappropriate to conclude on abstractions so remote both from the place that has grounded all these themes and from the customary realm of anthropological discourse. Theories about notions of value, state centralization, and the growth of capitalism have taken the discussion far from the realities of daily life for Transylvanian villagers, and have made their ethnic identities so heavily determined as to seem like straitjackets. But it was not quite so. It is well to be briefly reminded of this, and the reminder will be Petru, a Romanian from Binţinţi and this book's dedicatee, who appeared in chapter 6:

> Yes, sure we had to learn some Magyar in school before 1918—how to say "table," "chair," "stove,"—you know, things like that. But it was the Hungarian state then, and of course we had to learn Magyar. That's what the law said. You had to know it for the army—some of the officers didn't know Romanian, and how could we obey orders if we didn't know their language?

In other words, just because he learned Magyar didn't mean he turned into a Magyar; he simply used it when he had to. Petru learned Russian also, as a prisoner of war, and some German from the Germans who served with him in the Austro-Hungarian army; but these learnings did not change his identity, they merely made life easier. "We were all mixed up together: Germans, Romanians, Magyars. . . ."

During the First World War Petru found it very handy to be from a multinational empire: it gave him many more options than he might otherwise have had.

> We saw that the Russians always favored the Czech prisoners over everyone else, and whenever prisoners were needed as laborers, the Czechs got the cushiest jobs. Once they came for a transport of Czechs to work, and my two buddies and I — a Romanian from Sebeş and a German from Sibiu, he was always wanting me to sing with him and his accent was terrible — well, we just slipped into that group with the Czechs and we ended up on a fine, huge estate with pretty girls and good food.

Later, given a scythe and asked to reap, he told his "hosts" disdainfully, "We Austrians never reap like this, we have *motors*."[16] On different occasions, confronted with unappealing menial tasks he suddenly "became" not just an Austrian but an ex-officer; and encouraged to enroll in a training program and join the Red Army he "became" suddenly an illiterate Romanian, averring that Romanians in Austria had poor schools. What, indeed, was he (aside from quickwitted)? He seems to have given a consistent answer to only one question: when asked about his religion, he was always Orthodox. This stood him in good stead in Russia and got him days off from work for the saints' festivals he would have been celebrating at home.

Such multiple possibilities are and have long been commonplace in this part of Europe. Although the environment has always allowed options, however, individuals also have had stabilized identities, and the stabilization has occurred chiefly within tiny communities like Binţinţi, where being Austrian or Czech or Russian has been irrelevant. Year in and year out, one "was" a Romanian peasant in interaction with Germans and Magyars. (Even so, a few Romanians did "become" Magyars over the course of their lifetimes; yet for the most part they were still Romanians, as far as everyone was concerned.) "Being" a Romanian peasant meant many things, which tended to hang together over time. It meant large amounts of diminishing returns to one's labor, frequent sharecropping and some stealing, clever stratagems for getting by, celebrating saints' days, speaking Romanian mostly, worrying about hospitality to guests, preferring cattle, valuing sociability and good times, mourning one's dead properly — and it meant these and other things, year in and year out, in constant juxtaposition with clearly alternative ways of being that were not Romanian. There was "being" Magyar, which meant (from the Romanian point of view) being quick-tempered and ready to take offense (and raise an insurrection), being belligerent, civilized but arrogant and cruel, dressing finely, drinking heavily and gambling, speaking Magyar, being Catholic or Calvinist. What Romanian could seriously admire most of that? And there was "being" German, which meant being stingy, brisk and efficient, unsociable, perseverant and hardworking, orderly and disciplined at the expense of having a good time, cold-hearted to one's children, more civilized than Romanians, richer, speaking German, being Lutheran, calculating every cent . . . Some of those weren't so bad, but on the whole . . . (Germans saw little to desire in what they thought of as "being" Romanian, too.) Better to be crafty than stingy or belligerent, to move ahead through cunning,[17] rather than through plodding enterprise or hotheaded confrontation. There was a long history behind these characteristics and others thought to pertain to each group, but the characteristics also had their daily experience; and even as they were transformed through time, they sharpened in opposition to the characteristics of others encountered day by day during the course of a mundane existence.

Being Romanian has also meant centuries of being survivors, principally by mechanisms other than overt conflict, as many of their proverbs show.[18] "Sit still and shut up if you want to survive." "The sword does not cut off a head that is bowed." "To flee is shameful, but it's healthy." "Be brother to the devil until you're across the bridge." "Silence is like honey." "The docile lamb suckles from two ewes." Germans and Magyars are disdainful of this approach, which they view as cowardly. Easy for them to say, having always had some degree of access to opportunity, to history, and to power. But it is noteworthy that nearly two millennia after the Roman legions retreated from Transylvanian soil, a population speaking a Latin language still survives among a sea of Slavic speakers and despite Hungary's determined efforts at magyarization.

Henry Roberts observed (1951: conclusions) that one of Romania's greatest difficulties has been that ideas and institutions borrowed or imposed, largely from the West, have not proved apt to solving Romania's problems. Ideas and institutions were both borrowed and imposed that had developed as solutions in other places— France, or Germany—without appropriate modification to make them Romanian solutions. Roberts also comments that although

Leninism is another such imposition, it is at least closer to Romanian realities than are other borrowed ideas, for Lenin modified Marxism to fit Russia, a society whose history more closely conforms to Romania's than do Western histories. This similarity need not lead to conscientious adoption of everything Soviet, including the Stalinist model so closely imitated in Romania's collectivization and forced industrial development. One could nevertheless agree, following Roberts, that the present attempt shows at least as much promise of solving Romania's economic backwardness as would the imposition of Western parliamentary democracy and unfettered capitalism.

Romanians have managed their survival capably enough through the centuries; they deserve the opportunity to create their own solutions, insofar as possible, although it would be utopian to expect all international influences on that process to cease. These solutions would be the sounder, the more collective, and the more wisely shaped if villagers like those in Binţinţi and other similar places were encouraged to find and to contribute their voice, for they too have something to offer even though centuries of subordination have persuaded them otherwise. What they might contribute has a past that endows it with particular meanings, which this exposition has sought to clarify; and it has a present fundamentally transformed, in many respects, over anything the past might have been expected to produce. Although these villagers' past and present will inspire their voice, it does not wholly determine their message. Perhaps the breadth of the setting within which their story has been told here may encourage them to recognize the importance of what they have to say.

Notes

Introduction

1. I am indebted to Germaine A. Hoston for her help in clarifying for me some of the arguments on the state in Marxist writings.

2. Jane F. Collier did me the favor of insisting on this point, which is now my opinion but began as hers.

3. While this entity is commonly referred to as the Habsburg *Empire,* I consider its behavior to be perfectly consonant with treating it as an aspirant state in the European state system of its day.

4. For those who insist on a functional interconnection among parts of a society, including between a society and its state, it is impossible to consider organizational forms being adopted because of some global imperative. But the workings of the modern world are such that global interactions always affect developments internal to any society. I would modify Thomas and Meyer's position only by saying that the internal organization of different societies will condition the degree to which the standard state form is successfully adopted. Among the mechanisms to which one can point, to suggest how international pressures help to standardize the organizational form of the state, are the frequency with which new constitutions (whether of older or of new states) are modeled after the constitutions of early Western states, as Romania's in 1923 was modeled after that of France; and the insistence by international lending institutions, such as the International Monetary Fund and the World Bank, that prospective borrowers adopt a prespecified organization of ministries and bureaus before funds can be approved.

5. The discovery that dependency theory had frequently appeared as a "native" understanding of the world's workings was the first bit of information that led me to wonder at its analytic validity. I regard participants' views as important information about their societies and about the positions of those people in them, but not as apt scientific models.

6. The choices are arguable for many reasons; not least of them is that "feudalism" as a social system could not possibly have disappeared overnight with the legislation abolishing serfdom. I regard the society as having been in a long transformative process that makes changes in labels more or less undatable. To speak of "feudalism" through 1848 is merely a convenient solution to a complicated problem.

7. I am grateful to Ewa K. Hauser for clarifying the meanings of "nationalism" and "ethnicity" from the Eastern European (Polish) point of view.

8. My thanks to Sidney W. Mintz for the suggestion that I include this section in my work and for conversations that produced some of the ideas in it. Conversations with Emily Martin helped further to clarify my thoughts.

9. The grants most commonly used for field research in Romania are IREX (International Research and Exchanges Board) and Fulbright grants. Both involve the U.S. and Romania in treaty-like agreements spelling out the obligations of both sides to researchers and attaching those researchers to specific scientific institutions, mediated on the Romanian side by direct government sponsorship.

10. Talented and discerning Western scholars have found it possible to attempt fair renderings after many years of study—for example, Hitchins in his outstanding works on Transylvanian history (1969, 1977). But even these efforts have not been

immune to criticism from other scholars of talent and discernment (see Deak 1979:360 n. 20, on Hitchins).

11. I might add here that in parts of my discussion of local ethnic relations (as opposed to nationality problems in Transylvania as a whole), I sometimes write less sympathetically of the Germans than of the Romanians. This reflects no personal bias whatever against the Germans: my German informants were wonderfully helpful and my friendships with local Germans were of real emotional importance. But I believe that throughout history, the German position was generally more favorable than that of Romanians, who have always needed friends to help rectify the injustices of their situation.

12. For nonspecialists, I point out that the term "informant" is anthropology's technical term for the persons from whom we learn about the society we study. It has no implications of clandestine research or of intelligence operations.

13. In the interests of fairness, I wish to state that, to my knowledge, no Romanian suffered any such retribution on account of association with me, and the three research assistants I employed all went on to the careers they had intended. I know only that my correspondence with some persons was monitored, something that can happen in the U.S. as well.

14. Technically, it is incorrect to use "communism" and "socialism" interchangeably, as I do in this paragraph—reflecting common public usage of the terms. The Eastern bloc countries and the Soviet Union all regard themselves as socialist, "on the road" to true communism; none of them claims to be actually communist yet. One might question the extent to which they are properly termed "socialist," (hence my occasional reference to "so-called socialist states"), just as one might question whether the West is properly called "capitalist" in the present. I do not intend to engage these questions.

15. I am grateful to John Murra for conversations that made me think about this issue of the "voice" to use in presenting the social history of Binţinţi.

1: Sugar by the Kilogram

1. I am deeply indebted to Michael Cernea for giving this chapter a close critical reading. Regrettably, I could not incorporate everything he would have wished. David Kideckel also provided detailed criticism, for which I am grateful.

2. The commune is an administrative unit in Romania, usually consisting of a central settlement plus four to twelve villages. Since 1945, communes have been redrawn several times (Helin 1967). Communes have existed as administrative units in Transylvania since at least 1918, but they were smaller than at present, often comprising a single village. Romanian communes today are smaller than those in China, rarely contain much diversity in economic activities (such as rural industry), and are not major units in economic planning.

3. The following joke speaks to the prevalence of theft. An exchange between two villagers, it employs a pun on the simple past tense of the verb *to be* (*fură*), meaning *he was* and homonymous with a word meaning *he steals*.

"Mă Ioane, de unde or fi venind Relu? (Hey John, where could Aurel be coming from?)" — Fură pă la sfat azi (He was [stealing] at the People's Council today).

"La sfat? Mai fură alţi p'acolo? (The People's Council? Were there others [stealing] there?)" — Ba da, fură mulţi: preşedintele, secretarul, brigadierii . . . toţi ăiă fură. (Why yes, there were many [stealing]: the president, secretary, brigade-leaders . . . all of those were there [stealing]).

4. About 15% of German deportees from Romania died in Soviet labor camps, primarily in the Ukraine; the rest were released between 1945 and 1951, over

half of them going to places other than Romania—largely West Germany, and some to Austria and East Germany (Paikert 1967:259). The reasons for this deportation of Germans are arguable and doubtless complex. Once Germans returned to homes in Romania, it became much more difficult, if not impossible, for them to emigrate to West Germany; hence they had to endure the hardships described in the text. One might wonder why any returned to Romania at all. First, many had left spouses, children, or parents when they were deported, and they were anxious to reunite with their families. Second, although ethnically "German," most of these people thought of themselves as citizens of a Transylvanian, not a German, homeland.

5. According to Montias (1967:89), peasants identified as chiaburi usually had more than fifteen hectares, hired labor, and rented out part of their lands to other peasants; some people were named chiaburi by virtue of owning other important means of production, such as stills, flour mills, threshers, etc. Almost none of the chiaburi of Binţinţi met all these criteria.

6. This jingle goes, in the original, "Trăiască draga găină, că din curul tău iese lumină." It had additional verses less well remembered.

7. During the period 1970–1976, the mean value of exports from industry— machine-building, chemical industries, and industrial consumer goods—was 50% of the volume of exports, while the mean value of agricultural products exported, whether raw or processed, was 26% (Tsantis and Pepper 1979:578–579). This contrasts with a mean value of 55% for agricultural exports in 1950 (ibid.:259).

8. Tsantis and Pepper give the following tables (1979:583), which show the diversity of Romanian import and export patterns clearly.

	EXPORTS				IMPORTS			
Commodity group	CMEA coun- tries	Other socialist coun- tries	Devel- oped market econ- omies	Devel- oping coun- tries	CMEA coun- tries	Other socialist coun- tries	Devel- oped market econ- omies	Devel- oping coun- tries
Total exports	38.8	7.2	31.0	23.0	37.2	6.4	40.5	15.9
Machinery and equipment	35.4	45.4	6.6	27.8	48.9	19.4	36.3	0.8
Fuel, mineral raw materials, and metals	18.8	23.0	33.4	12.5	35.2	29.5	31.8	68.3
Chemicals, fertilizers, and rubber	6.2	23.8	7.6	18.8	3.6	4.2	10.3	4.0
Building materials	3.1	2.9	2.1	3.8	1.0	2.4	1.4	0.1
Vegetable and animal raw materials	4.9	2.0	6.5	9.8	3.9	9.7	8.1	19.9
Live animals	—	—	—	0.1	0.1	—	1.6	—
Unprocessed foodstuffs	4.1	0.2	8.0	7.1	0.9	3.6	9.6	2.7
Other foodstuffs	7.9	0.7	15.6	11.6	2.2	10.5	0.8	3.0
Industrial con- sumer goods	19.7	2.0	20.3	8.6	4.3	20.7	1.6	1.1

Source: Data supplied by the Romanian authorities during discussions with the authors.

9. A Romanian engineer gave me the best explanation I heard for the state's birth control policy: since the state aims at autarky, it must develop industrial capacity in far more branches of activity than it otherwise would, which means more labor, and given that the system still rests on labor-intensive more than on capital-intensive production, it requires even more labor.

10. One is struck by the "capitalist" tone of these concerns, which emphasize efficiency and mechanization rather than the equity that socialist ideology usually emphasizes.

11. A "day's worth of work" (*zi-muncă*) is not as simple a measurement as it might appear. Calculation of "days worked" rest on a set norm that represents the amount of work a normal worker would accomplish in a day, but it is possible to work much harder and rack up extra days. Some tasks are also rated as more taxing than normal jobs and thus count more than one day per actual day.

12. I received slightly different figures from various officials for the amounts planted to vegetables and fodder crops; the differences are partly accounted for by their applicability to different years. All gave more or less the same figures for cereals, however.

13. Not all personal plots are plowed in this manner. Some peasants plow with a pair of milk cows; a few households have horses used for this purpose and rent their services to others; some also contract for plowing by tractor legally through the CAP, paying a fee to have a tractor come when the work necessary to the CAP has been completed.

14. One villager reported that villagers were delighted with the new system in its first year, because the production targets set were modest and were easily surpassed, gaining workers terrific incomes. The next year production targets were reset, this time at the levels achieved the year before, since it had been verified that these levels could be reached.

15. The revised production targets possibly coincide with the state's reduction of incentives, mentioned on p. 46.

16. It is possible to market produce privately in Romania. In the marketplace of any market town, one will see both stalls with state produce and stalls or tables at which individual farmers sell their goods. The prices are controlled by the state and at least some items (animals) cannot be sold without obtaining a market ticket in advance, for a fee.

17. For example, to use one year's prices, pigs might sell for 28 lei/kg in the market and 12 lei/kg on contract. A 120-kg pig would sell for 3,360 in the market, 1,440 on contract. A farmer sells his own pig; he then buys another with his three cocontractors, paying 840 lei, receiving 360, and losing 480 on the deal. This makes his net income from pig transactions 2,880, as against the 1,440 he would have made on contract alone: exactly double.

18. The favorable position of this village with relation to industrial employment doubtless contributes to the poor motivation of its agricultural work force and is another reason why its CAP should not be taken as exemplifying collectivized agriculture in Romania more generally.

19. In addition to the labor force reported in the table, there were 154 persons aged 65 or over, about one-fifth of whom claim to work occasionally in the CAP.

20. The source of these data is a census conducted by the village schoolteacher at the request of the commune. I do not know how the job categories were determined and presume that they were self-declared. About 10% of the women were listed as "housewife," and most of them are persons who would have been likely

to prefer a fancier designation than "CAP member." My own interviews confirmed that there are persons who are inscribed in the CAP but work no more than their plots. According to new rules being gradually enforced in the late 1970s, retention of the usufruct plot will be made contingent on work in the CAP.

21. An additional 7% of the households consist of one widowed parent and a junior couple. Because of the advantages of the extended family form, it is possible that patterns of commuting will lead to a gradual increase in the frequency of extended over nuclear family forms — quite the opposite of what is usually predicted as a concomitant of industrialized economies.

22. The product destinations reported for industry near Binţinţi are unofficial; their source is villagers who work in positions of some authority in the factories in question.

23. This statement rests on numerous conversations concerning the status of various kinds of employment in the past, and on an occupational-ranking task performed for present jobs by twenty informants. If the results of their rankings are pooled, the mean rank for CAP peasant was 43 out of 45; only "unskilled laborer" and "nightwatchman" were lower.

24. There are a few enterprises that are privately owned: one-man trades such as carpenter, roofer, or tailor, practiced by persons working out of their homes instead of in factories.

25. I had no evidence that either of the last two examples had actually been done by villagers, although both are reportedly common in Romania. At most, I heard of two village families who were worrying how much they would have to save up to assure their children's success on the university entrance exams, and other villagers whose children had succeeded without benefit of bribes calmed their fears.

26. There were two exceptions: Germans who had served in the Romanian rather than the German army, into which many of Romania's Germans were enrolled through Romania's initial pact with Hitler. After the coup that toppled Romania's fascist military dictatorship and broke the alliance with the Nazis, Germans taken into the armed forces served in the Romanian army and were not "enemies of the people"; hence their lands were not expropriated in 1945.

27. Further detail on the issues discussed in this section may be found in Verdery 1978.

28. Not all Romanians were insouciant on the topic of German-Romanian relations, of course. A number of villagers were polled concerning their attitudes toward interethnic marriages, and a quarter of the Romanians — nearly all of them elderly — voiced some objection.

29. Spellings were noted down from the signatures on birth and death registrations in the civil registers. I include as "German spelling" a Romanian-like variant of Philippe (Filipp), which appeared as early as 1893 on Hungarian documents. (Ordinarily, the substitution of "F" for "Ph" marks a shift toward Romanian spelling.)

30. One might expect intermarriage to rise merely as a consequence of moving to cities. Given the size of the German population in Binţinţi in recent years, however, it is only in cities (those having a substantial number of Germans, true of many of the urban centers to which persons from Binţinţi have migrated) that Germans will find a marriage pool sufficiently large to make a German spouse a reasonable possibility. The percentages for intermarriage for Binţinţi are similar to those reported for another community of Germans and Romanians (McArthur 1976).

31. To illustrate the effects of occupational title on ethnic identifications: Romanians habitually clarified any unclear personal reference to a German by adding "that German" except when the person held a high occupational title, in which case the clarification was almost invariably "the professor" or "the engineer" without reference to germanness.

32. These minority Councils were created in the wake of the Soviet invasion of Czechoslovakia. They gave the state greater control over minority activities and were probably intended to reduce the likelihood that minorities in Romania would create internal agitation justifying fraternal intervention by the Soviets (Turnock 1974:25). Similar tightenings of control on a number of fronts appeared in the wake of the 1956 revolution in Hungary.

33. I do not have complete figures on German emigration, but the following will give a hint of its magnitude. The Munich-based *Siebenbürgische Zeitung* for October 31, 1979, reports record immigrations during 1978–79 from Eastern Europe and gives breakdowns by country for the month of September, 1979. If one (hesitantly) multiplies the figure for Romania by twelve, the result is 10,500–11,000 German emigrants for that year.

2: On the Side of the Emperor

1. My beginning this discussion with the eighteenth century does not imply a timeless past until this date, marking a sudden transformation. The time selected is a convenience, chosen because Transylvania's incorporation into the Habsburg Empire commences then.

2. In this book I use the terms "aristocracy" and "nobility" more or less interchangeably, although strictly speaking the former is a subset of the latter. I sometimes write "latifundists," meaning nobles with middle-to-large estates; I imply nothing about the degree of modernization in their farming practices by using this term. Differentiation within the category of "nobles" is indicated, following usage prevalent in historical writing on Hungary, with the terms "magnates" (or great aristocracy) and "gentry" (or lesser nobility), the latter including professionals such as lawyers. These terms refer first to title, the magnates bearing titles and the gentry not, but also generally to differences in wealth, the gentry usually owning under 5,000 hectares. The grouping of nobles into "magnates" and "gentry" appears to have been a categorization employed by these nobles over several centuries. Further details may be found in Király 1969:25ff.

3. The deceased Miklós Macskásy was to be found in Binţinţi in the first place because he, along with a large number of other Magyar nobles from southeastern Hungary, took refuge in Transylvania once the Turkish forces began their depradations of the Hungarian Plain. (The Macskásys originated in Tinkova, in Hungary, west of what were then the limits of the Transylvanian principality.) The Turks extended their campaigns into Transylvania, frequently along the Mureş River valley containing Binţinţi.

4. The Macskásy Collection, located in the Romanian State Archives in Cluj-Napoca, Romania, comprises the papers of the Transylvanian gentry family Macskásy, who owned properties in Binţinţi (and other villages) from the mid-1600s to the mid-1800s. I briefly examined about two-thirds of the 400 documents relating to their Binţinţi estates. For assistance in this task I wish to thank Liviu and Maria Ursuţiu, of the Academy Library, and also Alexandru Matei, Director of the Archive, for his generosity in putting a battery of translators at my disposal. Lucia Şerdan and Ion Dordea bore most of the burden of this assignment, with admirable grace and dispatch.

My translations of the documents quoted in the text are extremely loose and should be read as such. They are made on the basis of nothing more than brief notes taken on translations from Latin and Hungarian, sometimes only on summaries rather than full translations. I note also that I have occasionally combined information from more than one document in my translations, so as to complete the picture I wish to present. I have included nothing that was not found in the documents, however, and to the best of my understanding of the material, I have rendered the content of the documents accurately. I have adopted a consistent form throughout for persons named in the documents, although different records often give the names in different forms (e.g., "Farkas" appears sometimes in its latinized German variant, "Wolfgangus").

5. The centralization of a Transylvanian "state" under Bethlen should not be read as implying growth in the economy—to the contrary. Overall, the late sixteenth and early seventeenth centuries were a time of reduced trade, owing to the bankruptcy of the Spanish Habsburg king and the consequent decline in urban development in central Europe, as well as to larger changes in global trading patterns.

6. These three simple labels obscure a legion of complexities that it would not repay us to examine. Boundaries around each unit were changed several times during the course of the eighteenth and nineteenth centuries; parts were withdrawn in 1761 for the Military Border, and later reincorporated; in addition to the Counties there was a thing called the Partium, which I have assimilated to the Counties in my discussion. Nothing in my description should be taken as more than an approximation of the true state of affairs at any given time.

7. The main difference between the administrative regimes of the Counties and of the other areas was that the former was the only area where feudal relations were expressly permitted. The success with which feudalism was excluded varied from one to another of the remaining administrative zones.

8. Among the complexities omitted are varying degrees of freedom and autonomy among the Romanian mountain populations along the Southern Carpathians. The work of Sam Beck and Steven Randall clarifies the ways in which these areas differed from the overall picture I present for Transylvania.

9. In this book I seek to avoid cumbersome phrasing and misleading expressions by means of the following strategy: when I wish to refer to people living on the territory of Hungary but not in Transylvania, I use the word "Hungarian"; in referring to people living in Transylvania I use the word "Transylvanian," even when I am including people who happen to think of themselves as "Hungarians"; when I wish to speak of all the people in Hungary and Transylvania who think of themselves as "Hungarians," I use the word "Magyar." By this device I can separate the "Hungarian nobility" (nobles based in Hungary) from the "Transylvanian nobility" (Hungarian-speakers based in Transylvania), and when I wish to discuss the actions taken by nobles in both Hungary and Transylvania I speak of them as "the Magyar nobility." Sometimes—and this is always clear from the context— I use "Magyar" to refer only to the "Hungarians" in Transylvania without those in Hungary as well. Thus, the word "Hungarian" in the text never refers to persons in the population of Transylvania, and the word "Magyar" refers either to all those in Hungary and Transylvania who considered themselves ethnically Hungarian or to those so considered only within Transylvania, the context making clear which meaning is intended. While this procedure may seem confusing at first sight, it works reasonably well and is preferable to the constant periphrasis otherwise necessary.

10. The translations of this and the two preceding documents are loose and very abbreviated renderings of Latin sources. I have retained a hint of the prolonged and tortuous phrasings characteristic of the originals.

11. I wish to thank Leon Marfoe for the initial suggestion that the Habsburgs may have had a special buffer policy for Transylvania.

12. I give here a tax list from 1720 rather than from a later period because this is the only document I have to show taxation in Binţinţi. Documents I saw in the Romanian State Archive branch in Deva show taxes being assessed in kind for villages near Binţinţi as late as the 1850s.

13. I am uncertain how Ferencz Olasz could have the power to excuse his serfs of taxes. Professor David Prodan tells me, however, that the granting of tax exemptions was a common practice among nobles who wished to attract new labor to their estates — they would promise a few years' tax relief in exchange for a peasant's contracting himself into perpetual servitude.

14. This enquiry, referred to as the Cziráky conscription, was consulted and copied in full in the Hungarian State Archives (Magyar Országos Levéltár) in Budapest. The information for Binţinţi is found in volume 9 of the conscription, pp. 95-122. The enquiry consisted of nine separate questions, and peasants' responses were recorded in both Hungarian and Romanian. Citations from the Cziráky conscription in this and the following chapter are referenced in the text as "Cziráky, Question X."

15. Cziráky, Question 7. The document clearly refers not to taxes per se but to tithes. I use it nonetheless to illustrate processes that were at work to deprive the state of revenues due it in one form or another. My translation is a complete rendering of the exact response of the serfs, from the document's Romanian version.

16. The figures from which I derive the overrepresentation of Transylvania's nobles among convicted revolutionaries are these: Deak (1979:335) reports that 199 of the 666 convicted revolutionaries born in the various lands of the Hungarian Crown were from Transylvania (29.9%), and the 1850 populations of Transylvania and all of Hungary including Transylvania were about 2,100,000 and 13,800,000, respectively (Transylvania is therefore 15.2%). The nobles constituted roughly the same proportion of the population in both Transylvania and Hungary.

17. The argument that the empress was truly expressing "enlightened" and humanitarian views is somewhat undercut by the fact that the conditions of serfdom were about as bad in the regions administered directly by the Crown, without the intervention of a local nobility, as they were elsewhere. One can assume that if the state were more concerned than the nobles about humane treatment, serfs of the state would have had a more pleasant life than they did (see, for example, Daicoviciu and Constantinescu 1965:155).

18. My summary of Horea's revolt is based almost entirely upon Prodan (1971, 1979). While I have cited him specifically in the text in support of certain points, I acknowledge here that a great deal of what I say is drawn from his work. All translations are my own.

19. I have exercised some license in selecting the examples given in the text. All the complaints I cite are in fact documented by Prodan, but he does not give them in specific connection with the emperor's visit (his examples there do not refer to the villages with which I am concerned).

20. I should emphasize that although Prodan's data and analyses are the foundation upon which I interpret the significance of the rebellion, the interpretation and wordings are almost solely my own. Prodan would probably disagree with parts of how I have chosen to understand some of his evidence.

21. The peasants of southern Transylvania were more resistant to the Uniates than were those in the northern parts. A glance at maps of the distribution of religions in Transylvania (for example, the map shown in the 1910 Hungarian census) shows a clear patterning in the locations of Orthodox (i.e., Uniate-resistant) and Uniate peasants, with the former concentrated in southern Transylvania and the latter in the north. Among the possible reasons for this distribution—as yet unsolved—are the proximity of Protestant Saxons to Romanians in the south (Protestants being clearly averse to the extension of Catholicism), and the influence of other Orthodox persons such as Greek merchants in the southern areas (Meteş 1920:207–208). It is not clear exactly how these groups might have exercised their influence on the Romanian peasants, however, to make them resist the Union.

22. The emperors also unsuccessfully tried other tacks, such as attempting to force the Transylvanian Diet into revoking Transylvania's historical religious toleration, and appointing to the office of Count of the Saxons a Roman Catholic, in 1774 (the Count had always been elected and had, since the Reformation, always been Protestant) (Seton-Watson 1963:170–171).

23. The list included just about every village within a large radius of Binţinţi, and many along the southern Carpathians (see note 21 above).

24. I say "relative failure" because many areas in northern Transylvania did not offer resistance to the Union and remained Uniate until the Communist period in Romania.

25. Cheresteşiu suggests (1966:359–360) that the chain of events leading to Hungary's reaction ought to be extended *upwards* as well as downwards. He would have us see the effect of Hungarian nationalism on Hungary's minorities as having begun not just in Hungary's response to Austria but in Austria's own ambitions to be included within a Greater Germany, an idea emanating from the expansionist designs of some of Germany's statesmen.

26. The anti-Josephine nationalism of late-eighteenth-century Magyars was not the first nationalism to erupt on Transylvanian soil. In the late 1500s and early 1600s, the Saxons, whose niche in trade and commerce was being infringed upon by the entry of foreign traders, created what was probably Transylvania's first ethnic movement. This had nothing to do with Habsburg state-building, although it may have been provoked by state-like centralization within Transylvania. The subject will be taken up in more detail in chapter 3.

27. Emperor Francis was heard to voice the classic formulation of *divide et impera*. As a principle of government, he claimed, "My people are foreign to one another—so much the better. I send Hungarians into Italy and Italians into Hungary. From their antipathy is born order and from their mutual hatred peace" (cited in Cheresteşiu 1966:138; my trans.). Such notions, however, were not consistently followed in practice, a fact that underscores the complexity of the processes involved in decision-making by "the state."

28. The language I use in this final discussion comes from the sociological study of organizations, as exemplified particularly in the work of J. D. Thompson (1967).

3: *Serfs of the Magyars*

1. The two proverbs at the head of this chapter are in current circulation among my informants.

2. Empress Maria Theresa inherited a huge state debt when she ascended the throne in 1740, and 60% of this was foreign, much of it to England. The English allotted large subsidies to the empire over the next several years of her reign (Macartney 1968:48).

3. The development of textiles in the empire was part of the "second industrial revolution" that occurred throughout Europe between 1800 and 1870. As Europe's core economies shifted from producing textiles to specializing in capital-goods industries based on coal, iron, and railway building, textile production migrated from core to semi-peripheral economies (see Rubinson 1978:43). One gets a sense of this by looking at the relative growth of cotton-spinning industries between 1850 and 1920 (Mitchell, *European Historical Statistics*, p. 258). While the percentage increase in the number of cotton spindles declined in England throughout this period, trends in the Habsburg Empire were generally up, through the early 1900s, and the empire's production gained ground against the production of the second-ranked producers above it (first France, then Germany after 1861).

4. Strictly speaking, the Hungarian Kingdom does not include Transylvania between 1691 and 1867. In my description here, I distinguish between events restricted to Hungary and those applicable also to Transylvania by *always* adding "and Transylvania" in the latter instances, cumbersomeness notwithstanding.

5. In sticking with the term "feudal," I am explicitly disagreeing with Immanuel Wallerstein and others who see all Eastern European "feudalisms" as forms of capitalism and who would call the "serfdoms" of these areas "coerced cash-crop labor" (Wallerstein 1974). As summarized in note 7 below and in my arguments about "feudalism" in the text, my view is rather different from theirs.

6. My emphasis on the central role of consumption and display in feudal systems accords with the way several others have written of these systems, among them Banaji (1977) and Therborn (1978:71). Bourdieu (1977:171-183) provides a general framework within which this position could be expanded.

7. There is no generally accepted explanation for the refeudalization of Hungary in 1514—few have even struggled with the question. As I read the secondary sources, this development was the climax of a reassertion of the power of the lesser nobility over both the sovereign and the magnates. A number of events around the turn of the century had served to weaken monarchical authority vis-à-vis the nobles. At the same time, the cattle trade to urban centers in the Holy Roman Empire steadily increased, and prices even more so: the number of cattle exported between 1450 and 1540 grew by 1,779%, and their value rose by 6,529% (Pach 1970:242). Nobles involved in this trade were mostly owners of great and a few medium estates. It was not they, however, but the lesser nobles that produced the reimposition of serfdom in 1514; the magnates were not especially in favor of it. I see as the cause of this the gentry's reaction to much more attractive terms that newly enriched magnates could offer to scarce labor which the gentry also required for cultivating the grain they consumed or sold on local markets. Thus, although the refeudalization was indeed sparked by aristocratic involvement in international trade, serfdom was *not* the labor form most suited to exporting foodstuffs from the periphery, as Wallerstein would have it (1974:87), but rather the form suited to those producing at home.

8. The author was Baron Lőrincz Orczi, and the poem was entitled "Arrival in Tokaj in Winter" (quoted in Marczali 1910:86).

9. I generally refer to southern Transylvania as the locus of commercial growth and the seat of the Saxons. Although it is true that most Saxon activities were concentrated there, my usage is somewhat loose. A large piece of Saxon territory was found in northeastern Transylvania, the region known today as Bistriţa. Products moved eastward from Bistriţa to Moldavia through mountain passes much as they moved from the southern cities through the mountains into Wallachia. Proportionately speaking, however, the latter set of exchanges was much more significant in volume than the former.

10. While it is true that mining and metallurgy were the major industries in the region, my use of the word "Transylvania" is a bit misleading here. The sources upon which I rely tend to use this label for the whole area west of the Carpathians, rather than just for the intermontane plateau that constituted the old Transylvanian principality. Among the largest of the iron works were in what should be called the Banat, as against Transylvania proper. The most important of the properly Transylvanian centers of mining and metallurgy is in the county of Hunedoara, where I conducted my research.

11. The discussion in this section owes much to a recent paper by Ángel Palerm (1980).

12. Skepticism is also bred by the mechanical view of many Romanian scholars concerning capitalism: any sign of wage labor or of commodity production is ipso facto proof of capitalist penetration, without respect to the perhaps very noncapitalist system in which these forms may be found. In general, I believe, one can understand these scholars' concern with eighteenth-century capitalist development as partly motivated by a desire to heighten the analytic power of the idea of "class struggle," upon which they rely (as I do not) to explain Horea's revolt in 1784.

13. Botezan claims that in the 1780s about 47% of the population in the area of Horea's revolt was unable to supply itself adequately with food—a figure he gets from the historian Berlasz (Botezan n.d.:310) and uses to prove the existence of an internal cereals market. I regard this figure as much too high, given that he includes in it social categories that did have some access to land (priests, for example, who usually received a holding alongside their parish, and the category translated "day laborers," which contained a number of peasants with access to enough land to feed themselves quite well). The figure does not, in any case, tell us anything about the existence of cash supplies, since many exchanges were made in kind.

14. This speculation parallels Prodan's view (1967:579–586) of the feudal economy two centuries earlier: that the market played a minimal role in the reassertion and intensification of Transylvanian feudalism, which was instead fueled by its own dynamic together with the devaluation of precious metals. Although the situation had clearly changed in the intervening two centuries, I remain as skeptical of the market's role in the 1700s as Prodan is for the 1500s.

15. My information about the occupations of the nobility of Binţinţi comes from a number of sources, including notations in the genealogies mentioned in note 22 below, in the proceedings of the Jankovich Commission, in the Macskásy documents, and in Kemény's *Possessionaria*.

16. The Macskásy archive contains thousands of documents arranged primarily by the estate to which they pertain. The files for their estate in Binţinţi, the second

largest of all their estate files, contains just under 400 documents, dating from the 1660s to 1820. I had inadequate time to consult the complete file and therefore concentrated on the items from 1700 onward.

17. I use the word "pawn," which seems as satisfactory as any, although "collateral" may be closer to the intent of the participants at the time. Lands pawned by serfs might include the land they worked as serfs — that is, their usufruct holding — for which they were supposed to procure a letter of permission from their overlord before pawning it (a few such letters are found in the Macskásy archives); the lands might also include areas that the serfs themselves had cleared and that were technically their own property.

18. I say "declared holdings" here because many serfs underreported the amounts of land to which they held use rights (see Grimm 1863:72). The lower limit (1.75 hectares) is probably close to accurate, but the richest serfs in all likelihood had more than the 9-hectare maximum that appears in the tables of the Cziráky conscription.

19. It is possible that labor norms did vary within the ranks of any one lord's serfs. The language of the declarations, however, says "Landlord so-and-so has X serfs . . . Each one gives . . ." implying that the burdens are the same for all. It is important to note here that these labor obligations refer only to those people considered true urbarial serfs, with a plot of land in the village, upon which their house was constructed, and an urbarial holding of taxable status. Other kinds of dependent peasants in the village at this time are not included in this set of declarations.

20. This conclusion derives from Banaji (1977:19), who posits a wide variation in the degree of a noble's control over the process of production according to how much land was at the disposal of the serf. Banaji's own survey of data for various feudal systems shows a range of 10 to 100 acres for the "subsistence plot" of the peasant. For Binţinţi in 1820, one-third of the peasants fall below Banaji's 10-acre "minuscule" lower limit (remember, however, that serfs are not declaring all their lands, yet their totals include both arable lands and hayfields); the maximum declared holding is 23 acres, and no one but urbarial serfs are represented. Thus, there may be a fair number of peasants with nothing. My peasant informants of 1974 regarded 2.85 hectares as the minimum size of a self-sufficient farm for a family of four in the mid-1900s. The mean declared size of holding for the peasants represented in 1820 was 4.2 hectares. Given the inclusion of hayfields in this figure, and given differences in technology between 1820 and the 1940s, this statistic indicates a peasantry kept very close to the absolute margin of subsistence by its lords.

21. It is not out of the question that maize yields were higher in part because more maize was planted on peasant plots than on allodia, which were usually devoted to other things. (Botezan [n.d.:300] says that by 1795, maize was making progress "even on allodia," but he is quick to add that maize meal had not yet become the staple of the peasant diet.) The implication of this proposal is that one can see in high maize yields (aside from differences in the nature of the crops) a glimmer of the higher motivation a serf must have felt when working his own lands as opposed to those of the landlord. I have only one very insignificant piece of data concerning the relative proportions of maize land on serf as opposed to noble lands, but it is in the right direction. From a 1786 estate conscription that lists fields as "upper rotation," "lower rotation," and "maize fields," I calculated the percentages of maize fields to total lands for serf holdings and for the land-

lord's allodia. For seven serfs the mean ratio of maize lands to total holdings was 0.31 and for the allodia it was 0.21. The actual ratio of land planted to maize as opposed to land planted to other crops in any year would be higher than this, for in "total holdings" are included the full surface area, only half of which was planted in any one year; maize fields were, however, planted annually (MC #2918).

22. I reached this conclusion by noting all surnames found in the Macskásy documents (which often refer to other noble families), the conscription from 1820 and data from various sources referring to Horea's revolt, the lists in Grimm (1863), the village land records from the late 1870s, and my informants' recollections, and then trying to link them to one another using the genealogies of Nagy (1857-1865), Kempelen (1911-1932), Böjthe (1891), and Kelemen (MS), as well as the records of deaths from 1896 onward, in the civil registers of vital statistics.

23. See note 28 below for an explanation of how I derived the village's 1820 population.

24. I calculated the figures on fragmentation from MC #470, #485, #2827, #2918. I emphasize that these figures include arable land only, since hayfields are usually listed with a designation of the volume of hay produced (cartloads) rather than a surface measure.

25. The source for these figures is the collection of worksheets for the consolidation of fields in the village of Geoagiu, 1882. These worksheets (in five bound volumes) are located in the Romanian State Archive, Deva branch, Hunedoara County. My thanks to the director, Mr. Ion Frăţilă, and to Vasile Ionaş for finding these sheets and putting them at my disposal.

26. Source: Nachweisung der Hauptergebnisse der Gemeinde Voranschläge im Kronlande Siebenbürgen in den Gemeinden des Brooser-Bezirks im Jahre 1859/60. Romanian State Archives, Deva branch, Tax files for the Prefecture of Hunedoara and the district of Orăştie. Folder 5, sheets 45-54.

27. A similar timing for the shift from "regular" to "irregular" serfs appears in Csetri and Imreh (1972:174). They observe that statistics from 1767 on reveal a continual decline in the proportion of urbarial serfs in the overall population, and they attribute this decline to the growth of other categories preferable to urbarial serfs as labor.

28. I arrived at this figure in the following manner. The Dosa conscription of 1805 lists 85 Romanian families for Binţinţi; the 1820 Cziráky conscription lists 42 serf families, excluding the irregular categories. Csetri and Imreh's (1972) figures show a population decline of 21.7% between the two years 1808 and 1821, for the Counties of Transylvania (the effects of a terrible famine in 1815-1817 account for most of this population loss, which was worse in the Counties than elsewhere in Transylvania). Using 21.7% as a guideline, I arrive at a probable 67 families of Romanians in Binţinţi in 1820, which means that 25 families, or 38% of the village, are missing from the 1820 list. To arrive at estimates of the number of persons in the village at this time, I multiply the number of families by 4.1, which is the ratio of persons to families for this village in censuses of 1787 and 1857.

29. As late as the 1870s, when the offical property registers were begun in Binţinţi — well after emancipation, be it noted — approximately 15% of Binţinţi peasant households have a label (*Curialisbirtok*) that betrays their origins in one of these irregular serf categories.

30. I consulted the conscriptions and censuses referred to in the Hungarian State Archives, file Vegyes Összeírások, F49. The information in the text is drawn

primarily from two documents dated 1713 and 1724 (#14/2 and #15/3). My thanks to Dr. Zsolt Trócsányi for informing me of these items and putting them at my disposal.

31. Two unclear notations on this document might possibly mean that the grain was sold in the city of Deva and the wine in Binţinţi. I have reported figures in bushels and gallons, calculated roughly rather than exactly, for the numbers given in the documents in Metzen (1.74 bushels) and Eimer (14.95 gallons) (conversions from Blum 1948:247).

32. It is not out of the question, though highly unlikely, that the figures for maize could be amounts stored whole, on the cob, rather than kernels. Prodan (personal communication) assumes that the figures refer to kernels, and I follow his opinion.

33. Most of the indemnification tables give no more than a breakdown into "damages in kind" and "damages in property." Only a small number further itemize the damages in kind. For the County then called Hunyad-Zarand, damages in kind amounted to 41% of total damages (Jankovich Commission, fasc. VI, no 684).

4: "We've Been Here All Along"

1. This comment by Pál Macskásy (a direct lineal descendant of the original Miklós Macskásy and Sara Gámány of Binţinţi) is quoted in Baritĭu (1890:268-269).

2. This piquant anecdote was told me by Prof. David Prodan. The simplicity (and hence the delightfulness) of the peasant's reply comes across poorly in English; the Romanian is, "Apăi, noi, nu, că sîntem de aici."

3. To posit the imitation of state forms is consonant with the overt admiration of people like Széchenyi and Baritĭu for English constitutional principles.

4. The story of this revolution is told in Istvan Deak's excellent book (Deak 1979), from which I have drawn some of my description.

5. The views of the predominantly gentry revolutionaries and of the more conservative magnates interestingly parallel divergences of analysis in current neo-Marxist circles. The gentry propounded a version of "dependency theory," seeing the backwardness of their economy as the inevitable result of Austrian "colonialism," whereas the critics among the magnates—Széchenyi foremost among them—attributed economic underdevelopment to the behavior of the landed upper classes in Hungary.

6. Except where a published source is noted, these views from Binţinţi are the recollections of elderly informants.

7. According to the Austrian census of 1850, the population of Transylvania was 26% Magyar, 9% German, and 60% Romanian.

8. During the revolutionary period, the Habsburgs finally reciprocated the Saxon view that as "Germans" they should regard each other as allies. The Saxons had been pressing this view since at least 1791, when rules for voting in the Transylvanian Diet were revised and the Saxons no longer had *equal* but only *proportional* say in decisions. This made them seek separate influence with the Court, since they could no longer greatly influence the outcome in the Diet directly, but until 1848 the Habsburgs had often failed to take the Saxons' side.

9. The best histories of the Romanian national movement are the outstanding works by Hitchins (1969, 1977).

10. Relative to magnate-owned estates, gentry estates tended to have a higher proportion of urbarial lands, which went to peasants after 1848, and a lower proportion of allodial lands, which remained with the noble.

11. The state's active encouragement of new cattle breeds helped cause a precipitous drop in retention of older stock. In 1884, 80% of all Hungary's cattle were older indigenous breeds; in 1911, 28% were (Gaál and Gunst 1977:40).

12. In addition to the domestic capital accumulations that helped to develop Hungarian agriculture, modernization was enhanced by loans made by Austrian financiers directly to magnates, with the express objective of raising technological endowments in agriculture (Berend and Ránki 1974*b:*42).

13. Berend and Ránki note that foreign capital declined in Hungary from 60% in 1900 to 36% in 1913 (Berend and Ránki 1974*a:*103). They conclude their analysis of development in Eastern Europe by observing that in the east-central areas, foreign investment seems clearly to have accelerated domestic capital accumulation and contributed to development, while in the Balkans this was not true (ibid.:111).

14. Much of this discussion rests on literature that is not easy to synthesize. Contemporary Romanian scholarship on Transylvania consistently underemphasizes the nationalist contribution to economic developments, as part of the Romanian view that class is the important variable, not ethnicity. In addition, any given article tends to discuss a sector of the economy in isolation from others; hence, it is difficult to make statements about the relative development of the various sectors. The narrow, sectoral approach enables scholars interested in proving that peasants had no opportunity for industrial wage labor, say, to emphasize underindustrialization of the economy, while those interested in the growth of the working class may emphasize successful industrialization. See also notes 15 and 19.

15. Recent Romanian historiographers tend to emphasize the colonial exploitation of Transylvania's industrial development and to write as if industry were thereby retarded. I emphasize the interaction of colonial and indigenous developments and see considerable evidence for growth—which was, nevertheless, poorly integrated within the economy as a whole.

16. My source for this description of Mihu's life and activities is Mihu 1938, except where otherwise noted.

17. Source: Tax files, Fond prefectura, jud. Hunedoara, folder 2/1887, sheet 83. Romanian State Archives, Deva branch.

18. The biographical information on Karl Wolff comes from an article in the 1980 *Neuer Weg* Calendar (Bucureşti: Neuer Weg Verlag), pages 87–89. The article is entitled "Mein Sinnen und Streben gehört dem Volk," and is signed by Reimar Ungar.

19. Among the most important obstacles to achieving an overview of Transylvanian agriculture is that, partly from nationalist motives, statistical and scholarly publications from Hungary often do not list data for Transylvania separately and publications from Romania use the label "Transylvania" to include the Banat—the most commercialized agrarian area of the region adjacent to historical Transylvania. Romanian scholarship therefore includes many statistics that show more agricultural commercialization than I believe to have occurred within the *narrower* territorial definition of Transylvania. Yet Hungarian statistical aggregations do not help us to prove this readily. I do not mean to imply that Transylvanian scholars are falsifying the picture—far from it—only that for political reasons they are using territorial definitions different from mine.

20. Source: See note 17 above.

21. The history of Lajos Kovács was given to me by one of my German informants (unlike my histories of the Magyar nobles, which come from published sources).

22. I have no indications of Count Lázár's own wealth, but his widow appears in Grimm's listing for 1848 (Grimm 1863) with 150 serf holdings, which puts her in the top 7% of the Transylvanian nobility in terms of wealth.

23. Source: Tax files. Prefectura Orăştie. Folder 11/1860, sheet 129. Romanian State Archives, Deva branch. This letter merits some further comments. First, delay in paying taxes was one of several forms of Magyar resistance against the reimposition of central authority. Count Lázár may have been engaging in this form of resistance with his request for postponement — that is, his request does not necessarily reflect insolvency. Second, Prof. Istvan Deak, who was kind enough to translate this letter for me, commented that poor Mr. Novak was probably a Czech or Galician Pole imported by the Austrians "to introduce order into the Transylvanian pigsty," and that Novak was probably fired after this incident with Count Lázár. I have given only a summary of the letter, since its style is redundant and excessively ornate.

24. Source: see note 17 above; folder 7/1871, sheet 22.

25. I am indebted to Maria Ursuţiu, of the Romanian Academy Library in Cluj, for translating the biographies of the Lázár family for me.

26. The notations I have interpreted to mean continued bondage are of two forms. One lists a noble property owner and a peasant couple, preceded by the term *Megosztott Tulajdon* (joint property); after the peasants' names is a note saying "owner of buildings and having use rights to lands." The second gives this plus *Curialisbirtok* (noble property), after which there is usually, although not always, a specification of this kind: "the one enjoying use rights must give 25 days' manual labor per year" or "must pay 20 forints a year to avoid the labor obligations upon which this property is based." Both of these forms of notation contrast with the most prevalent form, in which no noble name appears on the records at all. The "joint property" form appears for 17% of the households, the "noble property" form for 20% of them.

I owe a debt of gratitude to the Romanian Ministry of Justice for permission to copy the land records and to the office of the State Notary for Hunedoara County, which provided invaluable assistance in facilitating my access to the records and translating some of the terms.

27. Comparisons across these two censuses are difficult, since they did not use quite the same criteria to define units (see Eddie 1967:299-300). The censuses are more comparable for smaller than for larger properties, but at the top range the error from comparison is, if anything, conservative when property concentration is at issue. Figures from the two censuses show that between 1895 and 1910, the percentage of the agricultural surface area held by properties over 575 hectares remained stable (18% — over three-fourths of this in communal or institutional rather than in private hands), while the percentages in the next several categories below this declined (all together, properties between 29 and 575 hectares decreased from 21% to 12% of the surface). Between 1895 and 1916, properties below 5.75 hectares increased from 19% to 45% of the agricultural surface. (Sources: Eddie 1967:300, for 1895; and Hungary 1920:326, for 1910 and 1916.)

28. I emphasize that this discussion refers to the Counties, since feudal relations did not exist, for the most part, in the Saxon lands. I also emphasize that I cannot discuss for the Counties the overall range of peasant activities, for example,

rural industry, which we know to have been important in the Szekler lands but concerning which little is known for the enserfed population. See Hintz 1846.

29. I have found no figure in the literature to suggest how many peasants remained virtual serfs after 1848. My figure of 15% is derived as follows. Data in Csetri and Imreh (1974:154) show a probable agrarian population of about 85% of the total population for the early 1800s, and as of 1821 the population of free peasants had reached 27%. Multiplying the number of families impropriated after 1848 (173,781) by five (the figure used by Transylvanian historians for this purpose) yields 868,905 persons, or 45% of Transylvania's 1857 population count (impropriation occurred in 1854, hence the 1857 population count is adequate). This percentage may be a bit high, since there is some argument about whether five or something smaller is the best multiplicand for population statistics. Adding this 45%-or-less figure (serfs given property) to the 27% of the population who were free peasants gives us 72% to subtract from the 85% of the population that is in agriculture. I use the round figure 15% as the result. When Kovács (1972: 41-43) writes that 30% of the population remained under feudal relations, he means 30% of the population that had been subject to feudal conditions, not 30% of the total Transylvanian population, and he refers to the larger definition of "Transylvania," which included more irregular serfs than does the unit I am using.

30. Compensations were determined as the annual value of a serf's obligations minus one-sixth of that value (for administrative costs), times twenty. Values were determined by prices used in tax assessments (information from Grimm 1863:124). The enormity of the sums that resulted from this calculus led many observers to accuse the Court of trying to curry favor with the nobility (Baritïu 1890:692). Grimm (1863) offered a careful and extensive refutation of this idea. If one recalls that Transylvania's feudal obligations were heavier than anywhere else in the empire, it should not be surprising that the assessed damages were the highest in the empire.

31. The emigration to Romania began earlier and continued later than the emigration to the U.S., which was concentrated in the period 1901-1914. The 210,000 emigrants of 1901-1914 were 16.9% Magyar, 14.5% Saxon, and 68.3% Romanian (Hungary 1920:82).

32. Figure 4-1 suggests an additional area in which ethnic identity may have distorted the occupational structure: through preferential hiring of workers from the same nationality as a firm's owners and administrators (mostly Germans and Magyars). The percentages of each nationality differ for commerce as compared with industry, but within each of those sectors the ethnic representation of "independent owners" is very similar to the representation for "workers."

5: Paying Like a German

1. The first document now known to refer to Binţinţi is dated 1291 and records the sale of the village from its original owner, "Benchench," a Szekler, to the Count of the Saxon community of Kelling (Cîlnic) (Zimmermann and Werner 1892:185-186).

2. With the village's acquisition by the Count of Kelling, Saxon colonists were doubtless brought in (G. Gündisch, personal communication); Prodan finds documentary mention of *hospites* who he believes were Saxons, later in the village's history (Prodan, personal communication); and as of the 1890s, Germans were again present in the community.

3. There have also occasionally been Jews resident in Binţinţi, but I know little about them and will exclude them from my discussion here, as I have from my larger historical treatment as well.

4. My sources of information about the Magyars in Binţinţi are several elderly Romanian informants, aged 75 years or older in 1974, many of them relying on what they had been told rather than on what they themselves had seen.

5. One German informant recalled a time in the interwar period when butter sold for 40 lei/kg while wage labor was paid at 40 lei/day. His own butter yield at the time was 2½ kg/cow/week, for 3 cows, which gave him a weekly income of 7½ day-laborers' wages.

6. One of my elderly informants provided me with further evidence that labor exchanges might be rooted in the combination of serf households for draft labor. The verb for these labor exchanges in the present is *"a se ortăci,"* which most villagers understand as meaning simply to associate for work. One old man, however, in responding to my questions about who associated with whom in earlier times, would respond to some names thus: "How could he have had exchange partners? He didn't have any animals."

7. I have nothing more than one informant's recollection that Frau Müller did not loan cash at interest, an activity that Jane Schneider reminds me we might expect of someone like this. My informant was perhaps too young to have been a possible borrower in Frau Müller's heyday, but his recollection may still be accurate.

8. The source for this figure is annual prices in the Statistical Annual for Hungary from 1910 through 1918 (*Magyar Statisztikai Évkönyv*).

9. I say "two-thirds of all marriage partners" rather than speaking of marriages because I calculated marriages by sex of the individuals contracting them, believing that this procedure gives the most accurate representation of endogamy and exogamy and allows us to see differential patterns of marital movement across space for the two sexes. Here are the specific figures for Romanian marriages, 1895-1920:

Sex of Binţinţi Partner	Marriage Type						
	Endogamous		Spouse Marries In		Local Marries Out		
	N	%	N	%	N	%	T
Male	90	76.9	20	17.1	7	6.0	117
Female	90	63.4	16	11.3	36	25.4	142
T	180	69.5	36	13.9	43	16.6	259

The figures come from the parish and civil registers for Binţinţi.

10. For purposes of comparison with the marriage patterns of Romanians, I give here the data for Germans according to the form in footnote 9. The data come from the records kept in the Binţinţi Lutheran Church and cover the period 1897 to 1930.

Sex of Binţinţi Partner	Marriage Type						
	Endogamous		Spouse Marries In		Local Marries Out		
	N	%	N	%	N	%	T
Male	27	72.9	5	13.5	5	13.5	37
Female	27	60.0	1	2.2	17	37.8	45
T	54	65.9	6	7.3	22	26.8	82

11. Landlords *tended* to impose obligations by household (M. Ursuţiu 1979:236) and therefore to maximize the number of households at their command. Scholars have also noted that from 1714 on, many landlords sought to make *robot* apply to each working adult rather than each household (Giurgiu 1972:105); I suspect this may represent the landlord's response to peasant strategies aimed at maintaining extended households.

12. Hungarian law from as early as the thirteenth century provides for the descent of noble property to sons, or in their absence, for one-fourth of it to daughters (Paget 1850, I:400). It was also Hungarian custom for the youngest son to stay in the parental household (ibid.). Botezan notes (n.d.:49) that the custom of descent of the parental house to the youngest son is recorded for serfs in feudal times.

13. This argument is borrowed from Blum (1948:84), who sees behind many customs of the feudal period, including periodic reallotment of portions in the common pasture, this same concern to safeguard against repossession. Trócsányi makes a similar argument (see Botezan 1976:275).

14. Based on about 80% of the deaths recorded in Binţinţi for the years 1851–1870 (the oldest registers for the village, partly destroyed), average age at death in these years was 23.9 years for the total sample and 45.6 years for those who reached age ten.

15. Pascu and Gherman (1960:177) report the following information about inheritance under feudalism in a village north of Binţinţi. If a widow remarried a serf from her own village, she retained her right to serve as her children's guardian until their majority and to use her dead husband's possessions in this role. If she remarried a serf from another village or a propertyless day laborer, the lord took her children and gave them into someone else's care.

Information of this sort and of the kind provided by Kula (1972) suggests a hypothesis concerning the remarriage of widows in southeastern Europe. In some parts of Mediterranean Europe—Greece, for example—there are strong social proscriptions concerning the remarriage of widows, whereas notions of this sort are completely absent in Transylvania. I propose that the presence or absence of widow remarriage as socially accepted practice varies with the earlier presence or absence of a demesne economy with powerful landlordly influence over the behavior of serfs. Widow remarriage was integral to maintaining viable work units in this economy and may have been enforced (less likely in other economies), perhaps eventually becoming custom.

16. Daniel Chirot objects that my speculations are weakened by the fact that inheritance patterns among Romanians in regions other than Transylvania—regions with different histories and social structures—were similar to those in Transylvania. Because I do not believe that like effects always have like causes, I disagree with him. I find it plausible that similar inheritance forms could result from different conditions, each form being adequately explained with reference to its context. I would not, in any case (and neither would Chirot), explain the similarities as something inherent in Romanian character.

17. I must emphasize that this conclusion applies to Transylvania's Swabian Germans more than to Saxons, about whom my information is limited; Saxon patterns may nonetheless support the conclusion also (see F. H. Barth 1978:93).

18. I have already observed that German farm sizes in the 1890s ranged from about 9 to about 45 hectares, and that Romanians rarely had more than 10 hectares. This is to be compared with table 6-5, which shows Germans still overrepresented among Binţinţi's wealthy peasants, as of 1939 — 45 years and a major land reform later.

19. I do not present this argument and the data supporting it, because my confidence in the data is rather low; I will, however, explain the basis upon which my sentence in the text is derived. The figures used to estimate socioeconomic mobility were, for 1890, a list of the number of lots each household possessed in the village pasture; since not all households appear in this list, it does not provide a complete picture of the distribution of assets for that year. For 1920, the data consist of the mean rank that seven elderly informants assigned to the residents of the community as they could be recalled for the immediate postwar period. This method is obviously risky, since informants' recollections of the standing of families years earlier cannot be very reliable. To assess mobility, I took all offspring in 1920 who had parents in the 1890 list, standardized the scores for the two lists, and subtracted offspring's score from parent's score. The resulting figures were assigned to four categories of mobility: high or low upward mobility and high or low downward mobility.

20. Khera (1973), in a very interesting article, comes to similar conclusions for the relations among siblings under partible and impartible regimes for a present-day Austrian community.

21. My informants are not the only ones to hold this view; scholars agree with them. For example, Negoescu (1919:148) writes that the most impressive Romanian farms are found in the area between Braşov and Orăştie, where Romanians are neighbors of Germans and especially of Swabians, and that poorer farming practices are found where Romanians are intermixed with Magyars.

22. The last four paragraphs of this interview were delivered almost without interruption by a single informant (born 1891), in response to my questioning her why Romanians didn't rise up.

23. The tendency of serfs to regard themselves as owners rather than mere users of their feudal portion is noted by a number of Transylvanian scholars (Răduţiu, personal communication). It is especially evident in the language serfs used when replying to the questions of the two feudal conscriptions of 1785 and 1820: they called their portion *moşia* (the word used also for feudal estates), and referred to themselves as *gazda* (a label appropriate to an independent farm owner but not to a dependent serf); many questioned in 1785 believed their land was theirs to alienate as they chose; and they referred to feudal obligations not as *robot* (dues) but merely as "work" (*slujba, lucru*) (see Botezan and Schilling (1973:214).

24. The source for my estimate of the percentage of voters in Binţinţi is a list I collected from an elderly informant who seemed to have a special interest in this subject and claimed to remember what villagers from Magyar times were able to vote. This informant proved fairly reliable on a number of other questions, and although I would not use the data to try to clinch any arguments, they seem adequate for estimating how many Romanian households participated in the political process before 1918.

25. Istvan Deak has pointed out to me that Romanians were not necessarily or always harassed in connection with voting: often the Hungarian government sought to "buy" a pro-government vote by building roads or other public works specifically in the areas of non-Magyar voters, who might be wooed from voting with the radical parties sometimes favored by Magyar voters. For every Romanian peasant chased from the polls in Binţinţi, there was probably a radical (pro-Kossuth) Magyar peasant being chased away by government supporters, in other parts of Transylvania. This corrective reminds one to be cautious about generalizing to

all of Transylvania's peasants from those in this particular community, located near centers of high Romanian Nationalist activity.

6: *Peasants into Gentlemen*

1. For readers unaccustomed to Transylvanian history, the interwar period is especially confusing because everything now has a new referent, from the terms "state," "elite," "bourgeoisie," etc. to the term "Transylvania" itself. In the Hungarian Kingdom before 1918, "Transylvania" referred to 15 counties enclosed by the Carpathian arc and the Western Mountains, the region coterminous with the old and once-autonomous principality of Transylvania, while other areas such as those known as the Banat, Maramureș, etc. were parts of Hungary proper. After 1918, there developed a tendency for *all* the areas won from Hungary— including all of Transylvania plus parts of several Hungarian counties, some of them comprising the area known as the Banat—to be referred to as "Transylvania." Strictly speaking, separate designations for these areas should be retained, for generalizations true of agriculture in Transylvania are often not true of the Banat. In the present chapter, I have used the term in its broader sense, however, largely because many of the Romanian sources I cite do not differentiate Transylvania in its narrow sense from other areas. When I wish to be explicit that I am referring to the narrow sense, that is made clear in the text (e.g., "in Transylvania excluding the Banat").

2. Roberts observes that since the Romanian king was one of the country's most powerful industrial interests, the period of the royal dictatorship exemplifies the Romanian state at its closest to being the "arm of the bourgeoisie" (Roberts 1951:206).

3. It appears that yields did indeed drop after this reform. Warriner (1939:153) attributes this partly to the fact that landlords no longer provided sharecropping peasants with select seeds.

4. The term "rural overpopulation" is often used without recognizing the extent to which it is a function of social, economic, and technological factors—that is, as if arable land were a natural resource rather than a social one. Roberts argues that nevertheless, one *can* speak of an absolute excess of population in the Romanian countryside (1951:41–47, 334–335). Interwar governments had various ideas about how to solve the problem of rural overpopulation, but the most delightful was that of the National Peasants, who, in a wonderful reversal of history, proposed creating cottage industry to absorb rural labor (Șandru 1975:304).

5. Even in the present, one finds among Bințințeni an attitude in which labor time is not included in calculating costs. The family with whom I stayed in 1979 returned from market one Saturday very pleased at the price they had received for their pig. When I asked if the price made up for all the food the animal had been fed and all the time involved in feeding it, they replied that those things did not matter, what counted was that they had 3,000 lei more in income.

6. I argued this point vainly with one informant, against whom I was unwittingly taking the position of capitalist machine industry; when I pointed out all the implements that farming could employ, none of which were found in the village, and talked about chemical fertilization and other facets of modern agriculture, he remained firm in his belief that villagers did just as well without all that and their technique could not have been improved upon.

7. Even there, Macartney suggests, the new regime discriminated against non-Romanians by placing government contracts only with Romanian firms and by giving preferential credit arrangements to Romanian banks and industries while denying good terms to others (Macartney 1937:320–322). He also recognizes, however (ibid.: 323), that because the Regat government was dominated by non-Transylvanians, policy toward minorities was more lax than it would have been had Transylvanian Romanians (with more of an axe to grind) had more say in it.

8. The discussion in the remainder of the chapter contains a potential terminological confusion to which attention should be called. On the one hand, there is the "middle peasant" (usually signaled by quotation marks) who was an object of government policy; on the other, there are well-to-do or rich or wealthy, middle, and poor peasants from Binţinţi, categories that reflect how villagers spoke of their social environment. The well-to-do peasant of Binţinţi, however, was barely even "middle," according to government standards; no Romanian peasant from the village had more than 13 hectares in 1939, and even the Germans, who were the truly rich ones in the village, had a maximum of 25 hectares in that year.

9. Similar patterns of migration are reported from the study of Drăguş, investigated by the Gusti school, where it was found that there was almost no migration from that village into cities in Transylvania before the war, most of the movement being to the U.S. and (less) to cities in the Regat (Bărbat 1944:139).

10. I feel confident in labeling these untraceable persons as poor because most of them appear with very few pasturage lots in the listing that was drawn up in the 1880s, when pasture space was divided according to the number of plots each household had. Those with only 1 to 4 "rights" to pasture were marginal, when compared with families having 93 or 71 "rights" (the amounts accruing to the two richest villagers of that day).

11. Given the state of the Transylvanian economy at the time, it would be reasonable to expect that some of these migrants became part of a floating rural proletariat (Hitchins, personal communication). Indeed, many families arrived in Binţinţi in precisely this way. I do not have any informants' reports to this effect, however; all referred to "the city" as the destination of their families' earlier migrants.

12. My 30 prewar migrants are doubtless only a small proportion of villagers who left before 1918; they are merely the ones whose careers are remembered by persons still living in the village in the 1970s.

13. Interviews are the only source of my information about migrants. In creating tables 6-1 and 6-2, I have had to take some liberties that should be explained. I learned dates of departure for only some of the migrants and therefore had to estimate the rest. This was done by categorizing the migrants according to type of migration; using the cases for which a date of departure was known so as to calculate an average age of migration for the different types (persons going to high school only, persons entering the urban labor pool, etc.); and using this average age to figure probable dates of departure for the remaining migrants.

These two tables set the form used throughout the chapter. In every case the variable placed along the vertical dimension of the table is the independent variable; when this is given in the form of dates, they stand for temporal processes presumed to cause variation in the variable arrayed across the top of the table. Percentages are calculated on the totals for each row, and arrows are drawn to show changes in the frequency of the dependent variable across categories of the independent variable.

14. Indicators of wealth come from the listing of the numbers of pasture lots each person held in the late 1880s (see note 10 above); a listing constructed for 1920, in the absence of any other data, by asking seven elderly informants to rank all households in the village as of that time with respect to their economic standing; and property censuses from 1939 and 1948. Each of these lists was divided into eight parts, but when the data were processed the top octiles generally showed similar patterns and were therefore combined to form a top quartile. Trends within the remaining six octiles were often diverse, but for purposes of the present discussion a division into "top quartile" (for well-to-do peasants) and "remaining three quartiles" (for middle and poor peasants) seems adequate. The unsatisfactory character of the 1920 list makes the results less trustworthy than one might wish, but at least an outline of trends can be discerned using these indicators.

15. I did not include in my calculations some offspring sets from complex multiple marriages (one man, for example, had three wives and sired 14 children, between 1873 and 1911. Classifying this offspring set was problematic, so it was left out). I also eliminated offspring sets for which the number of offspring reaching age 15 was not reliably known, as happened when children were born for whom neither a death registration nor a marriage registration exists and no villagers from that family survive in the present to verify that these children did in fact grow up. These offspring sets are included only in the rough calculation of child mortality, reported on p. 299, and the uncertainty surrounding the fates of the children born but not traceable is the reason for my saying that "at least" 45% of all children born did not reach age 15.

16. The mean Romanian family size of 2.74 children contrasts sharply with the mean size of surviving offspring sets for Germans before the war: 5.4, which drops to a mean of 2.2 after the war.

17. I arrived at these percentages by adding all children ever born to couples during the three time periods and dividing this into all the children for each time period who survived to age 15. For explanation of "at least 45%," see the end of note 15 above.

18. It should be noted that as phrased here, the periods do not coincide with those defined for the table on fertility trends. Couples *married* between 1890 and 1915 did not necessarily bear all their children within those same years, although for the interwar period, when couples tended to have their one or two children fairly soon after marriage, the discrepancy between the ways of reporting child mortality and fertility trends is not very great. In looking at mortality trends, I have preferred to emphasize couples rather than offspring set sizes, so as to capture the new environment faced by couples considering the size of their families after the war.

19. Fertility control did not appear completely out of the blue in 1918. It is clear in both aggregate statistics and data from Binţinţi that fertility control had been increasing among some sectors of the population before the war. For example, Manuila (1938:845) gives natality statistics for Transylvania that show a decline of about 24% in the rates of natality between 1875 and 1920, particularly evident for counties in southwest Transylvania (including Hunedoara). But against this 24% drop over 45 years, we see a further drop of 20% — almost as much as before — in only 15 years, from 1920 to 1935. This suggests that fertility control was considerably stepped up after the war, although we cannot know if this was for the same or different reasons.

20. There are no major changes in age at marriage that could be used to explain changes in fertility. The age at marriage did rise slightly for both men and women, but by only 1 to 2 years, for both sexes. We know from the example of Ireland that later marriage can still be accompanied by high fertility, in any case.

21. Among the most common techniques of fertility control from before the war was one involving the use of a plant, known locally as *Pelin* (*Artemesia absinthium* L.), whose root was introduced into the vagina and left for a day or two to provoke infection and subsequent miscarriage, not infrequently followed by the woman's death. Another plant less often used is known as *Lemnul maicii domnului* (*Santolina chamoeparissus*). Pelin was being used, and causing death, as late as the early 1930s. A technique used more rarely was to attempt abortion with a spindle, which produced unintended and distressing results often enough to have been a last resort. One elderly informant learned a technique from a city prostitute and used it without ill effects several times; she shared it with only one other person, however — one of her sisters.

The expression used most often to describe fertility control in the interwar years was "to guard" (*păzi*), as in "We had no more children because I guarded my wife" (*am păzit-o pe nevasta*). This refers to coitus interruptus (also sometimes to abstinence) and could be initiated by women, through a timely pelvic jerk, as well as by men.

22. This argument fits with the finding that family limitation in pre-industrial Hungary was most widespread in the southeastern areas (Demény 1968), which happen to be areas of petty-commodity production on peasant farms rather than areas with a high concentration of latifundia. Where latifundia were more prevalent, fertility was much higher.

It should also be noted that U.S. restrictions on immigration closed off that very important source of employment.

23. The source for this information about the reform in Binţinţi is records of the reform in the Deva branch of the Romanian State Archives. My thanks to Ion Frăţilă and Vasile Ionaş, who located the documents for me. In the text of my discussion I say "about" 350 hectares, "about" 125 people, etc., because the original distribution of reform lands was challenged by a group of villagers who thought it had been carried out unfairly, and in reallotting portions all the figures on the document were revised in sometimes indecipherable ways, with totals and subtotals not in full agreement.

24. Although a cash economy did become more widely generalized during the interwar years, it is important to note that many habits from the earlier under-commercialized economy persisted. Villagers remember that many items were still exchanged through barter, as described in chapter 5 — hill peasants with firewood, fruit, brandy or wooden barrels, wanting produce in exchange. I suspect that this barter economy may have been rejuvenated by the depression, but informants do not date their recollections specifically to that period.

25. The source of this property distribution is an undated list in the archives of the People's Council in Geoagiu. By comparing the way persons are listed (who was listed as still alive, who was "widow" X, etc.) with the dates of death in the civil registers, I arrived at a tentative date of 1939.

The results shown in the text have been modified over the original listing in two ways. First, I show only the properties of Romanians and Germans resident in the community at the time; I have left out the properties of people who were absent (some of their lands were available for sharecropping) as well as communal property. Second, I have altered the original list by combining properties that were listed separately for parents and offspring but that I believe were farmed as a unit by parents and offspring. In most of these cases, the house number identifying the proprietors was the same. The separate listings almost certainly mean that the census was taken from notarial records in which parents' donations to a child at marriage had been registered in that child's name even if he or she was co-resident.

26. Louis Golomb, in an ingenious discussion of complementarities in the agricultural practices of neighboring ethnic groups in Malaysia, also reports having received numerous and not always logical responses when he asked for explanations. His conclusion, after assessing the pros and cons of the rationality of the different practices, is that what is ultimately at stake is a more or less unconscious ethnic adaptation in which complementarity rather than isolated rationality is the determinant: what Thais and Malays do is best understood as ways of avoiding conflict with one another, within limits. While I admire Golomb's sensitivity and intelligent handling of the problem, I do not find his conclusions adequate for my own case (Golomb 1978).

27. Wealthier Romanian peasants depart from the pattern described in several ways. Those who fattened cattle regularly, as poorer peasants could not always manage to do, often bought scrawny animals at market, fattened them for three or four months on fodder crops alone without resort to common pasture and often without using them first for plowing, and then sold them, to buy another scrawny pair a few months later. This pattern implied sowing more fodder on one's fields than one would who marketed fattened cattle only on occasion. It also, however, implies that rich peasants would not engage in abuses of common pasturage, since they regarded the finest fattening as that which excluded summer pasture. This is one example in which commercialization by richer peasants does not necessarily take place at the expense of the poor.

28. This is not to say that all peasants could now keep cows and fatten oxen, thanks to the common pasture, but merely that more people could do so than before. In any case, 100 hectares of summer pasture (for a village that had 600 head of cattle in 1941) is not an ideal amount; it is simply more than other villages had, and more than Binţinţeni had had before.

29. I am indebted to Christopher Chase-Dunn for raising this idea and setting me on the train of thought that led to the analysis in this paragraph.

30. I owe this observation to Ira Lowenthal.

31. It is possible that with piecemeal purchases, Germans were gradually creating fragmented farms, rather than the large expanses of intact fields they acquired in the 1890s. While I did not question them directly on the consolidation of their farms, however, Germans more often mentioned buying not just 1-hectare pieces but chunks of 3 to 5 hectares, on the rare occasions when such chunks came onto the market; Romanians always spoke of picking up fractions of a hectare here and there.

32. Village Germans may have had a glimmer of this change when several members of the community, noninheriting offspring who had been apprenticed to urban trades and had ostensibly left the village, returned during the early years of the depression and settled onto the small patches of land that "quasi impartibility" had endowed them with. Germans with whom I spoke in 1974 believed

that the unemployment of these people had something to do with discrimination against them; no one viewed it as part of the same crisis that was depressing their agricultural markets.

33. In the text I refer only to responses to a specific set of interviews, and not to the countless times Romanians mentioned Germans' former wealth and advancement in informal conversation.

34. In this paragraph I report data given in the census, but I cannot be certain that all declarations recorded in this census were accurate. Several informants, when questioned, said that at the time of the census people did not know it was a prelude to collectivization. Nonetheless, the regime was unfamiliar, some of its rhetoric was already clear, and peasants *may* have underdeclared those things they saw as having an ideological significance for the new regime. Wage labor may have been one such thing, and fancy agricultural implements another.

35. I heard very little to suggest that Germans lent money to much of anyone, certainly not often to Romanians. Any serious practice of usury on their part would doubtless have come up in my 16 months with these peasants. Nonetheless, some degree of informal lending must have taken place, presumably among Germans, for one informant, whose reliability and memory proved consistently outstanding, claims to have remembered overhearing quarrels occasioned by the conversion of debts. The conversion was most fully enforceable in public institutions, but even informal arrangements were encouraged to conform. My informant implies that not everyone who had lent money informally was disposed to comply.

36. Conversations with Romanians who had engaged in wage labor for Germans during these years reveal a surprisingly unhostile attitude toward their employers; the recollections are often warm. Perhaps these Romanians, far from seeing the relationship as exploitative, were grateful at having local opportunities for income supplements that allowed them to remain peasants.

37. This phrasing is drawn from Arturo Warman's (1980) outstanding analysis of similar developments among the peasants of Morelos, Mexico. Warman's view of the processes he describes for Morelos has influenced my analysis in this chapter strongly.

38. The basis for this statement is a number of conversations I had with informants in 1979-80, concerning their perceptions of the possibilities open to them in the interwar period and of the obstacles to achieving those possibilities. All informants could think of obstacles to success in the prewar years or in the period since 1945, but almost none could think of anything that stood in the way during the interwar years: only two persons, from among the village's most destitute, saw obstacles, in the fact that rich people had the land and didn't want to sell it and poor people had a hard time getting bank loans to buy land.

39. This report from German informants could be colored by hindsight, but my experience with them persuades me that the facts, at least — an initial stint in the Romanian army, then transfer to the German army — are probably correct for those who reported this. Several kinds of pressure inclined Germans to join Hitler's troops, even though some Binţinţi Germans say they would much rather not have done so. Within the Saxon organization there was a powerful Nazi faction, which was able to generate considerable moral suasion toward the Nazi cause. Germany itself also vigorously recruited troops among Transylvania's Germans, until the 1944 coup overthrew the pro-Hitler Romanian government and precluded such activities.

40. Until the early 1960s, Romania practiced a fair degree of reverse discrimination in university student enrollments. Children from the upper classes (which included the *chiaburi*) were handicapped on their entrance exams or penalized by denial of scholarship funds. For several years, then, talented children among the poorer peasantry had a chance to catch up with the wealthier families who had begun the trend toward educating offspring.

Conclusion: That's How It's Always Been

1. Very few points in this chapter are referenced, for nearly all have been made, with appropriate citations, earlier in the book.

2. My references to "peasants" in these concluding observations apply primarily to Romanian villagers, since the Germans entered Binținți very late in the period covered during this discussion.

3. Peasants' perceptions of state power did not necessarily follow perfectly with increments in it. Because of the Hungarian state's active discrimination against Romanians, the power of this state was probably perceived as greater than it really was, relative to the power of states that came before and after it. Peasants seem to have had almost no perception of the role of the interwar state in setting the conditions of agricultural production; in contrast, they perceive the socialist state as having tremendous visibility, less for its continued role in setting prices than for the ubiquity of the Party in the media and the presence of the CAP in their midst. Because peasants do not appear to have seen the hand of the interwar state in fixing market prices and so forth but chiefly in the agrarian reform and the conversion of debts, they tend to attribute a benevolence to the interwar state that my interpretation suggests is quite misplaced. This makes one wonder about further meanings for Adam Smith's reference to capitalism's "invisible hand."

4. The trends outlined for the Germans clearly do not refer to those in Binținți, but to the ethnic identifications of the Saxon community into which Binținți Germans were integrated upon their arrival.

5. This information comes from Binținți Germans who now live in West Germany and from a German minister who discussed with me the reasons his parishioners give when seeking counsel with him about their desire to emigrate.

6. Because of this possibility, I see no "paradox" in Anderson's (1974:40) observation that Absolutism paradoxically strengthened the aristocracy while protecting the interests of the nascent bourgeoisie.

7. This phrasing suggests that the state is systematically related to the process of accumulation. In the cases at hand, I agree with this view; but I prefer not to see the state as merely part of the global logic of accumulation, as does Chase-Dunn (1980); rather, I wish to endow states (at least theoretically) with a measure of potential autonomy in this process of accumulation.

8. To make this observation is not necessarily to take a specific position on the nature of socialist states in a capitalist world economy—i.e., whether Eastern European regimes are a form of state capitalism, state socialism, a transitional form between capitalism and socialism, etc.

9. Throughout this discussion I beg a major question: precisely which interest groups most fully influenced the policies of "the state" during these different times? Was it really a capitalist bourgeoisie that was responsible for determining the

conditions of peasants' lives, or was it really the "state"? I am not competent to unravel the intricacies of governmental processes in all these states at different times so as to answer this question, but I adhere to the idea that there was never a single group setting state policy without internal opposition and bargaining of some sort.

10. The analysis here, as in parts of chapter 3, is influenced by Palerm (1980).

11. As suggested in chapters 3 and 4, the relative backwardness of Transylvanian agriculture had several causes. Among them were ecological factors, the character of investment opportunities in the economy, and the fact that the main markets for agriculture were in the western part of the empire, which gave Hungarian producers a competitive edge the Transylvanians could never surpass, while across the Carpathians was another specialized agrarian export economy also.

12. To say that under socialism, state and bourgeoisie are one and the same is not to deny the existence of conflicts within the managerial class—the contention between "red" and "expert," as the Chinese call it, or between the "technocratic and bureaucratic elites." In Romania, however, there seems to be enough mixing of the two to justify saying that a collaboration of both runs the economy for the state.

13. While one can point to the very different meanings of formal similarities in their historical contexts, there remains the separate question of why serfdom seems an appropriate metaphor for villagers today. It, rather than capitalism, seems to provide them with the quintessential image of exploitation. I will leave the reader to ponder what this implies.

14. It is reasonable to ask, given the numerous scenarios for the encounter between developed and traditional social systems (see p. 361 above), why in this case we find that "tradition" is being reinforced or created, rather than wiped out. I suspect the answer is the class associations of different cultural systems in a period when the class structure was undergoing great transformation; but I believe the ideological component—the meanings of natio and feudal privilege—played a significant part as well.

15. I owe a great debt to Beatriz Lavandera, Pirkko Graves, and John Murra for important contributions to the form of this conclusion.

16. What is most delightful about this piece of identity manipulation on Petru's part is that he had never seen a mowing machine or heard that such a thing existed; he made it up on the spot. All he needed for this invention was some idea of agricultural machinery (he may have gotten this from Binţinţi Germans) and the association of "Austrian" with "more advanced and civilized."

17. Although cunning and cleverness are traits associated with Romanians from all parts of the country, jokes involving regional stereotypes suggest that cunning is more completely associated with Romanians from the Romanian Kingdom than from Transylvania, whose Romanians are stereotyped as being perhaps more sophisticated but somewhat duller of wit than "Regăţeni."

18. The original forms of these proverbs, most of which were collected from informants (two came from a book of proverbs in which many I collected also appear), are as follows, in order as in the text:

Rabdă şi taci dacă vrei să trăieşti.

Capul ce s-apleacă sabia nu-l taie.

Fugă-i ruşinoasă dar e sănătoasă.

Fă-te frate cu dracul pînă treci podul.

Tăcere e ca miere.

Mielul blînd suge la doi oi.

References Cited

Documents or Unpublished Primary Statistical Sources, with Location

Binţinţi civil and parochial registers of births, deaths, and marriages. Commune Office, Geoagiu.

Binţinţi land registers (*Cartea Funduară*). Romanian State Notary, Deva.

Binţinţi property register, ca. 1939. Commune Office, Geoagiu.

Binţinţi property register, 1948. Romanian State Archives, Bucureşti.

Kelemen, Lajos, *Genealogie*. MS in Romanian State Archives, Cluj.

Kemény, József C. *Transilvania Possessionaria*. MS in Romanian Academy Library, Cluj.

Macskásy Collection, catalogued by Liviu and Maria Ursuţiu (1974). Romanian State Archives, Cluj.

Miscellaneous conscriptions and censuses, including Conscriptio Cziráky-ana, for Binţinţi and nearby villages. Hungarian State Archives, Budapest.

Miscellaneous personal papers of Binţinţi Mayor Dumitru Vlaicu, 1880s to 1890s. Vlaicu Museum, Binţinţi.

Miscellaneous tax and property files for Orăştie prefecture and Hunedoara County. Romanian State Archives, Deva.

Report of the Jankovich Commission on Horea's revolt. Microfilm, Hungarian State Archives, Budapest.

Published Works

Anderson, Perry
    1974 Lineages of the absolutist state. London: NLB.

Andorka, Rudolf
    1976 The peasant family structure in the 18th and 19th centuries. Acta Ethnographica Academiae Scientiarum Hungaricae 25:321–348.
    1979 Family reconstitution and types of household structure. *In* Time, space, and man, ed. J. Sundrin and E. Söderlund, pp. 11–33. Stockholm: Almquist and Wicksell.

Anonymous
    1936 Entstehung und Geschichte von Benzenz. Siebenbürgische-Deutsches Tageblatt (Sibiu), nr. 18949.

Ardant, Gabriel
    1975 Financial policy and economic infrastructure in modern states and nations. *In* The formation of national states in Western Europe, ed. C. Tilly, pp. 164–242. Princeton: Princeton University Press.

Austria, Statistische Zentralkommission
    1831 Tafeln zur Statistik der Österreichischen Monarchie, Vol. 4.

Axenciuc, V.
1966 Evoluţia economiei româneşti în anii 1918–38. Analele Institutului de Studii Istorice şi Social-Politice de pe lînga CC al PCR
6:3–18.
Banaji, Jairus
1977 Modes of production in a materialist conception of history. Capital and Class 3:1–44.
Bărbat, Al.
1944 Drăguş: un sat din Ţara Oltului (Făgăraş): manifestări economice.
Bucureşti: Institutul de Ştiinţe Sociale al României.
Baritĭu, George
1889– Parti alese din istori'a Transilvaniei pre doue sute de ani din
1891 urma. Vol. 1 (1889), Vol. 2 (1890), Vol. 3 (1891). Sibiu: W.
Krafft.
Barth, F. H.
1978 Marriage traditions and customs among Transylvanian Saxons.
East European Quarterly 12:93–110.
Barth, Fredrik, ed.
1969 Ethnic groups and boundaries. Boston: Little, Brown.
Bassa, Beniamin
1970 Transportul sării pe Mureş in secolele XVIII–XIX. Sargetia
7:141–149.
Báthory, Ludovic
1976 Dezvoltarea social-economică a comunei Gîrbou (judeţul Sălaj)
între anii 1820–1848. Anuarul Institutului de Istorie din Cluj
19:331–340.
Berend, Iván T., and György Ránki
1974a Economic development in East-central Europe in the 19th and
20th centuries. New York: Columbia University Press.
1974b Hungary: a century of economic development. New York: Barnes
and Noble.
Berlin, Isaiah
1976 Vico and Herder: two studies in the history of ideas. New York:
Viking Press.
Bloch, Marc
1961 Feudal society. 2 vols. Chicago: University of Chicago Press.
Blum, Jerome
1948 Noble landowners and agriculture in Austria, 1815–1848. Baltimore: Johns Hopkins Press.
1957 The rise of serfdom in Eastern Europe. American Historical
Review 62:807–836.
1978 The end of the old order in rural Europe. Princeton: Princeton
University Press.
Böjthe, Ödön
1891 Hunyadmegye sztrigymelléki részének és nemes családainak tör-
ténete, tekintettel a birtokviszonyokra. Budapest: Müller Károly.

Boli-Bennett, John
1980 Global integration and the universal increase of state dominance, 1910–1970. *In* Sociological studies of the modern world-system, ed. Albert Bergesen, pp. 77–107. New York: Academic Press.

Boner, Charles
1865 Transylvania; its products and its people. London: Longmans, Green, Reader, and Dyer.

Botezan, Liviu
n.d. Contribuţii la studiul problemei agrare din comitatele Transilvaniei în perioada 1785–1820. Unpublished Ph.D. dissertation, Cluj University.
1970*a* Organizarea pămînturilor arătoare şi a fînaţelor iobăgeşti din Transilvania în perioada 1785–1820. Apulum 8:137–167.
1970*b* Situaţia rentei în bani din comitatele Transilvaniei în perioada 1785–1820. Studia Universitatis Babeş-Bolyai, Series Hist. 15: 31–49.
1976 Aspecte ale antrenării gospodăriilor ţărăneşti din Transilvania în economia de mărfuri între 1785–1820. Anuarul Institutului de Istorie din Cluj 19:137–156.

Botezan, L., and Constantin Enea
1970 Antrenarea gospodăriilor iobăgeşti din comitatul Hunedoara în economia de mărfuri, la începutul veacului al XIX-lea. Sargetia 7:151–161.

Botezan, L., and Roland Schilling
1970, 1971, 1973 Conscripţii urbariale hunedorene din 1785. Sargetia 7:121–140; 8:89–106; 10:213–230.

Bourdieu, Pierre
1977 Outline of a theory of practice. Cambridge: Cambridge University Press.

Braudel, Fernand
1958 Histoire et sciences sociales: la longue durée. Annales: Economies, Sociétés, Civilisations 13:725–753.

Braun, Rudolf
1978 Early industrialization and demographic change in the canton of Zürich. *In* Historical studies in changing fertility, ed. Charles Tilly, pp. 289–334. Princeton: Princeton University Press.

Brenner, Robert
1977 The origins of capitalist development: a critique of neo-Smithian Marxism. New Left Review 104:25–92.

Cernea, Mihail
1974 Sociologia cooperativei agricole. Bucureşti: Editura Academiei.
1975 The large-scale formal organization and the family primary group. Journal of Marriage and the Family 37:927–936.
1976 L'exploitation familiale des coopérateurs, projet social ou rémanence économique? *In* Sociologie rurale, ed. Placide Rambaud, pp. 131–135. The Hague: Mouton.

1978 Macrosocial change, feminization of agriculture, and peasant women's threefold economic role. Sociologia Ruralis 18:107–124.

Cernovodeanu, Paul
1972 Mercantilist projects to promote Transylvania's foreign trade at the beginning of the Habsburg domination. Journal of European Economic History 1:409–417.

Chase-Dunn, Christopher
1980 Socialist states in the capitalist world-economy. Social Problems 27:505–525.

Chase-Dunn, Christopher, and Richard Rubinson
1979 Cycles, trends, and new departures in world-system development. *In* National development and the world system, ed. John W. Meyer and Michael Hannan, pp. 276–296. Chicago: University of Chicago Press.

Chereşteşiu, Victor
1966 Adunarea naţională de la Blaj 3–5 (15–17) mai 1848; începuturile şi alcătuirea programului revoluţiei din 1848 din Transilvania. Bucureşti: Editura Politică.

Chirot, Daniel
1976 Social change in a peripheral society: the creation of a Balkan colony. New York: Academic Press.
1978a Neoliberal and social-democratic theories of development: the Zeletin-Voinea debate concerning Romania's prospects in the 1920's and its contemporary importance. *In* Social change in Romania, 1860–1940, ed. Kenneth Jowitt, pp. 31–52. Berkeley, Calif.: Institute of International Studies, University of California.
1978b A Romanian prelude to contemporary debates about development. Review 2:115–123.

Ciobanu, Virgil
1926 Statistica românilor din Ardeal făcută de administraţia austriacă la anul 1760–62. Anuarul Institutului de Istorie Naţională (Cluj) 3, extract, pp. 1–87.

Ciomac, Ion Luca
1931 Despre stările agrare din Transilvania sub regimul maghiar şi cercetări asupra situaţiei exploatărilor agricole, după reforma agrară. Bucureşti: Imprimeria Naţională.

[Ciura, Al.]
1920 Albumul Vlaicu. Orăştie: Tipografia "Libertatea."

Cohen, Abner
1969 Custom and politics in urban Africa: a study of Hausa migrants in Yoruba towns. Berkeley and Los Angeles: University of California Press.

Cohen, Ronald
1978 Ethnicity: problem and focus in anthropology. *In* Annual Review of Anthropology, ed. Bernard J. Siegel et al., pp. 379–403. Palo Alto, Calif.: Annual Reviews Press.

Cole, John W.
1981 Ethnicity and the rise of nationalism. *In* Ethnicity and nationalism in Southeastern Europe, ed. Sam Beck and John W. Cole, pp. 105-134. Amsterdam: University of Amsterdam Antropologisch-Sociologisch Centrum.

Cole, John W., and Eric R. Wolf
1974 The hidden frontier: ecology and ethnicity in an alpine valley. New York: Academic Press.

Collier, George A.
1975 Fields of the Tzotzil: the ecological bases of tradition in Highland Chiapas. Austin: University of Texas Press.

Coulon, Christian, and Françoise Morin
1979 Occitan ethnicity and politics. Critique of Anthropology 13-14: 105-123.

Cristea, Tiberiu
1929 Creşterea animalelor în Transilvania. *In* Transilvania, Banatul, Crişana, Maramureşul 1918-1928, pp. 387-446. Bucureşti: Cultura Naţională.

Csetri, Elek
1958- O încercare de eliberare a iobagilor din anul 1832. Anuarul
1959 Institutului de Istorie din Cluj 1-2: 179-189.

Csetri, Elek, and István Imreh
1966a Aspecte ale situaţiei şi dezvoltării oraşelor din Transilvania (1786-1848). Studia Universitatis Babeş-Bolyai, Series Hist 11:61-76.
1966b Asupra relaţiilor de proprietate feudală în Transilvania (1750-1848). Anuarul Institutului de Istorie din Cluj 9:109-125.
1972 Stratificarea socială a populaţiei din Transilvania la sfîrşitul orînduirii feudale (1767-1821). *In* Populaţie şi societate, vol. I, ed. Ştefan Pascu, pp. 139-238. Cluj: Editura Dacia.

Daicoviciu, Constantin, et al.
1961 Din istoria Transilvaniei, vol. I (2nd edition). Bucureşti: Editura Academiei Republicii Populare Romîne.

Daicoviciu, Constantin, and Miron Constantinescu
1965 Brève histoire de la Transylvanie. Bucureşti: Editura Academiei Republicii Socialiste România.

Dalton, George
1972 Peasantries in anthropology and history. Current Anthropology 13:385-406.

Deak, Istvan
1979 The lawful revolution: Louis Kossuth and the Hungarians, 1848-1849. New York: Columbia University Press.

de Etéd, Eugen Gagyi
1911 Documente istorice: Regulatio Diocesis Transilvanicae Disunitae anno 1805. Transilvania Revista. Asociaţiune pentru Literatura Română şi Cultura Poporului Româno. Anul 42:38-61 and 147-171.

Demény, Paul
1968 Early fertility decline in Austria-Hungary: a lesson in demographic transition. Daedalus 97:502-522.
Demian, J. A.
1809 Tableau géographique et politique des royaumes de Hongrie, d'Esclavonie, de Croatie, et de la grande Principauté de Transylvanie. 2 vols. Paris: S. C. L'Huillier.
Densuişianu, Nicolae
1884 Revoluţiunea lui Horia în Transilvania şi Ungaria 1784-1785. Bucureşti: Tipografia "Romanulu."
Deutsch, E., N. N. Constantinescu, A. Negrea, and A. Negucioiu
1964 Unele aspecte ale dominaţiei capitalului financiar în Transilvania în primele decenii ale secolului al XX-lea. *In* Destrămarea monarhiei austro-ungare 1900-1918, ed. C. Daicoviciu and M. Constantinescu, pp. 217-230. Bucureşti: Editura Academiei Republicii Populare Romîne.
Dobrescu, Vasile
1972 Din activitatea secţiei economice a "Astrei" (1900-1914). Studia Universitatis Babeş-Bolyai, Series Hist. 17:89-115.
Dobrogeanu-Gherea, Constantin
1910 Neoiobăgia. Bucureşti: Editura Librăriei SOCEC & Comp.
Domínguez, Virginia
1977 Social classification in Creole Louisiana. American Ethnologist 4:589-602.
Dordea, Ion, and Volker Wollmann
1978 Transportul şi comercializarea sării din Transilvania şi Maramureş în veacul al XVIII-lea. Anuarul Institutului de Istorie din Cluj 21:135-171.
Dragomir, Silviu
1920- Istoria desrobirei religioase a românilor din Ardeal în secolul
1930 XVIII. 2 vols. (Vol. 1, 1920; vol. 2, 1930). Sibiu: Tipografia Arhidiecezană.
Eddie, Scott
1967 The changing pattern of landownership in Hungary, 1867-1914. Economic History Review 20:293-309.
Egyed, Ákos
1962 Aspecte ale dezvoltării industriei mari din Transilvania între anii 1867-1873. Anuarul Institutului de Istorie din Cluj 5:145-177.
1968 Unele caracteristici ale dezvoltării industriei in Transilvania la sfîrşitul secolului al XIX-lea. Acta Musei Napocensis 5:251-264.
Eidheim, Harald
1968 The Lappish movement: an innovative political process. *In* Local-level politics, ed. Marc J. Swartz, pp. 205-216. Chicago: Aldine.
Emerson, R.
1962 Power-dependence relations. American Sociological Review 27: 31-41.

Enea, Constantin, and Liviu Botezan
1969 Unele aspecte ale obligaţiilor iobăgeşti pe domeniul Deva şi pe alte moşii din comitatul Hunedoara, la începutul veacului al XIX-lea. Sargetia 6:105-124.

Firth, Raymond
1950 The peasantry of Southeast Asia. International Affairs 26:503-514.

Forster, Robert
1970 Obstacles to agricultural growth in eighteenth-century France. American Historical Review 75:1600-1615.

Foster-Carter, Aidan
1978 The modes of production controversy. New Left Review 197:47-77.

Francisco, Ronald A., Betty A. Laird, and Roy D. Laird
1979 The political economy of collectivized agriculture. New York: Pergamon Press.

Frank, Andre Gunder
1967 Capitalism and underdevelopment in Latin America. New York: Monthly Review Press.

Frăţilă, Ion, and Vasile Ionaş
1979 Aportul populaţiei din judeţul Hunedoara la unirea Transilvaniei cu România. Sargetia 14:465-474.

Fried, Morton
1968 On the concepts of "tribe" and "tribal society." *In* Essays on the problem of tribe, ed. June Helm, pp. 3-20. Seattle: American Ethnological Society.

Frunzănescu, A.
1939 Evoluţia chestiunii agrare în România. Bucureşti: Imprimeria Naţională.

Gaál, László, and Péter Gunst
1977 Animal husbandry in Hungary in the 19th-20th centuries. Budapest: Akadémiai Kiadó.

Geertz, Clifford
1963 The integrative revolution: primordial sentiments and civil politics in the new states. *In* Old societies and new states, ed. C. Geertz, pp. 105-157. Glencoe, Ill.: Free Press.

Gellner, Ernest
1969 Nationalism. Chapter *in* Thought and change, pp. 147-178. Chicago: University of Chicago Press.

Gerard, E.
1888 The land beyond the forest: facts, figures, and fancies from Transylvania. New York: Harper & Bros

Giurgiu, Natalia
1972 Populaţia Transilvaniei la sfîrşitul secolului al XVIII-lea şi începutul secolului al XIX-lea. *In* Populaţie şi societate, vol. 1, ed. Ştefan Pascu, pp. 97-138. Cluj: Editura Dacia.

Göllner, Karl, and Marcel Ştirban
1971 Cîteva aspecte din conţinutul agrar al doctrinelor politice bur-

gheze din România în perioada dintre cele două războaie mondiale. Sargetia 8:173-178.

Golomb, Louis
1978 Brokers of morality: Thai ethnic adaptation in a rural Malaysian setting. Honolulu: University of Hawaii Press.

Golopenția, Anton, and D. C. Georgescu
1941 60 sate românești. Vol. II: Situația economică. București: Institutul de Științe Sociale al României.

Grimm, Josef A. Ritter von
1863 Das Urbarialwesen in Siebenbürgen. Vienna: Friedr. und Moritz Förster.

Gross, N. T.
1966 Industrialization in Austria in the nineteenth century. Unpublished Ph.D. dissertation, Economics, University of California, Berkeley.
1973 The Habsburg monarchy, 1750-1914. *In* The Fontana economic history of Europe, vol. 4: The emergence of industrial societies, ed. Carlo M. Cipolla, pp. 228-278. London: Collins/Fontana Books.

Gündisch, Gustav
1937 Urkundenbuch zur Geschichte der Deutschen in Siebenbürgen. Vol. IV:1416-1437. Hermannstadt: Krafft & Drotleff.

Gusti, D., et al.
1938 Enciclopedia României. București: Imprimeria Națională.

Halpern, Joel, and E. A. Hammel
1969 Observations on the intellectual history of ethnology and other social sciences in Yugoslavia. Comparative Studies in Society and History 11:17-26.

Hanák, Péter
1967 Hungary in the Austro-Hungarian monarchy. Austrian History Yearbook 3:260-302.
1975a Economics, society, and sociopolitical thought in Hungary during the age of capitalism. Austrian History Yearbook 11:113-135.
1975b The first attempt at the Austro-Hungarian compromise—1860. *In* Etudes Historiques Hongroises II, pp. 567-600. Budapest: Akadémiai Kiadó.

Hann, C. M.
1980 Tázlár: a village in Hungary. Cambridge: Cambridge University Press.

Hechter, Michael
1975 Internal colonialism: the Celtic fringe in British national development, 1536-1966. Berkeley, Los Angeles, London: University of California Press.

Helin, Ronald A.
1967 The volatile administrative map of Rumania. Annals of the Association of American Geographers 57:481-502.

Hintz, Johann
1846 Stand der privat-Industrie, der Fabriken, Manufakturen und Handlungen in Siebenbürgen im Jahre 1844. Archiv des Vereins für Siebenbürgische Landeskunde 2:422-451.

Hitchins, Keith
1969 The Rumanian national movement in Transylvania, 1780-1849. Cambridge, Mass.: Harvard University Press.
1977 Orthodoxy and nationality: Andreiu Şaguna and the Rumanians of Transylvania, 1846-1878. Cambridge, Mass.: Harvard University Press.
1979 Religion and Rumanian national consciousness in eighteenth-century Transylvania. Slavonic and East European Review 57: 214-239.

Hungary
1897- A magyar korona országainak mezőgazdasági statisztikája. 5 vols.
1900 Budapest: Pesti Könyvnyomda-Részvénytársaság.
1912- A magyar szent korona országainak 1910. évi népszámlálása.
1916 Multiple volumes. Budapest: Athenaeum.
1920 The Hungarian peace negotiations: report on the activity of the Hungarian peace delegation at Neuilly ˢ/S, from January to March 1920. Vol. 3A. Budapest: Victor Hornyánszky.

Imreh, István
1955 Despre începuturile industriei capitaliste din Transilvania în prima jumătate a secolului al XIX-lea. Bucureşti: Editura Academiei Republicii Populare Romîne.
1965 Contribuţia la problema utilizării forţei de muncă a iobagilor. Anuarul Institutului de Istorie din Cluj 8:127-172.

Ionaş, Vasile
1972 Conscripţiile urbariale ale satelor Ormindea, Meria, şi Lunca Cernii din anul 1820. Sargetia 9:112-141.

Iorga, Nicolae
1925 Istoria comerţului românesc. 2 vols. Bucureşti: Tiparul Românesc.

Iovanelli, Marcela Felicia
1975 Industria românească 1934-1938. Bucureşti: Editura Academiei Republicii Socialiste România.

Jackson, George D.
1966 Comintern and peasant in Eastern Europe, 1919-1930. New York: Columbia University Press.

Jászi, Oscar
1929 The dissolution of the Habsburg monarchy. Chicago: University of Chicago Press.

Jowitt, Kenneth
1971 Revolutionary breakthroughs and national development: the case of Romania, 1944-1965. Berkeley, Los Angeles, London: University of California Press.

Jude, Maria Magdalena
1974 "Amicul poporului" şi problema agriculturii raţionale. Acta Musei Napocensis 11:311-321.

Jude, Maria Magdalena, and Nicolae Cordoş
1976 Prima reuniune de agricultură la români transilvăneni. Acta Musei Napocensis 13:523-536.

Kahn, Joel
1980 Minangkabau social formations: Indonesian peasants and the world economy. Cambridge: Cambridge University Press.

Kann, Robert A.
1974 A history of the Habsburg empire, 1526-1918. Berkeley, Los Angeles, and London: University of California Press.

Katus, L.
1970 Economic growth in Hungary during the Age of Dualism (1867-1913): a quantitative analysis. *In* Social-economic researches on the history of East-Central Europe, pp. 35-127. Studia Historica Academiae Scientiarum Hungaricae, vol. 62. Budapest: Akadémiai Kiadó.

Kempelen, Béla
1911- Magyar nemes családok. Budapest: K. Grill.
1932

Kenyeres, Agnes
1969 Magyar életrajzi lexicon. Multiple volumes. Budapest: Akadémiai Kiadó.

Khera, Sigrid
1973 Social stratification and land inheritance among Austrian peasants. American Anthropologist 75:814-823.

Kideckel, David
1979 Agricultural cooperativism and social process in a Romanian commune. Unpublished Ph.D. dissertation, Anthropology, University of Massachusetts, Amherst.
1982 The socialist transformation of agriculture in a Romanian commune, 1945-62. American Ethnologist 9:320-340.

Király, Béla K.
1969 Hungary in the late eighteenth century: the decline of enlightened despotism. New York: Columbia University Press.
1975 Napoleon's proclamation of 1809 and its Hungarian echo. *In* Intellectual and social developments in the Habsburg empire from Maria Theresa to World War I, ed. Stanley B. Winters and Joseph Held, pp. 31-54. Boulder, Colo.: Eastern European Quarterly Monographs, no. 11.

Klein, Gustav Adolf
1929 Viaţa economică germană din Ardeal, Banat şi Satu-Mare. *In* Transilvania, Banatul, Crişana, Maramureşul 1918-1828, pp. 571-584. Bucureşti: Cultura Naţională.

Komlos, John
   1978 The Habsburg monarchy as a customs union: economic develop-
        ment in Austria-Hungary in the nineteenth century. Unpublished
        Ph.D. dissertation, History, University of Chicago.
   1981 Economic growth and industrialization in Hungary 1830–1913.
        Journal of European Economic History 10:5–46.
Kovács, József
   1972 Despre problema proprietăţii funciare din Transilvania in lumina
        legislaţiei. Studia Universitatis Babeş-Bolyai, Series Hist. 17:
        39–48.
   1973 Desfiinţarea relaţiilor feudale in Transilvania. Cluj: Editura
        Dacia.
Kula, Witold
   1972 The seigneury and the peasant family in eighteenth-century
        Poland. Annales: Economies, Sociétés, Civilisations 27:449–458.
   1976 An economic theory of the feudal system: towards a model of the
   [1962] Polish economy, 1500–1800. London: NLB.
Larionescu, Maria
   1980 Romanian agriculture within social and economic development
        strategy. Paper prepared for Conference on Rural Economy and
        Society in Contemporary Eastern Europe. Bellagio, Italy, 1980.
Lázár, Miklós
   1858 A gróf Lázár család. Kolozsvár: A Rom. Kathol. Lyceum Betüivel.
Leeds, Anthony
   1977 Mythos and pathos: some unpleasantries on peasantries. *In* Peas-
        ant livelihood, ed. Rhoda Halperin and James Dow, pp. 227–
        256. New York: St. Martins.
Levine, David
   1977 Family formation in an age of nascent capitalism. New York:
        Academic Press.
Levine, Robert A., and Donald T. Campbell
   1972 Ethnocentrism: theories of conflict, ethnic attitudes, and group
        behavior. New York: John Wiley.
McArthur, Marilyn S.
   1976 The "Saxon" Germans: political fate of an ethnic identity. Dia-
        lectical Anthropology 1:349–364.
Macartney, C. A.
   1934 Hungary. London: Ernest Benn.
   1937 Hungary and her successors: the Treaty of Trianon and its con-
        sequences. London: Oxford University Press.
   1962 Hungary: a short history. Edinburgh: Edinburgh University Press.
   1968 The Habsburg empire 1790–1918. London: Weidenfeld and
        Nicholson.
McNeill, William H.
   1964 Europe's steppe frontier, 1500–1800: a study of the eastward
        movement in Europe. Chicago: University of Chicago Press.

Madgearu, Virgil
  1940 Evoluţia economiei româneşti după războiul mondial. Bucureşti: Independenţa Economică.
Maior, George
  1906 Politica agrară la români: dezvoltarea chestiunii agrare în toate ţări locuite de români din secolele XVII, XVIII, XIX. Bucureşti: Institutul de Arte Grafice Carol Göbl.
Makkai, László
  1946 Histoire de Transilvanie. Paris: Les Presses Universitaires de France.
Małowist, Marian
  1958 Poland, Russia and western trade in the fifteenth and sixteenth centuries. Past and Present 13:26-39.
  1966 The problem of the inequality of economic development in Europe in the latter Middle Ages. Economic History Review 19: 15-28.
Manuila, Sabin
  1938 Aspects démographiques de la Transylvanie. *In* La Transylvanie, pp. 793-856. Bucureşti: Academia Română (for Cluj Institute of National History).
Marczali, Henrik
  1910 Hungary in the eighteenth century. Cambridge: Cambridge University Press.
Mayhew, Alan
  1973 Rural settlement and farming in Germany. New York: Barnes and Noble.
Mellor, Roy E.
  1975 Eastern Europe: a geography of the Comecon countries. New York: Columbia University Press.
Meteş, Ştefan
  1920 Relaţiile comerciale ale Ţerii-Româneşti cu Ardealul până în veacul al XVIII-lea. Sighişoara: W. Krafft.
Mihu, Ioan
  1938 Spicuiri din gîndurile mele politice, culturale, economice. Sibiu: Tiparul Tipografiei Arhidiecezane.
Miliband, Ralph
  1969 The state in capitalist society. New York: Basic Books.
  1973 Poulantzas and the capitalist state. New Left Review 82:83-92.
Mintz, Sidney
  1977 The so-called world system: local initiative and local response. Dialectical Anthropology 2:253-270.
Mitrany, David
  1930 The land and the peasant in Rumania: the war and the agrarian reform, 1917-1921. New York: Greenwood.

1951 Marx against the peasant: a study in social dogmatism. Chapel Hill: University of North Carolina Press.

Moga, Ioan
1973 Scrieri istorice, 1926-1946. Cluj: Editura Dacia.

Montias, John M.
1967 Economic development in communist Rumania. Cambridge, Mass.: MIT Press.

Moţa, Ioan
1936 Românii din Orăştie înainte de război. *In* Fraţilor Alexandru şi Ion L. Lăpědatu, pp. 525-537. Bucureşti: Imprimeria Naţională.

Mureşan, Hilde
1969 Date noi în legătură cu războiul vamal dintre România şi Austro-Ungaria (1886-91). Anuarul Institutului de Istorie din Cluj 12: 113-143.

Nagy, Iván
1857- Magyarország családai czimerekkel és nemzetrendi táblákkal. 12
1865 vols. Pest: Beimel J. és Kozma Vazul (vols. 1-3); Ráth Mór (vols. 4-12).

Neamţu, Al.
1970 Societăţile pe acţiuni şi provenienţa capitalului în industria extractivă din Transilvania în a doua jumătate a secolului XVIII. Acta Musei Napocensis 7:227-247.
1971 Forţa de muncă salariată în industria extractivă din Transilvania în secolul XVIII. Acta Musei Napocensis 8:251-266.

Negoescu, Cristu S.
1919 Ardealul nostru: Transilvania, Banatul, Crişana, Maramureşul — din punct de vedere geografic, economic, administrativ, şi mai ales financiar. Bucureşti: Tipografia "Gutenberg," Joseph Göbl.

Nuţu, Constantin, and Ákos Egyed
1961 Transilvania în primele două decenii ale secolului XX. Unirea Transilvaniei cu România. *In* Din istoria Transilvaniei. 1st ed., vol. 2. Bucureşti: Editura Academiei Republicii Populare Romîne.

Oţetea, Andrei, ed.
1970 The history of the Romanian people. New York: Twayne Publishers.

Pach, Zsigmond Pál
1968 The shifting of international trade routes in the 15th-16th centuries. Acta Historica Academiae Scientiarum Hungaricae 14: 287-321.
1970 The role of East-Central Europe in international trade. *In* Etudes Historiques I, pp. 217-264. Budapest: Akadémiai Kiadó.
1972 Sixteenth-century Hungary: commercial activity and market production by the nobles. *In* Economy and society in early modern Europe, ed. Peter Burke, pp. 113-133. New York: Harper & Row.

Paget, John
  1850 Hungary and Transylvania; with remarks on their condition, social, political, and economical. 2 vols. 1971 reprint. New York: Arno Press and the New York Times.
Paikert, G. C.
  1967 The Danube Swabians: German populations in Hungary, Rumania and Yugoslavia and Hitler's impact on their patterns. The Hague: Martinus Nijhoff.
Palerm, Ángel
  1980 Articulación campesinado-capitalismo: sobre la fórmula M-D-M. *In* Antropología y Marxismo, pp. 199–224. Sacramento, Mexico: Editorial Nueva Imagen.
Pamlényi, Ervin, ed.
  1975 A history of Hungary. London and Wellingborough: Collet's.
Pascu, Ştefan, and Traian Gherman
  1960 Urbariul satului Cetan din prima jumătate a secolului al XVIII-lea. Anuarul Institutului de Istorie din Cluj 3:171–255.
Pascu, Ştefan, C. C. Giurescu, J. Kovács, and L. Vajda
  1964 Unele aspecte ale problemei agrare în monarhia austro-ungară la începutul secolului al XX-lea (1900–1918). *In* Destrămarea monarhiei austro-ungare 1900–1918, ed. C. Daicoviciu and M. Constantinescu, pp. 11–91. Bucureşti: Editura Academiei Republicii Populare Romîne.
Pataki, József
  1973 Domeniul Hunedoara la începutul secolului al XVI-lea. Bucureşti: Editura Academiei Republicii Socialiste România.
Patnaik, Utsa
  1979 Neopopulism and Marxism: the Chayanovian view of the agrarian question and its fundamental fallacy. Journal of Peasant Studies 6:375–420.
Plakans, Andrejs
  1975 Seigneurial authority and peasant family life: the Baltic area in the eighteenth century. Journal of Interdisciplinary History 5:629–654.
Popa, Valeriu, and Nicolae Istrate
  1915 Transilvania, Banatul, Crişana, si Maramurăşul. Bucureşti: Tipografia F. Göbl.
Poulantzas, Nicos
  1978 Political power and social classes. London: Verso.
Prebisch, Raúl
  1950 The economic development of Latin America and its principal problems. New York: United Nations, Economic Commission for Latin America.
Preobrazhensky, Evgenii
  1971 Peasantry and the political economy of the early stages of indus-
  [1924] trialization. Reprinted in Peasants and peasant societies, ed. Teodor Shanin, pp. 219–226. Baltimore: Penguin Books.

Prodan, David
1944 Teoria imigraţiei românilor din Principatele Române în Transilvania în veacul al XVIII-lea. Sibiu: Tipografia "Cartea Românească din Cluj."
1958- Producţia fierului pe domeniul Hunedoarei în secolul XVII.
1959 Anuarul Institutului de Istorie din Cluj 1-2:29-124.
1967 Iobăgia în Transilvania în secolul al XVI-lea. Vol. I. Bucureşti: Editura Academiei Republicii Socialiste România.
1971 Supplex Libellus Valachorum. Bucureşti: Editura Academiei Republicii Socialiste România. (Citations are to English-language edition.)
1976 Urbariile Ţării Făgăraşului. Vol. II: 1651-1680. Bucureşti: Editura Academiei.
1979 Răscoala lui Horea. Bucureşti: Editura Ştiinţifică şi Enciclopedică. 2 vols.

Puskás, J.
1975 Emigration from Hungary to the United States before 1914. *In* Etudes Historiques Hongroises, II, pp. 65-103. Budapest: Akadémiai Kiadó.

Ragin, Charles
1979 Ethnic political mobilization: the Welsh case. American Sociological Review 44:619-635.

Rebel, Hermann
1983 Peasant classes: the bureaucratization of property and family relations under early Habsburg absolutism, 1511-1636. Princeton: Princeton University Press.

Retegan, Simion
1978 Mutaţii economice în satul românesc din Transilvania la mijlocul veacului al XIX-lea. Anuarul Institutului de Istorie din Cluj 21: 189-208.

Rey, Pierre Philippe
1973 Les alliances de classes: sur l'articulation des modes de production. Paris: Maspero.

Roberts, Henry L.
1951 Rumania: political problems of an agrarian state. New Haven: Yale University Press.

Romania, Direcţia Generală a Arhivelor Statului
1972 Îndrumător în Arhivele Statului judeţului Hunedoara. Bucureşti.

Romania, Institutul de Cercetări Economice al României
1936 Studii privitoare la preţuri şi rentabilitate în agricultura României. Bucureşti: Imprimeria Naţională.

Roseberry, William
1978 Peasants as proletarians. Critique of Anthropology 3:3-18.

Rostow, Walt W.
1960 The stages of economic growth, a non-Communist manifesto. Cambridge: Cambridge University Press.

Rothschild, Joseph
1974 East Central Europe between the two world wars. Seattle: University of Washington Press.
Rousseau, Jerome
1975 Ethnic identity and social relations in Central Borneo. *In* Pluralism in Malaysia, ed. Judith A. Nagata, pp. 32–49. Leiden: E.J. Brill.
Rubinson, Richard
1978 Political transformation in Germany and the United States. *In* Social change in the capitalist world economy, ed. Barbara H. Kaplan, pp. 36–74. Beverly Hills: Sage.
Şandru, D.
1975 Reforma agrară din 1921 în România. Bucureşti: Editura Academiei Republicii Socialiste România.
Schneider, Jane
1977 Was there a pre-capitalist world system? Peasant Studies 6:20–29.
Schneider, Jane, and Peter Schneider
1976 Culture and political economy in western Sicily. New York: Academic Press.
Seton-Watson, R. W.
1963 A history of the Roumanians, from Roman times to the completion of unity. n.p.: Archon Books (reprint).
Skinner, G. William
1978 Vegetable supply and marketing in Chinese cities. China Quarterly 76:733–793.
Skocpol, Theda
1979 States and social revolutions: a comparative analysis of France, Russia, and China. Cambridge: Cambridge University Press.
Smith, Carol A.
1981 Regional analysis in world-system perspective: a critique of three structural theories of uneven development. Paper prepared for Conference of the Society for Economic Anthropology, Bloomington, Ind.
Smith, Dennis
1978 Dominance and containment: an approach to modernization. Comparative Studies in Society and History 20:177–213.
Spigler, Iancu
1973 Economic reform in Rumanian industry. London: Oxford University Press.
Spufford, Margaret
1974 Contrasting communities: English villagers in the sixteenth and seventeenth centuries. Cambridge: Cambridge University Press.
Stinchcombe, Arthur
1961 Agricultural enterprise and rural class relations. American Journal of Sociology 67:165–176.

Stys, W.
1957 The influence of economic conditions on the fertility of peasant women. Population Studies 11:136–148.

Suciu, Petru
1929 Clasele sociale ale Româniilor din Ardeal. *In* Transilvania, Banatul, Crişana, Maramureşul 1918–1928. Bucureşti: Cultura Naţională.

Surdu, Bujor
1960 Liniile dezvoltării social-economice a Transilvaniei în secolul al XVIII-lea pînă la răscoala lui Horia. Anuarul Institutului de Istorie din Cluj 3:103–170.
1962 Aspecte privind rolul băncilor în consolidarea burgheziei romîneşti din Transilvania pînă la primul război mondial. Anuarul Institutului de Istorie din Cluj 5:179–202.
1964 Contribuţii la problema naşterii manufacturilor din Transilvania în secolul al XVIII-lea. Anuarul Institutului de Istorie din Cluj 7:147–237.

Szabad, György
1977 Hungarian political trends between the revolution and the compromise (1848–1867). Budapest: Akadémiai Kiadó.

Szinnyei, József
1900 Magyar irók élete és munkái. Vol. 7. Budapest: Hornyánsky Viktor Könyvkiadóhivatal.

Szuhay, Miklós
1965 L'évolution des cultures à charrue en Hongrie de 1867 à 1914. Nouvelles Etudes Historiques I:639–666.

Taylor, A. J. P.
1942 The Habsburg monarchy, 1815–1918. London: Macmillan & Co.

Therborn, Göran
1978 What does the ruling class do when it rules? London: NLB.

Thomas, George, and John W. Meyer
1980 Regime changes and state power in an intensifying world-state-system. *In* Studies of the modern world-system, ed. Albert J. Bergesen, pp. 139–158. New York: Academic Press.

Thompson, E. P.
1963 The making of the English working class. New York: Vintage.

Thompson, James D.
1967 Organizations in action. New York: McGraw-Hill.

Tilly, Charles
1975 The formation of national states in Western Europe. Princeton: Princeton University Press.
1978a From mobilization to revolution. Reading, Mass.: Addison-Wesley.
1978b Historical studies of changing fertility. Princeton: Princeton University Press.

Tóth, Zoltán
1955 Mişcările ţărăneşti din Munţii Apuseni pînă la 1848. Bucureşti: Editura Academiei Republicii Populare Romîne.

Trouillot, Michel-Rolph
   1982 Motion in the system: coffee, color and slavery in eighteenth-century Saint-Domingue. Review 5: 331-388.
Tsantis, Andreas, and Roy Pepper
   1979 Romania: the industrialization of an agrarian economy under socialist planning. Washington, D.C.: The World Bank.
Tucker, William James
   1886 Life and society in Eastern Europe. London: S. Low, Marston, Searle, and Rivington.
Turnock, David
   1974 An economic geography of Romania. London: G. Bell.
Ursuţiu, Liviu
   1977 Tranzacţii asupra iobagului şi asupra pămîntului pe domeniul Gurghiu (1652-1715). Marisia 7:125-139.
Ursuţiu, Liviu, and Maria Ursuţiu
   1974 Arhive familiale 3-7: repertorii. Biblioteca Academiei Republicii Socialiste România, Filiala Cluj-Napoca.
Ursuţiu, Maria
   1979 Structura familiei iobăgeşti pe domeniul Hunedoarei la sfîrşitul secolului al XVII-lea. Sargetia 14:233-242.
Vajda, Ludovic
   1965 Cu privire la pătrunderea capitalului austriac în industria minieră şi siderurgică a Transilvaniei între 1848 şi 1867. Studia Universitatis Babeş-Bolyai, Series Hist. 10:63-78.
   1967 Începuturile revoluţiei industriale în mineritul şi metalurgia din Transilvania. Anuarul Institutului de Istorie din Cluj 10:173-195.
   1972 Capitalul străin în industria minieră şi metalurgică a Transilvaniei (1867-1900). Acta Musei Napocensis 9:229-254.
Verdery, Katherine
   1978 The decline of corporate German ethnicity in Romania. Paper prepared for conference on Ethnicity and Economic Development, East and West. Ann Arbor, Mich.
   1979 Internal colonialism in Austria-Hungary. Ethnic and Racial Studies 2:378-399.
Voinea, Şerban
   1926 Marxism oligarhic: contribuţie la problema desvoltării capitaliste a României. Bucureşti: Editura I. Brănişteanu.
Wagner, Ernst
   1977 Historisch-statistisches Ortsnamenbuch für Siebenbürgen, mit einer Einführung in die historische Statistik des Landes. Köln: Böhlau Verlag.
Wallerstein, Immanuel
   1973 The two modes of ethnic consciousness in Soviet Central Asia. *In* The nationality question in Soviet Central Asia, ed. Edward Allworth, pp. 168-175. New York: Praeger.

1974 The modern world-system: capitalist agriculture and the origins of the European world-economy in the sixteenth century. New York: Academic Press.

1979 The capitalist world-economy. Cambridge: Cambridge University Press.

1980 The modern world-system, II: mercantilism and the consolidation of the European world-economy, 1600–1750. New York: Academic Press.

Warman, Arturo

1980 We come to object: the peasants of Morelos and the national state. Baltimore: Johns Hopkins Press.

Warriner, Doreen

1939 Economics of peasant farming. London: Oxford University Press.

Weber, Max

1946 Politics as a vocation. *In* From Max Weber: essays in sociology,
[1918] ed. H. H. Gerth and C. W. Mills, pp. 77–128. New York: Oxford University Press.

Wilson, William A.

1976 Folklore and nationalism in modern Finland. Bloomington: Indiana University Press.

Wolf, Eric R.

1966 Peasants. Englewood Cliffs, NJ: Prentice-Hall.

1969 Peasant wars of the twentieth century. New York: Harper.

Yambert, Karl A.

MS Peasant politics in Piura, Peru: a post-dependency perspective. Paper presented at the Annual Meeting of the American Anthropological Association, Washington, D.C.

Zagoroff, S. D., Jenö Végh, and Alexander D. Bilimovich

1955 The agricultural economy of the Danubian economies 1935–45. Stanford, Calif.: Stanford University Press.

Zeletin, Ştefan

1925 Burghezia română: originea şi rolul ei istoric. Bucureşti: Cultura Naţională.

Zimmermann, Franz, and Carl Werner

1892 Urkundenbuch zur Geschichte der Deutschen in Siebenbürgen. Vol. I: 1191–1342. Hermannstadt: Franz Michaelis.

1897 Urkundenbuch zur Geschichte der Deutschen in Siebenbürgen. Vol. II: 1342–1390. Hermannstadt: Franz Michaelis.

Zimmermann, Franz, and Georg Müller

1902 Urkundenbuch zur Geschichte der Deutschen in Siebenbürgen. Vol. III: 1391–1415. Hermannstadt: Franz Michaelis.

Index

Acord global. *See* Contract-payment system

Agrarian reform. *See* Land reform

Agricultural commodity production, 149-150, 153-155, 217-218, 250, 289, 336, 342, 357, 364, 366; in Binţinţi, 169-173, 213-214, 232-242, 258, 307, 310-316, 318, 334; in 18th-century Transylvania, 153-155, 364; under Hungarian state, 217-218, 250; in interwar Romania, 289

Agricultural modernization, 336, 342; in Binţinţi, 37-38, 234, 237, 241, 260, 311, 318-319, 323, 324; in Hungary and Transylvania, 173-174, 176, 196, 217, 332; in interwar Romania, 283, 286, 290-291, 332

Agricultural organization: for village Germans, 233-235, 239, 310-312, 314-320; for village Magyars, 232-233; for village Romanians, 233-238, 310-312, 314-320

Agricultural revolution, 129

Agriculture: field and crop rotation, 158, 162, 164, 173, 217; state investment in, 42, 46, 57, 327, 330-331, 356; subsistence, 233, 235-236, 241, 258, 283, 284, 307, 364; transfer of surplus from, 42-45, 54-55, 71, 200, 274, 275, 282, 286, 329, 332, 335, 343-344, 356, 362. *See also* Capitalist agriculture; Credit; Livestock production

Agro-Industrial Councils, 47, 52

Alba Iulia, 101, 103, 109

Alcohol production and distribution, 147, 154-155, 171, 172-173, 205, 213, 218

Allgemeiner Sparkassaverein, 207

Allodial lands, 160, 165, 169, 173, 219, 387 n. 10. *See also* Urbarial lands

Allodial serfs, 169-170, 219, 231, 252. *See also* Feudalism; "Irregular" serfs; Urbarial serfs

András II (Hungarian king), 81, 83, 89

Anthropological field research, 18-25; ethical issues in, 20-25

Anthropology: role of, 1, 11, 17-18, 26, 368

Apafi, Michael (Transylvanian prince), 81

Ardeleana bank, 206, 207

Aristocracy. *See* Gentry; Magnates; Nobility; Nobles

Army, 82, 90, 94-95, 98, 134, 358; Germans enter, during World War II, 334, 377 n. 26, 398 n. 39; as source of demand for agricultural commodities, 137, 154, 170; as source of Romanian employment, 226, 288, 294-295. *See also* Border Regiments

Aurel Vlaicu (new name of Binţinţi), 227, 273-274

Austria, 87, 107, 112, 115, 124, 194; as source of capital, 198, 202, 208; wool manufacture of, 138, 139

Austria-Hungary, 266, 276, 290

Austrian Military Border, 250

Austrian State Railroad Co., 204

Austro-Prussian War, 194

Austro-Romanian tariff war, 205

Austro-Turkish War, 112, 153, 154, 172

Autarky: of Habsburg economy, 128, 130, 353, 355; of Hungarian state, 223; of Romanian state, 275, 280, 285, 286, 289, 333; of socialist Romania, 40, 41, 42, 54-55, 57-58, 335, 349

Banaji, Jairus, 12, 135, 151, 384 n. 20

Banat, 169, 207, 276, 290, 383 n. 10, 387 n. 19, 393 n. 1

Bariţiu, George, 190

Barter, 241, 245, 396 n. 24

Barth, Fredrik, 362-363

Bem, Joseph (general), 186

Bethlen, Gábor (Transylvanian prince), 82, 341

Binţinţi: collectivized, 39; earliest documentary mention of, 231, 389 n. 1; labor force of, 59; located on map, 31; name changed, 227, 273-274; population figures for, 164-165, 234, 385 n. 28

Bismarck, Otto von (Prussian chancellor), 194
Blaj, mass meetings at, in 1848, 186, 187, 189
Bloch, Marc, 135
Blum, Jerome, 139
Boner, Charles, 217, 218
Border Regiments, 94–95, 102, 111, 154
Botezan, Liviu, 162, 163, 164, 165, 167
Brenner, Robert, 11
Bribery, 37, 52, 56, 62
Bucharest, 227, 297
Budapest, 226, 227, 245
Bureaucracy, 45, 288; of Habsburg Empire, 5, 90, 100, 104; modernization of, 5, 92, 100, 107; social composition of, 182, 195, 224, 276, 277, 287, 292, 297; and taxation, 90–95. *See also* Gentry, and access to public office; Nobles, and access to public office

Calvinism, 84, 87, 107, 110, 111, 231
CAP (Cooperative Agricolă de Producție). *See* Cooperative farm(s)
Capital. *See* Foreign capital; Merchant capital; Symbolic capital
Capitalism: and relation to noncapitalist economies, 9–13, 361; rent capitalism, 210, 233, 235; state capitalism, 277, 360, 368, 399 n. 8; in world-system theory, 10–12. *See also* Feudalism, and shift to capitalism
Capitalist agriculture: in Hungary, 182, 195–197, 199–200; underdeveloped in Transylvania, 342–345, 356–359, 366; underdeveloped in Transylvania before World War I, 175–178, 201, 210–224, 240, 253, 255, 383 n. 12, 387 nn. 14, 19, 400 n. 11; underdeveloped in Transylvania after World War I, 274, 286, 289–291, 307, 316, 323–325, 329–332, 334. *See also* Livestock production; Underdevelopment
Cattle: as main cash crop of Romanians in village, 242, 292, 312–317, 329, 331, 332, 397 n. 27. *See also* Livestock production

Ceaușescu, Nicolae (president of Romania), 33, 42, 74
Cernea, Mihail, 47
Charles VI (Habsburg emperor), 86, 87, 88, 89, 90
Chayanov, Alexander, 302–303
Chiaburi ("rural exploiters"), 36, 38–39, 334, 375 n. 5
Coalitions in state centralization, 5, 6, 82, 93, 95, 98, 99, 104–105, 112–113, 124, 173. *See also* State-building
Cole, John W., 253
Collective farm. *See* Cooperative farm(s)
Collectivization of agriculture, 43–45, 57, 340, 342, 343, 344, 371; in Binținți, 38–39, 334, 335. *See also* Cooperative farm of Binținți; Cooperative farms
Communal pasture, 56, 278, 290; in Binținți, 166–167, 215, 304, 314–315, 321, 397 n. 28
Communism, 374 n. 14. *See also* Socialism
Communist Party, 37, 47, 69; activities of, 39, 44, 45, 54, 69, 337
Compensation, 358; after 1848, 196, 219–220, 389 n. 30; after 1921, 279, 287; after 1945, 343. *See also* Land reform
Compromise of 1867, 194
Conservative Pary, 283
Constantinescu, Mitița, 326, 333
Contract-payment system (*acord global*), 46, 51, 52, 53, 376 n. 14. *See also* Portion
Contracts of agricultural goods to socialist state, 55–57
Cooperative farm of Binținți: establishment of, 38; German membership in, 63; and household composition, 46, 59; organization of, 48–58, 60; remuneration in, 51–52, 53; reputation of, 30, 32, 33, 34
Cooperative farms, 44, 47, 48, 73, 344, 360; labor remuneration in, 46, 47, 51–52, 53; problems of, 56, 57, 61, 62
Core, 10, 11. *See also* Periphery
Coulon, Christian, 351

Credit: in Hungary, 196–198, 217, 218, 220, 223–224; in Romania, 279, 280–281, 282–284, 289, 356. *See also* Agriculture, state investment in Crimean War, 138, 147

Crisis in seignorial revenues, 136–137, 138–140, 152–153, 156, 344, 366

Cugir, 309, 310, 334

Curialisbirtok (noble property), 216, 385 n. 29, 388 n. 26

Customs union, and internal customs line, 130, 132

Czechoslovakia, 40, 41

Cziráky conscription (conscription of 1820), 93, 153, 155, 161, 167, 169, 170, 238, 338, 380 nn. 14, 15, 384 n. 18

Dacian Empire, 29, 30

Dacians, 19, 70

Deak, Istvan, 121

Debt-conversion of 1932, 284, 285, 286, 331, 332, 333, 358

Dependency theory, 9–10, 13, 362, 373 n. 5

Depression of 1870s, 196, 197, 198–199, 358

Depression, Great, 58, 234; in Romania, 284, 285, 309, 312, 317, 318, 326, 331, 340, 359, 397 n. 32; and interwar politics, 277, 280, 281; and village agricultural strategies, 314; and world-system processes, 274–276, 301

Diploma Leopoldinum, 87

Display: by nobles, 73–74, 135, 136, 138, 151, 152, 156–158, 364–366, 382 n. 6; by present-day villagers, 61–62, 73–74. *See also* Symbolic capital

Divide et impera, 122, 123, 381 n. 27

Dowry, 246, 247, 291, 292, 304, 306

Dual Monarchy, 194, 195, 196, 197, 201, 202, 339. *See also* Habsburg Empire; Hungarian state

Eastern Europe: early industrialization of, 355; and ideas of ethnicity, 15–17; present-day states of, 276, 277, 278, 280, 337, 339, 368; research in (*see* Anthropological field research)

Eastern Orthodoxy. *See* Romanian Orthodoxy

East Germany, 41, 65

Edict of Toleration, 110, 111–112

Education of Romanians, 62; connection with nationalism, 295–299; in Habsburg Empire, 119; pre-World War I, 174, 206, 226, 228; post-World War I, 292, 293–299, 329, 335

Emancipation of serfs, 100, 167, 181, 195–196, 205, 211, 216, 223, 343; and categories of servile labor, 218–222; and concern with labor efficiency, 139, 173–174

England, 128, 130, 138

Enlightenment, The, 116–117, 124, 191, 349, 352

Ethnic identity, 14, 15; altered significance of, 66, 337, 345–351, 359; changes of, 64, 187–188, 260–261, 291, 345, 348, 363, 368–369; and education/occupation, 66, 68; German conceptions of, 67–70; individualization of, 15; and stereotypes of other groups, 64–66, 237, 242, 258–260, 262, 322, 369–370. *See also* Ethnicity; German-Romanian relations; Magyar-German relations; Romanian-Magyar relations; Triethnic relations

Ethnicity, 13–17, 72, 256–266, 354, 361–367; and class, 85–86, 182, 192, 225, 229, 287, 346–349, 351, 363–366, 400 n. 14; and class in pre-World War I Binţinţi, 230, 231, 242–245, 246, 256–257; and class in post-World War I Binţinţi, 311, 320–322, 325; conceptualization of, 13–14; and differences in agricultural organization, 232–243, 307–320; Eastern and Western European perspectives on, 15–17; and economic development, 361–367; and intergroup competition, 114–115, 144–145, 287, 319, 346–347, 352, 363–366; and intergroup competition in Binţinţi, 255, 269, 320–323, 337,

350; and kinship, 255; and language, 15, 65–69 passim, 84, 243, 337; and occupational/economic specialization, 225, 232–242, 287, 312–317, 347, 389 n. 32, 397 n. 26; and politicization of cultural differences, 114, 116–117, 345; and religion, 64, 66, 67, 84, 243; and trade monopolies, 144–145, 347; and village politics, 244, 255, 264–266, 325–327. *See also* Agricultural organization; Ethnic identity; Household; Inheritance; Nationalism; Stratification, rural

Ethnic relations. *See* German-Romanian relations; Magyar-German relations; Romanian-Magyar relations; Tri-ethnic relations

Fascism, 277–278, 297
Fertility control, 273, 274, 299–304, 306, 309, 329, 335, 344, 376 nn. 16, 19, 396 nn. 20, 21, 22
Feudal economy: continuities of, in subsequent practice, 73–74, 236, 237, 238–240, 242, 250–252, 258, 260–261, 315–316, 390 n. 6; and household/marriage form, 251, 252; peasant recollections of, 260–264. *See also* Feudalism
Feudalism: conceptualization of, for Eastern Europe, 133–136, 373 n. 6, 382 n. 5; land as foundation of, 151, 159, 233; and parallels with socialist system, 73–74, 360; and shift to capitalism, 342–345, 346–347, 353–354, 357–358, 363; and shift to capitalism in Habsburg Empire, 138–140, 145–150, 152, 173–174, 183, 184; and shift to capitalism in Hungary-Transylvania, 216–222; size of landholdings in, 161–162, 163–166, 384 n. 21; in Transylvania, characteristics of, 134, 135, 140, 151–174, 379 n. 7. *See also* Feudal economy; Feudal labor dues; Modes of production; "Second serfdom"; Urbarial regulations
Feudal labor dues, 101, 103, 150, 160–161, 168–169, 171, 384 n. 19. *See also Robot*

Feudal status groups, 16, 84, 135, 183, 345, 346, 347
Field research. *See* Anthropological field research
Fogarassy family, 232, 233, 257, 262, 263, 264, 268
Foreign capital: in Habsburg Empire, 147, 177, 193; in Hungary-Transylvania, 197–200, 202, 204–205, 206, 207, 208, 387 n. 13; in interwar Romania, 275, 280, 281, 286, 288–289, 327–333 passim
France, 90, 128, 129, 130, 283
Francis I (Habsburg emperor), 121, 122, 338
Frank, Andre Gunder, 9
French Revolution, 112
Full serf holding. See *Sessio*

Gaál, László, 218
Gentry, 224; and access to public office, 100, 111, 196, 220, 276; as opposed to magnates, 95–96, 173, 193, 194, 196, 386 n. 5, 387 n. 10. *See also* Bureaucracy; Nationalism, Magyar; Nationalism, Romanian; Nobility; Nobles
German-Magyar relations *See* Magyar-German relations
German-Romanian relations: in interwar period, 257–260, 269, 320–327, 328, 329, 350, 398 n. 36; pre-World War I, 185, 188, 232, 235, 236, 243–245, 253, 257–260, 265, 346–347, 348–349, 350; in socialist period, 33, 35, 38, 64–68, 71–72, 257–260, 334, 337, 346–347, 377 nn. 28, 30. *See also* Tri-ethnic relations
Germans: deported, 35–36, 374 n. 4; lands expropriated, 35–36, 63, 312, 334, 337, 347; as Romanian villagers' "serfs," 38, 73. *See also* Saxons
Germany, 128, 129, 137, 285, 286, 310, 398 n. 39
Godparenthood. *See* Ritual kinship
Golden Bull, 81, 89, 116
Grazcik, József, 213, 214, 216
Greece, 284, 316
Gunst, Péter, 218

Habsburg Empire, 5, 70, 79-181; bankruptcy of, 87, 128, 137, 379 n. 5; centralization of, imperfect, 104-105, 111-112, 121-122, 123-125, 339; centralization of, and nationalism, 120, 193; centralization of, and nobles' resistance, 80, 87, 89, 94-96, 116-119, 193, 212-213, 352, 355-356, 388 n. 23; centralization of, and peasant uprising, 99-106; becomes Dual Monarchy, 194; economic development in, 126, 127-133, 163, 339, 355; revenues of, 79-80, 90-93, 132, 339, 354; as "semi-periphery," 128, 176, 177-178, 382 n. 3; and special policies toward Transylvania, 89, 355. *See also* Horea's revolt; Hungary; State-building; Urbarial regulations

Habsburg state. *See* Habsburg Empire

Hechter, Michael, 362

Herder, Johann Gottfried von, 117, 352

Hitchins, Keith, 111, 373 n. 10

Hitler, Adolph, 333, 334, 347

Holy Roman Empire, 87

Horea's revolt, 99, 100-106, 119, 172, 188, 263, 342, 380 n. 18, 383 n. 12, 386 n. 33

Household: extended, 37, 59, 155, 248, 250, 251, 377 n. 21, 391 n. 11; nuclear 37, 59, 155; as unit of labor in cooperative farm, 46

Hungarian state, 194, 195, 200, 206, 220, 223-224, 265, 268, 339. *See also* State-building, and nationalism

Hungary: distorts Transylvania's economic development, 202-206, 220, 224; economic development in, 130-133, 137-140, 195-200, 339, 340; as Habsburg "colony," 132-133, 140, 182, 184, 198, 352, 386 n. 5, and imperial grain markets, 138, 199; incorporated into Habsburg Empire, 81, 87, 89; medieval kingdom of, 81-82, 194; refeudalization of, 382 n. 7; Revolution of 1848 in, 96, 132, 174, 182, 184-188, 189, 194, 223, 339. *See also* Hungarian state

Imreh, István, 172

Industrial revolution, 205

Industrialization, geographic distribution of, 130, 131, 141, 142-144, 153. *See also* Industries

Industries: in Habsburg lands, 129, 130, 131, 382 n. 3; in Hungary, 129, 140; in interwar Romania, 281; in socialist Romania, 40-42, 46, 60; in Transylvania, 141, 142, 145-150, 202-205, 383 n. 10

Industry, cottage, 147, 150, 155, 225, 302

Inheritance, 222, 233, 302, 344, 356; and class, 253, 298, 306, 335; and ethnic differences, 245-256; under feudalism, 96, 134, 135, 164, 252, 341, 391 nn. 12, 15; and migration, 253, 254, 255, 358; and village elites, 253-255. *See also* Agricultural organization; Stratification, rural

Intermarriage, 64, 65, 66, 68, 69, 243, 321, 337, 377 n. 30. *See also* Ethnic identity; Ethnicity

Internal market, 60-62, 71, 74, 233, 240, 285, 355, 357, 360, 383 nn. 13, 14; problems of, 45, 281, 282; problems of, in Transylvania, 148, 150, 151-156, 170, 176, 177, 201, 210-211, 217-218, 224

International Research and Exchanges Board, 373 n. 9

Interstate system, 7-8, 128, 176, 177-178, 182-183, 274-276, 280, 358, 359

Întovărăşire (peasant association), 38, 44

Iorga, Nicolae, 148

"Irrationality." *See* rationality in farming

"Irregular serfs," 169-170, 218, 220, 385 nn. 27, 29. *See also* Allodial serfs

Istanbul, 153

Italy, 49, 128, 129, 283, 316

Jews, 195, 213, 214, 235, 245, 277, 316, 317

Joint-stock companies, 147, 149, 205

Joseph II (Habsburg emperor), 79-80, 82, 98, 110, 120, 121, 154; and nobles, 104, 112, 152; reforms of, 99-100, 111-112, 152, 184, 352; and

Transylvanian peasantry, 100–101,
102, 103. *See also* Edict of Toleration;
Nationalism, Magyar; Nationalism,
Romanian
Josephine Reforms. *See* Joseph II,
reforms of

Kideckel, David, 48, 51
Kin ties, 49, 234, 238, 255
Kossuth, Louis, 185, 189
Kula, Witold, 135
Kun, Count István, 165, 209, 211, 227

Labor: exchanges (*a se ortăci*), 237,
240, 252, 310, 390 n. 6; intensifica-
tion, process of, 63, 308, 324–325,
332, 333, 343–345, 356, 358, 360
Labor dues. *See* Feudal labor dues;
Robot
Land reform, 291, 358; of 1945, 36, 43,
334; of 1921, 216, 273–315 passim,
329–343 passim; and Saxon organization, 319
Lázár, Count Kálmán, 187, 212–213,
388 nn. 22, 23
Legion of the Archangel Michael, 277
Leopold I (Habsburg emperor), 87
Leopold II (Habsburg emperor), 119
Lesser nobility. *See* Gentry
Liberal Party, 277, 280, 281, 283, 288,
289, 326, 327, 328, 333
Livestock production: in interwar
period, 275, 284, 289, 290, 310–316,
323, 332; pre-World War I, 137–
139, 153, 171–172, 196–197, 213–
218 passim, 232–242 passim; in
socialist period, 43, 49, 54, 55, 56–57
"Local response": and world-system
theory, 11, 367
London, 173
Lord-peasant relations. *See* peasant-
lord relations
Lutheranism, 64, 66, 84, 86, 87, 107,
231, 243, 347
Luxuries, 129, 130, 141, 152, 156, 157,
360, 365–366. *See also* Display, by
nobles

Macartney, C. A., 287, 288, 289
Machine-tractor stations (SMAs), 47,
52

Madgearu, Virgil, 327
Magnates, 95–96, 149, 173, 174, 193,
194, 196, 224, 386 n. 5, 387 n. 10.
See also Nobility; Nobles
Magyar-German (Saxon) relations, 186,
188, 189, 347. *See also* Nationalism,
Magyar; Nationalism, Saxon; Tri-
ethnic relations
Magyarization, 118–119, 121, 183, 189,
226, 227, 261, 265, 268, 347, 370.
See also Nationalism, Magyar
Magyar-Romanian relations. *See* Ro-
manian-Magyar relations
Magyars: religion of, 84; in Romanian
state, 69, 70, 287, 288, 348, 351, 352.
See also *Natio*, Magyar; Nationalism,
Magyar; Nobles
Makkai, László, 20
Marczali, Henrik, 139, 150
Maria Theresa (Habsburg empress),
79–80, 95, 97, 109, 111, 129, 139,
382 n. 2
Marriage: age at, 248, 251; residence
after, 246, 247, 251; types of, 247,
248, 273, 274, 304–306, 320, 329,
331, 390 nn. 9, 10
Matyás (Hungarian king), 341
Merchant capital, 340, 341, 356; in
Binţinţi, 235, 245, 307, 308, 312,
316–319 passim, 327–328, 333; in
Habsburg Empire, 146, 147, 148–149,
175, 177; in Hungary and Transylvania, 200–209, 211, 220, 229, 235;
in interwar Romania, 284, 286, 317–
318, 332
Metternich, Klemens von (Habsburg
chancellor), 121–122
Meyer, John W., 7, 373 n. 4
Migration: from Austria-Hungary, 293–
294, 389 n. 31; from Binţinţi, 293–
299, 306, 329; of Germans, from
socialist Romania, 69, 337, 351, 374
n. 4, 378 n. 33; from Transylvania,
93–95, 221–222, 250, 287, 358, 394
n. 9; within Transylvania, 246, 247,
248, 253, 255, 273, 274, 344
Mihu, Ioan, 206–207, 208–210, 214,
216, 225, 265, 266, 308
Mintz, Sidney, 11
Modes of production: articulation
among, 12–13, 48, 54–56, 136–137,

149–150, 197, 285, 331–332, 336, 355–358, 361–366, 393 nn. 5, 6; and world-system theory, 10–12

Moldavia, 383 n. 9

Morin, Françoise, 351

Mortality, 299–300, 252, 391 n. 14

Napoleonic wars, 130, 134, 138, 139, 147

Naşie. See Ritual kinship

Natio ("nation"): concept examined, 83–84, 116–119, 121, 190–191, 363, 400 n. 14; distribution of languages in, 84–85; of Magyars, 83, 87; and nationalism, 116–119, 121, 185, 190–192, 345, 363–364; none for Romanians, 348; of Saxons, 83, 84, 87, 145, 346; of Szeklers, 83, 84, 87. *See also* Nationalism

"Nation." See *Natio*

Nationalism, 13, 15–17, 72, 113, 345–350, 359, 361–362; and economic development, 361–362; and economic development in Hungary, 114–115, 185, 194–195, 200, 202, 206–210, 222–229, 366–367; and economic development in Romania, 356, 366–367; as ideology, 353–354; and language, 84, 118, 119, 120, 121, 262; as language for articulating conflict, 122–123, 183; manifestations at village level, 243, 256–257, 261–269; and social "revolution" of 1918, 274, 293, 296–297, 319–320. *See also* Ethnicity; Magyarization; *Natio;* Nationalism, Magyar; Nationalism, Romanian; Nationalism, Saxon; State-building

Nationalism, Magyar, 86, 115, 120, 223–229, 346; arouses reciprocal nationalisms, 188–190, 194–195, 225, 265, 296, 348, 349, 353; compared to Romanian, 190, 191–192, 260; and exclusion of Romanians, 118–119, 260, 262–263, 264, 267–268, 293, 349; and language, 121, 261, 368, 370; and role of nobles/gentry, 116–119, 184, 196, 212–213, 352, 365–366. *See also* Magyar-German relations; Magyarization; *Natio,* Magyar; Romanian-Magyar relations

Nationalism, Romanian, 225, 227, 348–350; aspires to inclusion, 120, 191, 260–261, 269, 322, 325, 349, 352; early development of, 115–116, 119–121, 367; from 1848, 187, 188, 189–190, 191–192, 354; in socialist period, 41, 55, 69–70; in village life, 207–210 passim, 263, 266–269, 293, 296, 322, 325–329, 350. *See also* Education of Romanians; German-Romanian relations; Magyarization; Romanian-Magyar relations

Nationalism, Saxon (German), 118, 144, 189, 260, 348, 350, 353, 381 n. 26. *See also* German-Romanian relations; Magyar-German relations; *Natio,* Saxon

National Peasant Party, 267, 277, 281, 283, 326, 327, 328, 393 n. 4

Nation-state, 9, 15, 79, 113, 347; and cultural homogenization, 114, 117, 194–195, 354–355, 361; emergence of, 4, 8, 115, 116–117, 127. *See also* Interstate system; Nationalism; State-building

Nazis, 64, 321, 348, 350, 351, 398 n. 39

Nobility: Austro-Bohemian, 132–133, 146, 176, 177, 352, 355; of Hungary, 80, 89, 95, 132; of Hungary, compared to that of Transylvania, 86, 87, 89, 96, 140–141, 164, 174, 188, 380 n. 16; of Hungary, emergence as separate estate, 81. *See also* Display; Gentry; Luxuries; Magnates; Nobles

Nobles: and access to public office, 136, 158–159, 182, 220, 224–225, 341, 348, 365, 366; augment supplies of land and labor, 166–170, 380 n. 13, 384 n. 17, 391, n. 11; bankruptcies of, 195–196, 207–208, 211–212, 234; industrial-commercial activities of, 132–133, 139, 146, 148–149, 152, 158, 173–174, 196, 205, 220, 225; lend grain to peasants, 136, 166, 168, 172, 360; and retention of semi-servile labor after emancipation, 219, 220–221, 222, 388 n. 26; in salt trade, 91; tax exemption of, 81, 90, 132, 137, 140, 169; use of term explained, 378 n. 2. *See also* Display; Feudalism;

Gentry; Magnates; Peasant-lord relations; State-noble relations
Nopsca, Baron László, 187, 188, 349
North American grain, 196, 199, 281

Orăştie, 170, 211, 235, 239, 266, 309, 310
Ottoman Empire, 70, 81, 82, 87-88, 128, 144

Paget, John, 139, 157, 158, 173
Palerm, Ángel, 383 n. 11, 400 n. 10
Palestine, 284, 316
Paris Peace Conference, 266
Peasant economy: under feudalism, 162-163, 170-171; under socialism, 52-57
Peasant-lord relations, 93, 96, 98, 100-106, 154, 156, 250-251, 252, 327-328, 341, 360. See also Feudalism; Peasant resistance; State-peasant relations
Peasant resistance: under Habsburg dynasty, 72, 93-94, 99-106, 108-110, 162, 173, 174, 250-251, 342, 367, 381 n. 21; under Hungarian state, 221, 263-264; in interwar Romania, 259, 268, 275; in socialist period, 37, 38, 43-44, 51, 53, 56-57, 72. See also Horea's revolt; Peasant-lord relations
Peasants, 359; definition of, 3; indebtedness of, 221, 275, 279, 283, 284, 294, 307, 308, 317-318, 326, 331, 333; and nationalism, 184, 186, 189-190, 207, 209-210, 225-227, 256-257, 261-269, 274, 296; as occasional labor in industry, 37, 60, 290, 303, 309, 323, 336; and perceptions of oppression and injustice, 232, 256-257, 261-269, 322, 327-328, 333; and postfeudal labor obligations, 216, 219, 220-221, 222, 343, 344, 388 n. 26, 389 n. 29; purchasing power of, 61, 285, 336; reconstitution of, 286, 295, 303, 330-331, 358; and relations between rich and poor, in Hungarian Transylvania, 168, 215, 236, 237-239, 255; and relations between rich and poor, in interwar Romania, 283-284, 321-323, 325; and relations

between rich and poor, in socialist period, 36; "traditionalism" of, 345, 357-358, 367. See also German-Romanian relations; State-peasant relations; Stratification, rural
"Peasant-workers," 58-61, 62, 63, 336
Periphery, 10, 11, 276, 280, 286. See also Core
Poland, 128, 135, 276
Poland-Lithuania, 176
Porţie. See Contract-payment system; "Portion"
"Portion" (porţie), 54, 336. See also Contract-payment system
Prague, 218, 331
Prebisch, Raúl, 9
Primogeniture, 248-249, 250. See also Inheritance
Private plot. See Usufruct plot
Prodan, David, 104, 105, 107, 156, 162, 171
Proletarization, 275, 283, 336, 359; government action in promoting, 329; retarded, 362; retarded, under Hungarian state, 211, 221, 222, 233, 241, 251; retarded, in interwar Romania, 279, 284, 286, 290, 293, 294-295, 298, 303, 306, 315, 317-335 passim, 343, 357-358; retarded, in socialist period, 36, 44, 48. See also Sharecropping
Property: consolidation of, 44, 215, 278-279, 283, 303-304; fragmentation of, 96, 156, 163-165, 176, 218-222 passim, 240, 248, 344, 397 n. 31. See also Inheritance
Protestantism, as anti-Habsburg, 107, 110-111, 381 n. 21
Prussia, 129

Quotas for agricultural delivery, 36-37, 38, 43, 334, 344

Rationality in farming: 43, 45, 279-280, 282, 284-285, 336; ethnically linked, 237-245 passim. See also Agricultural organization; German-Romanian relations
Red Army, 369
Reformation, 84

Regat, 277, 287, 288, 289, 290, 324. *See also* Romanian Kingdom; Romanian principalities; Romanian state

Ritual kinship (*naşie*), 36, 66, 238, 239, 241, 243

Roberts, Henry, 277, 282, 370

Robot (labor dues), 96, 97, 155, 157, 160–161, 173, 238, 251, 252, 391 n. 11. *See also* Feudal labor dues

Roman Catholicism, 67, 84, 87, 107–108, 111, 113, 231, 261

Romania: anthropological field research in, 18–25; economic development of, under socialism: 39–48, 278–286, 375 nn. 7, 8. *See also* Romanian Kingdom; Romanian principalities; Romanian state; Socialism

Romanian bourgeoisie, 206, 269, 289, 319

Romanian-German relations. *See* German-Romanian relations

Romanian Kingdom, 221, 227, 266–267, 268–269, 287, 290, 293; birth of, 354. *See also* Regat; Romanian principalities; Romanian state

Romanian-Magyar relations, 19–20, 69–70, 181, 185, 187–189, 287, 349, 352, 392 n. 25; in Binţinţi, 102, 186, 187–189, 209, 227, 233, 236, 256–257, 261–265, 267–269, 369–370. *See also* Magyarization; Nationalism, Magyar; Nationalism, Romanian; Tri-ethnic relations

Romanian Nationalist Movement, 208. *See also* Nationalism, Romanian

Romanian National Party, 209, 265, 267, 277, 325. *See also* Nationalism, Romanian

Romanian Orthodoxy, 64, 66, 86, 107, 110, 113, 120, 231, 237, 243, 248, 261, 296; as tolerated creed, 84, 87, 108

Romanian principalities, 107–108, 128, 148, 191. *See also* Moldavia; Regat; Romanian Kingdom; Romanian state; Wallachia

Romanian state, 70, 72, 268–269, 276–291 passim, 325, 327, 329, 332, 341; interwar political parties of, 267, 277–278, 297, 326, 329; revenues of, 339; and state-building, 282, 287, 292. *See also* Liberal Party; National Peasant Party; Regat; Romanian Kingdom; Socialism

Romans, 119

Rousseau, Jean-Jacques, 117

Russia, 64, 112, 129, 371

Russian Revolution, 278, 291

Salt: mines bought by state, 148; trade in, 90–91, 354

Sarmizegetusa (capital of Dacian Empire), 30

Saxon-Romanian relations. *See* German-Romanian relations

Saxons: arrival in Transylvania, 82; economy of, 83, 347; and Habsburgs, 146; opposed by Transylvanian nobles, 145; religion of, 84; textile industry of, 147, 205; and trade, 143–144, 146, 147–148; as Transylvania's "bourgeoisie," 85–86, 142–145, 182, 208, 227–229, 243, 245, 319–320, 337, 346–347, 348. *See also* Industrialization; *Natio*, of Saxons; Nationalism, Saxon

Sebeş, 170

"Second serfdom," 12, 137, 382 n. 7. *See also* Feudalism: Hungary

"Semi-periphery," 10, 128, 141, 145, 176, 177–178, 382 n. 3

Serfdom. *See* Feudal economy; Feudalism; Peasants

Sessio (full serf holding), 160, 165, 166, 167

Sharecropping, 38, 173, 210–222 passim, 232–236 passim, 240–241, 244–245, 279, 302–303, 310–311, 336. *See also* Proletarization, retarded

Sibiu, 105, 108, 109, 157, 207

Silesia, 129, 149

Singer sewing machine, 215, 309

Socialism: in present-day Romania, 20–24, 29–79, 334, 335–336, 337, 355, 358, 359; U. S. attitudes toward, 21–25 passim; use of term, 374 n. 14, 400 n. 12. *See also* Capitalism, state

Soviet Union, 22, 35, 39, 64, 73, 374 n. 14; relations with Romania, 44,

49, 276, 333, 337; and Romania's economic development, 40, 41

Sovroms (joint Soviet-Romanian companies), 40

State: autonomy of, 5, 7, 367-368, 399 n. 7; alterations in nature of, 4, 359; conceptualization of, 3-6, 359; constituent organizations of, 6; as object of competition, 7, 114, 224, 366; and policies for economic development, 340, 355-359, 362-367; and policies for economic development under Habsburg dynasty, 128, 129-130, 133, 146, 163, 176; and policies for economic development under Hungarian state, 195, 197-198, 220, 223-224, 387 n. 11; and policies for economic development in interwar Romania, 274, 275, 276-286, 288-290, 308, 314, 316, 317, 319, 328, 329-332; and policies for economic development in socialist period, 39, 40-48, 57, 71, 335-337; in relation to forms of economy, 13, 354-358, 362-368; socialist, 5, 41, 227, 336, 339, 340, 356, 368; and urban food supply, 43. *See also* Agriculture, state investment in; Credit; Hungarian state; Interstate system; Romanian state; State-building; State-noble relations; State-peasant relations

State-building, 3-8, 23, 25, 79, 339-340, 341, 345, 351-353, 354-359, 363, 364-367; defined, 4; and ethnicity, 15, 351-352, 361-367, 378 n. 32; under Habsburgs, 80, 95, 96, 99, 100, 123-125, 344; and nationalism, 351-352, 353, 354; and nationalism, under Habsburg dynasty, 113, 114-115, 117-118, 120-125, 350, 364-366; and nationalism, under Hungarian state, 182-183, 190, 193, 194, 224, 350, 366-367; and nationalism, in interwar Romania, 366-367, 394 n. 7. *See also* Habsburg Empire, centralization of; Nationalism; Peasant resistance

State Farms, 48, 49, 54, 56

State-noble relations, 80, 91-106, 134, 170, 196, 341-342, 365-366. *See also* Habsburg Empire, centralization of

State-peasant relations, 4, 5, 8, 339-342, 355, 356-359, 360, 367; under Habsburg dynasty, 93-95, 96, 98-99, 100-106, 111, 112, 124-125, 152, 177; under Hungarian state, 267-268, 399 n. 3; in interwar Romania, 232, 275, 283, 316, 325-328, 330-332; in socialist period, 39, 45, 52, 55, 60, 72, 337, 356-358, 360. See also *Supplex Libellus Valachorum*

"Stem heirs," 248-250. *See also* Inheritance

Stratification, rural, 242-243; in Hungarian Transylvania, 236-238; 245-246, 253-255; in Romanian Transylvania, 36, 62, 253-255, 291-299 passim, 301-307 passim, 311, 317-318, 320-325, 334-335, 394 nn. 8, 10. *See also* Agricultural organization; Ethnicity; Inheritance

Supplex Libellus Valachorum, 119-121, 191

Swabians, 207, 209, 243, 247, 250, 288

Switzerland, 171

Symbolic capital, 364-366

Szeklers, 82, 83, 84, 86. See also *Natio, of Szeklers*

Taxation, 90-95, 152, 170, 251, 275, 281, 286, 307-308, 331, 380 n. 12

Teutonic Knights, 82

Third World, 41, 280

Thomas, George, 7, 373 n. 4

Thompson, E. P. 257

Tisza, Count István, 209

Transylvania: administrative and territorial divisions of, 83, 142, 379 n. 6; arguments concerning history of and sovereignty over, 19-20, 32, 70; changes in social structure of, 182, 195, 221, 224-226, 227-229, 230, 345-351, 364; colonists settled in, 81-82, 83, 209, 211, 234; economic development in, 201-208, 210-211, 216-218, 342-345; economy of, under Magyars, 140-174; effects of incorporation by Habsburg, 175, 176-177, 257, 357; Habsburg efforts to catholicize, 107-111; incorporated into Habsburg Empire, 87, 89; incorporated into Hungarian state, 182;

incorporated into Romania, 192, 266–269, 273–279, 287–293, 296–298, 302–303, 319–320, 349, 350; industrial revolution in, 205; and issue of union with Hungary, 118, 185, 188–189, 191; partial autonomy within Habsburg Empire, 104, 164; population figures for, 380 n. 16, 389 n. 29; religions in, 84–85, 87; Revolution of 1848 in, 185–189; rise of nationalism in, 114–115, 116–117, 118, 121; and salt trade, 90–91, 97; semi-independent under Turkish rule, 82–83, 86; as "semi-periphery," 141, 145; social structure of, 83–86, 87, 114, 142, 243, 246, 253, 255, 257, 269, 273, 274; special imperial treatment of, 89, 97, 107, 156. *See also* Feudalism, in Transylvania; Nobility, of Hungary

Transylvanian Agricultural Society, 174

Treaty of Versailles, 276

Tri-ethnic relations, 69–70, 185–189 passim, 209, 257, 348, 352, 369–370. *See also* German-Romanian relations; Magyar-German relations; Romanian-Magyar relations

Tucker, William, 158

Turkey, 112, 129, 139

Turks. *See* Ottoman Empire

Ulászló (Hungarian king), 80–81

Ulrichhofer brothers, 209–210, 214, 215, 216

Ultimogeniture, 247, 249, 250, 251, 252. *See also* Inheritance

Underdevelopment, 8–13, 39–40, 41, 57–58, 280; in Hungary, 130–133, 140; theories of, 9–13. *See also* Capitalist agriculture, under-developed in Transylvania; Hungary, as Habsburg "colony"

Uniate Church, 108, 110–111, 119, 120, 231, 349, 350, 352, 367; clergy of, 110, 113, 119; motives for clerical conversion to, 108; resistance to, by peasants, 108–110. *See also* Nationalism, Romanian

Unitarianism, 84, 87, 107

United States, 21, 24, 221, 293, 294–295, 358

Urbarial lands, 160, 165, 169, 219, 223, 387 n. 10. *See also* Allodial lands

Urbarial regulations: under Habsburg dynasty, 97, 98, 100, 105–106, 112, 134, 138; in Hungary, 160, 161–162; in Transylvania, 97, 98, 105, 140, 152, 161, 338, 366. *See also* Habsburg Empire, centralization of

Urbarial serfs, 169, 170, 219, 231, 315, 385 n. 27. *See also* Allodial serfs; Feudalism

Urbarium. *See* Urbarial regulations

Usufruct plot: compared to serf's holding, 73; and cooperative farm membership, 32, 47–48, 63, 376 n. 20; under feudalism, 150, 160–161, 384 n. 21; in organization of Binţinţi economy, 51–60 passim; in socialist economy, 50, 51, 54, 55, 336, 359

Venice, 137

Vlaicu, Aurel (inventor), 30, 226–227, 266, 294, 296

Voievod (prince), 82

Wallachia, 93, 94, 141, 144, 145, 147, 148, 383, n. 9; exports grain to Transylvania, 51, 153

Wallerstein, Immanuel, 9–11, 128, 382 nn. 5, 7

Warman, Arturo, 13, 26, 362

Western Europe, 12, 111, 124; feudalism in, 134, 135; and ideas of ethnicity, 15–17; in relation to Transylvanian economy, 128, 144, 148; rise of nation-states within, 116, 117, 127

West Germany, 49, 69, 346, 348

Wheat: as German cash crop, 234, 312–317

Wilson, Woodrow (president), 266

Wolf, Eric R., 253

Wolff, Karl, 207–209, 212

World-system theory, 10–12

Zi-muncă (unit of remuneration) 46, 376 n. 11

Designer:	UC Press Staff
Compositor:	Freedmen's Organization
Printer:	Thomson-Shore
Binder:	Thomson-Shore
Text:	11/12 Baskerville
Display:	Baskerville II